Fruits Basket

Volume 8

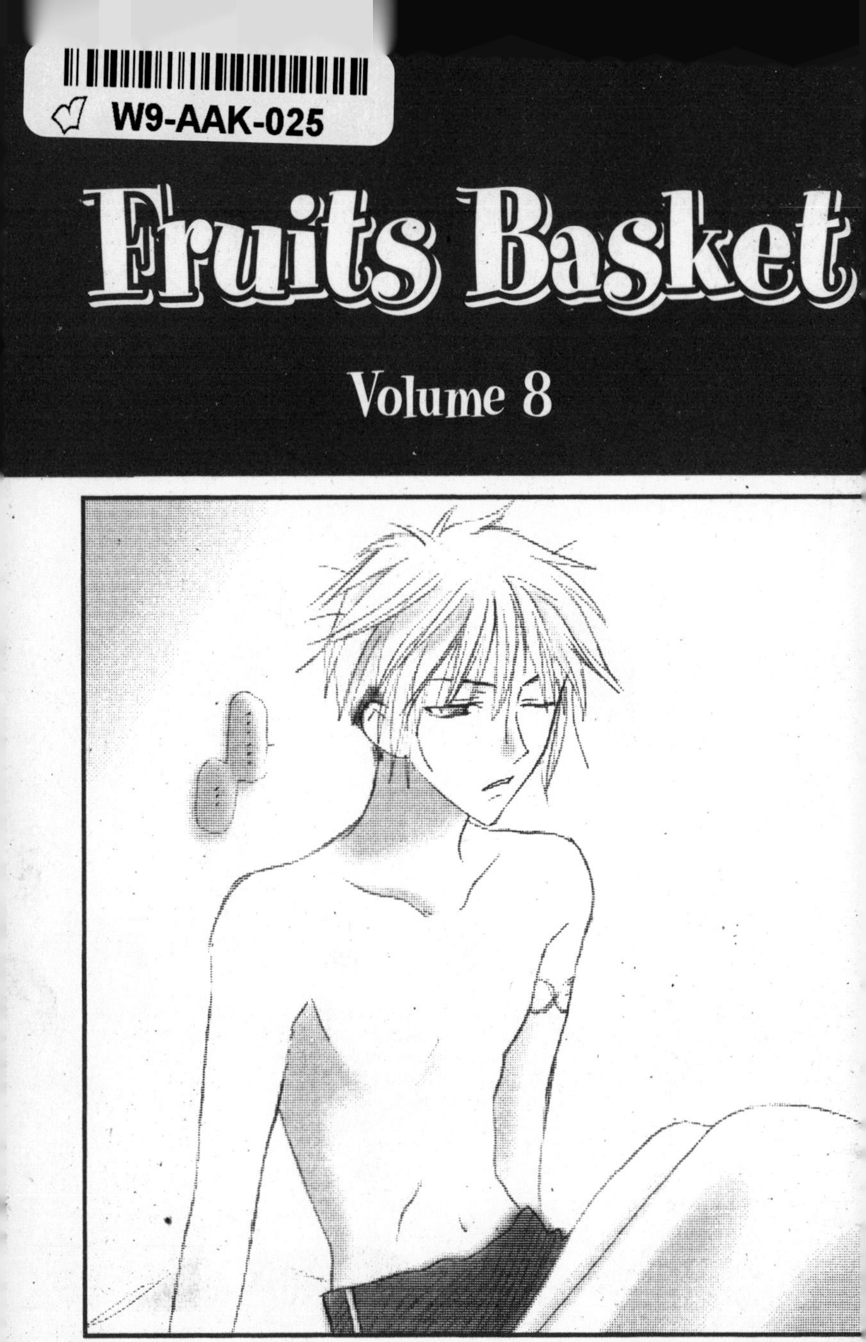

Natsuki Takaya

Fruits Basket Vol. 8
Created by Natsuki Takaya

Translation - Alethea Nibley and Athena Nibley
English Adaptation - Jake Forbes
Contributing Writer - Adam Arnold
Associate Editor - Peter Ahlstrom
Retouch and Lettering - Deron Bennett
Production Artist - James Lee and Jose Macasocol, Jr.
Cover Design - Gary Shum

Editor - Paul Morrissey
Digital Imaging Manager - Chris Buford
Pre-Press Manager - Antonio DePietro
roduction Managers - Jennifer Miller and Mutsumi Miyazaki
Art Director - Matt Alford
Managing Editor - Jill Freshney
VP of Production - Ron Klamert
Editor-in-Chief - Mike Kiley
President and C.O.O. - John Parker
Publisher and C.E.O. - Stuart Levy

A 🟢 **TOKYOPOP** Manga

TOKYOPOP Inc.
5900 Wilshire Blvd. Suite 2000
Los Angeles, CA 90036

E-mail: info@TOKYOPOP.com
Come visit us online at www.TOKYOPOP.com

FRUITS BASKET Vol. 8 by Natsuki Takaya
© 2000 Natsuki Takaya. All rights reserved.
published in Japan in 2002 by HAKUSENSHA, INC., Tokyo
English language translation rights in the
United States of America, Canada and the United Kingdom
arranged with HAKUSENSHA, INC., Tokyo through
Tuttle-Mori Agency Inc., Tokyo
English text copyright © 2005 TOKYOPOP Inc

All rights reserved. No portion of this book may be
reproduced or transmitted in any form or by any means
without written permission from the copyright holders.
This manga is a work of fiction. Any resemblance to
actual events or locales or persons, living or dead, is
entirely coincidental.

ISBN: 1-59532-403-8

First TOKYOPOP printing: April 2005
10 9 8
Printed in the USA

T 251594

Fruits Basket™

Volume 8

By
Natsuki Takaya

HAMBURG // LONDON // LOS ANGELES // TOKYO

Fruits Basket™

Table of Contents

STORY SO FAR...

Hello, I'm Tohru Honda and I have come to know a terrible secret. After the death of my mother, I was living by myself in a tent, when the Sohma family took me in. I soon learned that the Sohma family lives with a curse! Each family member is possessed by the vengeful spirit of an animal from the Chinese Zodiac. Whenever one of them becomes weak or is hugged by a member of the opposite sex, they change into their Zodiac animal!

I MET A STRANGE BOY WHO "KIDNAPPED" MY MOM! WE HAD A ROUGH START...
...BUT I KNOW THAT HIRO SOHMA HAS A GOOD HEART. HE CARES SO MUCH FOR KISA!
NOW, I WONDER WHICH MEMBERS OF THE ZODIAC I'LL ENCOUNTER THIS TIME...?

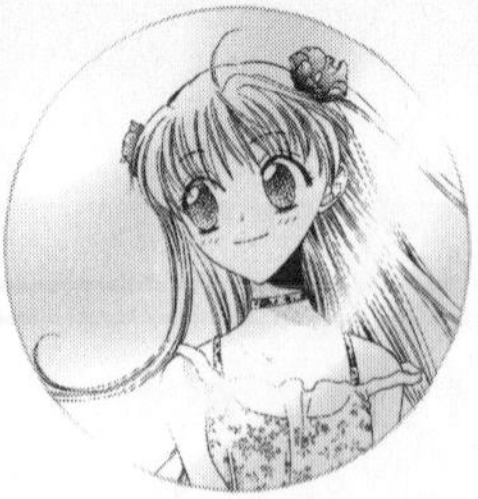

Tohru Honda

The ever-optimistic hero of our story. An orphan, she now lives in Shigure's house, along with Yuki and Kyo, and is the only person outside of the family who knows the Sohma family's curse.

Yuki Sohma, the Rat

Soft-spoken. Self-esteem issues. At school he's called "Prince Yuki."

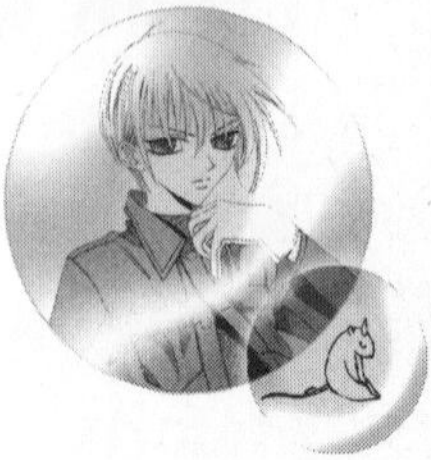

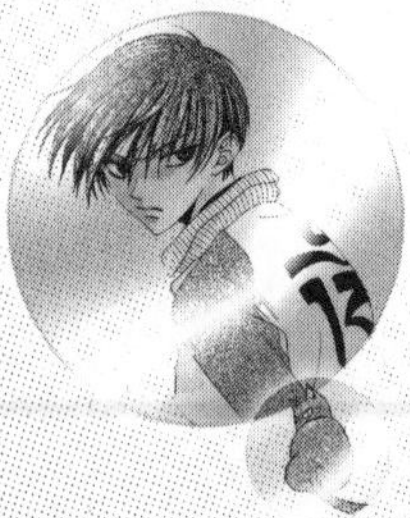

Kyo Sohma, the Cat

The Cat who was left out of the Zodiac. Hates Yuki, leeks and miso. But mostly Yuki.

Mabudachi Trio

Shigure Sohma, the Dog

Enigmatic, mischievous and a little perverted. A popular novelist.

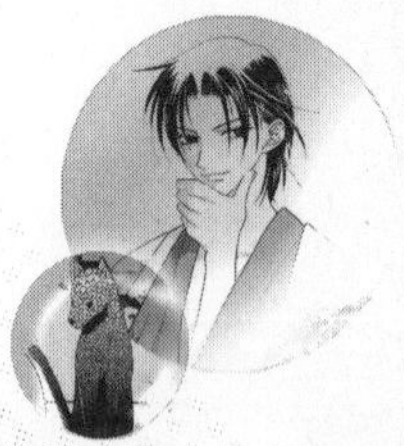

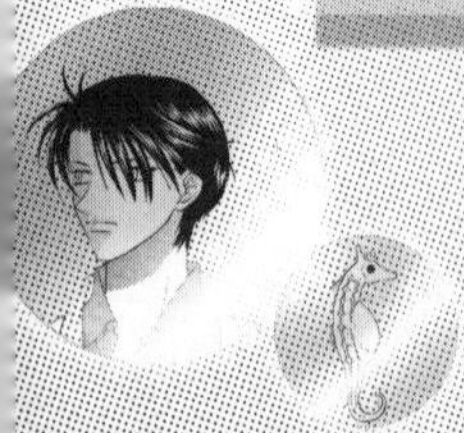

Hatori Sohma, the Dragon

Family doctor to the Sohmas. Only thing he can't cure is his broken heart.

Ayame Sohma, the Snake

Yuki's older brother. A proud and playful drama queen…er, king. Runs a costume shop.

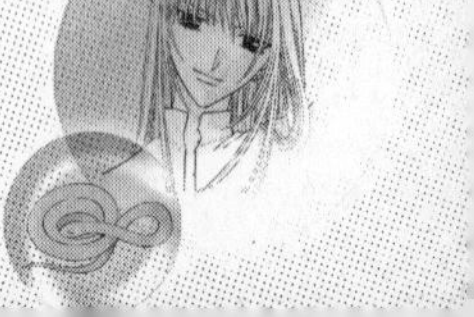

Fruits Basket Characters

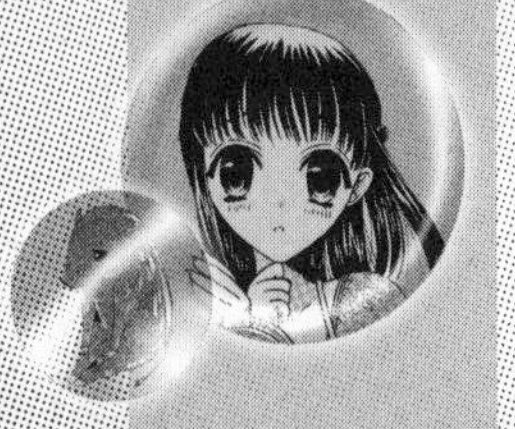

Kagura Sohma, the Boar

Bashful, yet headstrong. Determined to marry Kyo, even if it kills him.

Momiji Sohma, the Rabbit

Half-German. He's older than he looks. Mother rejected him because of the Sohma curse.

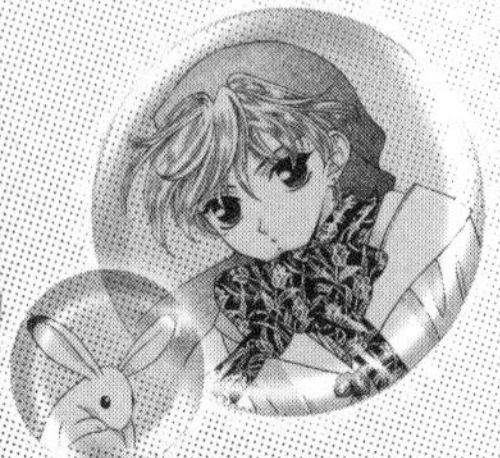

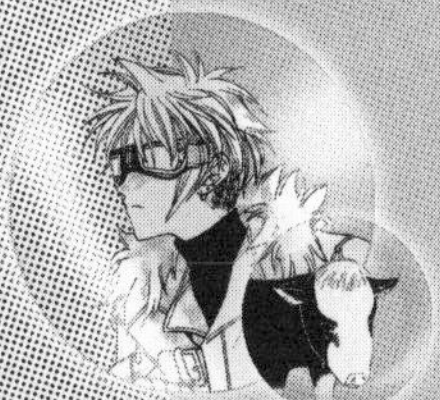

Hatsuharu Sohma, the Ox

The nicest of guys, except when he goes "Black." Then you'd better watch out.

Akito Sohma

The head of the Sohma clan. A dark figure of many secrets. Treated with fear and reverence.

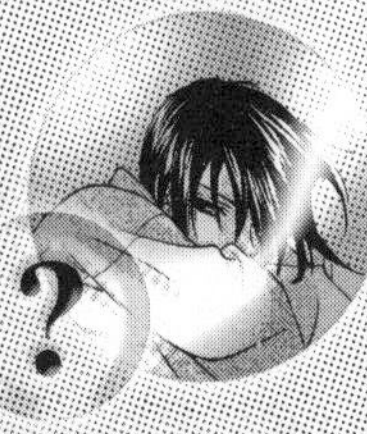

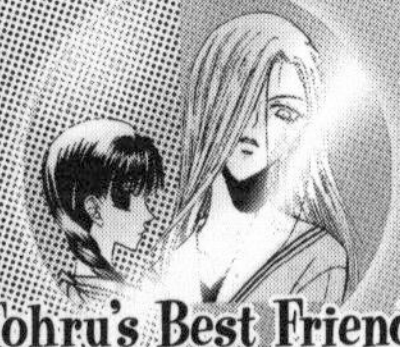

Tohru's Best Friends

Saki Hanajima

"Hana-chan." Can sense people's "waves." Goth demeanor scares her classmates.

Arisa Uotani

"Uo-chan." A tough-talking "Yankee" who looks out for her friends.

Kisa Sohma, the Tiger

Kisa became shy and self-conscious due to constant teasing by her classmates. Yuki, who has similar insecurities, feels particularly close to Kisa.

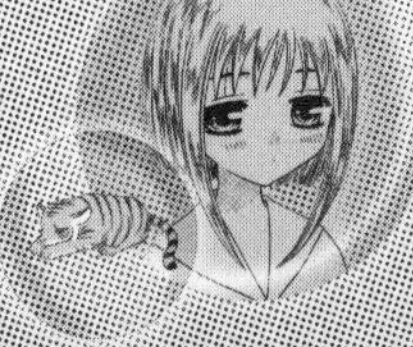

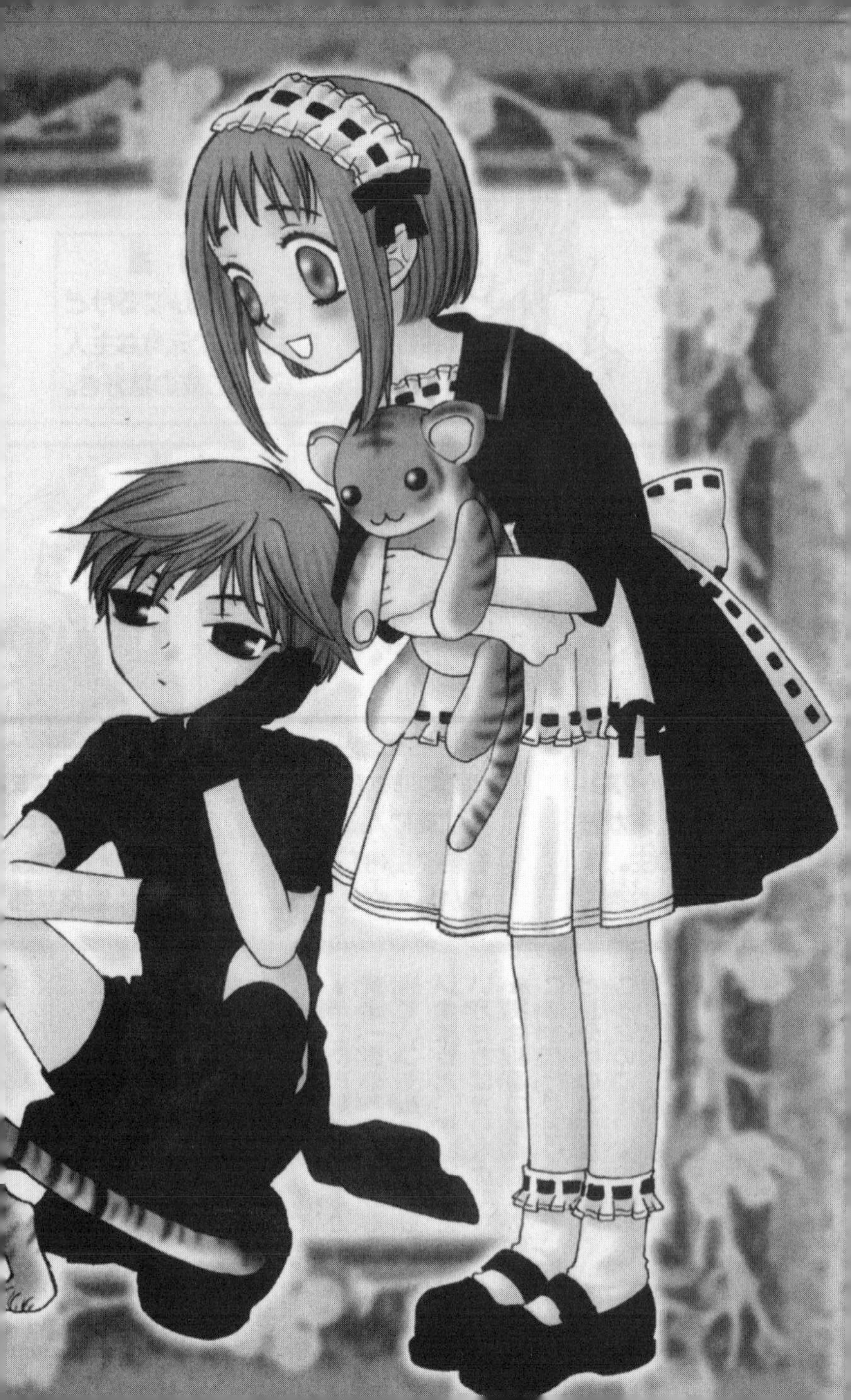

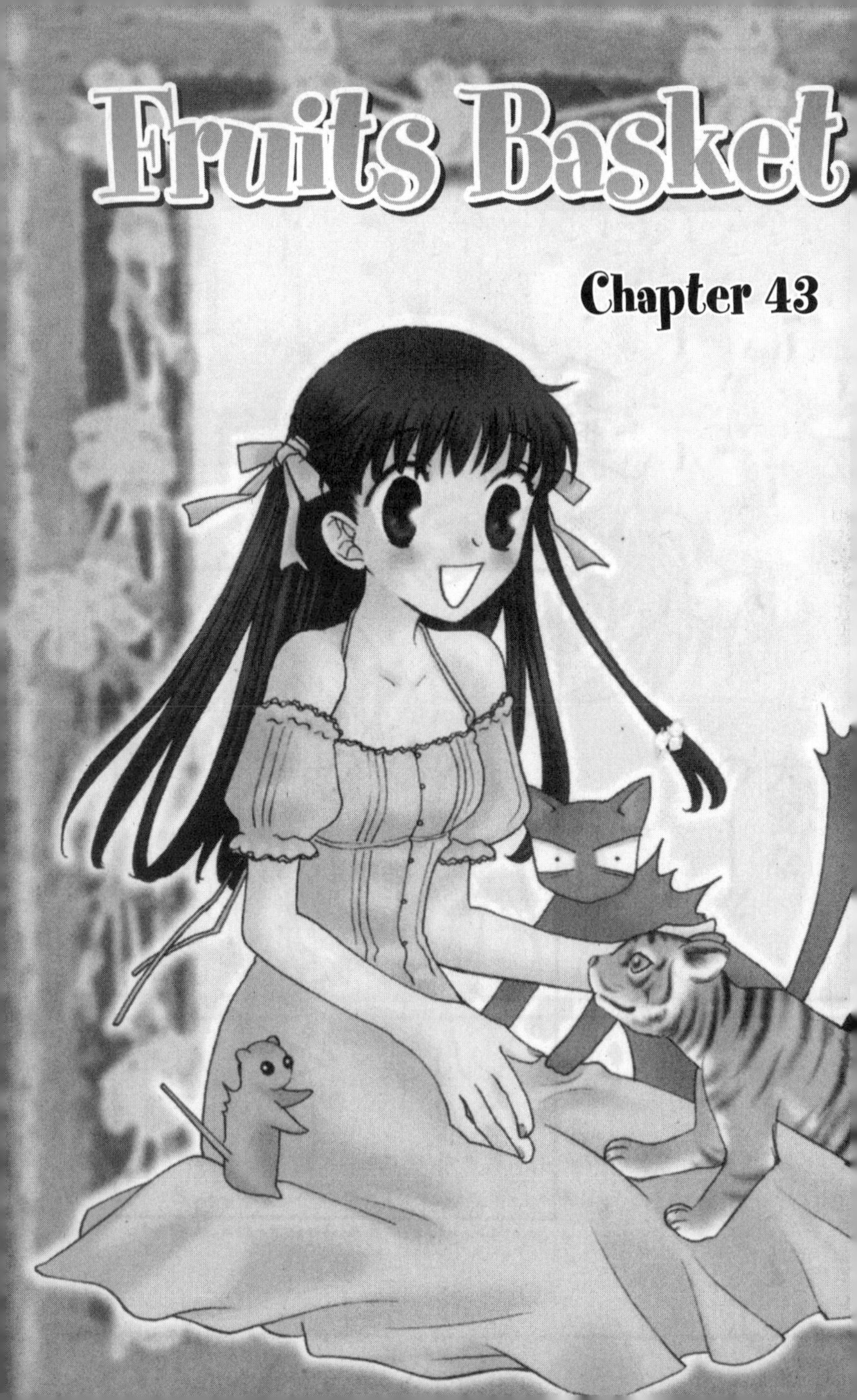
Fruits Basket
Chapter 43

Filler
Sketch

Shigure-san—even his teasing of Mitchan must be in moderation.

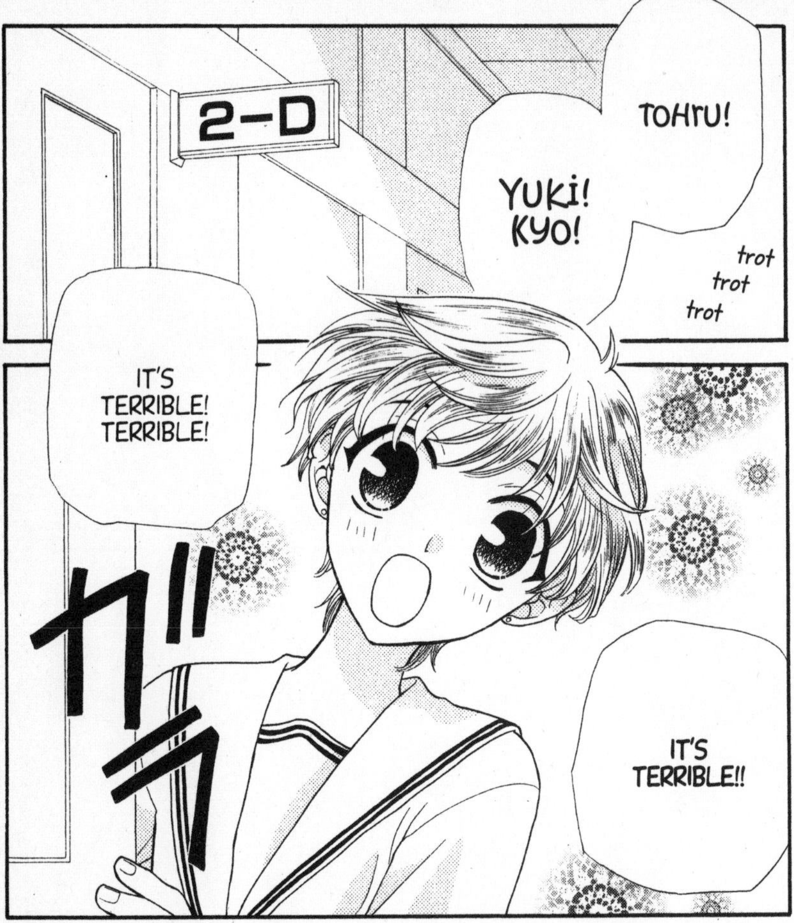
TOHRU!
YUKI! KYO!
trot trot trot
IT'S TERRIBLE! TERRIBLE!
ガラ
IT'S TERRIBLE!!

ULTRA-SPECIAL BLAH, BLAH, BLAH 1

Aaargh! I keep thinking I want to change the title of this section, but before I knew it, it had gotten to the twentieth volume. It's long... It's too long, this title...

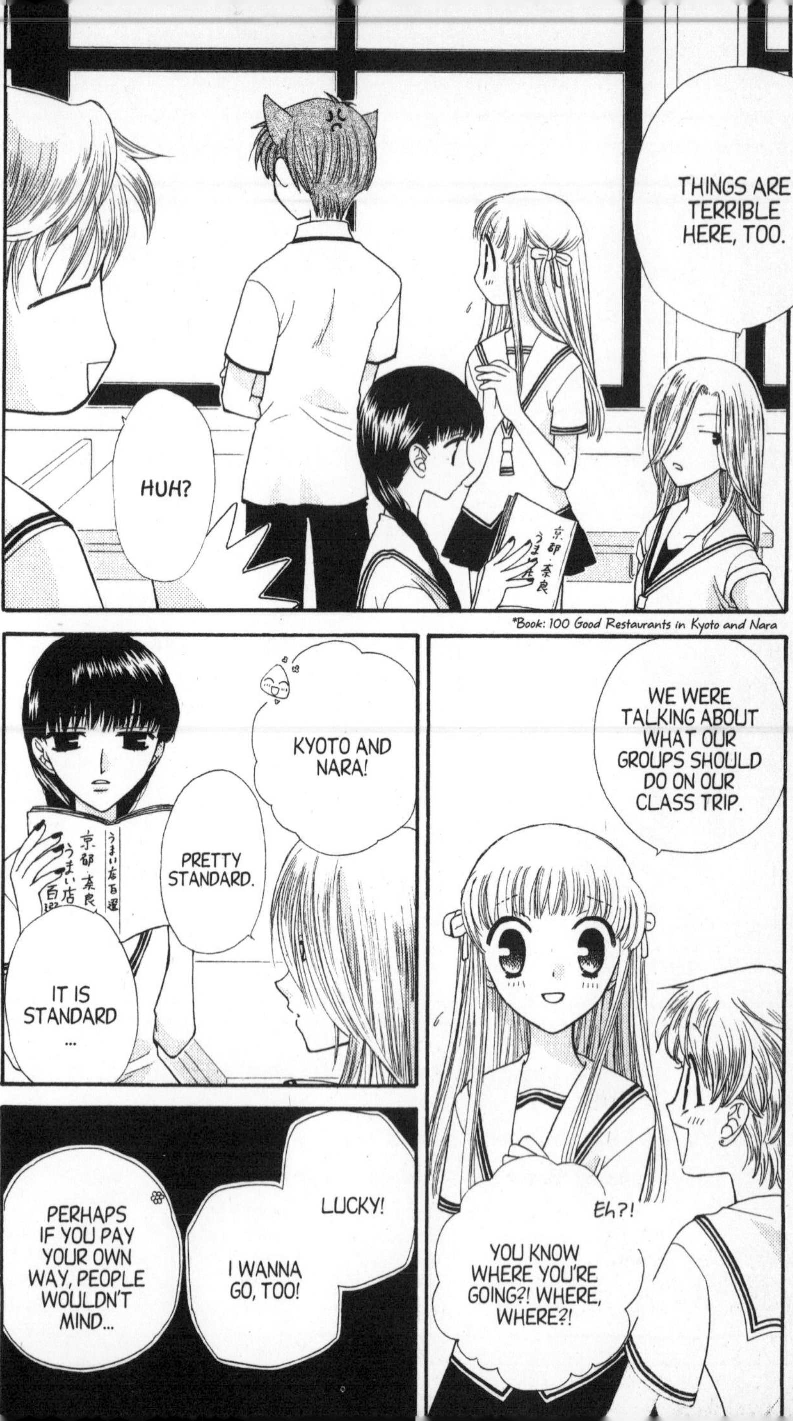
THINGS ARE TERRIBLE HERE, TOO.
HUH?
*Book: 100 Good Restaurants in Kyoto and Nara
WE WERE TALKING ABOUT WHAT OUR GROUPS SHOULD DO ON OUR CLASS TRIP.
Eh?!
YOU KNOW WHERE YOU'RE GOING?! WHERE, WHERE?!
KYOTO AND NARA!
PRETTY STANDARD.
IT IS STANDARD ...
LUCKY!
I WANNA GO, TOO!
PERHAPS IF YOU PAY YOUR OWN WAY, PEOPLE WOULDN'T MIND...

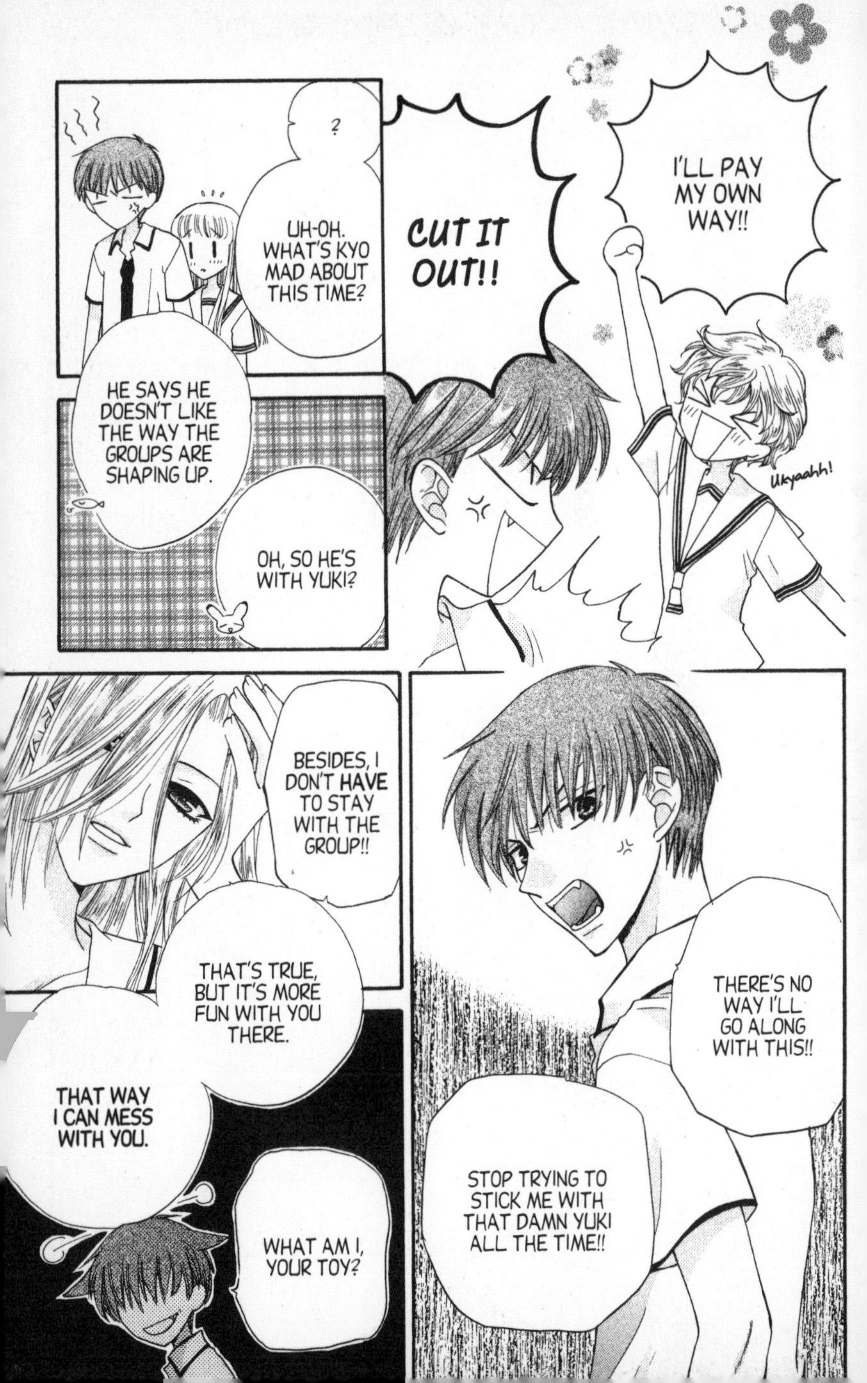
I'LL PAY MY OWN WAY!!
CUT IT OUT!!
Ukyaahh!
?
UH-OH. WHAT'S KYO MAD ABOUT THIS TIME?
HE SAYS HE DOESN'T LIKE THE WAY THE GROUPS ARE SHAPING UP.
OH, SO HE'S WITH YUKI?
THERE'S NO WAY I'LL GO ALONG WITH THIS!!
STOP TRYING TO STICK ME WITH THAT DAMN YUKI ALL THE TIME!!
BESIDES, I DON'T HAVE TO STAY WITH THE GROUP!!
THAT'S TRUE, BUT IT'S MORE FUN WITH YOU THERE.
THAT WAY I CAN MESS WITH YOU.
WHAT AM I, YOUR TOY?

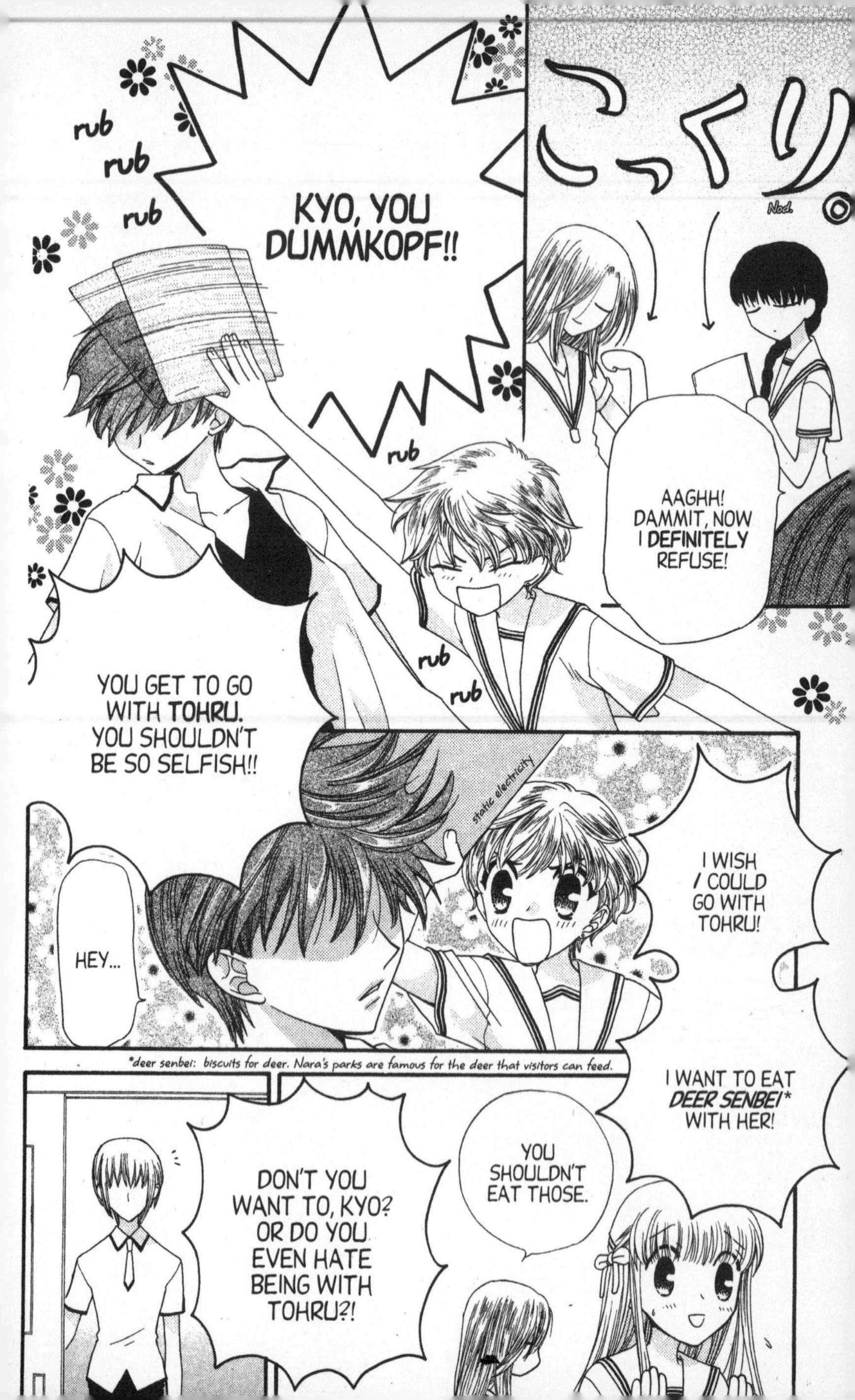
こっくり
Nod.
AAGHH! DAMMIT, NOW I DEFINITELY REFUSE!
KYO, YOU DUMMKOPF!!
rub rub rub
rub
rub rub
YOU GET TO GO WITH TOHRU. YOU SHOULDN'T BE SO SELFISH!!
I WISH I COULD GO WITH TOHRU!
static electricity
HEY...
I WANT TO EAT DEER SENBEI* WITH HER!
YOU SHOULDN'T EAT THOSE.
DON'T YOU WANT TO, KYO? OR DO YOU EVEN HATE BEING WITH TOHRU?!

*deer senbei: biscuits for deer. Nara's parks are famous for the deer that visitors can feed.

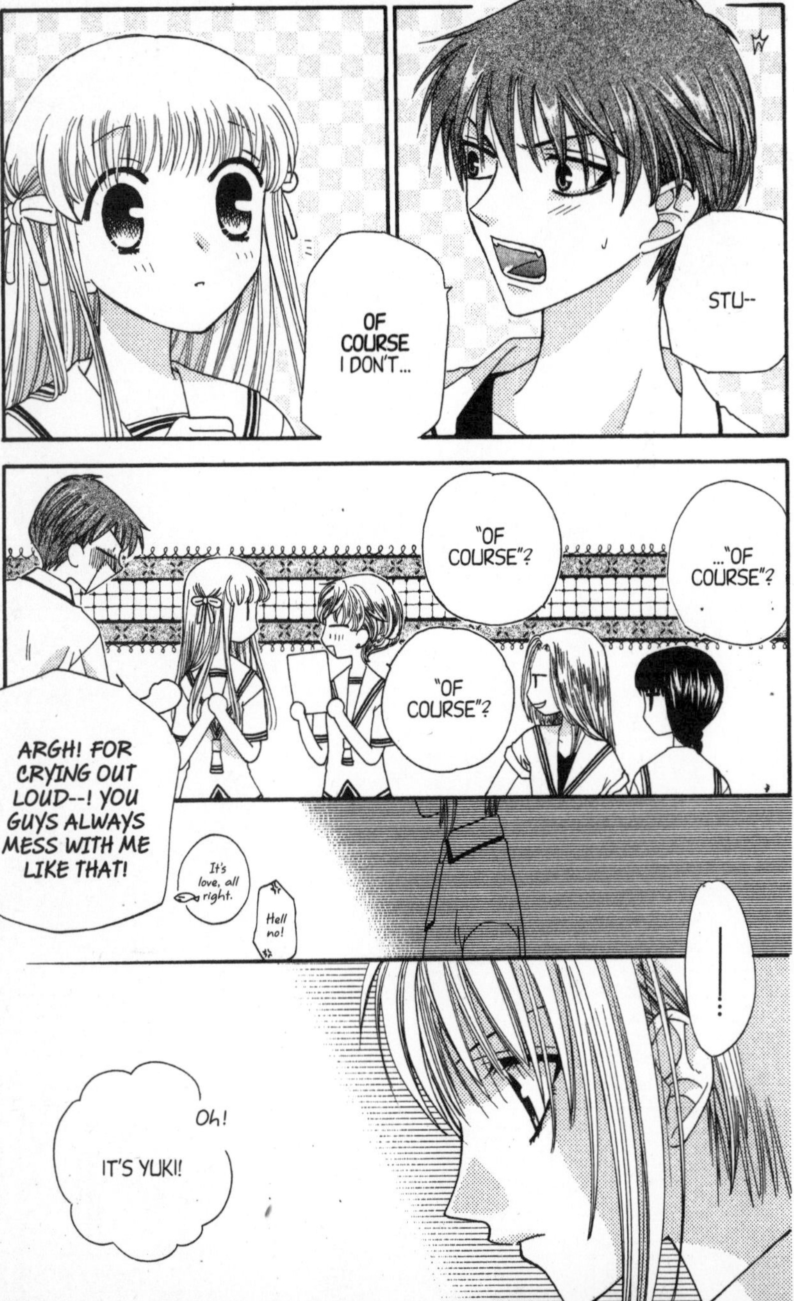
STU--
OF COURSE I DON'T...
..."OF COURSE"?
"OF COURSE"?
"OF COURSE"?
ARGH! FOR CRYING OUT LOUD--! YOU GUYS ALWAYS MESS WITH ME LIKE THAT!
It's love, all right.
Hell no!
--...!
Oh!
IT'S YUKI!

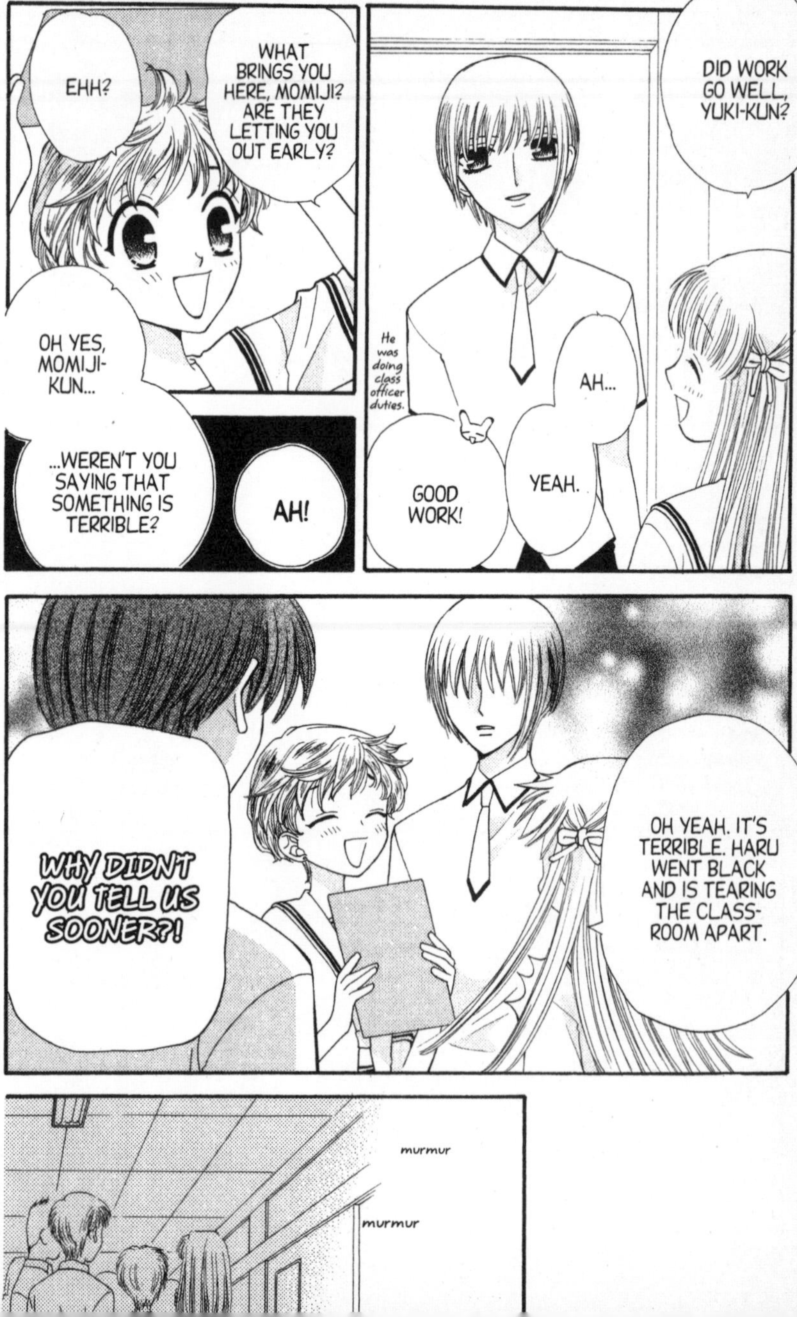
DID WORK GO WELL, YUKI-KUN?
AH...
YEAH.
He was doing class officer duties.
GOOD WORK!
WHAT BRINGS YOU HERE, MOMIJI? ARE THEY LETTING YOU OUT EARLY?
EHH?
OH YES, MOMIJI-KUN...
AH!
...WEREN'T YOU SAYING THAT SOMETHING IS TERRIBLE?
OH YEAH. IT'S TERRIBLE. HARU WENT BLACK AND IS TEARING THE CLASS-ROOM APART.
WHY DIDN'T YOU TELL US SOONER?!
murmur
murmur

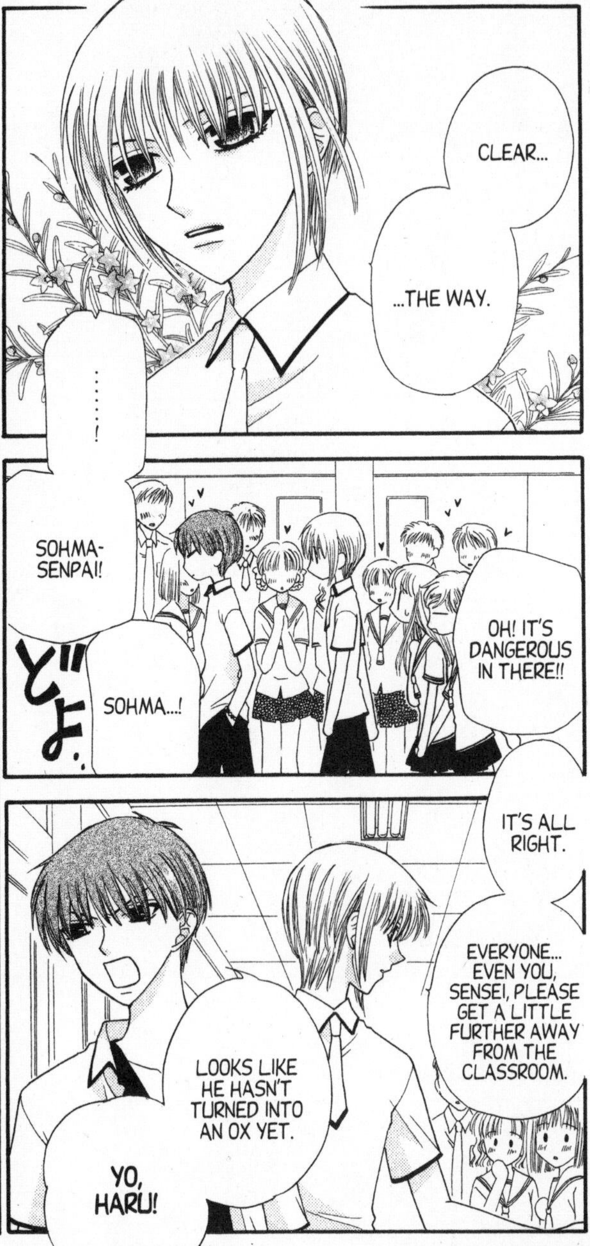
CLEAR...
...THE WAY.
......!
OH! IT'S DANGEROUS IN THERE!!
SOHMA-SENPAI!
SOHMA...!
どよ.
IT'S ALL RIGHT.
EVERYONE... EVEN YOU, SENSEI, PLEASE GET A LITTLE FURTHER AWAY FROM THE CLASSROOM.
LOOKS LIKE HE HASN'T TURNED INTO AN OX YET.
YO, HARU!

Fruits Basket 8: Part 1

Hajimemashite and konnichiwa! It's Takaya again. We're up to volume 8. This makes the twentieth manga volume by me (in Japan, at least). Woo-hoo! Clap clap! And decorating the cover of this momentous 20th volume is Hatsuharu. And the reason is... it's just his turn (To put it frankly). Haru is one of the kids who is really easy to draw. His personality comes out so well. And with that, please, enjoy Furuba volume 8!

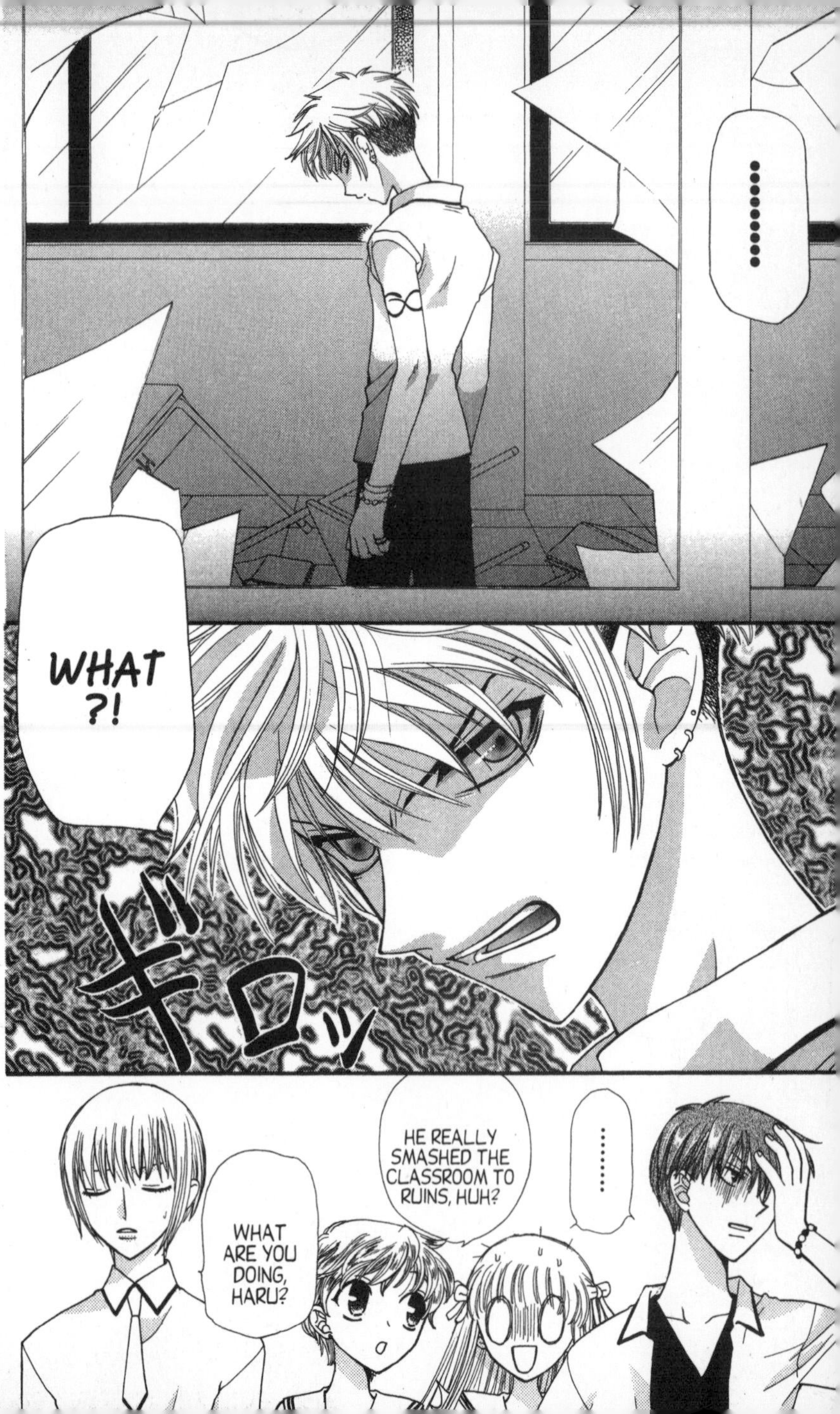
....
WHAT ?!
ギロッ
......
HE REALLY SMASHED THE CLASSROOM TO RUINS, HUH?
WHAT ARE YOU DOING, HARU?

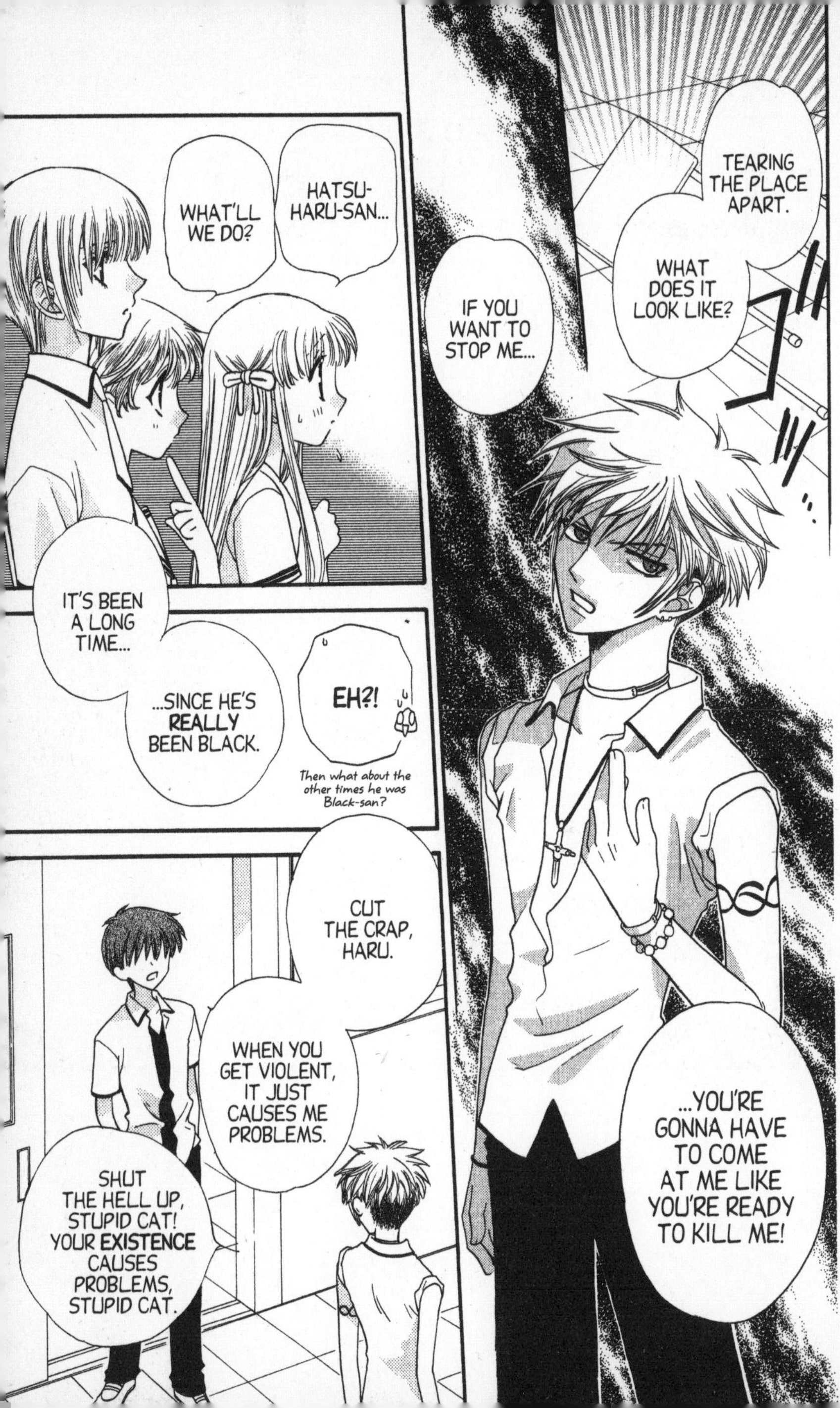
TEARING THE PLACE APART.
WHAT DOES IT LOOK LIKE?
IF YOU WANT TO STOP ME...
...YOU'RE GONNA HAVE TO COME AT ME LIKE YOU'RE READY TO KILL ME!
HATSU-HARU-SAN...
WHAT'LL WE DO?
IT'S BEEN A LONG TIME...
...SINCE HE'S **REALLY** BEEN BLACK.
EH?!
Then what about the other times he was Black-san?
CUT THE CRAP, HARU.
WHEN YOU GET VIOLENT, IT JUST CAUSES ME PROBLEMS.
SHUT THE HELL UP, STUPID CAT! YOUR **EXISTENCE** CAUSES PROBLEMS, STUPID CAT.

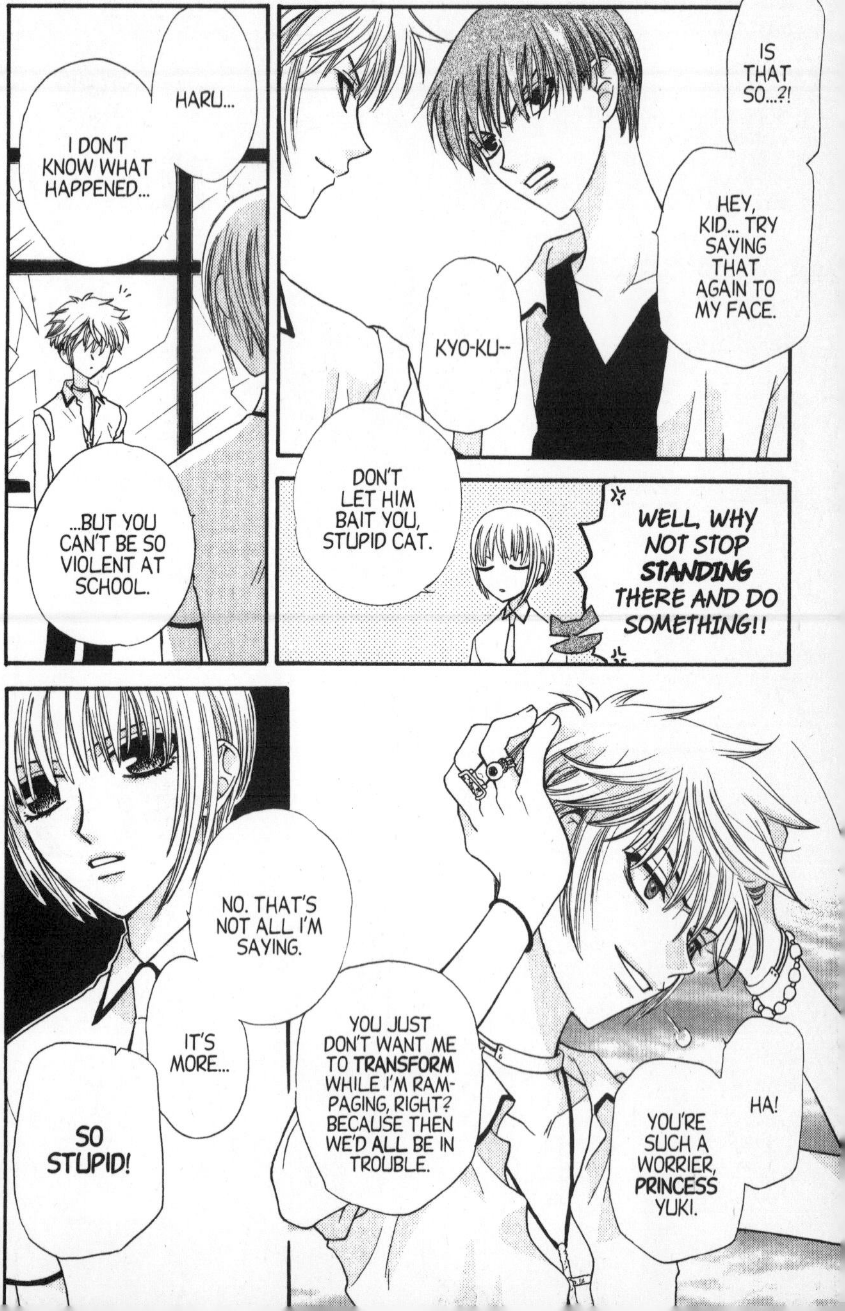
IS THAT SO...?!
HEY, KID... TRY SAYING THAT AGAIN TO MY FACE.
KYO-KU--
WELL, WHY NOT STOP STANDING THERE AND DO SOMETHING!!
DON'T LET HIM BAIT YOU, STUPID CAT.
HARU...
I DON'T KNOW WHAT HAPPENED...
...BUT YOU CAN'T BE SO VIOLENT AT SCHOOL.
HA!
YOU'RE SUCH A WORRIER, PRINCESS YUKI.
YOU JUST DON'T WANT ME TO TRANSFORM WHILE I'M RAMPAGING, RIGHT? BECAUSE THEN WE'D ALL BE IN TROUBLE.
NO. THAT'S NOT ALL I'M SAYING.
IT'S MORE...
SO STUPID!

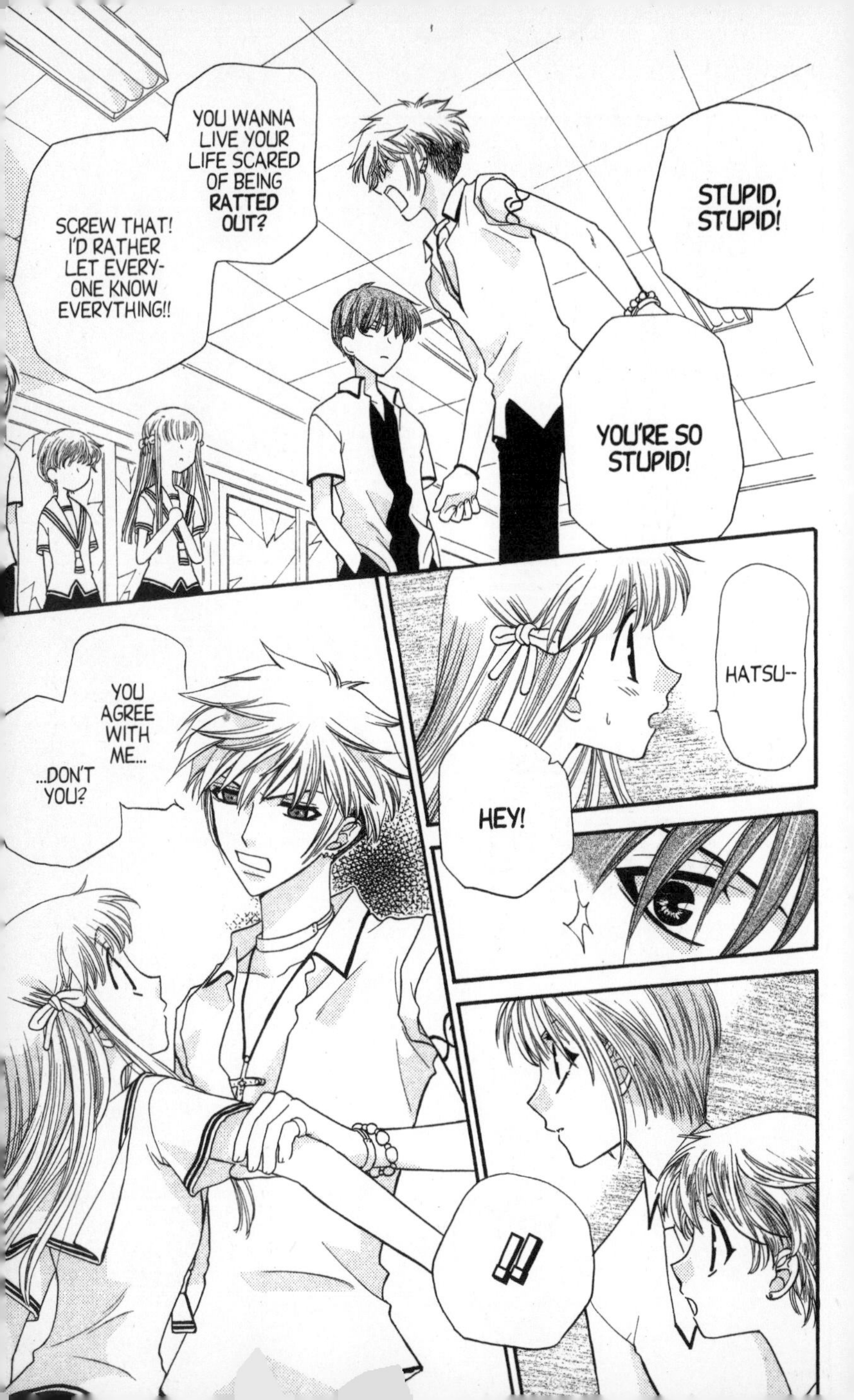

STUPID, STUPID!
YOU'RE SO STUPID!
YOU WANNA LIVE YOUR LIFE SCARED OF BEING **RATTED** OUT?
SCREW THAT! I'D RATHER LET EVERY-ONE KNOW EVERYTHING!!
HATSU--
HEY!
!!
YOU AGREE WITH ME...
...DON'T YOU?

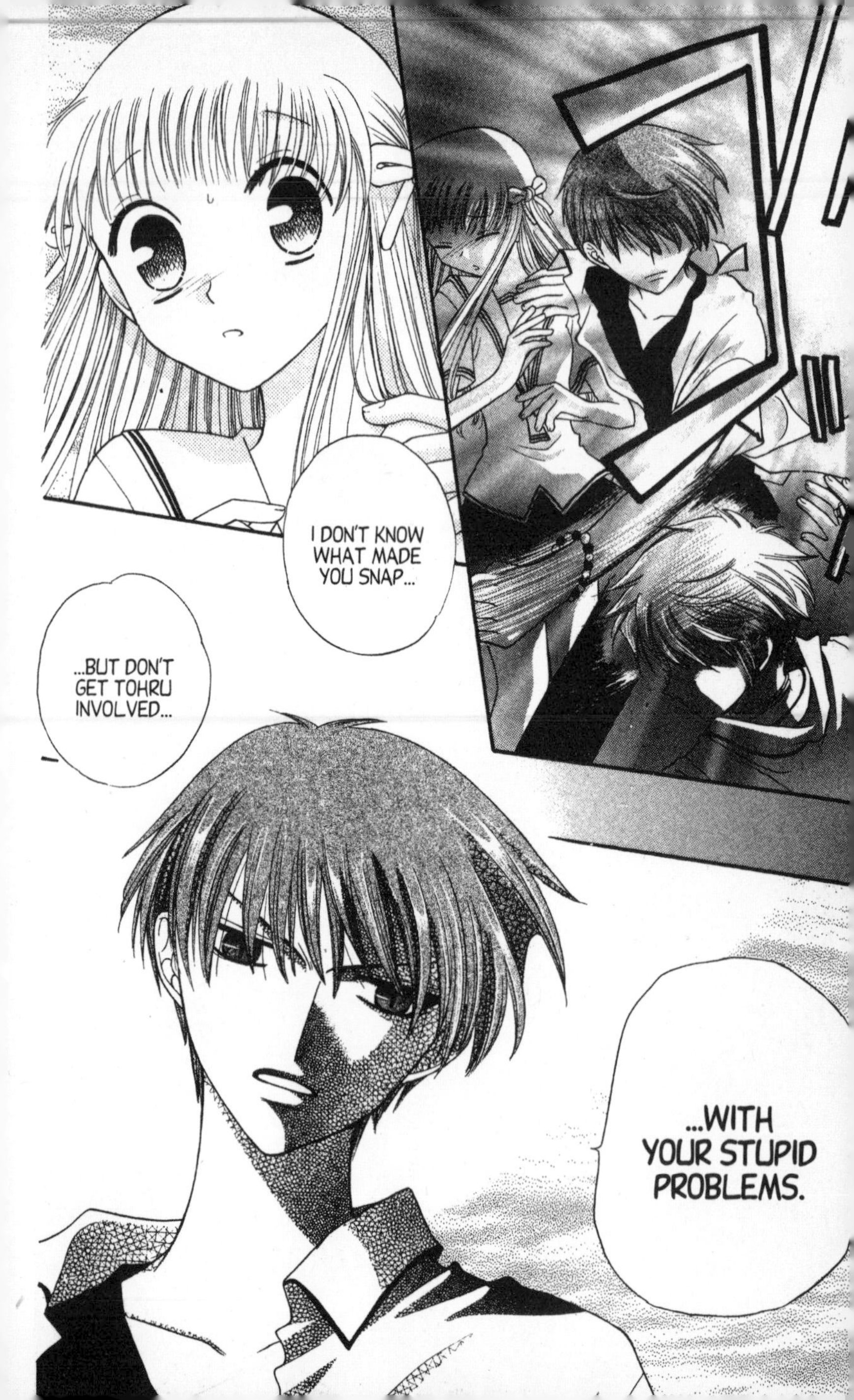
I DON'T KNOW WHAT MADE YOU SNAP...
...BUT DON'T GET TOHRU INVOLVED...
...WITH YOUR STUPID PROBLEMS.

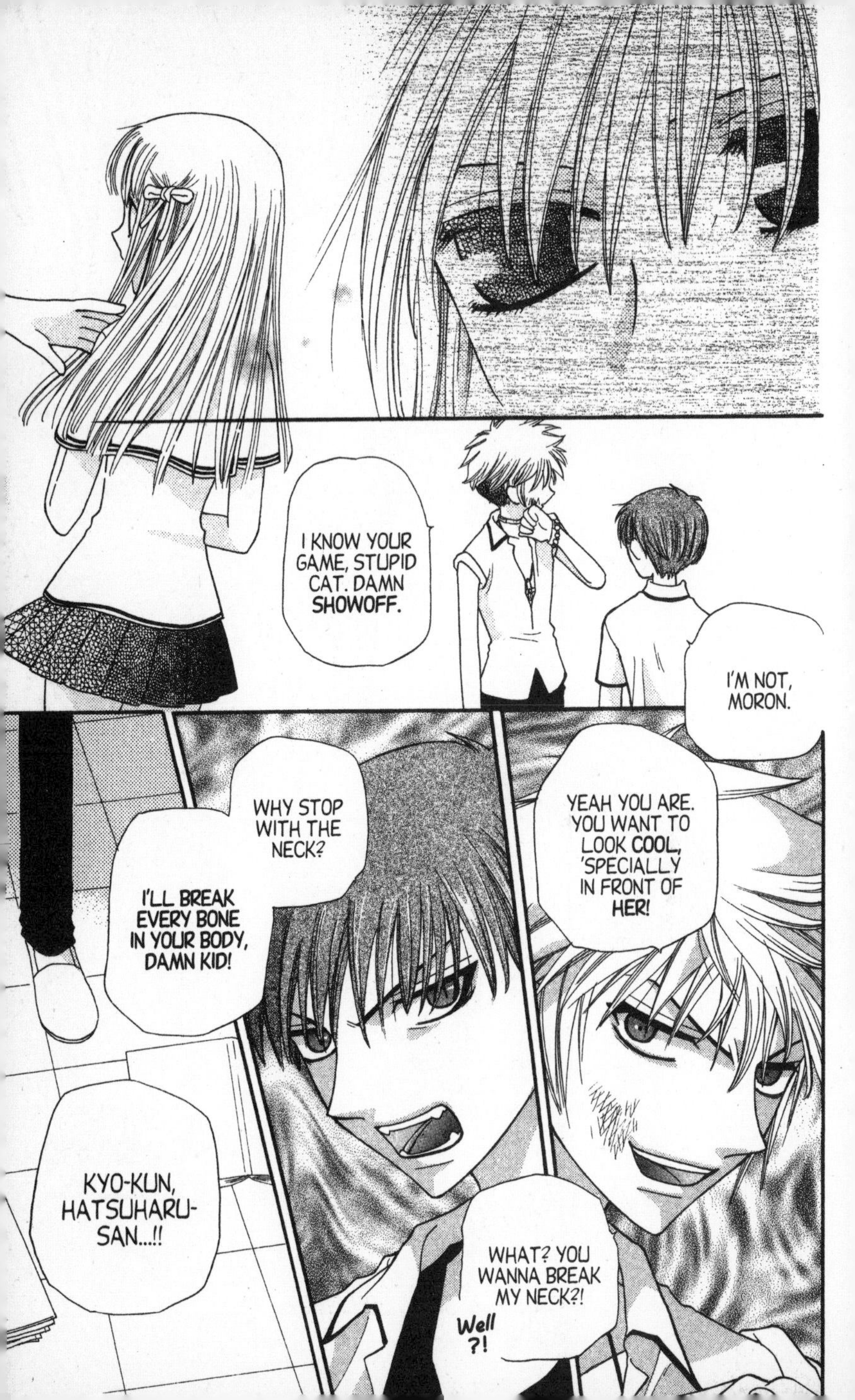
I KNOW YOUR GAME, STUPID CAT. DAMN SHOWOFF.
I'M NOT, MORON.
YEAH YOU ARE. YOU WANT TO LOOK COOL, 'SPECIALLY IN FRONT OF HER!
WHAT? YOU WANNA BREAK MY NECK?!
Well ?!
WHY STOP WITH THE NECK?
I'LL BREAK EVERY BONE IN YOUR BODY, DAMN KID!
KYO-KUN, HATSUHARU-SAN...!!

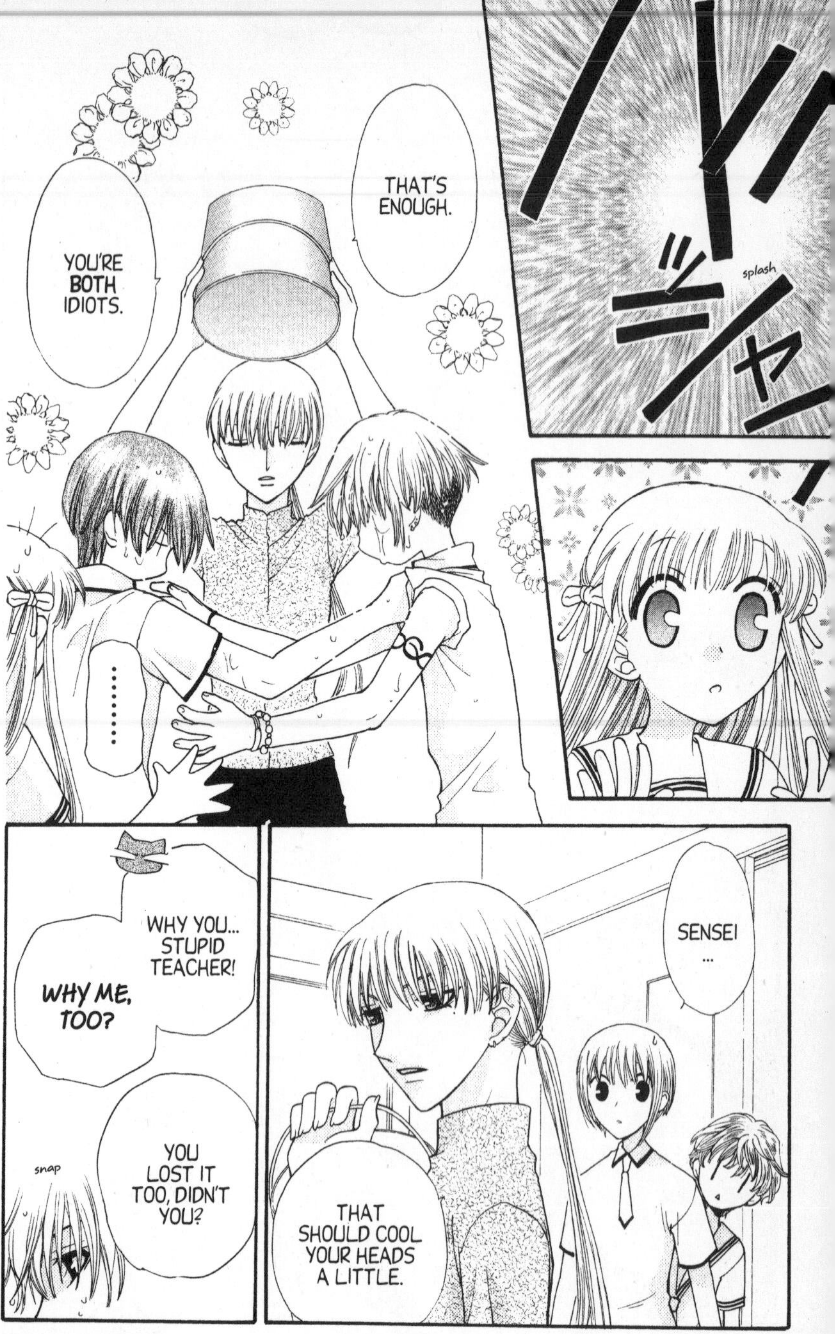
splash
THAT'S ENOUGH.
YOU'RE BOTH IDIOTS.
....
SENSEI ...
THAT SHOULD COOL YOUR HEADS A LITTLE.
WHY YOU... STUPID TEACHER!
WHY ME, TOO?
YOU LOST IT TOO, DIDN'T YOU?
snap

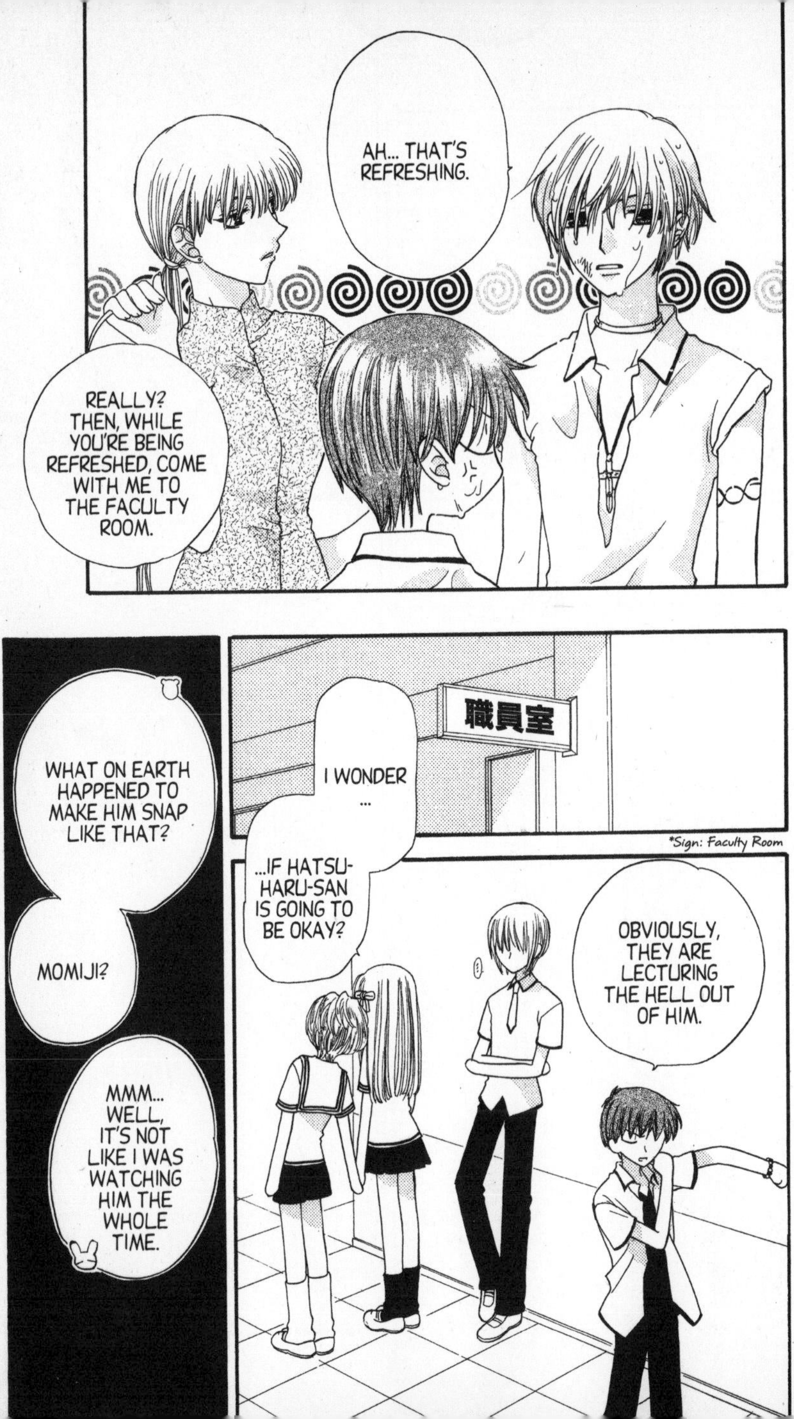
AH... THAT'S REFRESHING.
REALLY? THEN, WHILE YOU'RE BEING REFRESHED, COME WITH ME TO THE FACULTY ROOM.
職員室
I WONDER ...
...IF HATSU-HARU-SAN IS GOING TO BE OKAY?
*Sign: Faculty Room
OBVIOUSLY, THEY ARE LECTURING THE HELL OUT OF HIM.
WHAT ON EARTH HAPPENED TO MAKE HIM SNAP LIKE THAT?
MOMIJI?
MMM... WELL, IT'S NOT LIKE I WAS WATCHING HIM THE WHOLE TIME.

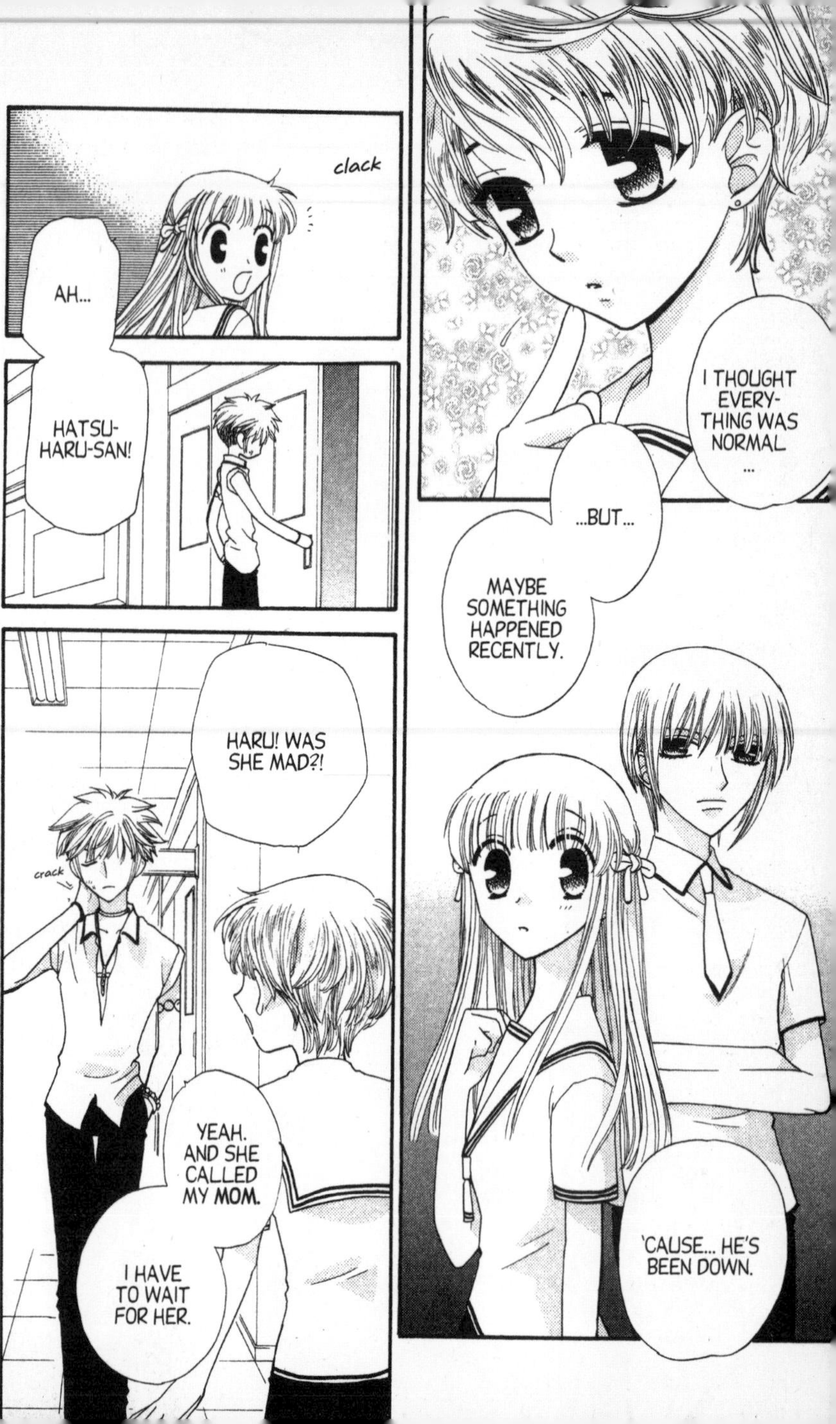
I THOUGHT EVERY-THING WAS NORMAL ...
...BUT...
MAYBE SOMETHING HAPPENED RECENTLY.
'CAUSE... HE'S BEEN DOWN.
clack
AH...
HATSU-HARU-SAN!
HARU! WAS SHE MAD?!
crack
YEAH. AND SHE CALLED MY **MOM**.
I HAVE TO WAIT FOR HER.

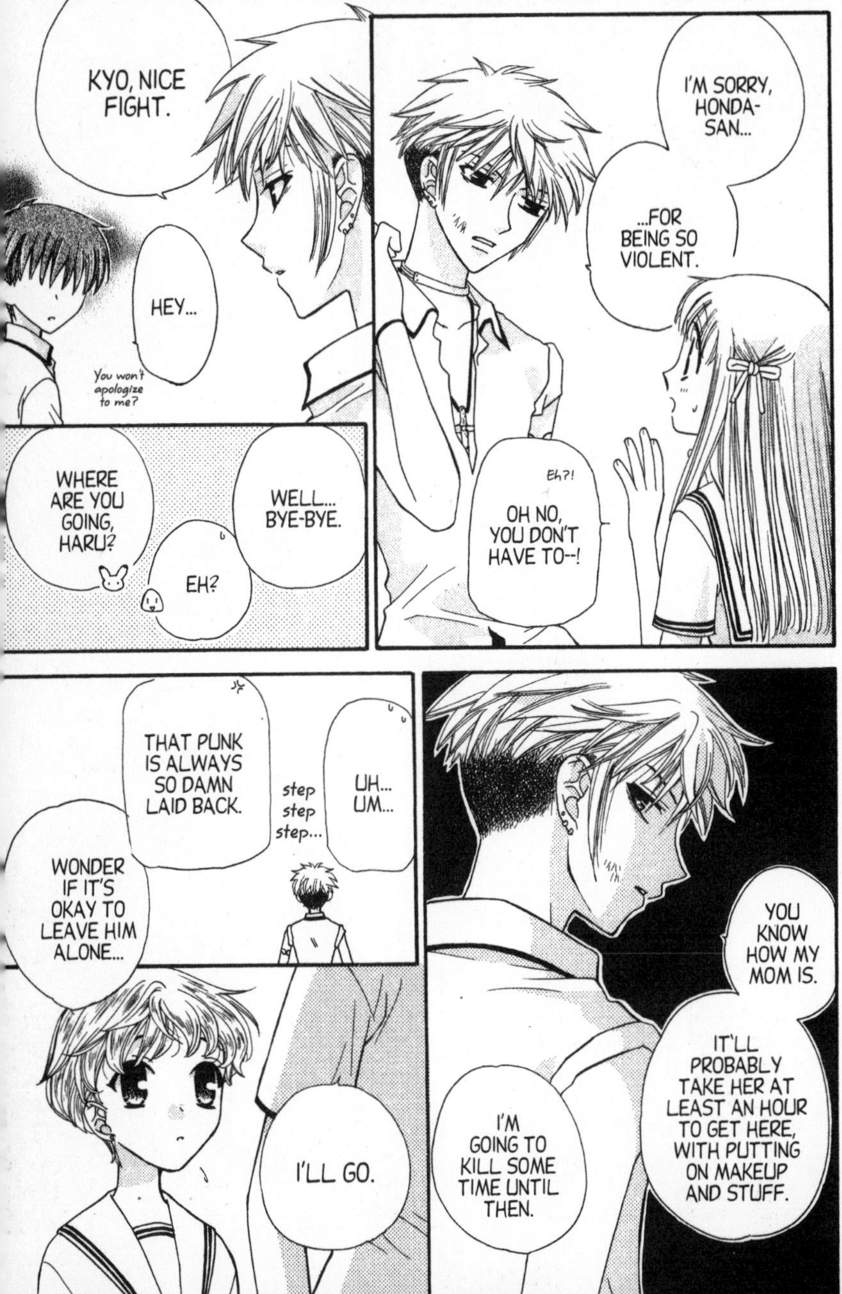
I'M SORRY, HONDA-SAN...
...FOR BEING SO VIOLENT.
Eh?!
OH NO, YOU DON'T HAVE TO--!
KYO, NICE FIGHT.
HEY...
You won't apologize to me?
WELL... BYE-BYE.
EH?
WHERE ARE YOU GOING, HARU?
YOU KNOW HOW MY MOM IS.
IT'LL PROBABLY TAKE HER AT LEAST AN HOUR TO GET HERE, WITH PUTTING ON MAKEUP AND STUFF.
I'M GOING TO KILL SOME TIME UNTIL THEN.
UH... UM...
step step step...
THAT PUNK IS ALWAYS SO DAMN LAID BACK.
WONDER IF IT'S OKAY TO LEAVE HIM ALONE...
I'LL GO.

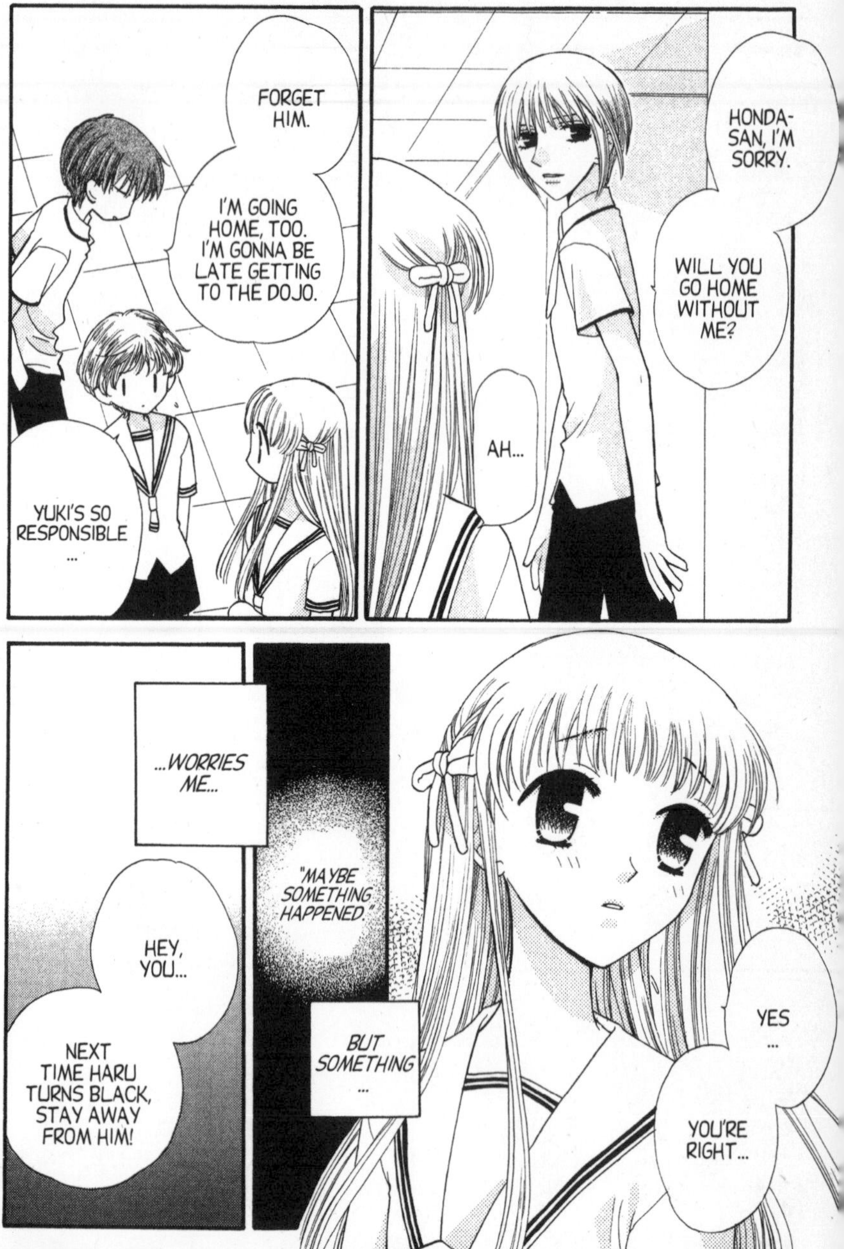
HONDA-SAN, I'M SORRY.
WILL YOU GO HOME WITHOUT ME?
AH...
FORGET HIM.
I'M GOING HOME, TOO. I'M GONNA BE LATE GETTING TO THE DOJO.
YUKI'S SO RESPONSIBLE ...
YES ...
YOU'RE RIGHT...
BUT SOMETHING ...
"MAYBE SOMETHING HAPPENED."
...WORRIES ME...
HEY, YOU...
NEXT TIME HARU TURNS BLACK, STAY AWAY FROM HIM!

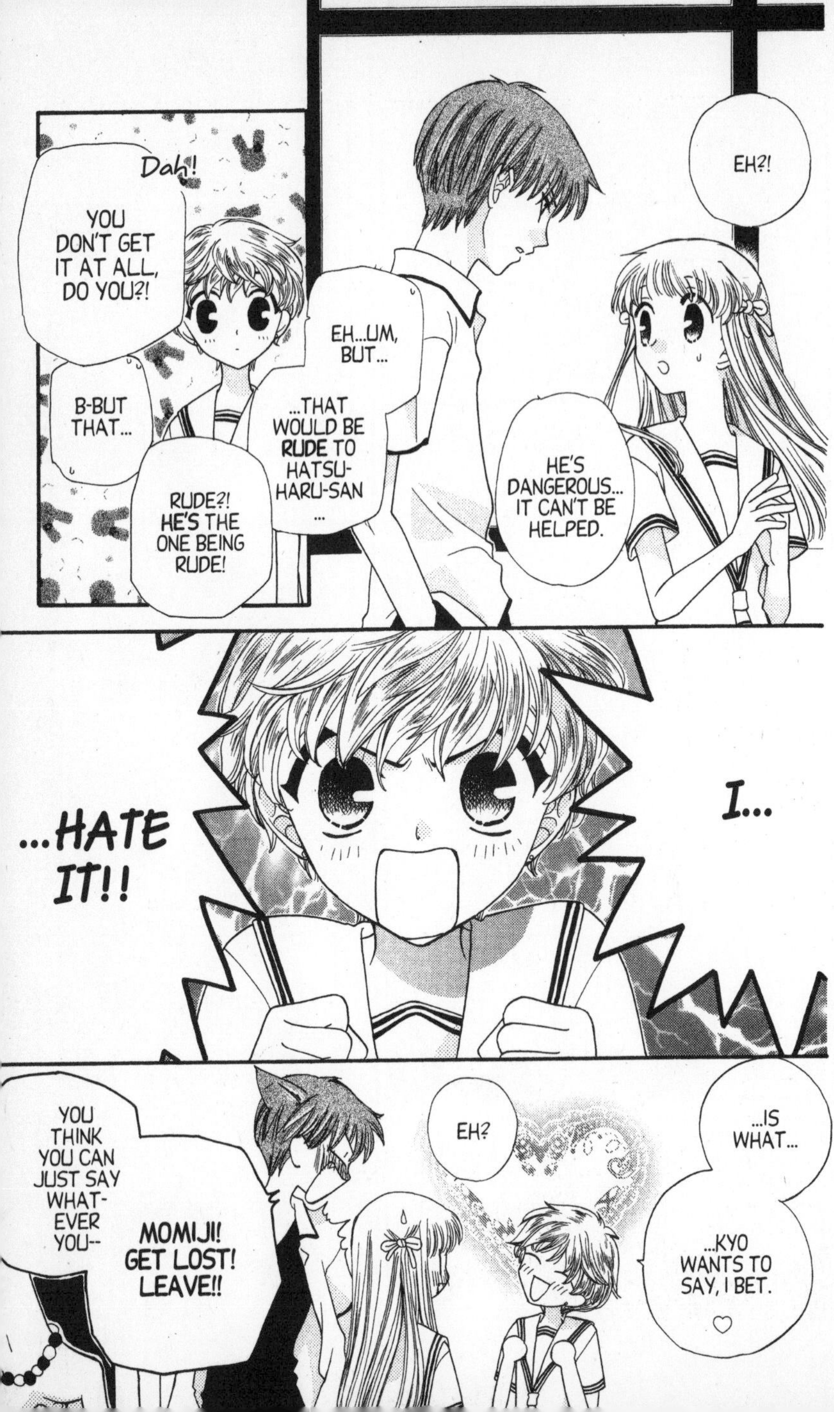
EH?!
HE'S DANGEROUS... IT CAN'T BE HELPED.
EH...UM, BUT...
...THAT WOULD BE RUDE TO HATSUHARU-SAN...
Dah!
YOU DON'T GET IT AT ALL, DO YOU?!
B-BUT THAT...
RUDE?! HE'S THE ONE BEING RUDE!
I...
...HATE IT!!
...IS WHAT...
...KYO WANTS TO SAY, I BET. ♡
EH?
YOU THINK YOU CAN JUST SAY WHATEVER YOU--
MOMIJI! GET LOST! LEAVE!!

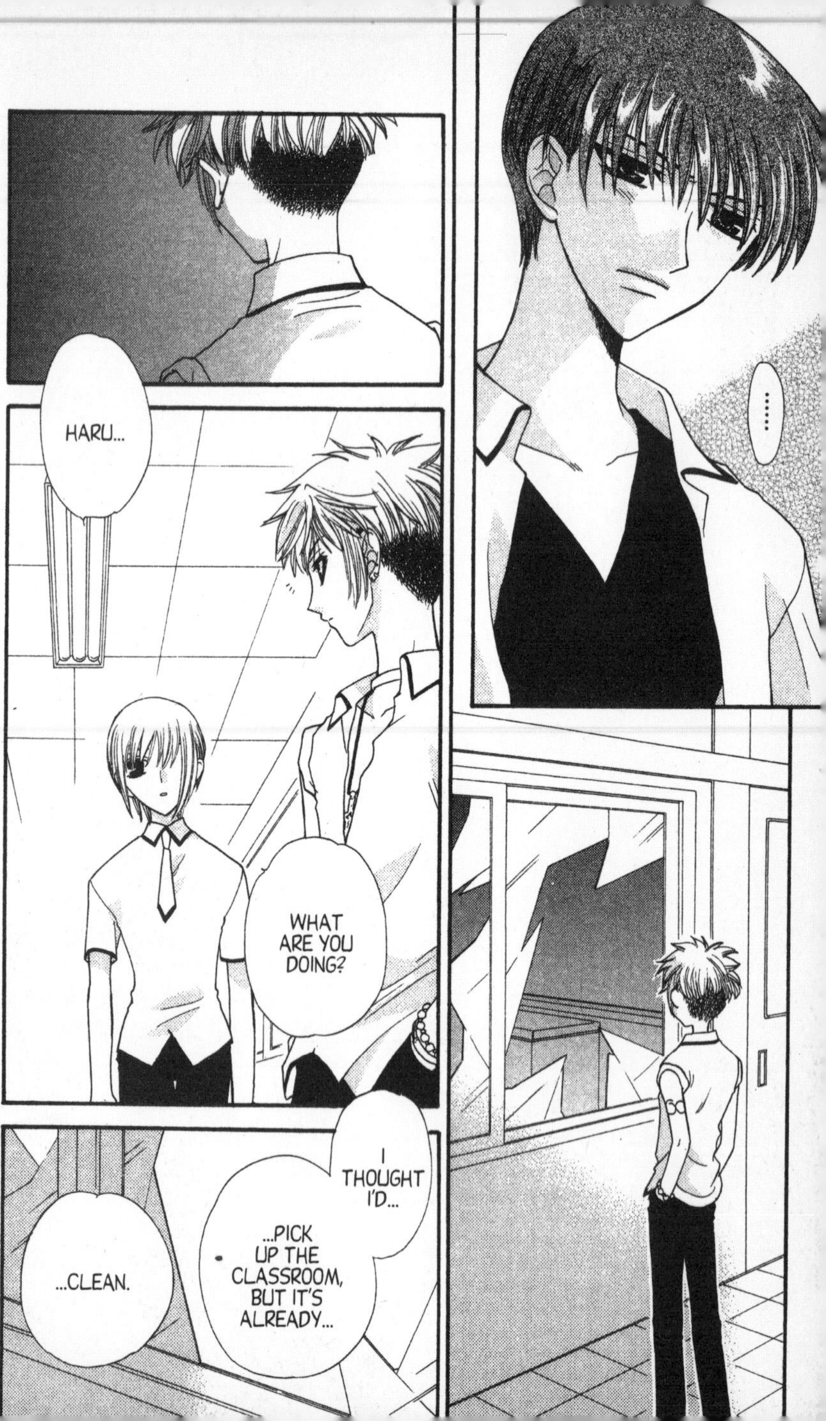
......
HARU...
WHAT ARE YOU DOING?
I THOUGHT I'D...
...PICK UP THE CLASSROOM, BUT IT'S ALREADY...
...CLEAN.

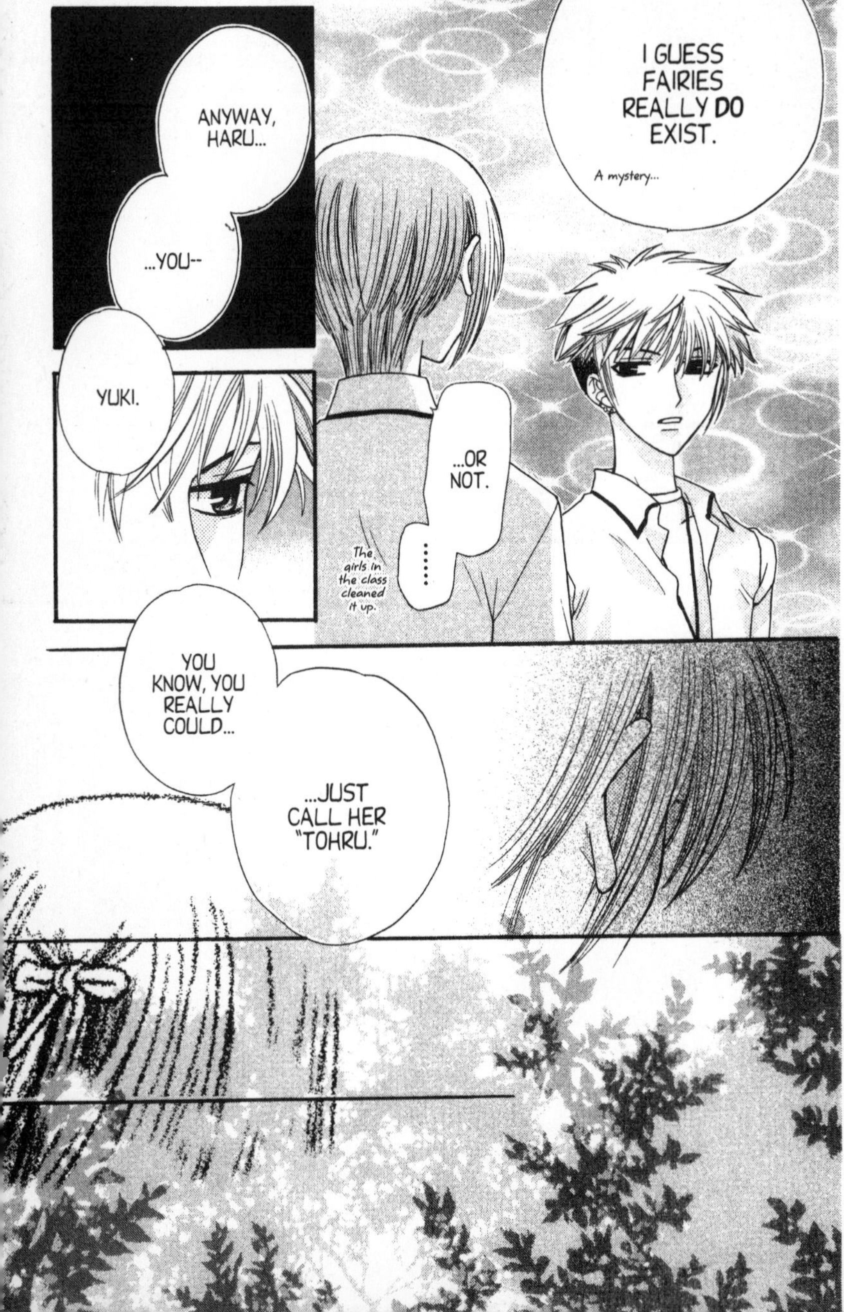
I GUESS FAIRIES REALLY DO EXIST.
A mystery...
...OR NOT.
......
The girls in the class cleaned it up.
ANYWAY, HARU...
...YOU--
YUKI.
YOU KNOW, YOU REALLY COULD...
...JUST CALL HER "TOHRU."

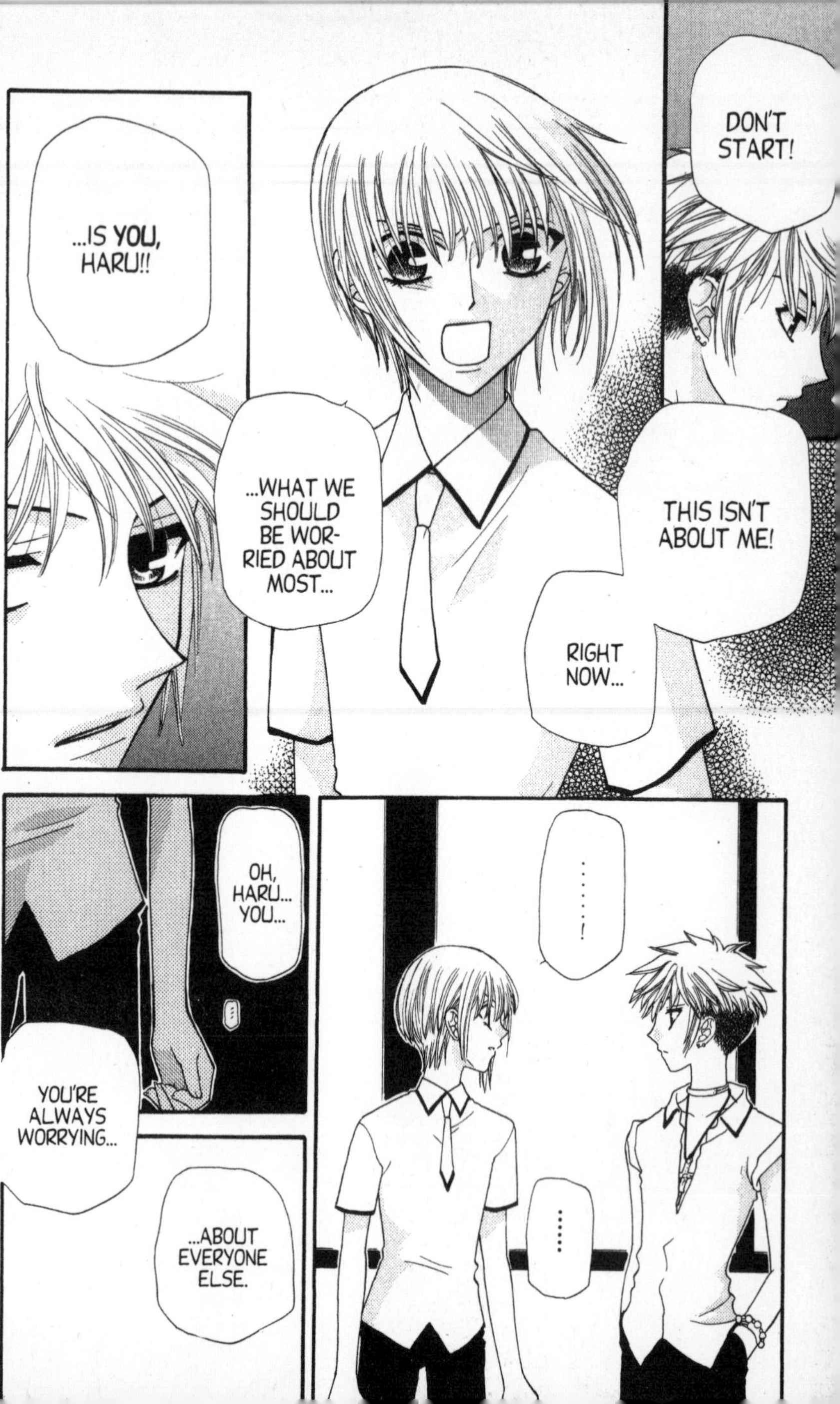
DON'T START!
THIS ISN'T ABOUT ME!
RIGHT NOW...
...WHAT WE SHOULD BE WORRIED ABOUT MOST...
...IS YOU, HARU!!
......!
......
OH, HARU... YOU...
...
YOU'RE ALWAYS WORRYING...
...ABOUT EVERYONE ELSE.

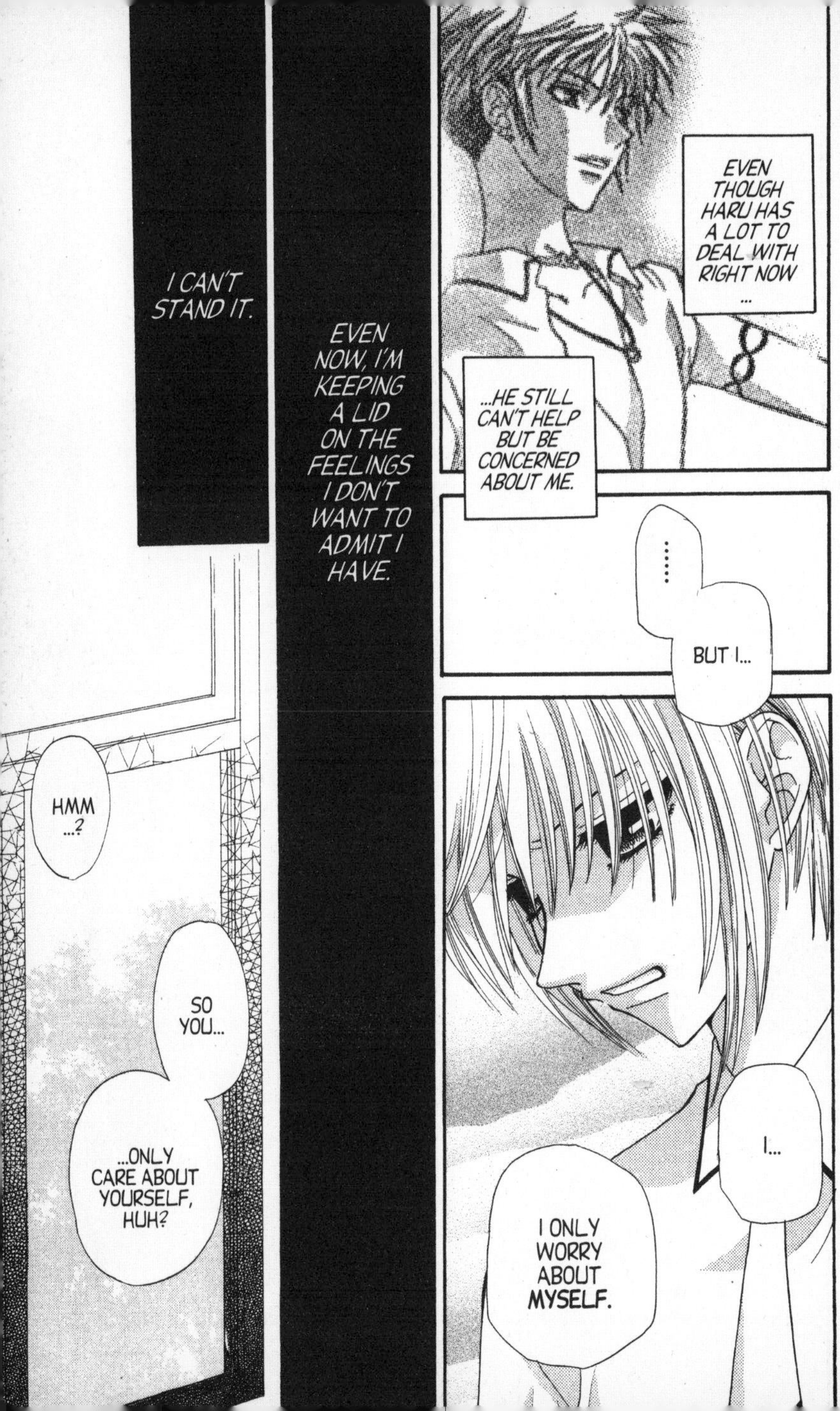
EVEN THOUGH HARU HAS A LOT TO DEAL WITH RIGHT NOW ...
...HE STILL CAN'T HELP BUT BE CONCERNED ABOUT ME.
......
BUT I...
I...
I ONLY WORRY ABOUT MYSELF.
EVEN NOW, I'M KEEPING A LID ON THE FEELINGS I DON'T WANT TO ADMIT I HAVE.
I CAN'T STAND IT.
HMM ...?
SO YOU...
...ONLY CARE ABOUT YOURSELF, HUH?

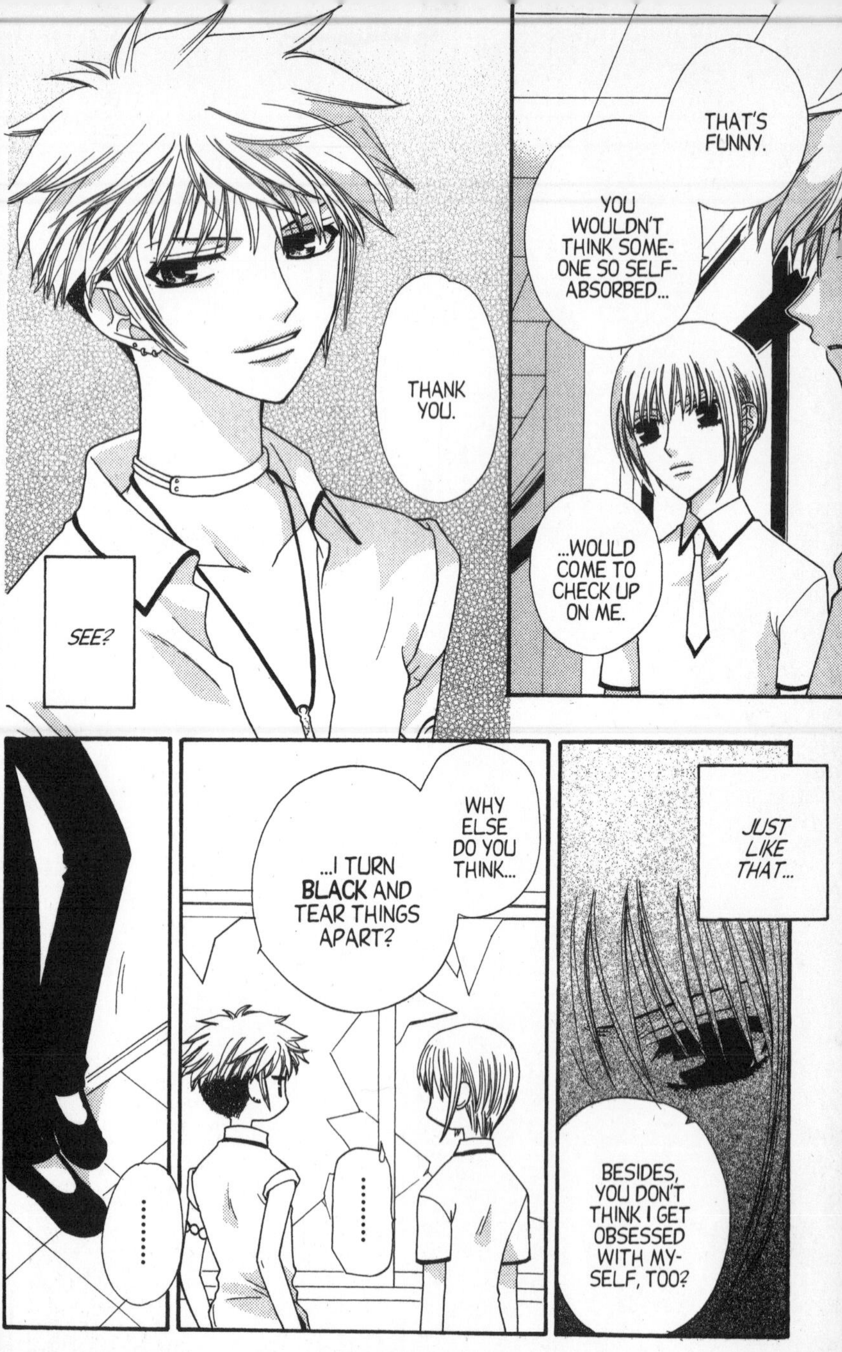
THAT'S FUNNY.
YOU WOULDN'T THINK SOME-ONE SO SELF-ABSORBED...
...WOULD COME TO CHECK UP ON ME.
THANK YOU.
SEE?
JUST LIKE THAT...
BESIDES, YOU DON'T THINK I GET OBSESSED WITH MY-SELF, TOO?
WHY ELSE DO YOU THINK...
...I TURN BLACK AND TEAR THINGS APART?
....
....

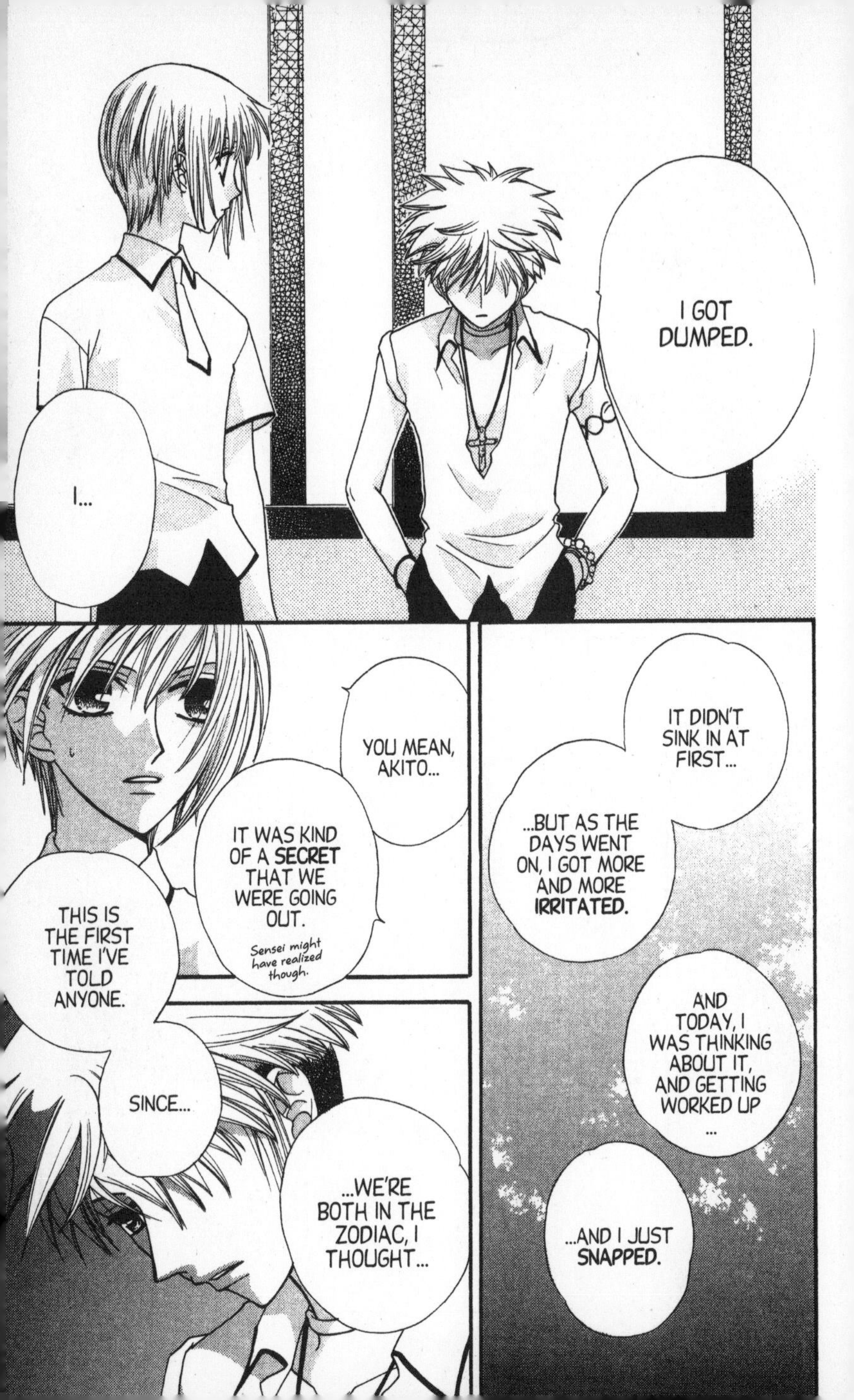
I GOT DUMPED.
I...
IT DIDN'T SINK IN AT FIRST...
...BUT AS THE DAYS WENT ON, I GOT MORE AND MORE IRRITATED.
AND TODAY, I WAS THINKING ABOUT IT, AND GETTING WORKED UP ...
...AND I JUST SNAPPED.
YOU MEAN, AKITO...
IT WAS KIND OF A SECRET THAT WE WERE GOING OUT.
Sensei might have realized though.
THIS IS THE FIRST TIME I'VE TOLD ANYONE.
SINCE...
...WE'RE BOTH IN THE ZODIAC, I THOUGHT...

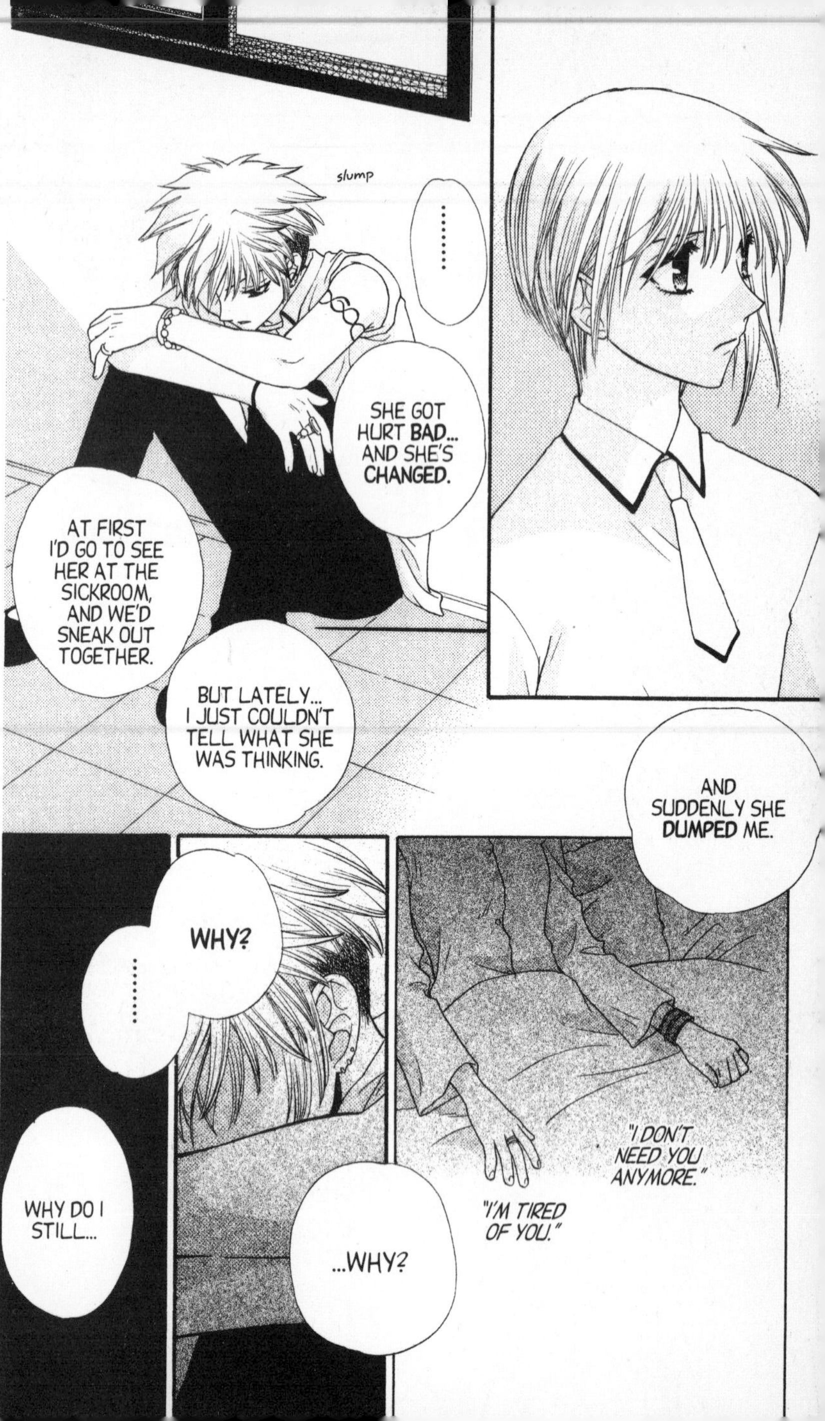
slump
....
SHE GOT HURT BAD... AND SHE'S CHANGED.
AT FIRST I'D GO TO SEE HER AT THE SICKROOM, AND WE'D SNEAK OUT TOGETHER.
BUT LATELY... I JUST COULDN'T TELL WHAT SHE WAS THINKING.
AND SUDDENLY SHE DUMPED ME.
"I DON'T NEED YOU ANYMORE."
"I'M TIRED OF YOU."
WHY?
....
...WHY?
WHY DO I STILL...

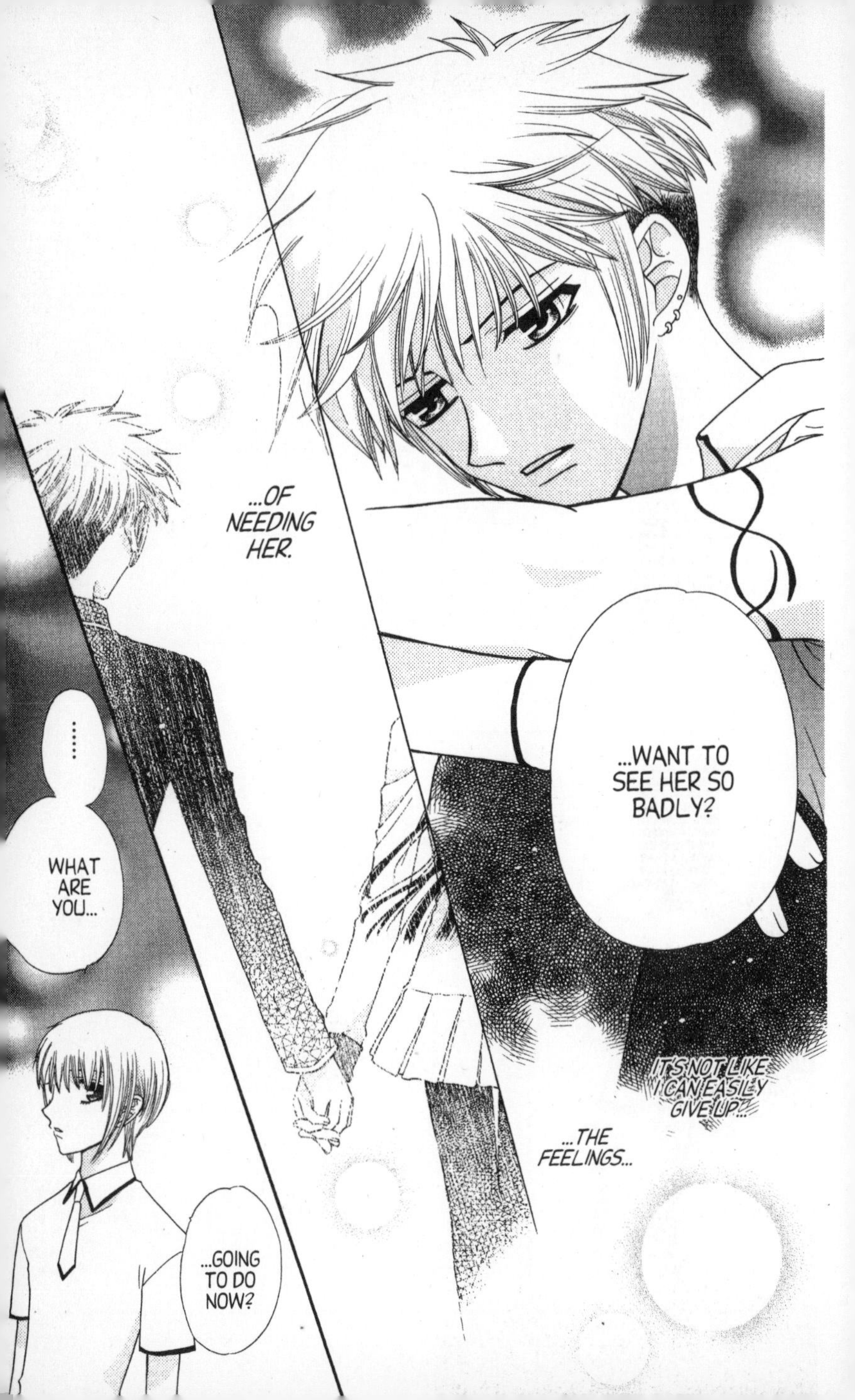
...WANT TO SEE HER SO BADLY?
IT'S NOT LIKE I CAN EASILY GIVE UP...
...THE FEELINGS...
...OF NEEDING HER.
......
WHAT ARE YOU...
...GOING TO DO NOW?

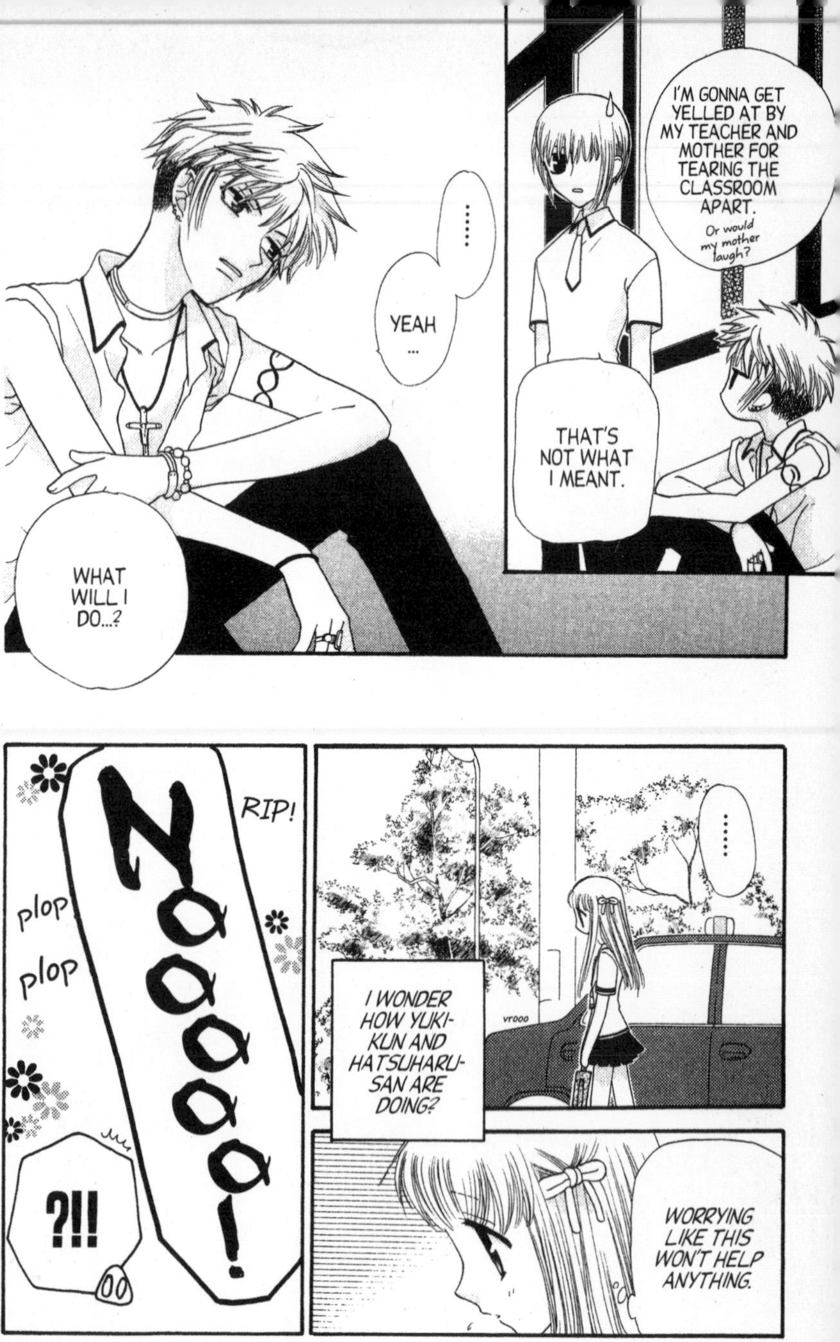
I'M GONNA GET YELLED AT BY MY TEACHER AND MOTHER FOR TEARING THE CLASSROOM APART.
Or would my mother laugh?
THAT'S NOT WHAT I MEANT.
......
YEAH ...
WHAT WILL I DO...?
......
I WONDER HOW YUKI-KUN AND HATSUHARU-SAN ARE DOING?
vrooo
WORRYING LIKE THIS WON'T HELP ANYTHING.
RIP!
Nooooo!
plop
plop
?!!

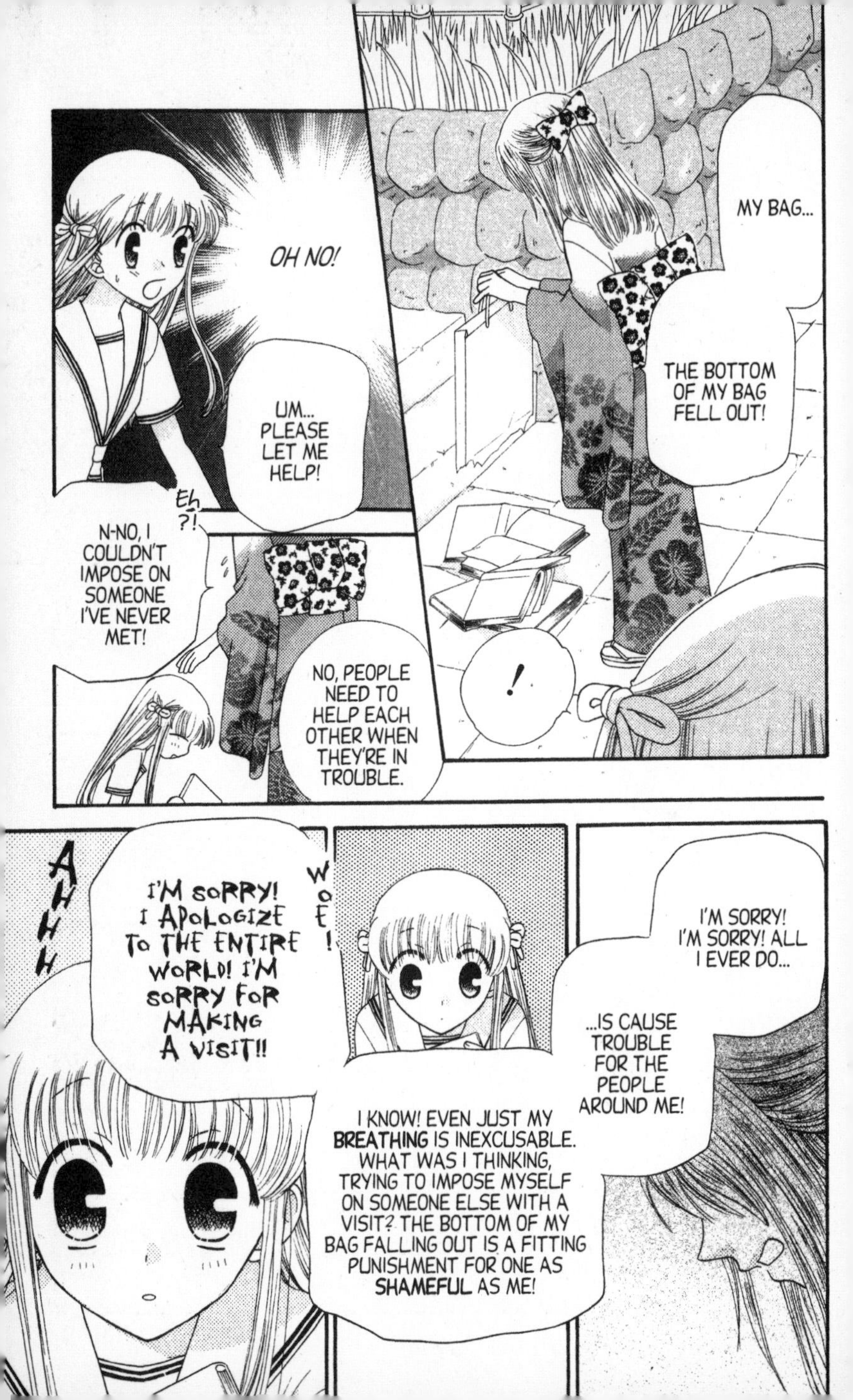
MY BAG...
THE BOTTOM OF MY BAG FELL OUT!
!
OH NO!
UM... PLEASE LET ME HELP!
Eh?!
N-NO, I COULDN'T IMPOSE ON SOMEONE I'VE NEVER MET!
NO, PEOPLE NEED TO HELP EACH OTHER WHEN THEY'RE IN TROUBLE.
I'M SORRY! I'M SORRY! ALL I EVER DO...
...IS CAUSE TROUBLE FOR THE PEOPLE AROUND ME!
I KNOW! EVEN JUST MY BREATHING IS INEXCUSABLE. WHAT WAS I THINKING, TRYING TO IMPOSE MYSELF ON SOMEONE ELSE WITH A VISIT? THE BOTTOM OF MY BAG FALLING OUT IS A FITTING PUNISHMENT FOR ONE AS SHAMEFUL AS ME!
WOE!
I'M SORRY! I APOLOGIZE TO THE ENTIRE WORLD! I'M SORRY FOR MAKING A VISIT!!
AHHH

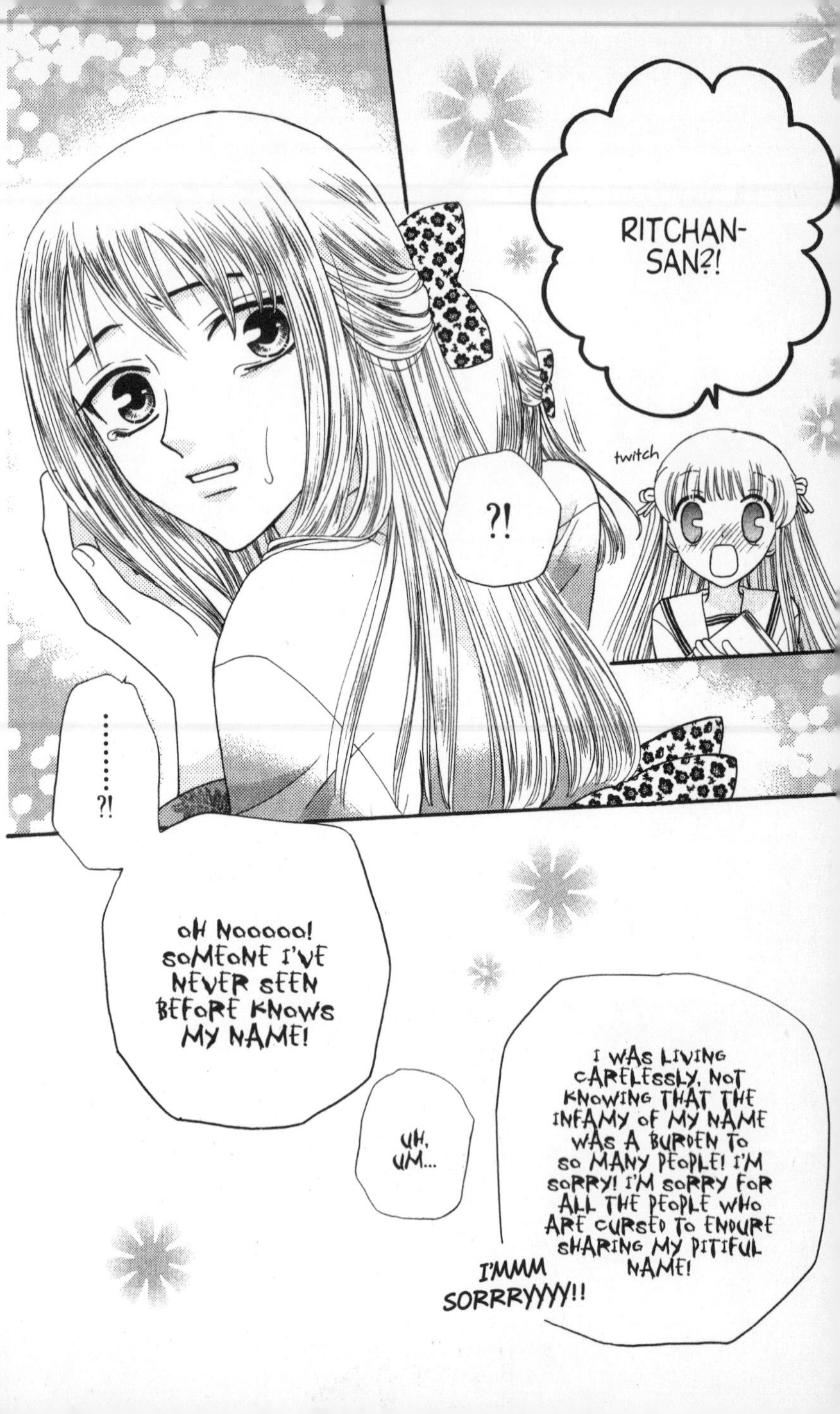
RITCHAN-SAN?!
twitch
?!
......?!
OH NOOOOO! SOMEONE I'VE NEVER SEEN BEFORE KNOWS MY NAME!
UH, UM...
I WAS LIVING CARELESSLY, NOT KNOWING THAT THE INFAMY OF MY NAME WAS A BURDEN TO SO MANY PEOPLE! I'M SORRY! I'M SORRY FOR ALL THE PEOPLE WHO ARE CURSED TO ENDURE SHARING MY PITIFUL NAME!
I'MMM SORRRYYYY!!

Chapter 44

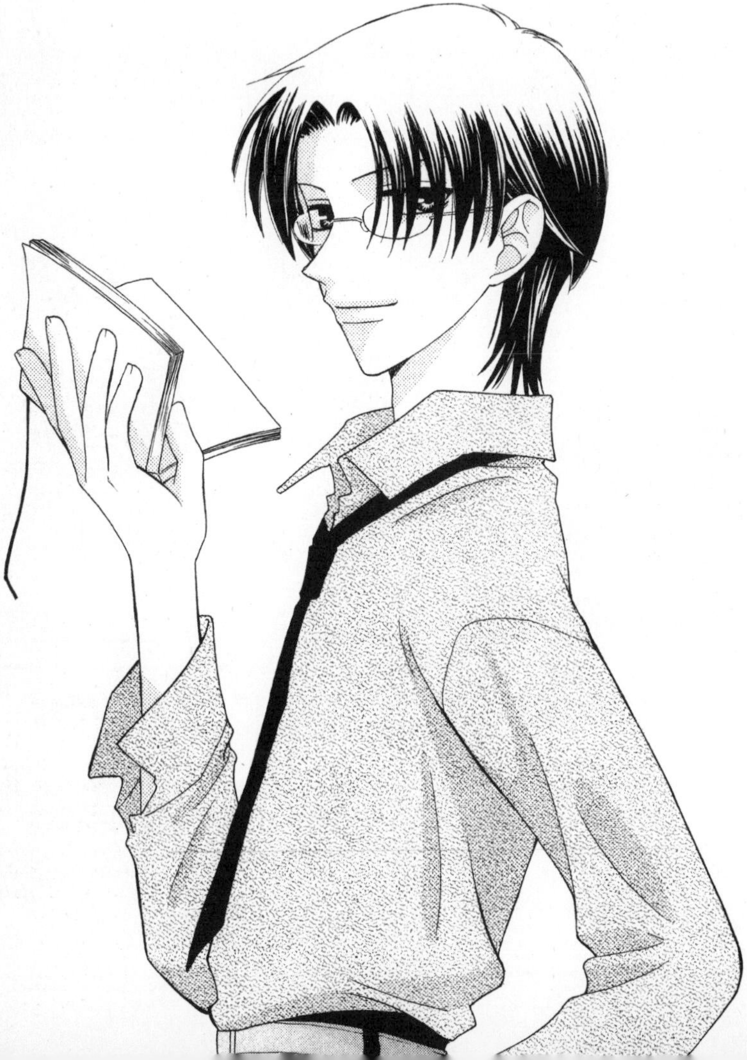

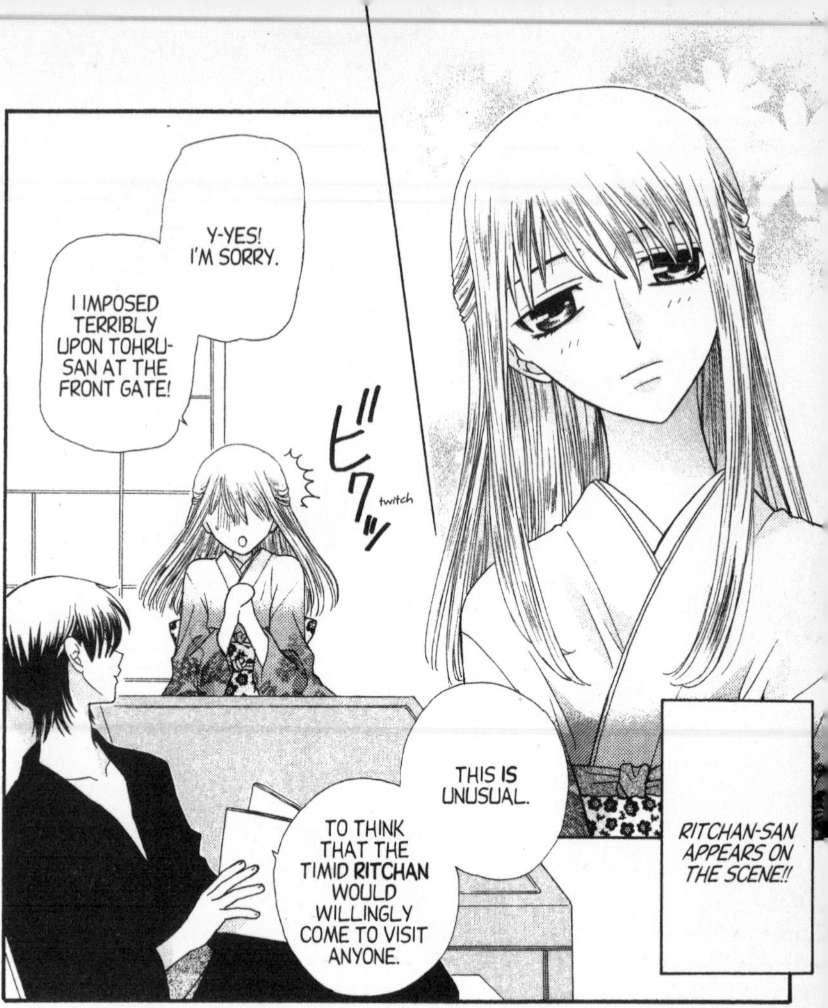
RITCHAN-SAN APPEARS ON THE SCENE!!
THIS IS UNUSUAL.
TO THINK THAT THE TIMID RITCHAN WOULD WILLINGLY COME TO VISIT ANYONE.
ビクッ
twitch
Y-YES! I'M SORRY.
I IMPOSED TERRIBLY UPON TOHRU-SAN AT THE FRONT GATE!

UL-SPE (I'LL ABBREVIATE IT AT LEAST!)
BLAH BLAH BLAH 2

Now that Ritsu has shown up, there are very few members of the Zodiac left. But Ritchan sure is energetic... (laugh).

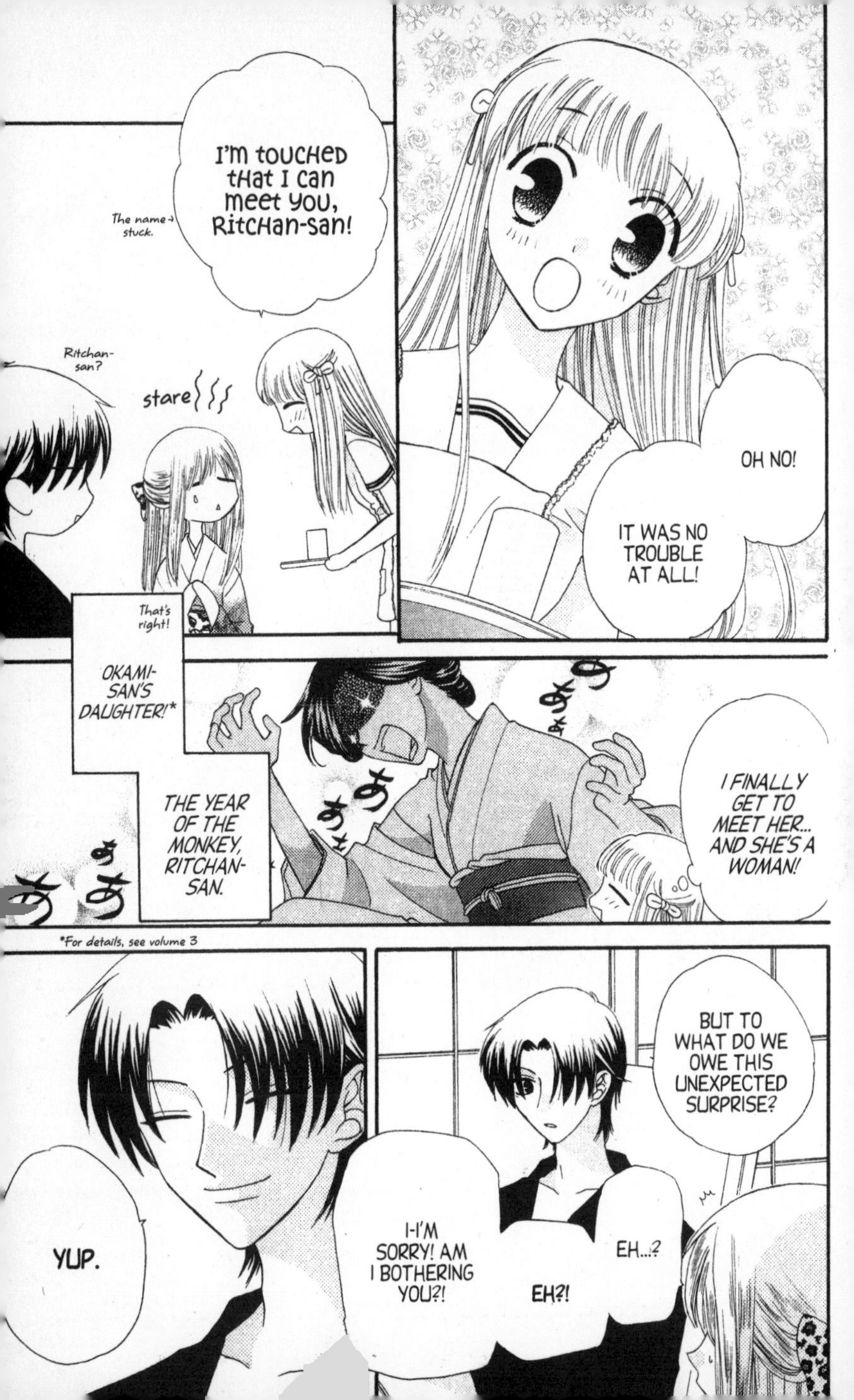
OH NO!
IT WAS NO TROUBLE AT ALL!
I'M TOUCHED THAT I CAN MEET YOU, RITCHAN-SAN!
The name stuck.
Ritchan-san?
stare
That's right!
I FINALLY GET TO MEET HER... AND SHE'S A WOMAN!
OKAMI-SAN'S DAUGHTER!*
THE YEAR OF THE MONKEY, RITCHAN-SAN.
BUT TO WHAT DO WE OWE THIS UNEXPECTED SURPRISE?
EH...?
EH?!
I-I'M SORRY! AM I BOTHERING YOU?!
YUP.

*For details, see volume 3

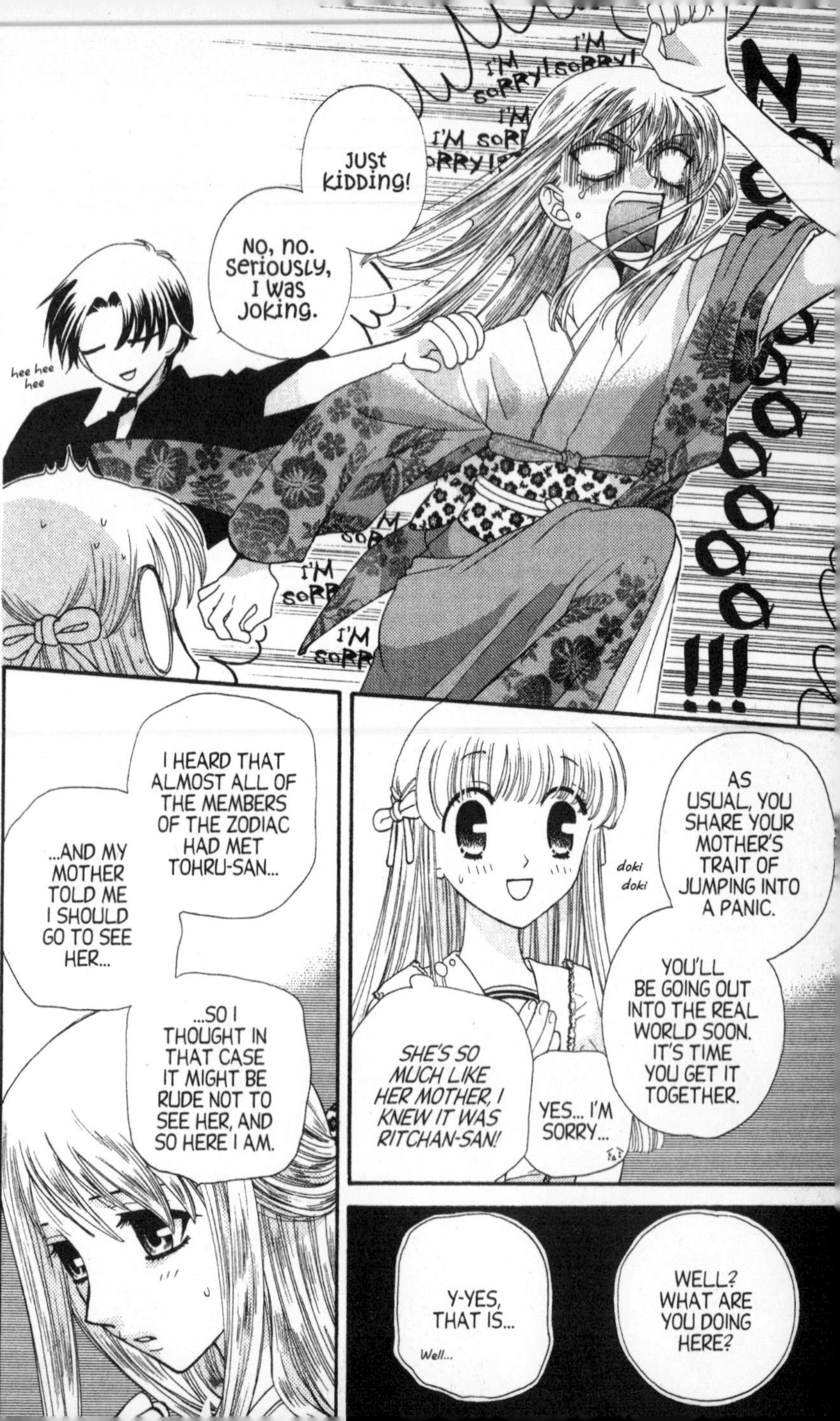
NOOOOOOOO!!!
I'M SORRY! SORRY!
I'M SORRY!
I'M SORRY!
I'M SORRY!
JUST KIDDING!
No, no. Seriously, I was joking.
hee hee hee
I'M SORRY
I'M SORRY
I'M SORRY
AS USUAL, YOU SHARE YOUR MOTHER'S TRAIT OF JUMPING INTO A PANIC.
doki doki
YOU'LL BE GOING OUT INTO THE REAL WORLD SOON. IT'S TIME YOU GET IT TOGETHER.
YES... I'M SORRY...
SHE'S SO MUCH LIKE HER MOTHER, I KNEW IT WAS RITCHAN-SAN!
WELL? WHAT ARE YOU DOING HERE?
Y-YES, THAT IS...
Well...
I HEARD THAT ALMOST ALL OF THE MEMBERS OF THE ZODIAC HAD MET TOHRU-SAN...
...AND MY MOTHER TOLD ME I SHOULD GO TO SEE HER...
...SO I THOUGHT IN THAT CASE IT MIGHT BE RUDE NOT TO SEE HER, AND SO HERE I AM.

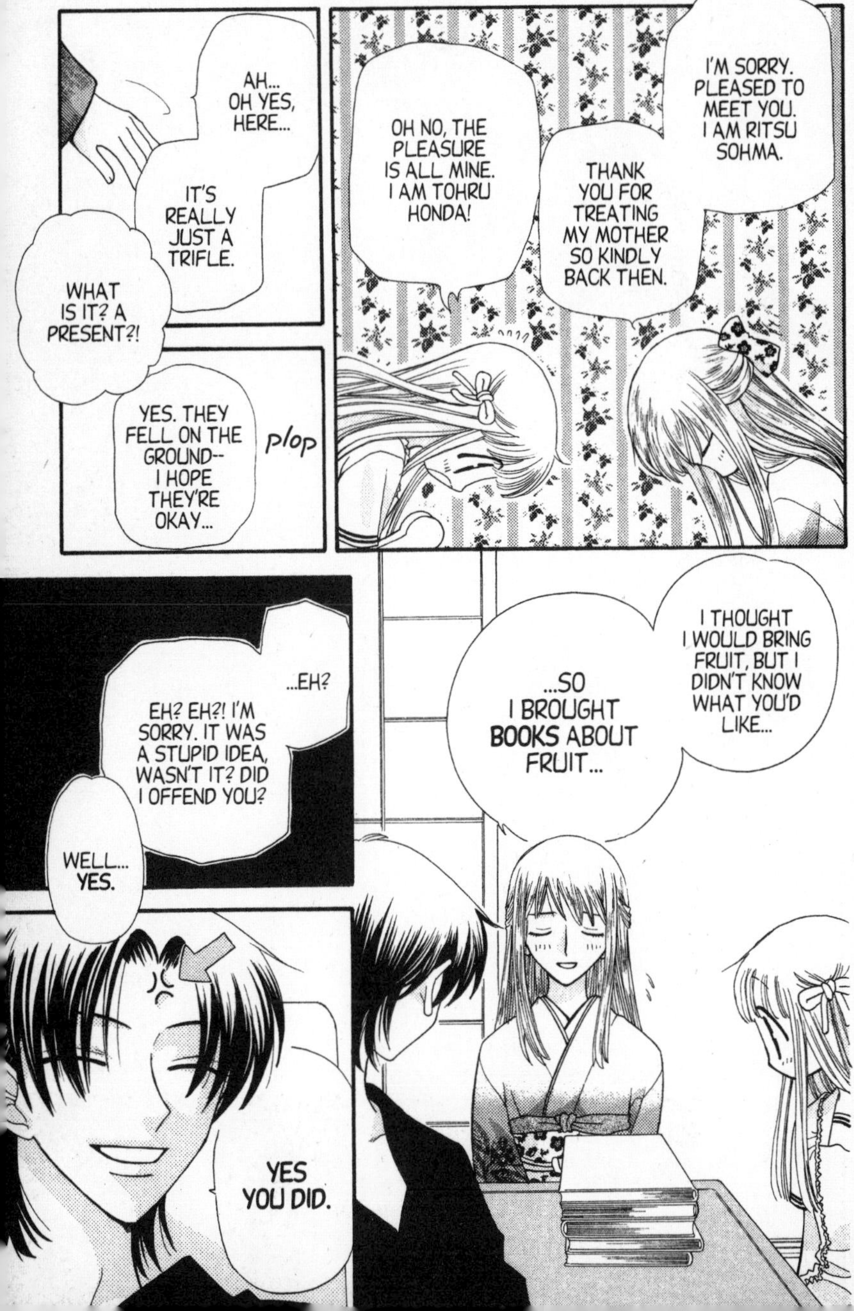
I'M SORRY. PLEASED TO MEET YOU. I AM RITSU SOHMA.
THANK YOU FOR TREATING MY MOTHER SO KINDLY BACK THEN.
OH NO, THE PLEASURE IS ALL MINE. I AM TOHRU HONDA!
AH... OH YES, HERE...
IT'S REALLY JUST A TRIFLE.
WHAT IS IT? A PRESENT?!
plop
YES. THEY FELL ON THE GROUND-- I HOPE THEY'RE OKAY...
I THOUGHT I WOULD BRING FRUIT, BUT I DIDN'T KNOW WHAT YOU'D LIKE...
...SO I BROUGHT BOOKS ABOUT FRUIT...
...EH?
EH? EH?! I'M SORRY. IT WAS A STUPID IDEA, WASN'T IT? DID I OFFEND YOU?
WELL... YES.
YES YOU DID.

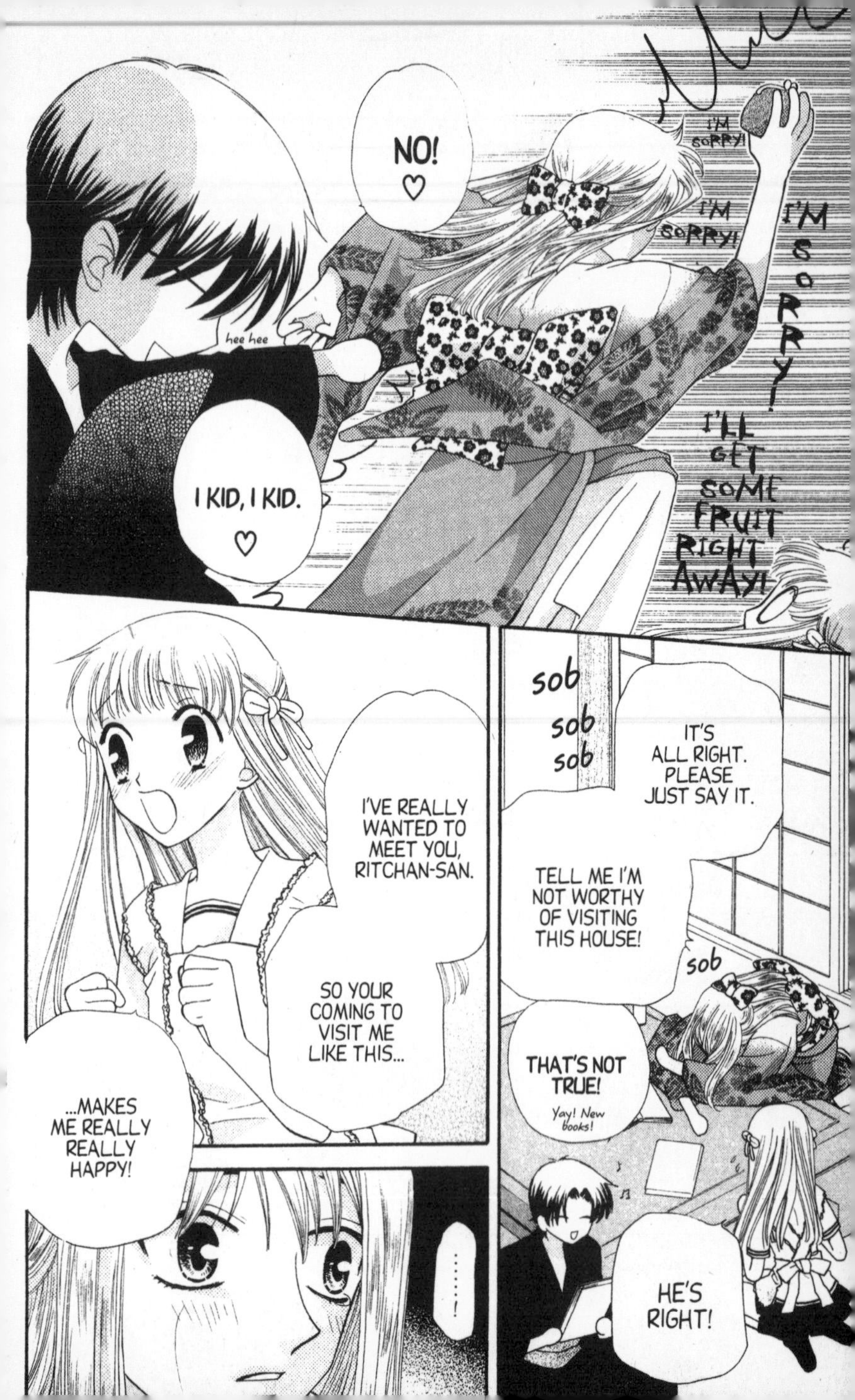
I'M SORRY!
I'M SORRY!
I'M SORRY!
I'LL GET SOME FRUIT RIGHT AWAY!
NO! ♡
hee hee
I KID, I KID. ♡
sob
sob
sob
IT'S ALL RIGHT. PLEASE JUST SAY IT.
TELL ME I'M NOT WORTHY OF VISITING THIS HOUSE!
sob
THAT'S NOT TRUE!
Yay! New books!
HE'S RIGHT!
I'VE REALLY WANTED TO MEET YOU, RITCHAN-SAN.
SO YOUR COMING TO VISIT ME LIKE THIS...
...MAKES ME REALLY REALLY HAPPY!
......!

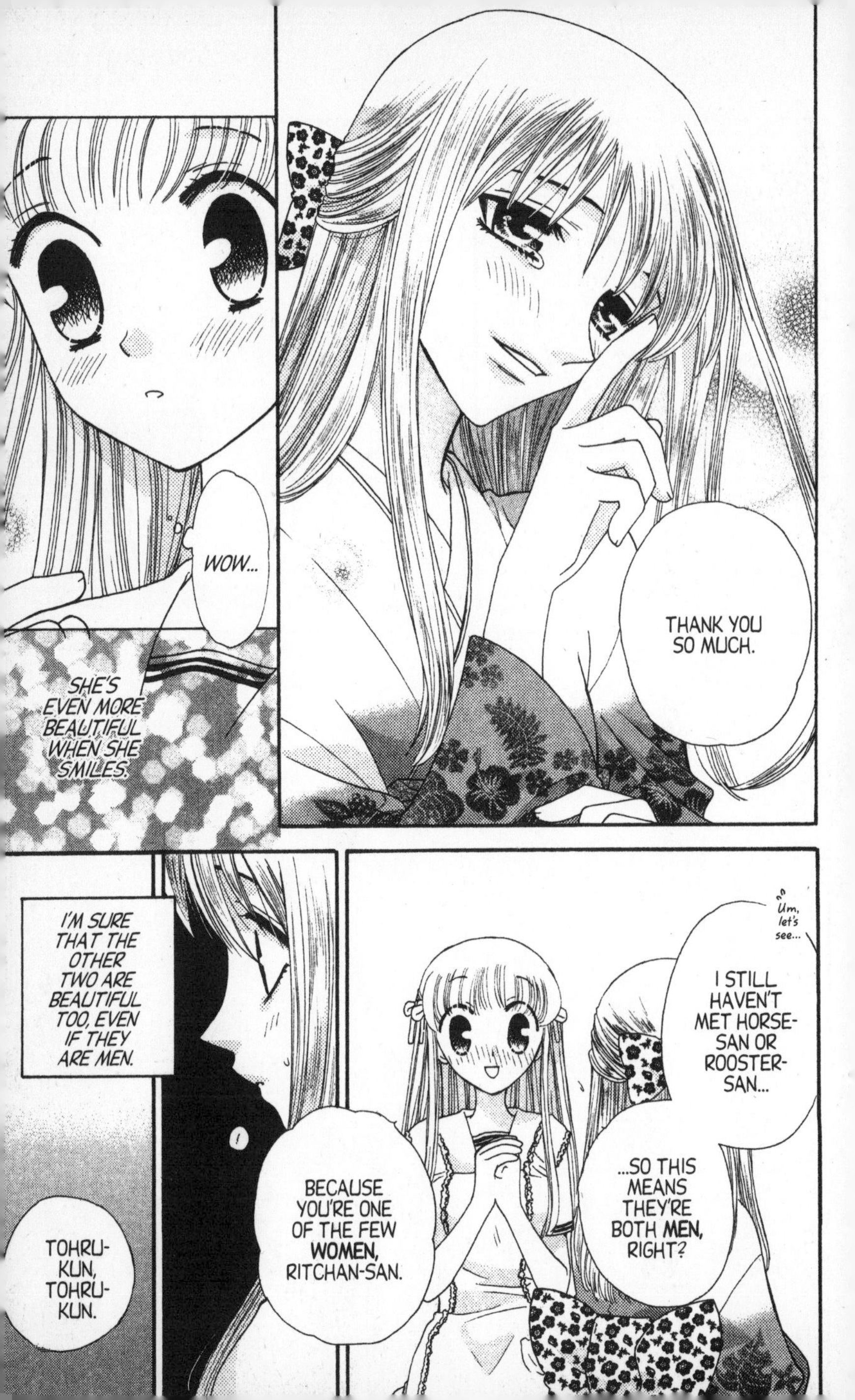
THANK YOU SO MUCH.
WOW...
SHE'S EVEN MORE BEAUTIFUL WHEN SHE SMILES.
Um, let's see...
I STILL HAVEN'T MET HORSE-SAN OR ROOSTER-SAN...
...SO THIS MEANS THEY'RE BOTH MEN, RIGHT?
BECAUSE YOU'RE ONE OF THE FEW WOMEN, RITCHAN-SAN.
I'M SURE THAT THE OTHER TWO ARE BEAUTIFUL TOO, EVEN IF THEY ARE MEN.
!
TOHRU-KUN, TOHRU-KUN.

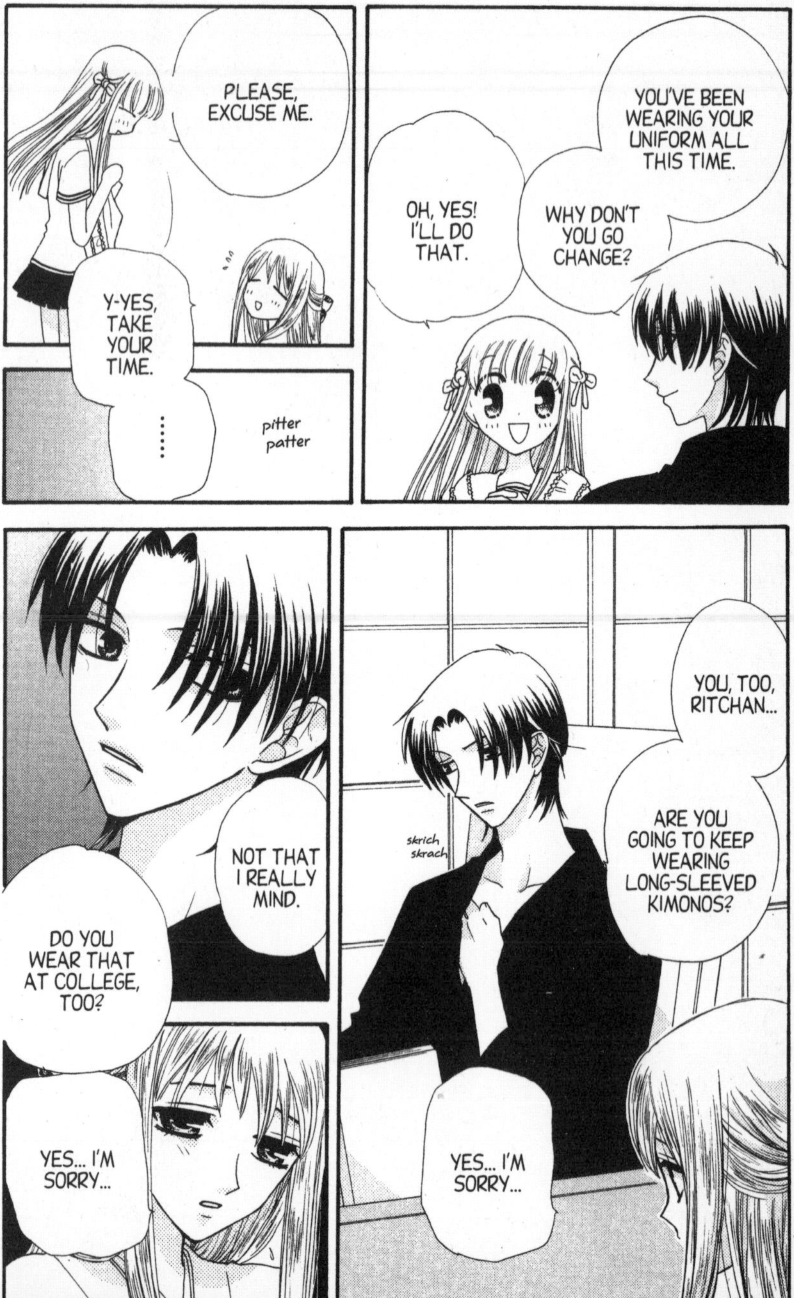
YOU'VE BEEN WEARING YOUR UNIFORM ALL THIS TIME.
WHY DON'T YOU GO CHANGE?
OH, YES! I'LL DO THAT.
PLEASE, EXCUSE ME.
Y-YES, TAKE YOUR TIME.
......
pitter patter
YOU, TOO, RITCHAN...
ARE YOU GOING TO KEEP WEARING LONG-SLEEVED KIMONOS?
skrich skrach
YES... I'M SORRY...
NOT THAT I REALLY MIND.
DO YOU WEAR THAT AT COLLEGE, TOO?
YES... I'M SORRY...

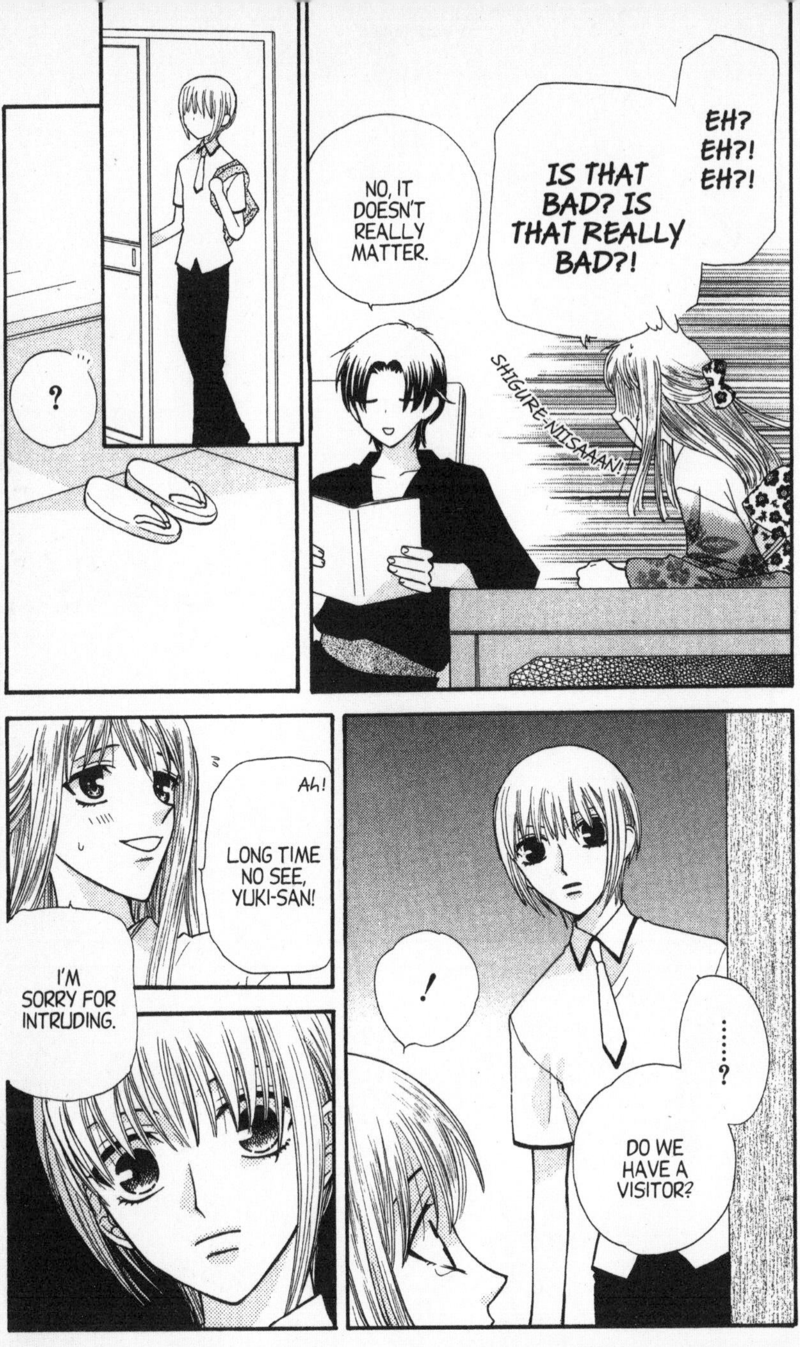
EH? EH?! EH?!
IS THAT BAD? IS THAT REALLY BAD?!
SHIGURE-NIISAAAN!
NO, IT DOESN'T REALLY MATTER.
?
……?
DO WE HAVE A VISITOR?
!
Ah!
LONG TIME NO SEE, YUKI-SAN!
I'M SORRY FOR INTRUDING.

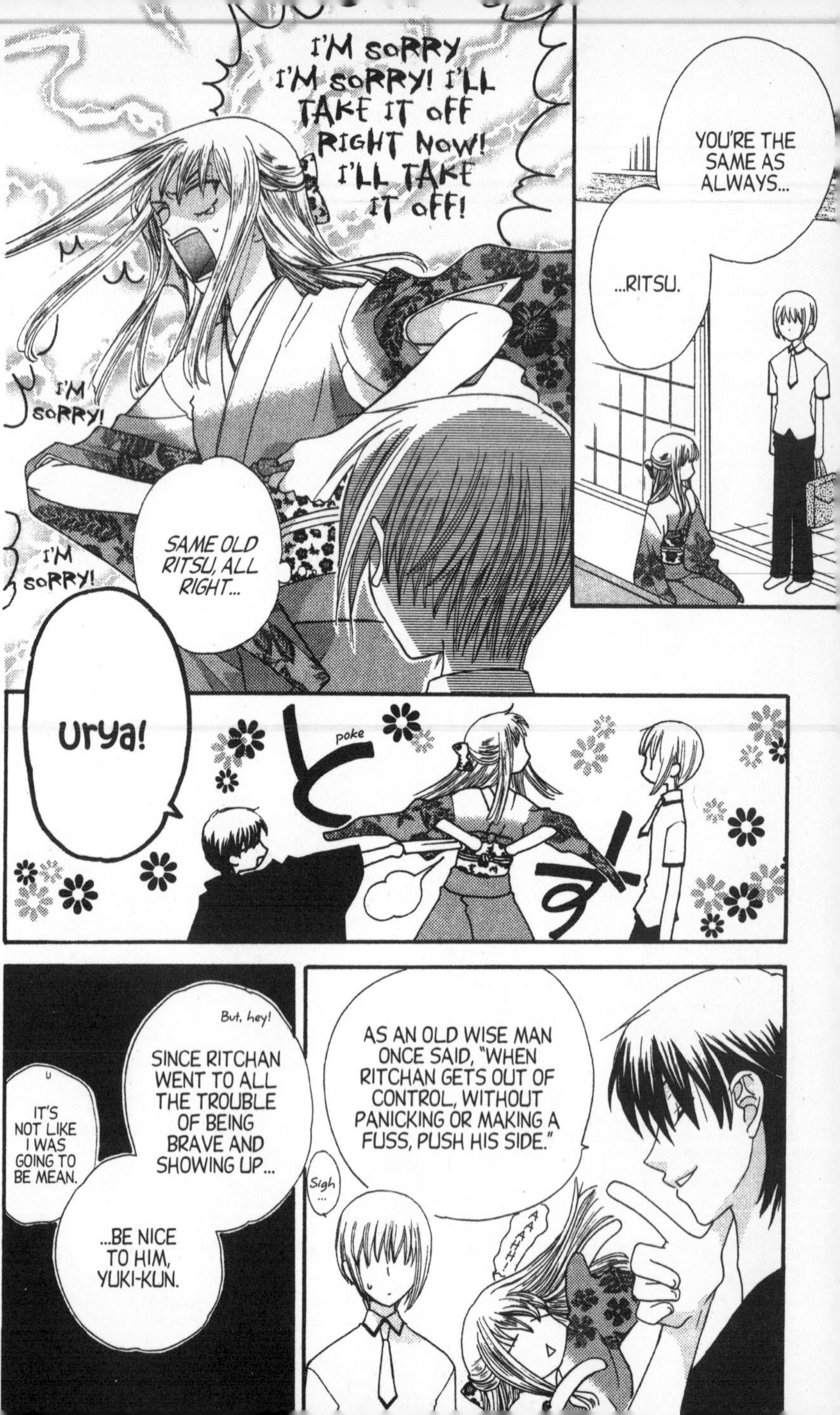

YOU'RE THE SAME AS ALWAYS...
...RITSU.
I'M SORRY I'M SORRY! I'LL TAKE IT OFF RIGHT NOW! I'LL TAKE IT OFF!
SAME OLD RITSU, ALL RIGHT...
I'M SORRY!
I'M SORRY!
Urya!
poke
AS AN OLD WISE MAN ONCE SAID, "WHEN RITCHAN GETS OUT OF CONTROL, WITHOUT PANICKING OR MAKING A FUSS, PUSH HIS SIDE."
Sigh...
But, hey!
SINCE RITCHAN WENT TO ALL THE TROUBLE OF BEING BRAVE AND SHOWING UP...
...BE NICE TO HIM, YUKI-KUN.
IT'S NOT LIKE I WAS GOING TO BE MEAN.

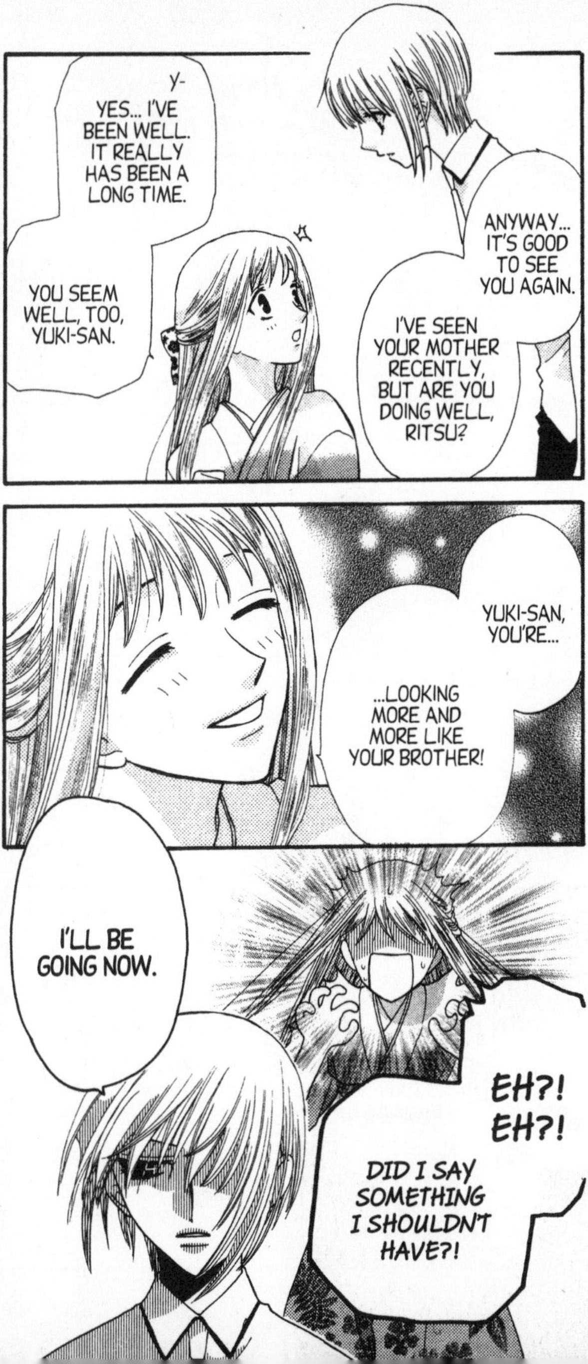
ANYWAY... IT'S GOOD TO SEE YOU AGAIN.
I'VE SEEN YOUR MOTHER RECENTLY, BUT ARE YOU DOING WELL, RITSU?
Y- YES... I'VE BEEN WELL. IT REALLY HAS BEEN A LONG TIME.
YOU SEEM WELL, TOO, YUKI-SAN.
YUKI-SAN, YOU'RE...
...LOOKING MORE AND MORE LIKE YOUR BROTHER!
I'LL BE GOING NOW.
EH?! EH?!
DID I SAY SOMETHING I SHOULDN'T HAVE?!

Fruits Basket 8: Part 2

My handwriting in volume seven is really, really small. A friend of mine teased me about it. but then, I tease **myself** about it.

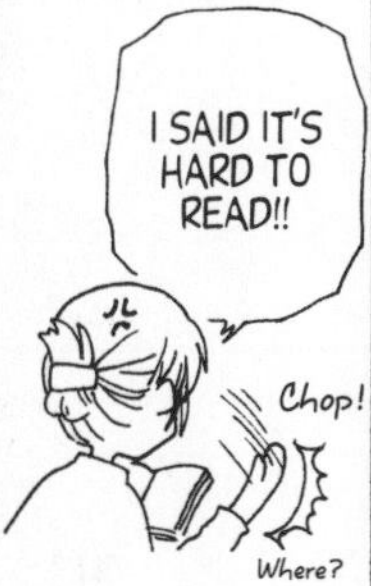
I SAID IT'S HARD TO READ!!
Chop!
Where?

It seems it's still hard for me to write bigger since the surgery. I feel like my writing was never that big to begin with. Even signing my name, my handwriting gets smaller as time goes on.

This time I'm writing bigger! or am I...?

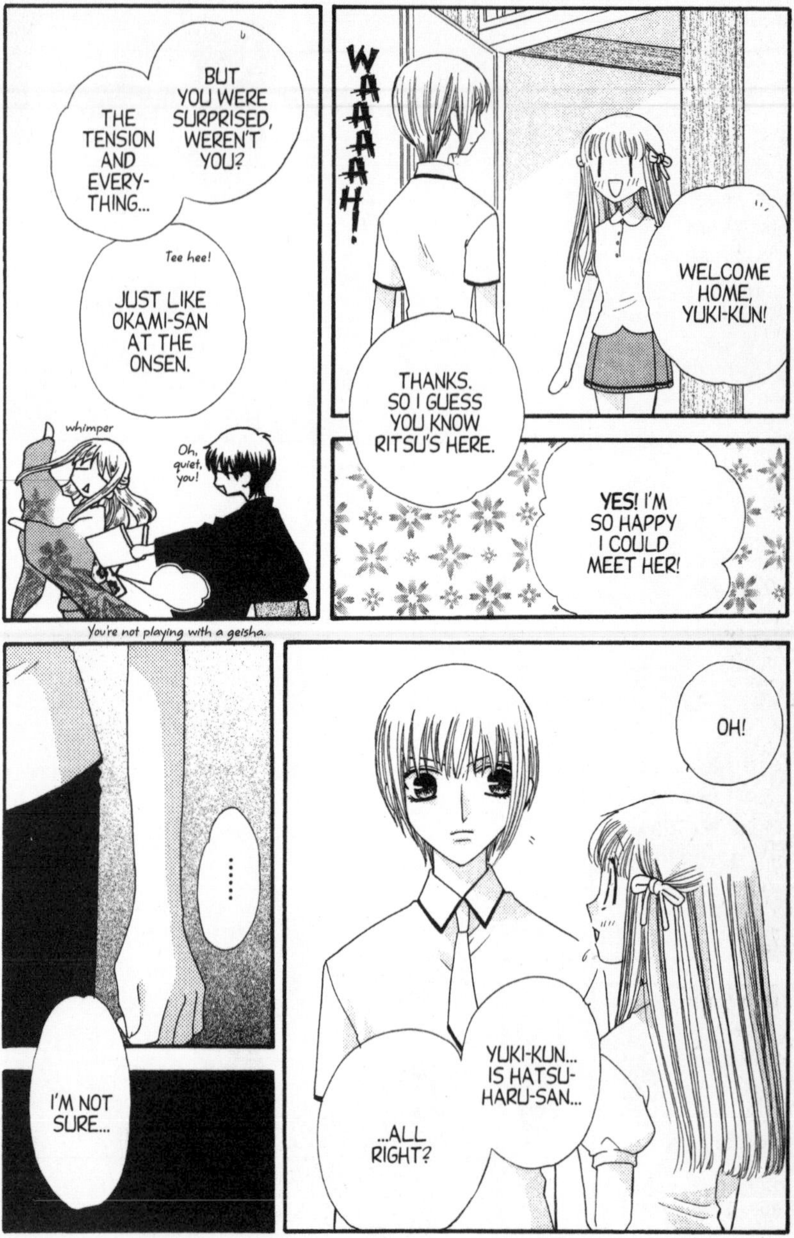
WAAAAH!
WELCOME HOME, YUKI-KUN!
THANKS. SO I GUESS YOU KNOW RITSU'S HERE.
YES! I'M SO HAPPY I COULD MEET HER!
BUT YOU WERE SURPRISED, WEREN'T YOU?
THE TENSION AND EVERY-THING...
Tee hee!
JUST LIKE OKAMI-SAN AT THE ONSEN.
whimper
Oh, quiet, you!
You're not playing with a geisha.
OH!
YUKI-KUN... IS HATSU-HARU-SAN...
...ALL RIGHT?
......
I'M NOT SURE...

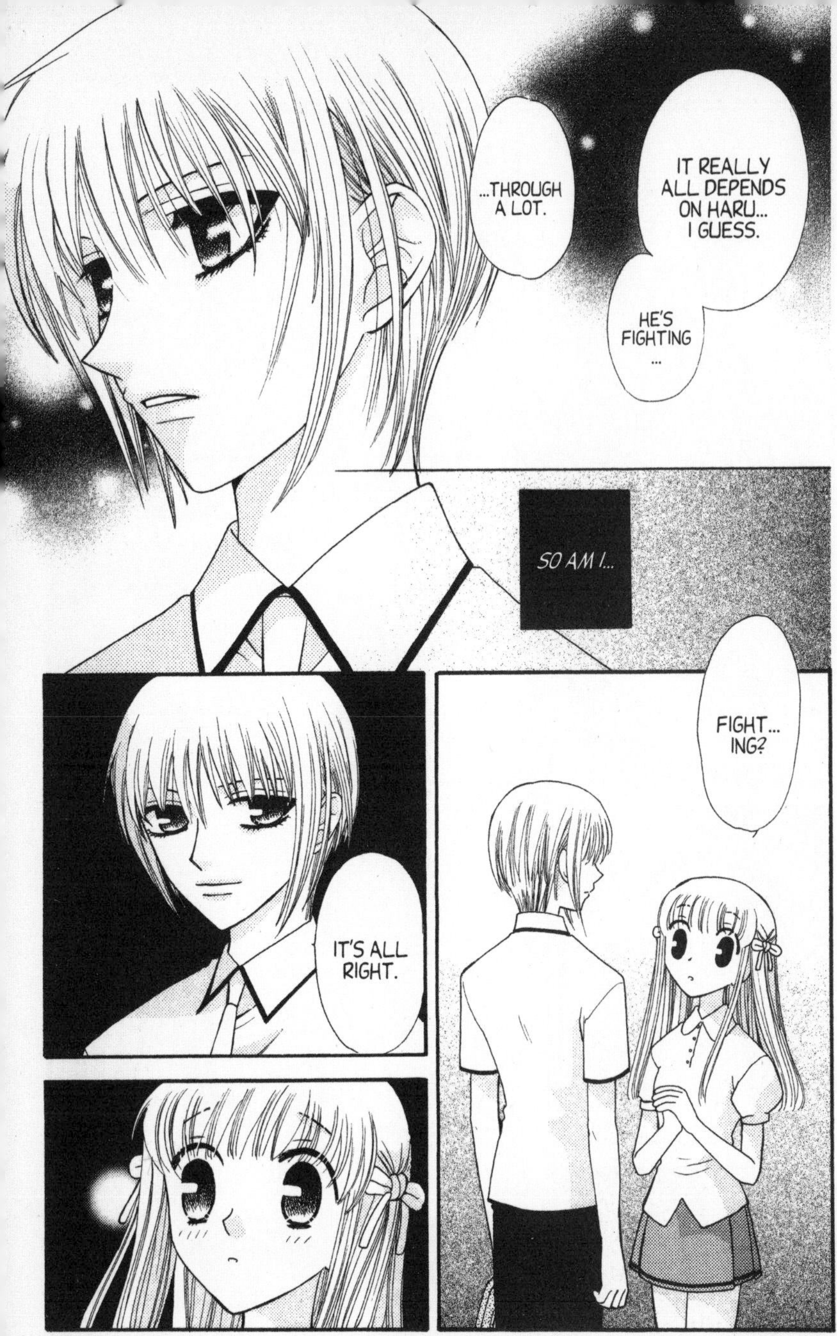
IT REALLY ALL DEPENDS ON HARU... I GUESS.
HE'S FIGHTING ...
...THROUGH A LOT.
SO AM I...
FIGHT... ING?
IT'S ALL RIGHT.

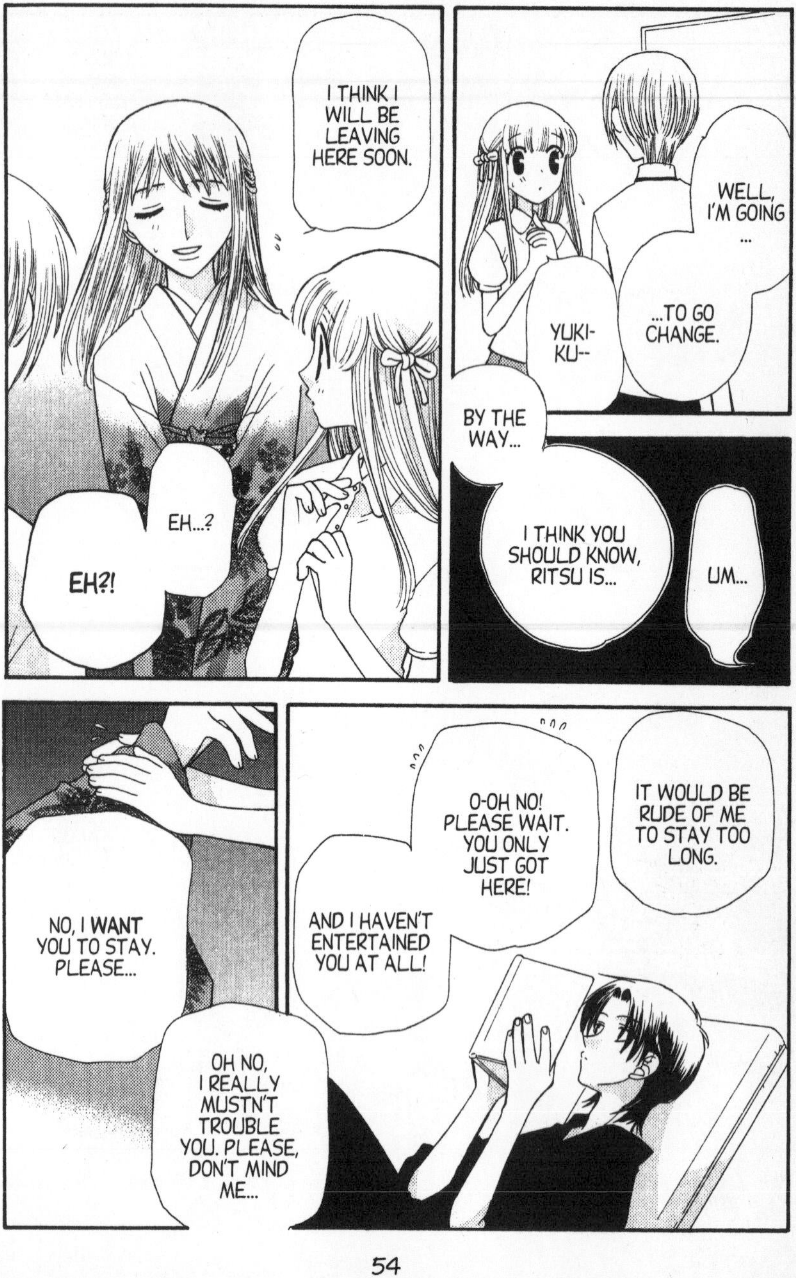
WELL, I'M GOING ...
...TO GO CHANGE.
YUKI-KU--
BY THE WAY...
I THINK YOU SHOULD KNOW, RITSU IS...
UM...
I THINK I WILL BE LEAVING HERE SOON.
EH...?
EH?!
IT WOULD BE RUDE OF ME TO STAY TOO LONG.
O-OH NO! PLEASE WAIT. YOU ONLY JUST GOT HERE!
AND I HAVEN'T ENTERTAINED YOU AT ALL!
NO, I WANT YOU TO STAY. PLEASE...
OH NO, I REALLY MUSTN'T TROUBLE YOU. PLEASE, DON'T MIND ME...

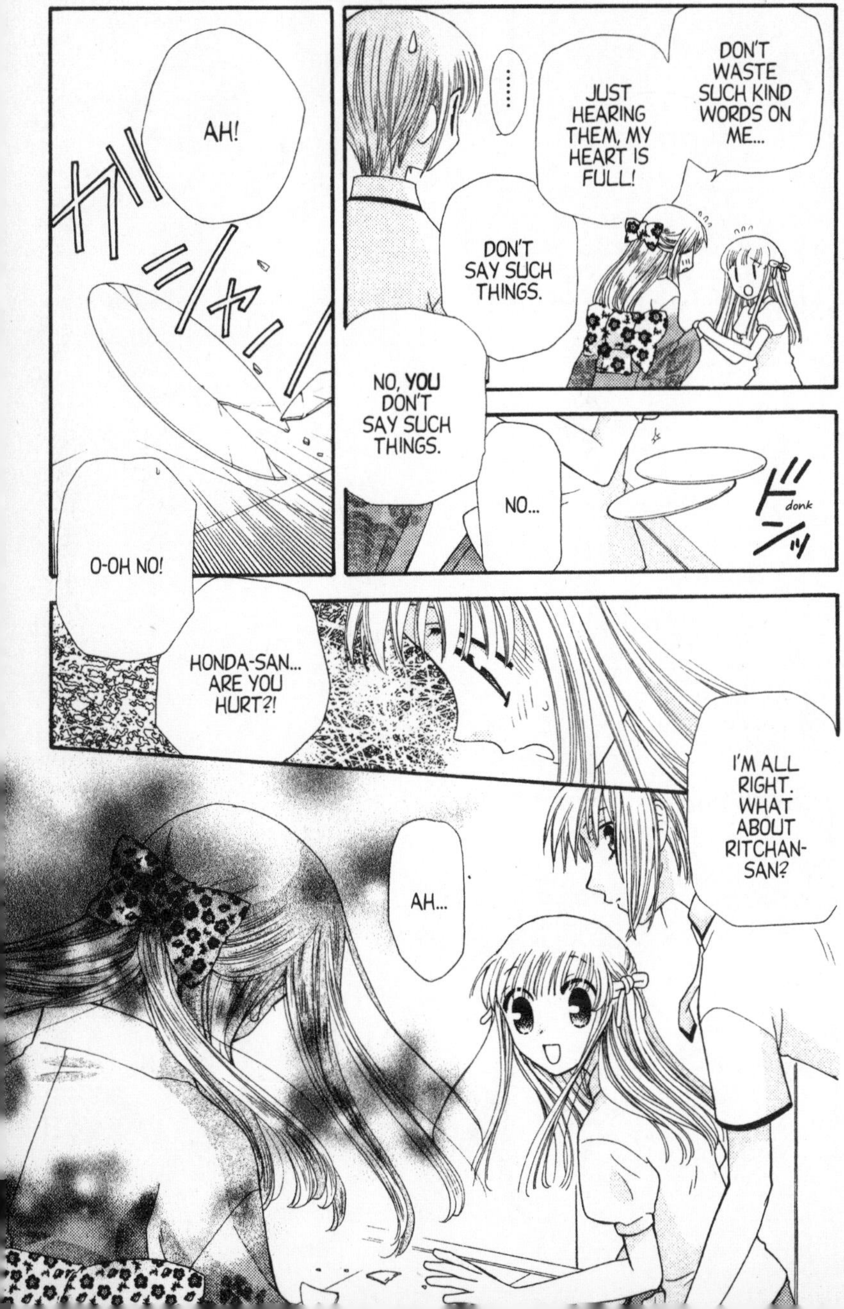
DON'T WASTE SUCH KIND WORDS ON ME...
JUST HEARING THEM, MY HEART IS FULL!
......
DON'T SAY SUCH THINGS.
NO, **YOU** DON'T SAY SUCH THINGS.
NO...
donk
AH!
O-OH NO!
HONDA-SAN... ARE YOU HURT?!
I'M ALL RIGHT. WHAT ABOUT RITCHAN-SAN?
AH...

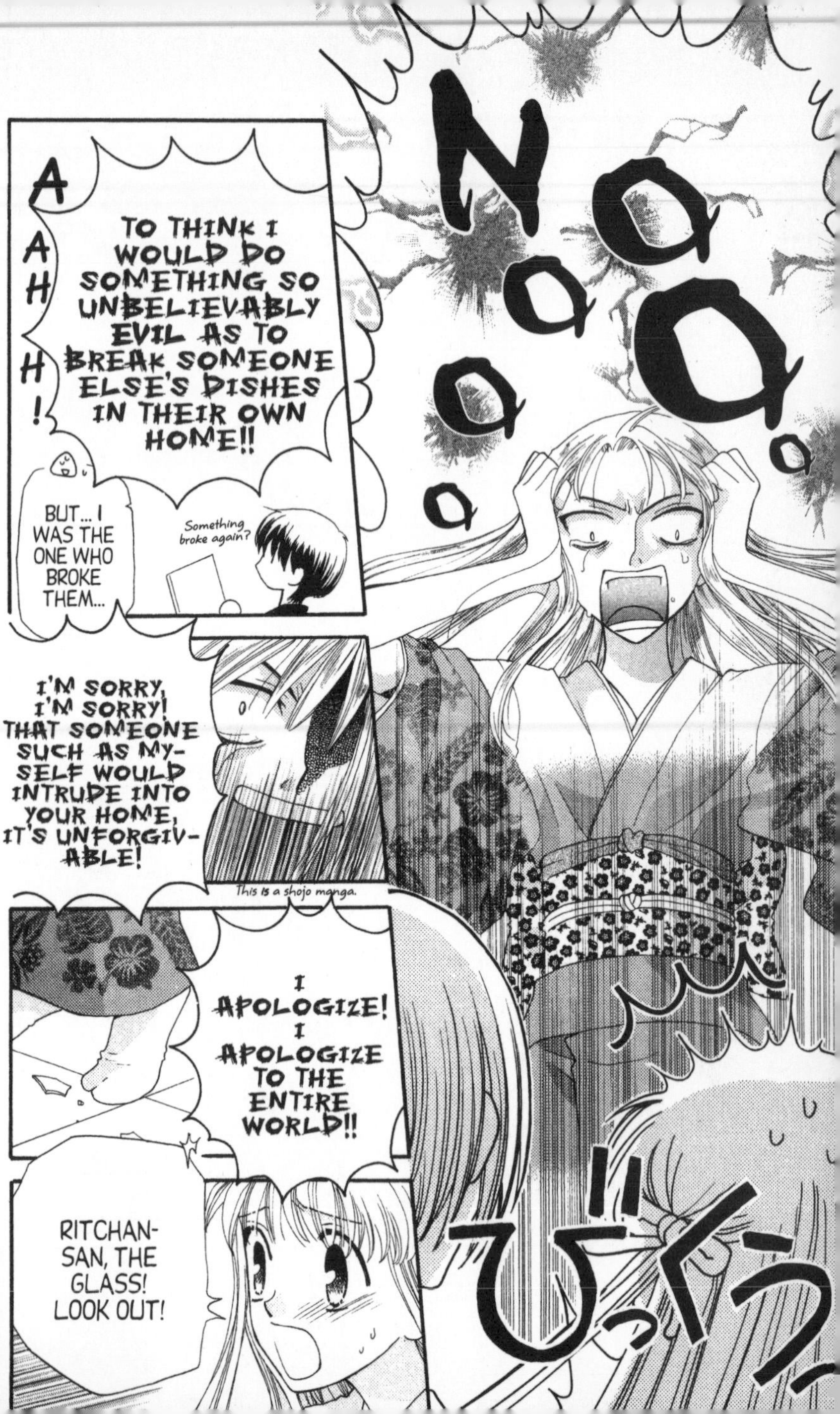
NOOOOOO
AAHH!
TO THINK I WOULD DO SOMETHING SO UNBELIEVABLY EVIL AS TO BREAK SOMEONE ELSE'S DISHES IN THEIR OWN HOME!!
Something broke again?
BUT... I WAS THE ONE WHO BROKE THEM...
I'M SORRY, I'M SORRY! THAT SOMEONE SUCH AS MY-SELF WOULD INTRUDE INTO YOUR HOME, IT'S UNFORGIV-ABLE!
This is a shojo manga.
I APOLOGIZE! I APOLOGIZE TO THE ENTIRE WORLD!!
RITCHAN-SAN, THE GLASS! LOOK OUT!

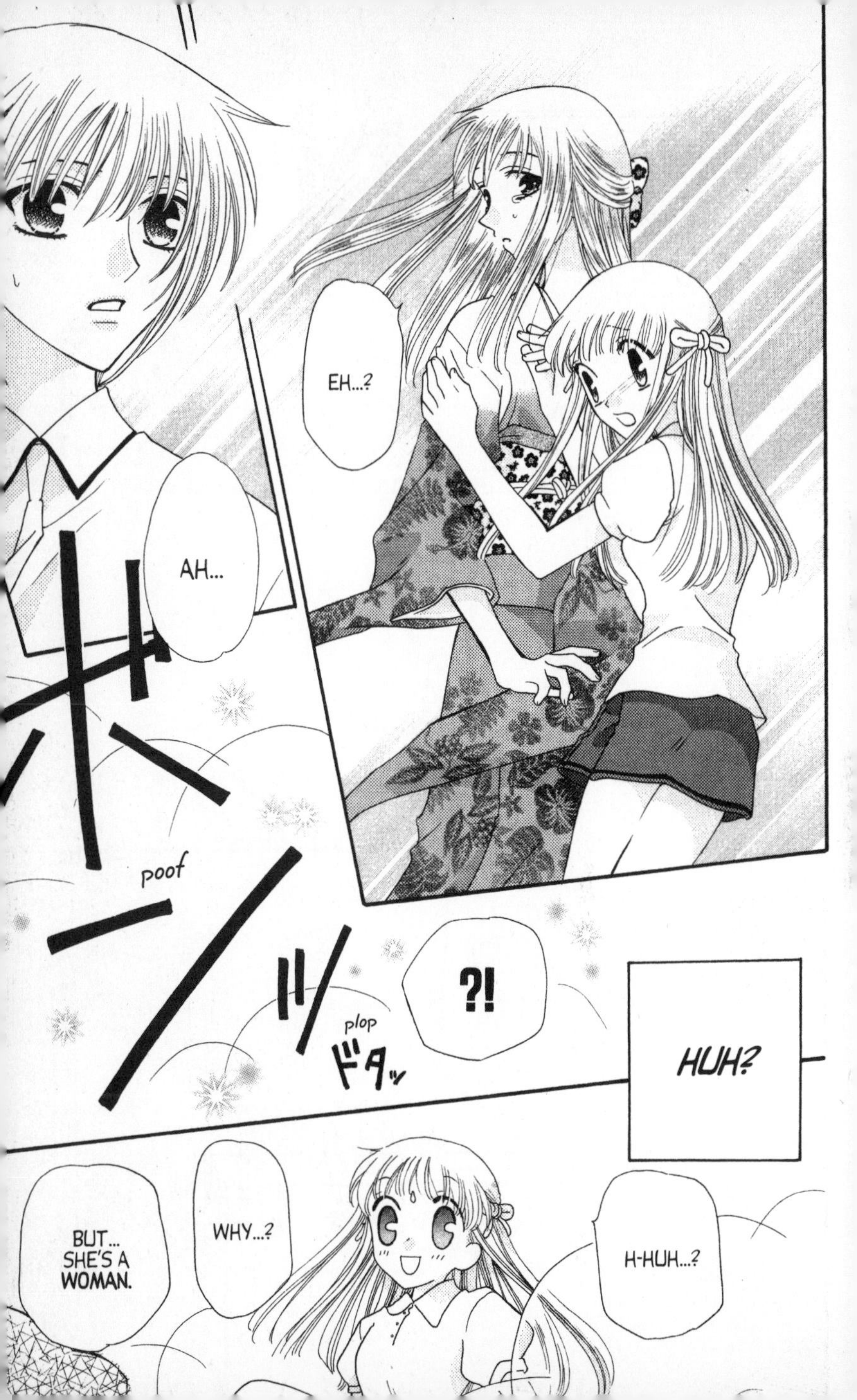
EH...?
AH...
ボン
poof
HUH?
?!
plop
ドタッ
H-HUH...?
WHY...?
BUT... SHE'S A WOMAN.

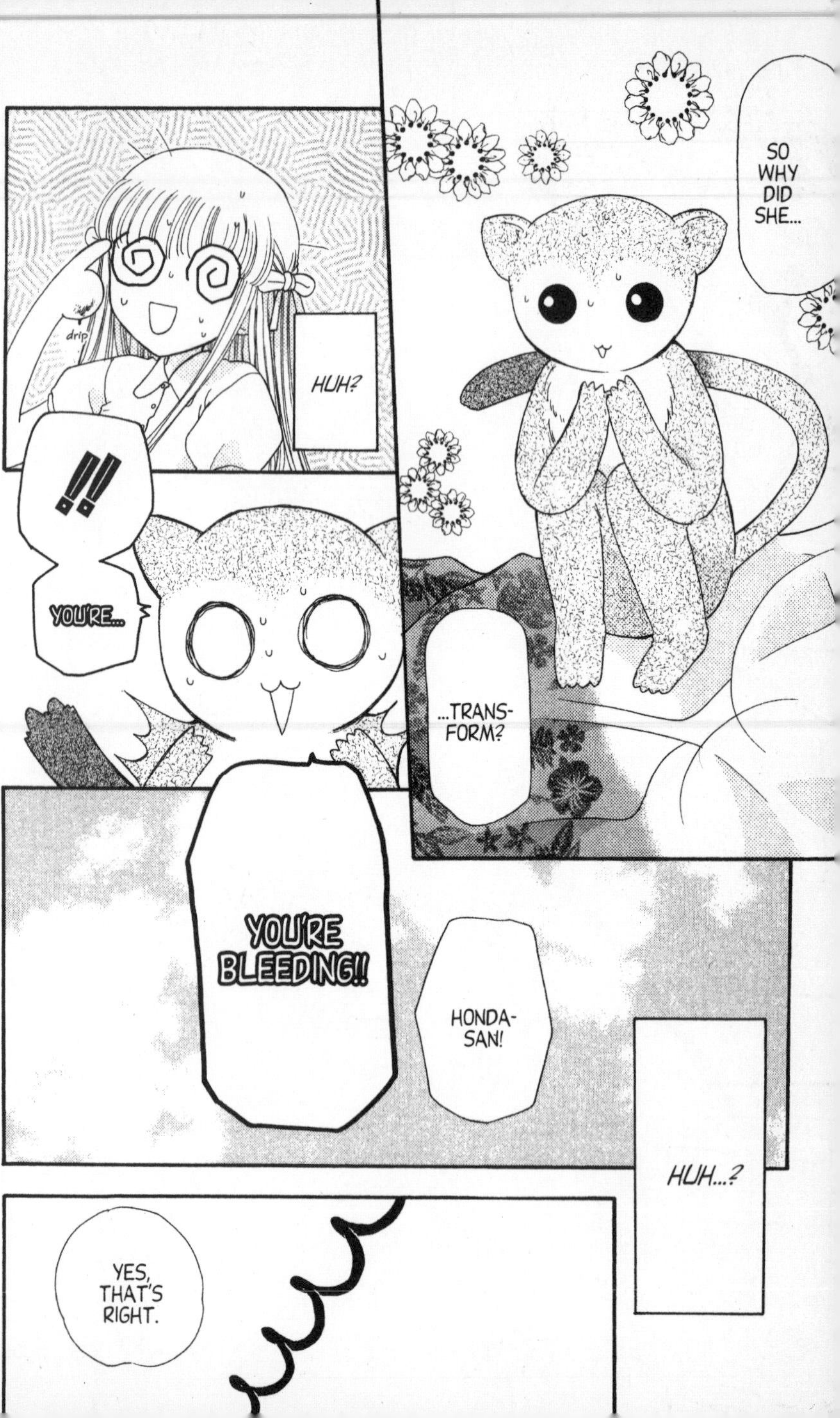
SO WHY DID SHE...
...TRANS-FORM?
HUH?
!!
YOU'RE...
YOU'RE BLEEDING!!
HONDA-SAN!
HUH...?
YES, THAT'S RIGHT.

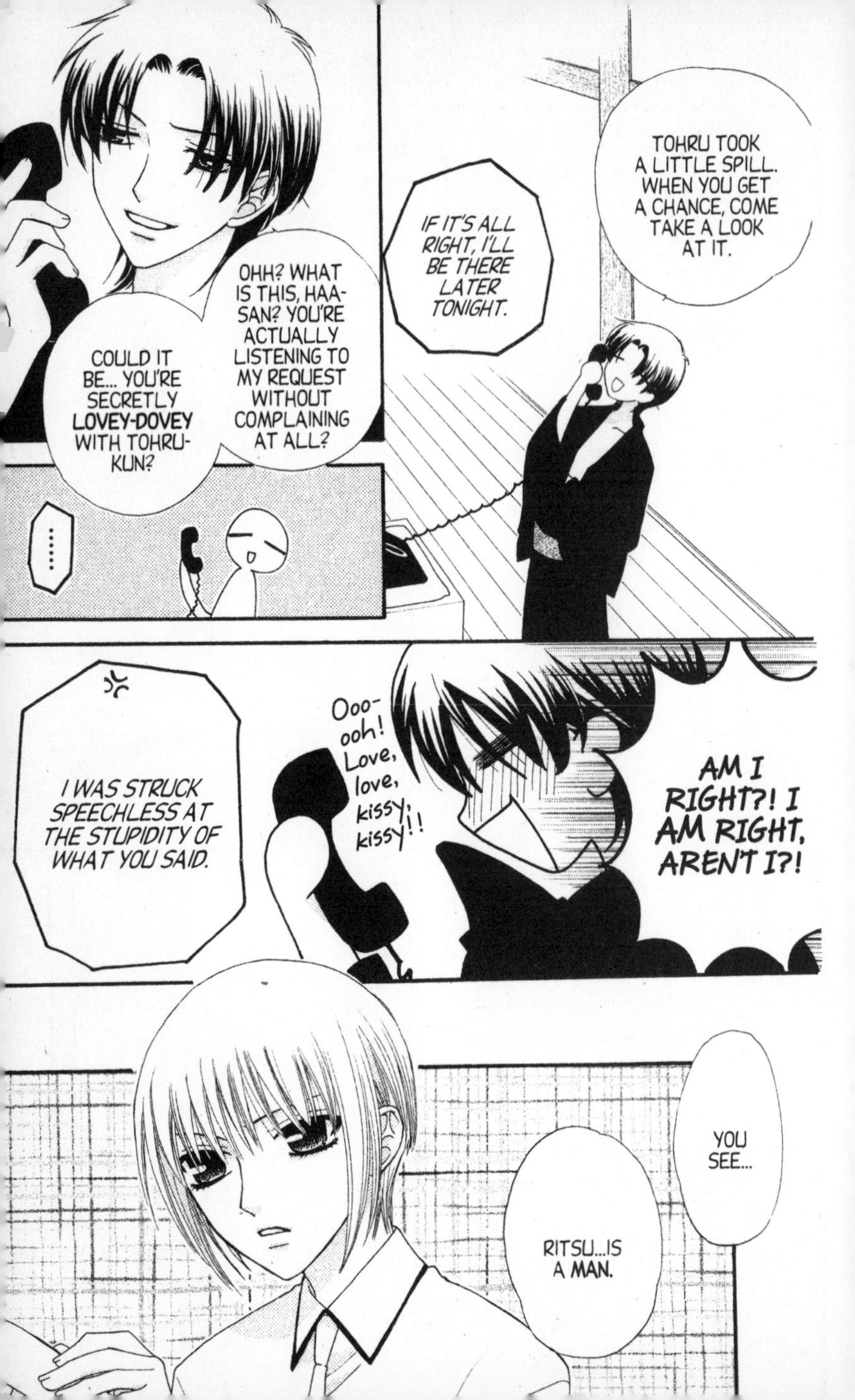
TOHRU TOOK A LITTLE SPILL. WHEN YOU GET A CHANCE, COME TAKE A LOOK AT IT.
IF IT'S ALL RIGHT, I'LL BE THERE LATER TONIGHT.
OHH? WHAT IS THIS, HAA-SAN? YOU'RE ACTUALLY LISTENING TO MY REQUEST WITHOUT COMPLAINING AT ALL?
COULD IT BE... YOU'RE SECRETLY **LOVEY-DOVEY** WITH TOHRU-KUN?
......
AM I RIGHT?! I AM RIGHT, AREN'T I?!
Ooo-ooh! Love, love, kissy, kissy!!
I WAS STRUCK SPEECHLESS AT THE STUPIDITY OF WHAT YOU SAID.
YOU SEE...
RITSU...IS A MAN.

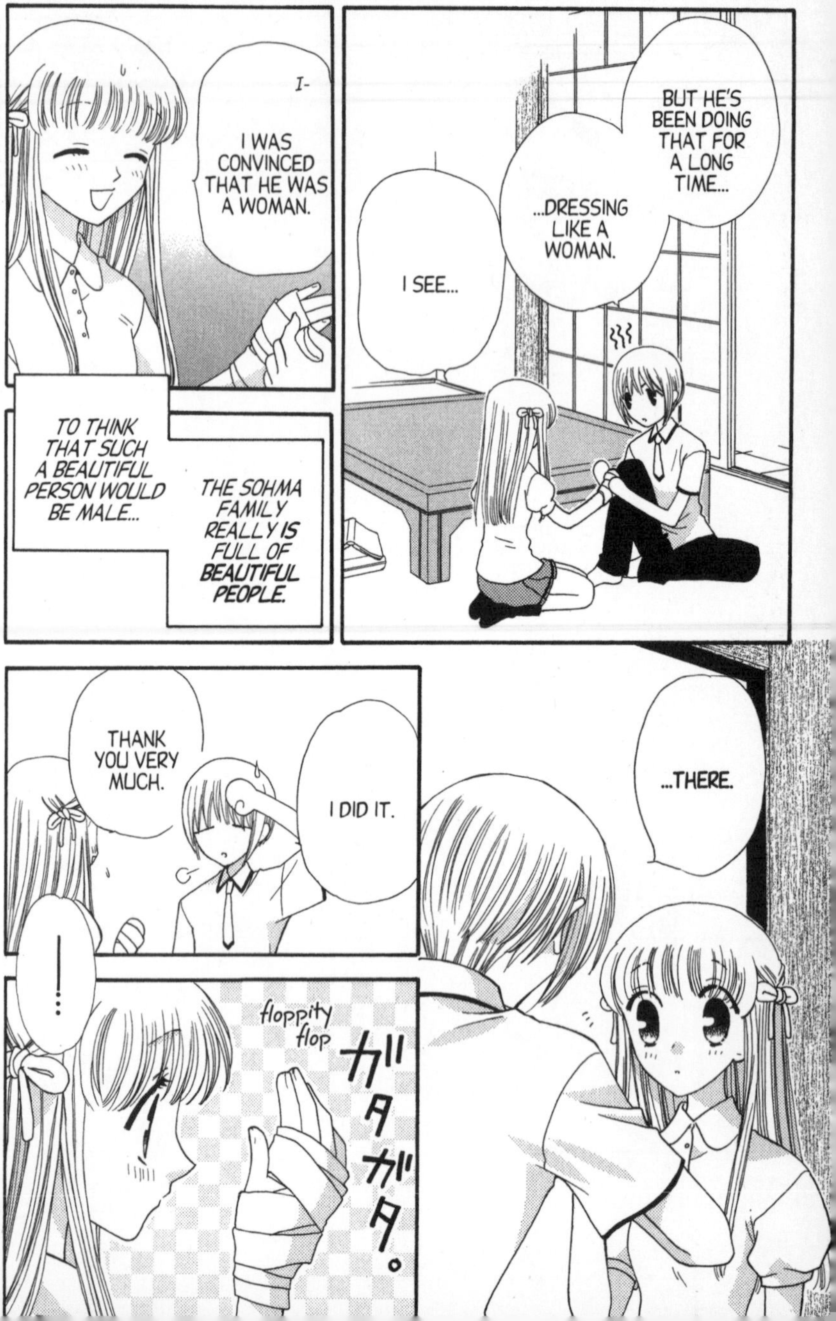

BUT HE'S BEEN DOING THAT FOR A LONG TIME...
...DRESSING LIKE A WOMAN.
I SEE...
I-
I WAS CONVINCED THAT HE WAS A WOMAN.
TO THINK THAT SUCH A BEAUTIFUL PERSON WOULD BE MALE...
THE SOHMA FAMILY REALLY IS FULL OF BEAUTIFUL PEOPLE.
...THERE.
I DID IT.
THANK YOU VERY MUCH.
...!
floppity flop
ガタガタ。

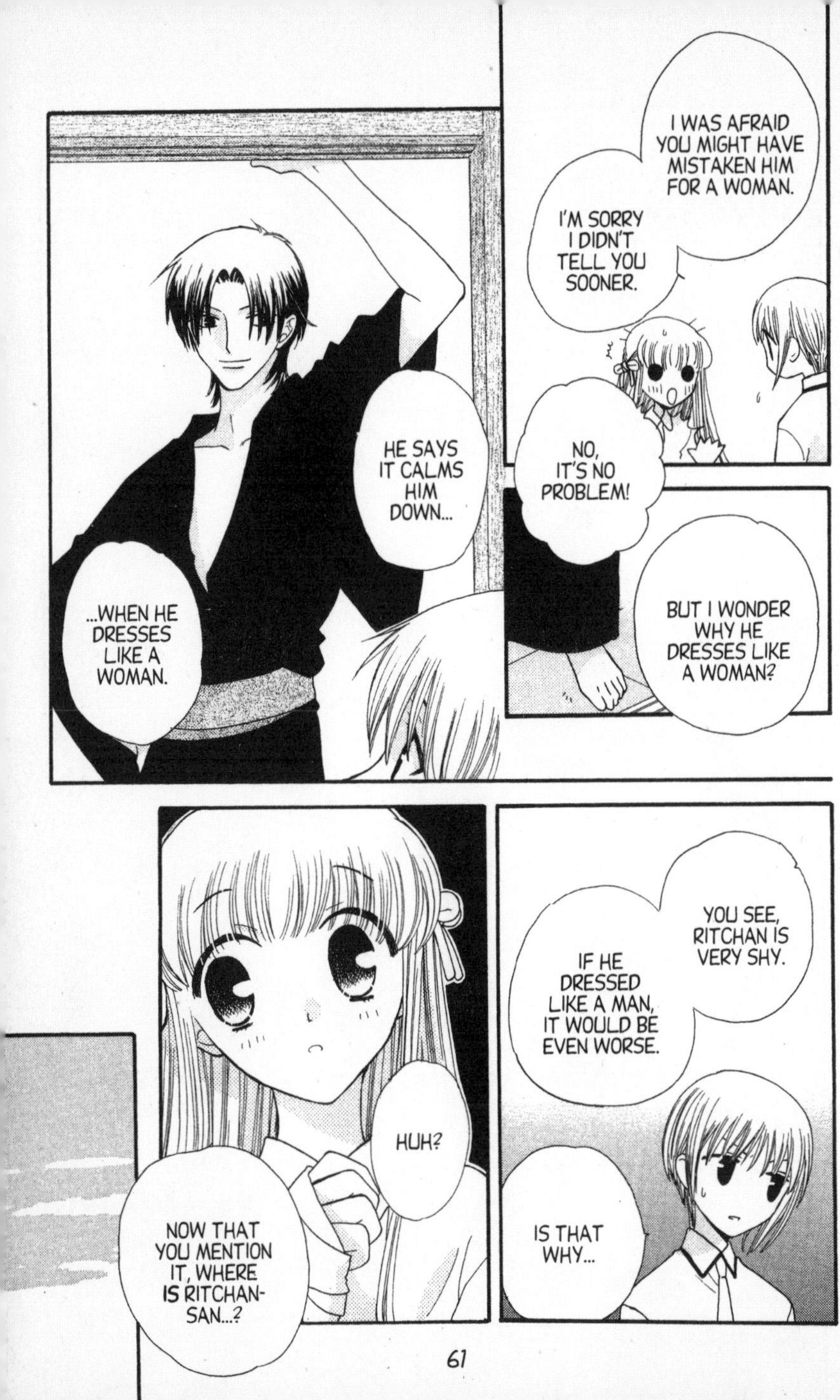
I WAS AFRAID YOU MIGHT HAVE MISTAKEN HIM FOR A WOMAN.
I'M SORRY I DIDN'T TELL YOU SOONER.
NO, IT'S NO PROBLEM!
BUT I WONDER WHY HE DRESSES LIKE A WOMAN?
HE SAYS IT CALMS HIM DOWN...
...WHEN HE DRESSES LIKE A WOMAN.
YOU SEE, RITCHAN IS VERY SHY.
IF HE DRESSED LIKE A MAN, IT WOULD BE EVEN WORSE.
IS THAT WHY...
HUH?
NOW THAT YOU MENTION IT, WHERE IS RITCHAN-SAN...?

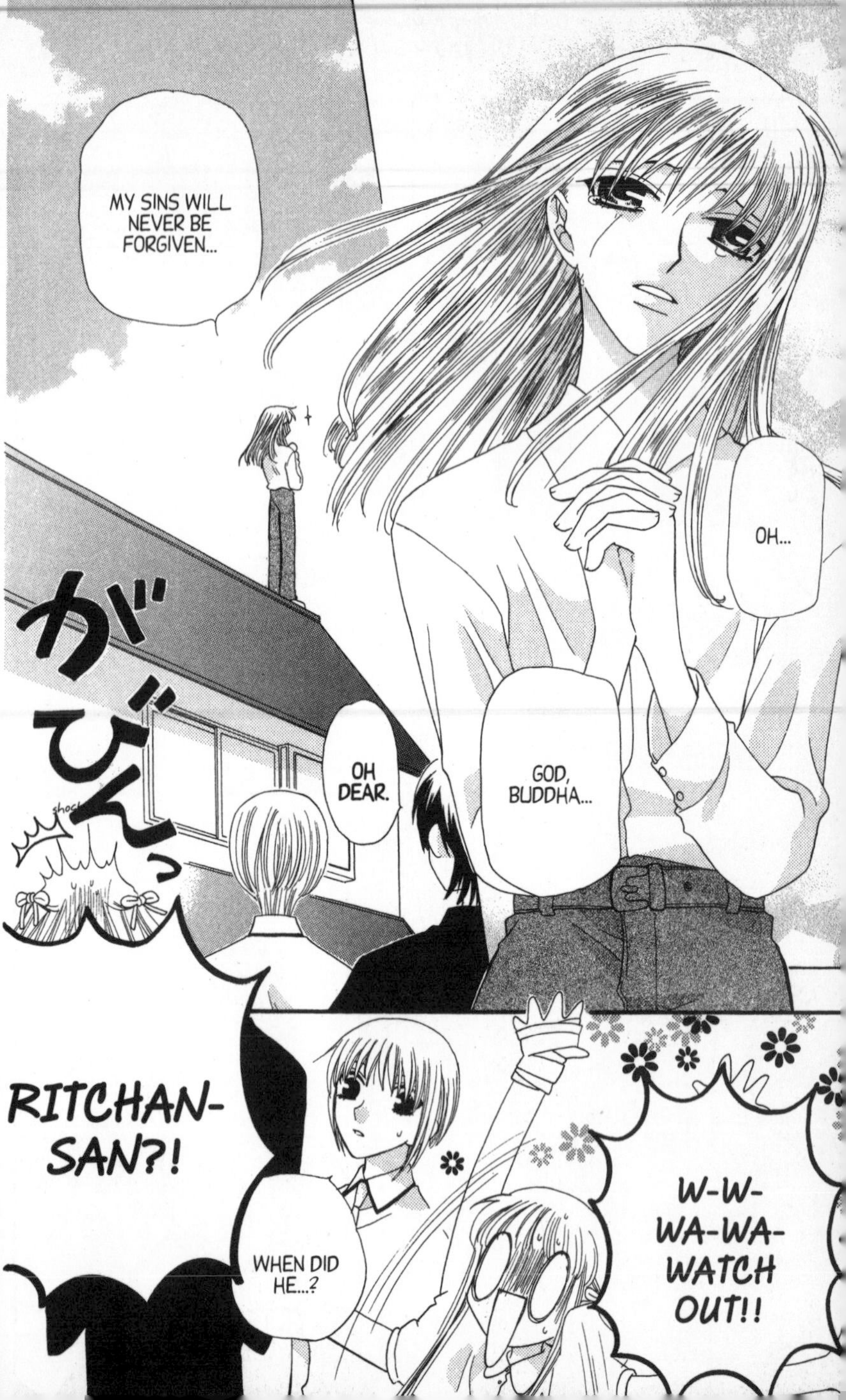
OH...
GOD, BUDDHA...
MY SINS WILL NEVER BE FORGIVEN...
OH DEAR.
がびんっ
shock
RITCHAN-SAN?!
W-W-WA-WA-WATCH OUT!!
WHEN DID HE...?

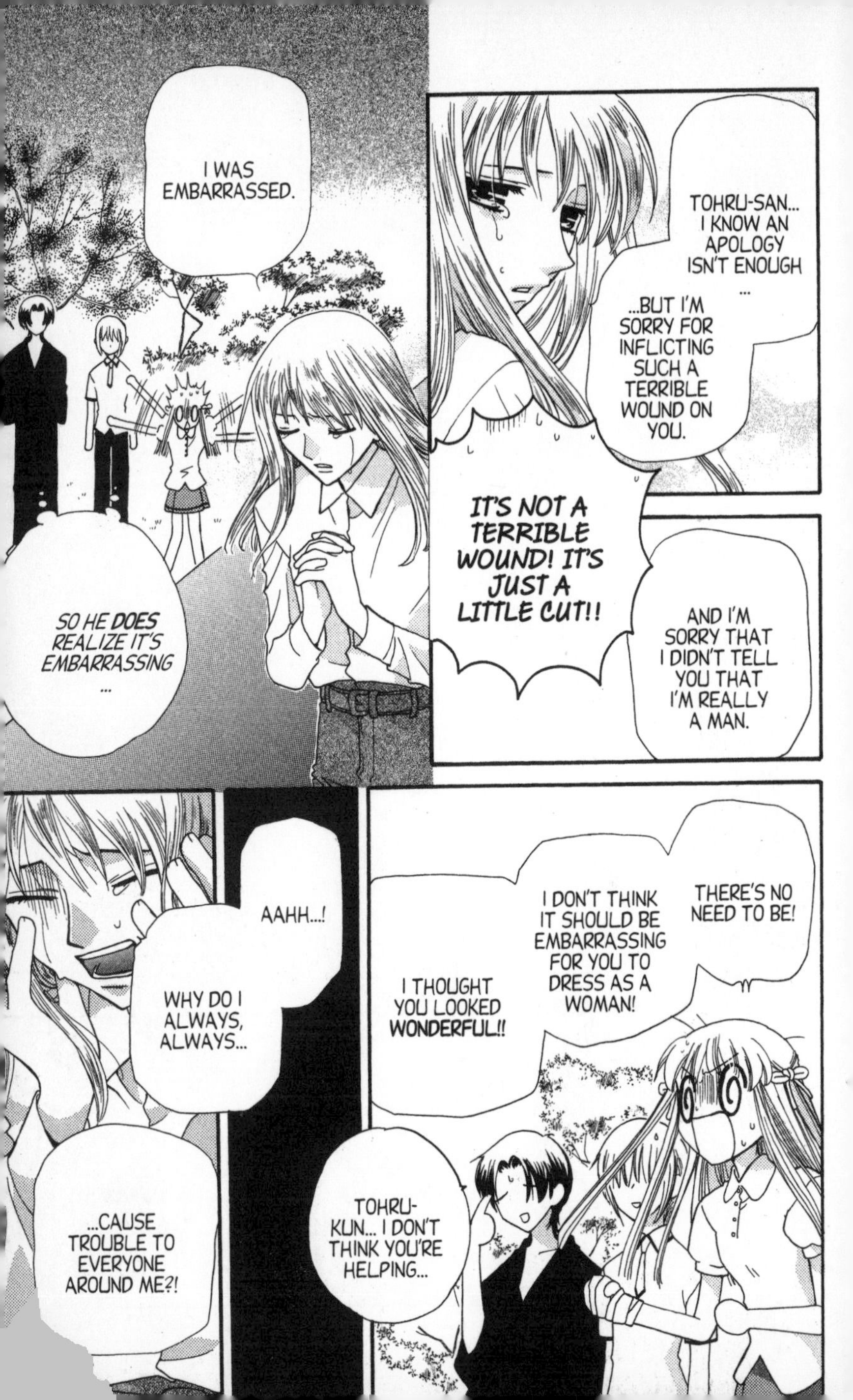
TOHRU-SAN... I KNOW AN APOLOGY ISN'T ENOUGH ...
...BUT I'M SORRY FOR INFLICTING SUCH A TERRIBLE WOUND ON YOU.
IT'S NOT A TERRIBLE WOUND! IT'S JUST A LITTLE CUT!!
AND I'M SORRY THAT I DIDN'T TELL YOU THAT I'M REALLY A MAN.
I WAS EMBARRASSED.
SO HE DOES REALIZE IT'S EMBARRASSING ...
THERE'S NO NEED TO BE!
I DON'T THINK IT SHOULD BE EMBARRASSING FOR YOU TO DRESS AS A WOMAN!
I THOUGHT YOU LOOKED WONDERFUL!!
TOHRU-KUN... I DON'T THINK YOU'RE HELPING...
AAHH...!
WHY DO I ALWAYS, ALWAYS...
...CAUSE TROUBLE TO EVERYONE AROUND ME?!

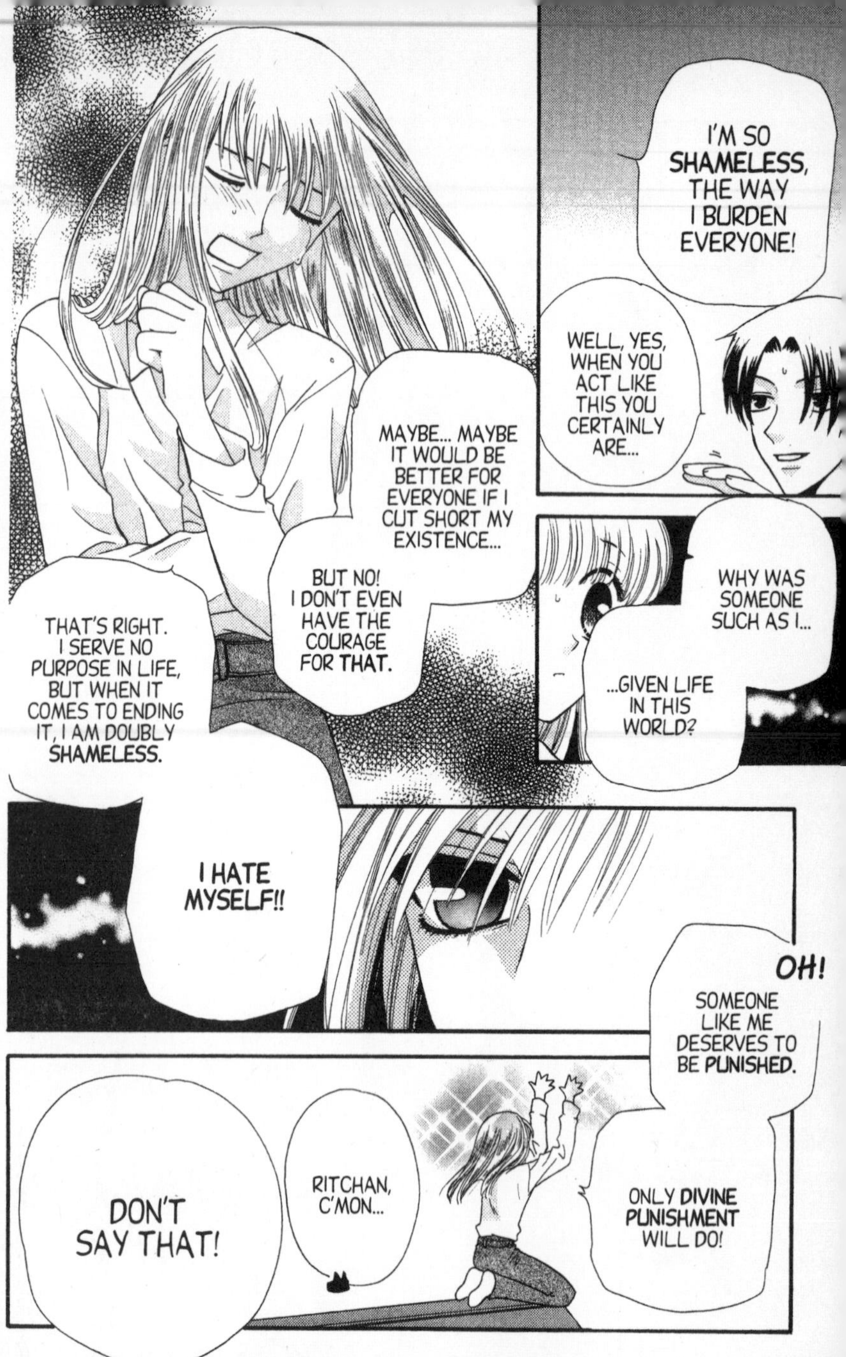
I'M SO SHAMELESS, THE WAY I BURDEN EVERYONE!
WELL, YES, WHEN YOU ACT LIKE THIS YOU CERTAINLY ARE...
WHY WAS SOMEONE SUCH AS I...
...GIVEN LIFE IN THIS WORLD?
MAYBE... MAYBE IT WOULD BE BETTER FOR EVERYONE IF I CUT SHORT MY EXISTENCE...
BUT NO! I DON'T EVEN HAVE THE COURAGE FOR THAT.
THAT'S RIGHT. I SERVE NO PURPOSE IN LIFE, BUT WHEN IT COMES TO ENDING IT, I AM DOUBLY SHAMELESS.
I HATE MYSELF!!
OH!
SOMEONE LIKE ME DESERVES TO BE PUNISHED.
ONLY DIVINE PUNISHMENT WILL DO!
RITCHAN, C'MON...
DON'T SAY THAT!

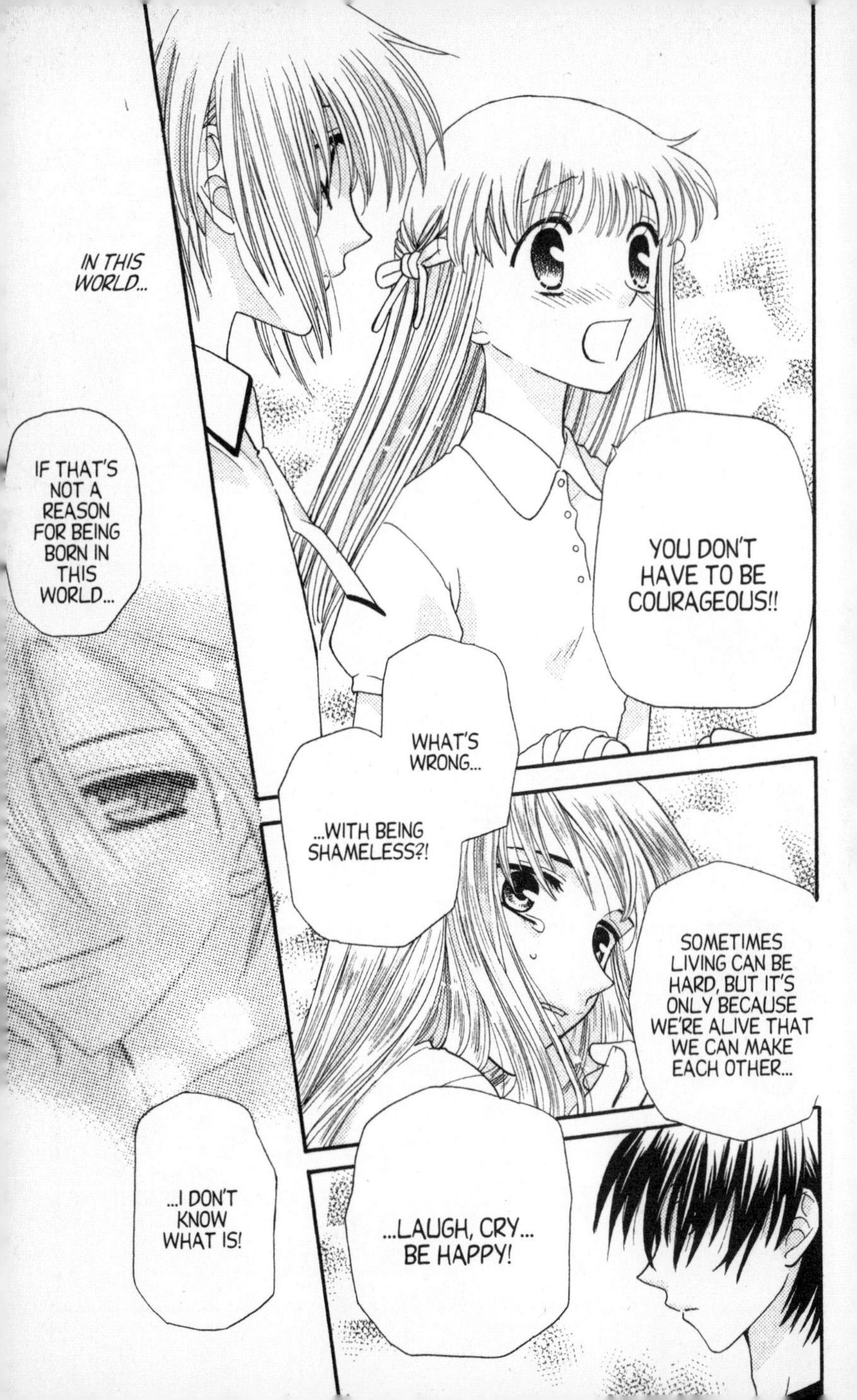
YOU DON'T HAVE TO BE COURAGEOUS!!
WHAT'S WRONG...
...WITH BEING SHAMELESS?!
SOMETIMES LIVING CAN BE HARD, BUT IT'S ONLY BECAUSE WE'RE ALIVE THAT WE CAN MAKE EACH OTHER...
...LAUGH, CRY... BE HAPPY!
IN THIS WORLD...
IF THAT'S NOT A REASON FOR BEING BORN IN THIS WORLD...
...I DON'T KNOW WHAT IS!

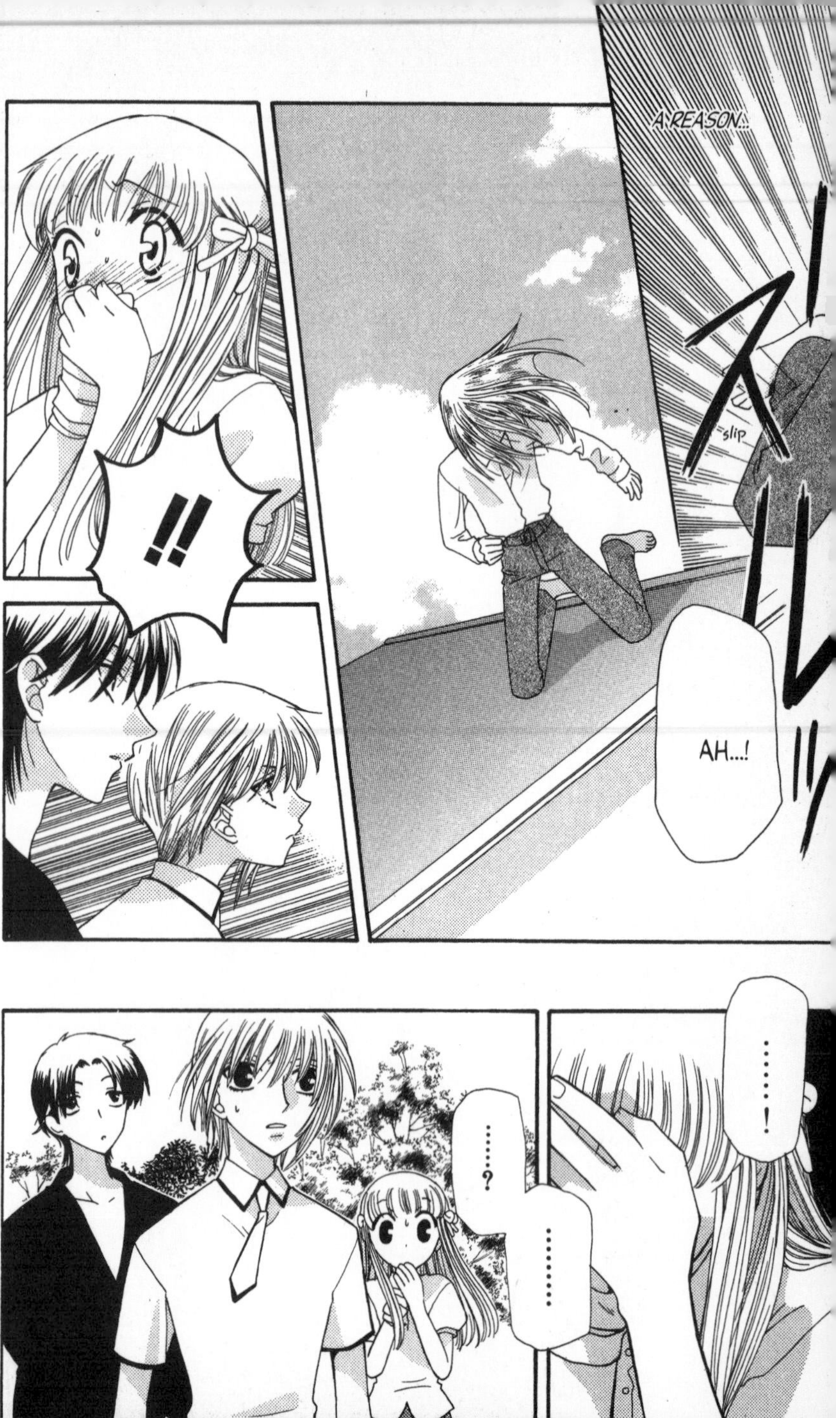
A REASON...
slip
AH...!
!!
......!
......?
....

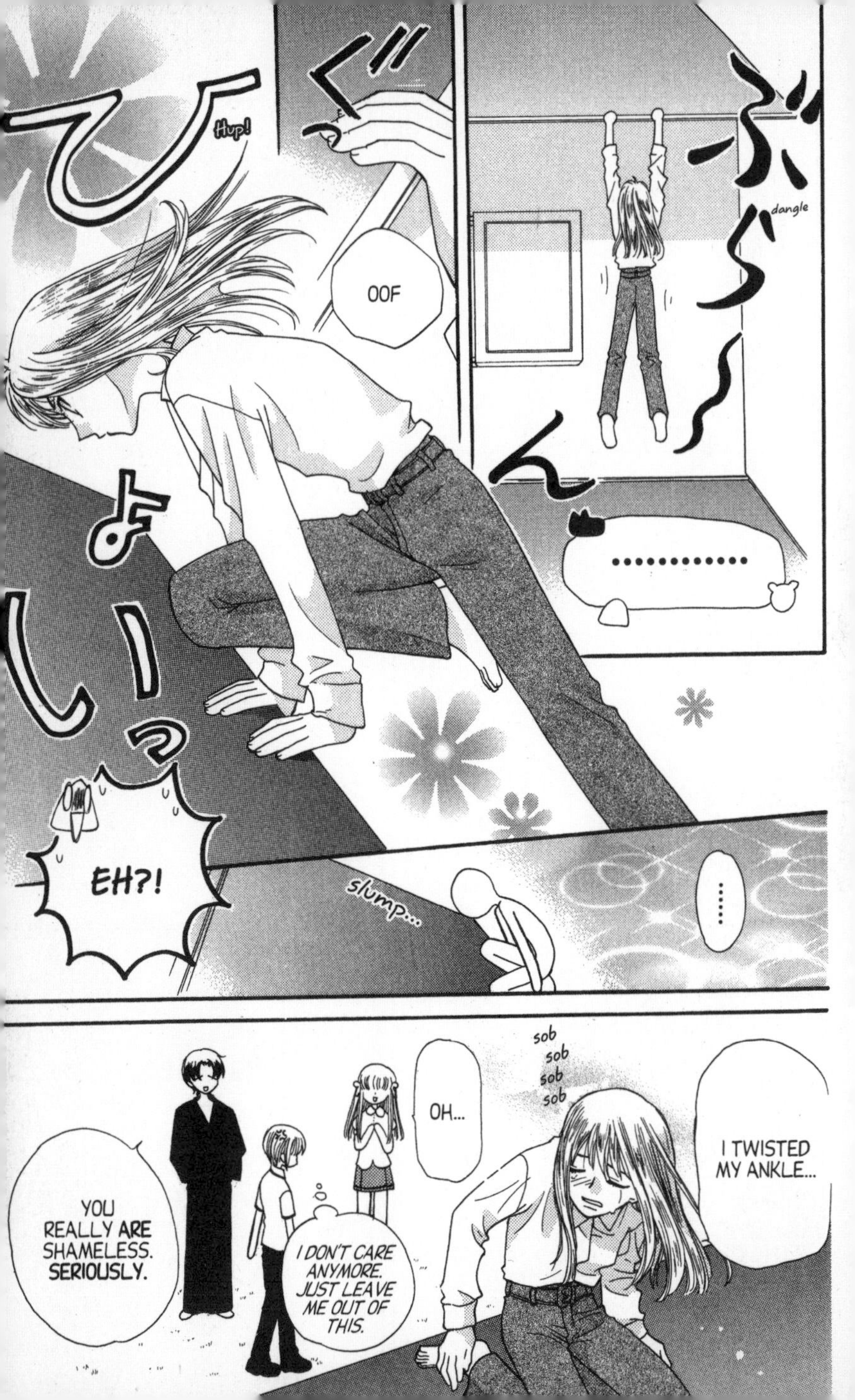

dangle
....
Hup!
OOF
EH?!
......
slump...
I TWISTED MY ANKLE...
sob sob sob sob
OH...
I DON'T CARE ANYMORE. JUST LEAVE ME OUT OF THIS.
YOU REALLY ARE SHAMELESS. SERIOUSLY.

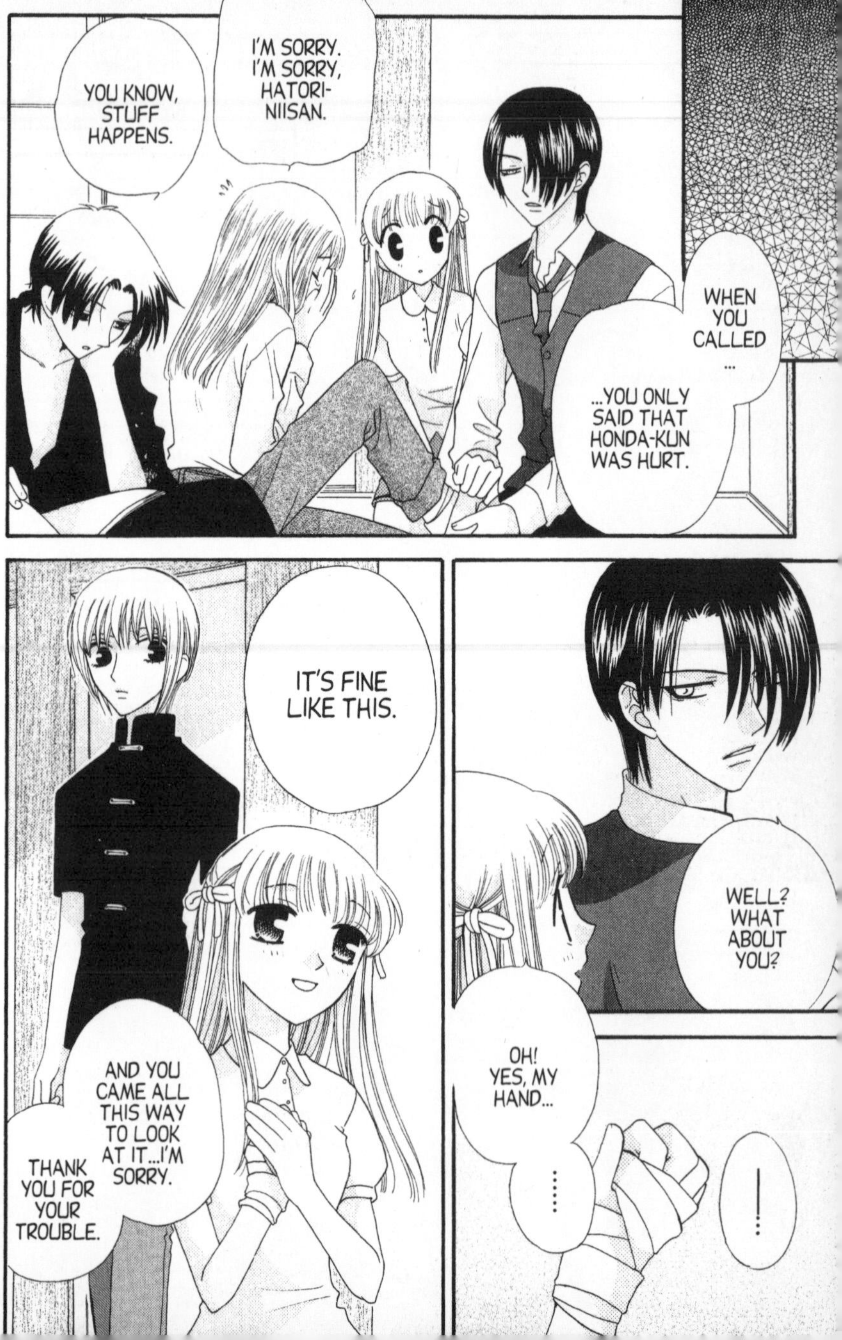
WHEN YOU CALLED ...
...YOU ONLY SAID THAT HONDA-KUN WAS HURT.
I'M SORRY. I'M SORRY, HATORI-NIISAN.
YOU KNOW, STUFF HAPPENS.
WELL? WHAT ABOUT YOU?
OH! YES, MY HAND...
!......
......
IT'S FINE LIKE THIS.
AND YOU CAME ALL THIS WAY TO LOOK AT IT...I'M SORRY.
THANK YOU FOR YOUR TROUBLE.

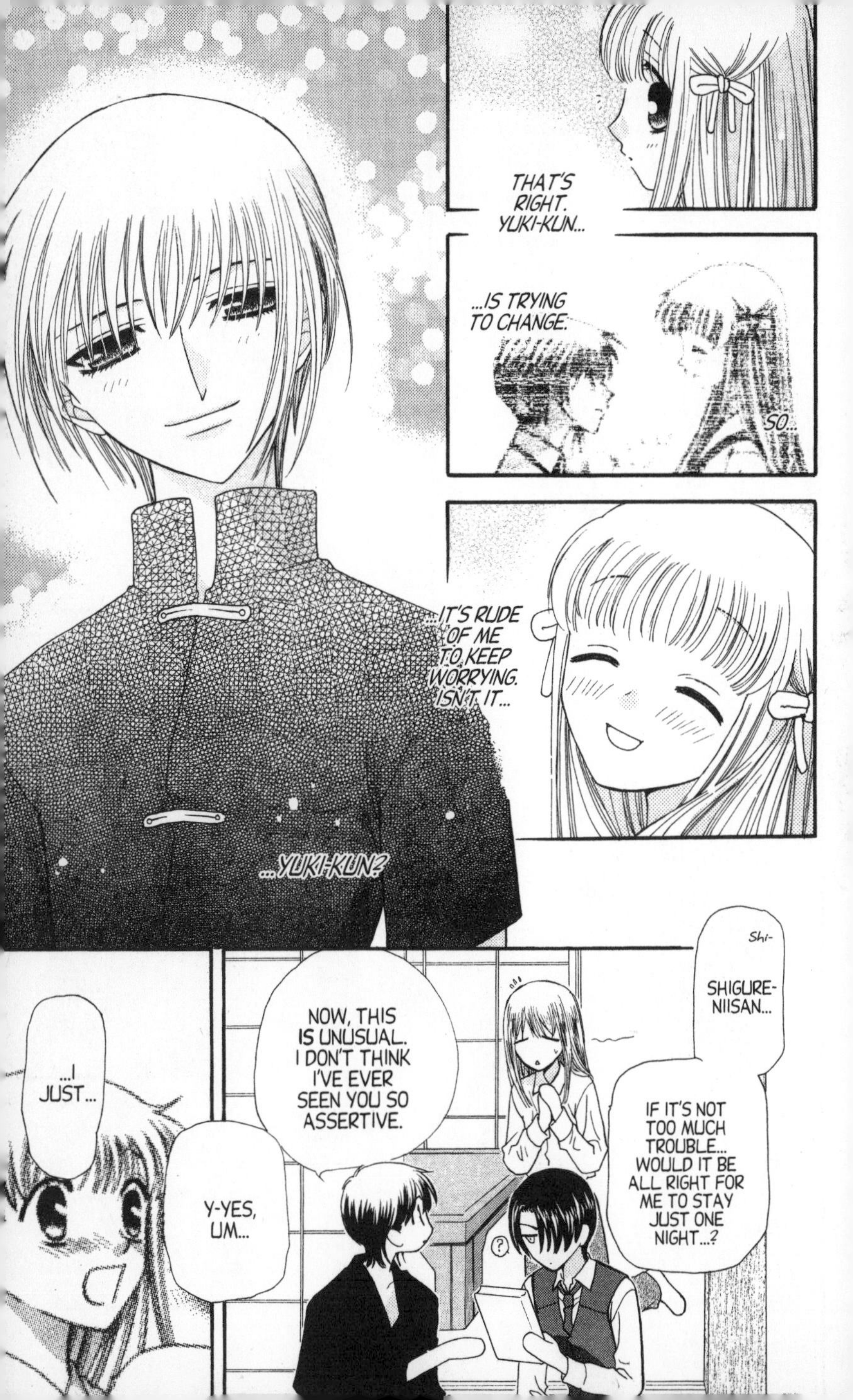
THAT'S RIGHT. YUKI-KUN...
...IS TRYING TO CHANGE.
SO...
...IT'S RUDE OF ME TO KEEP WORRYING, ISN'T IT...
...YUKI-KUN?
Shi-
SHIGURE-NIISAN...
IF IT'S NOT TOO MUCH TROUBLE... WOULD IT BE ALL RIGHT FOR ME TO STAY JUST ONE NIGHT...?
NOW, THIS IS UNUSUAL. I DON'T THINK I'VE EVER SEEN YOU SO ASSERTIVE.
Y-YES, UM...
...I JUST...

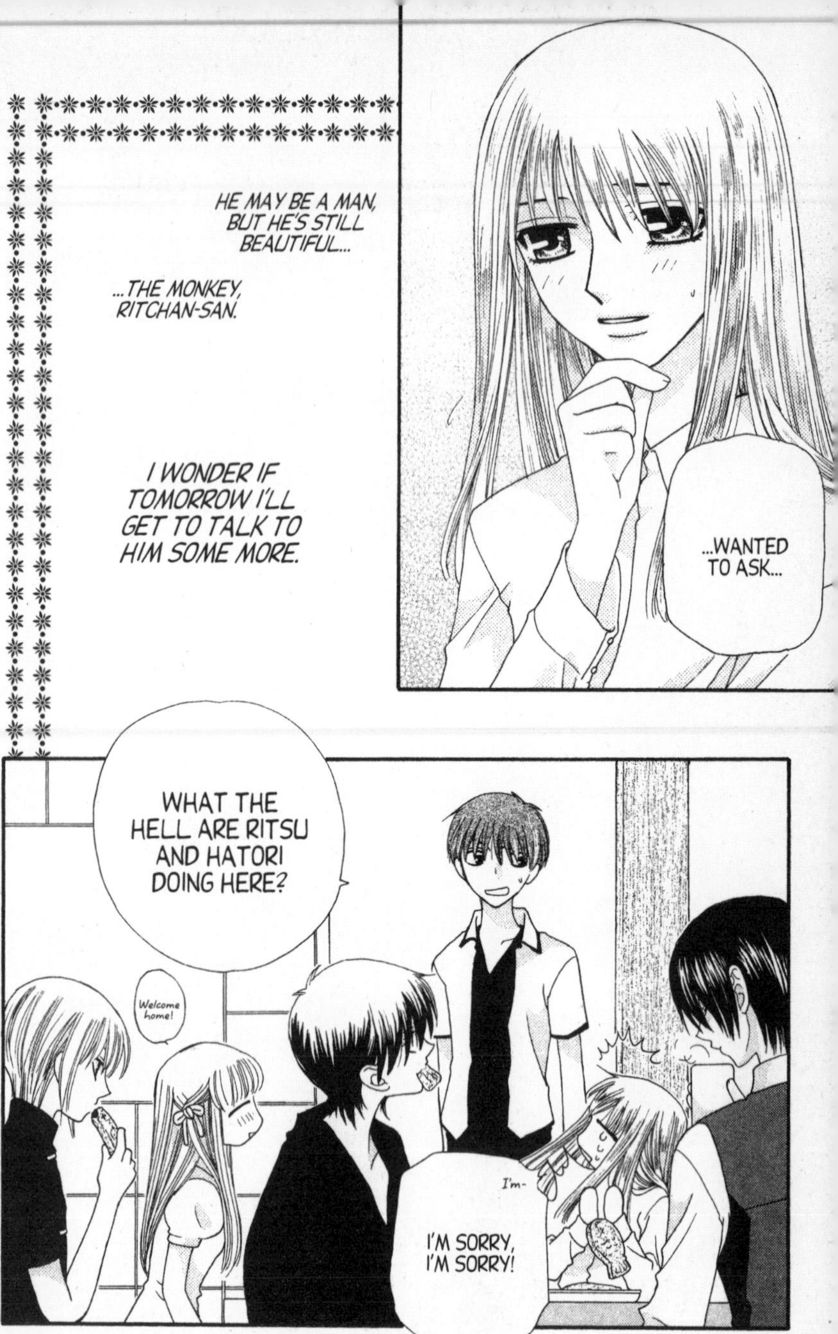
...WANTED TO ASK...
HE MAY BE A MAN, BUT HE'S STILL BEAUTIFUL...
...THE MONKEY, RITCHAN-SAN.
I WONDER IF TOMORROW I'LL GET TO TALK TO HIM SOME MORE.
WHAT THE HELL ARE RITSU AND HATORI DOING HERE?
Welcome home!
I'm-
I'M SORRY, I'M SORRY!

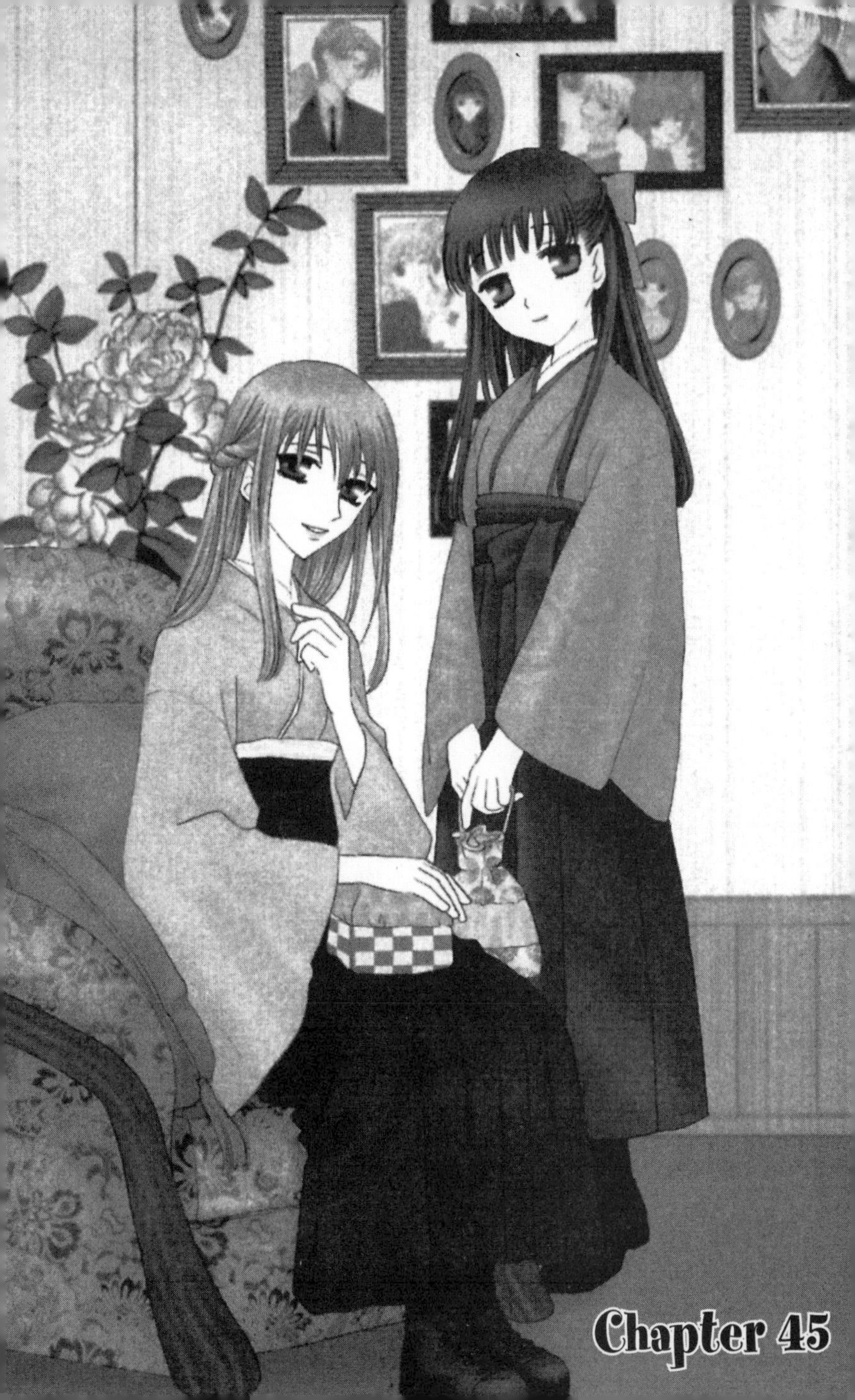
Chapter 45

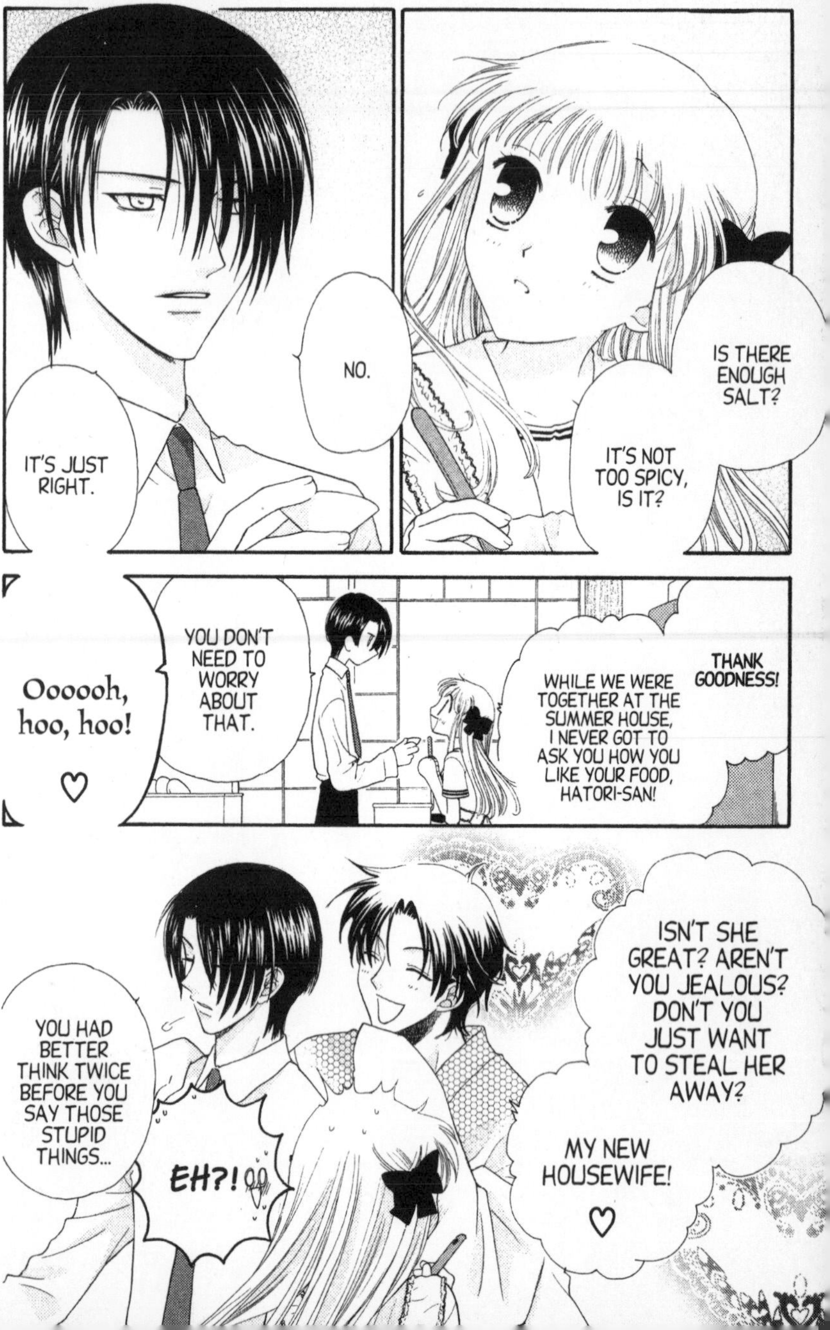
IS THERE ENOUGH SALT?
IT'S NOT TOO SPICY, IS IT?
NO.
IT'S JUST RIGHT.
THANK GOODNESS!
WHILE WE WERE TOGETHER AT THE SUMMER HOUSE, I NEVER GOT TO ASK YOU HOW YOU LIKE YOUR FOOD, HATORI-SAN!
YOU DON'T NEED TO WORRY ABOUT THAT.
Oooooh, hoo, hoo! ♡
ISN'T SHE GREAT? AREN'T YOU JEALOUS? DON'T YOU JUST WANT TO STEAL HER AWAY?
MY NEW HOUSEWIFE! ♡
EH?!
YOU HAD BETTER THINK TWICE BEFORE YOU SAY THOSE STUPID THINGS...

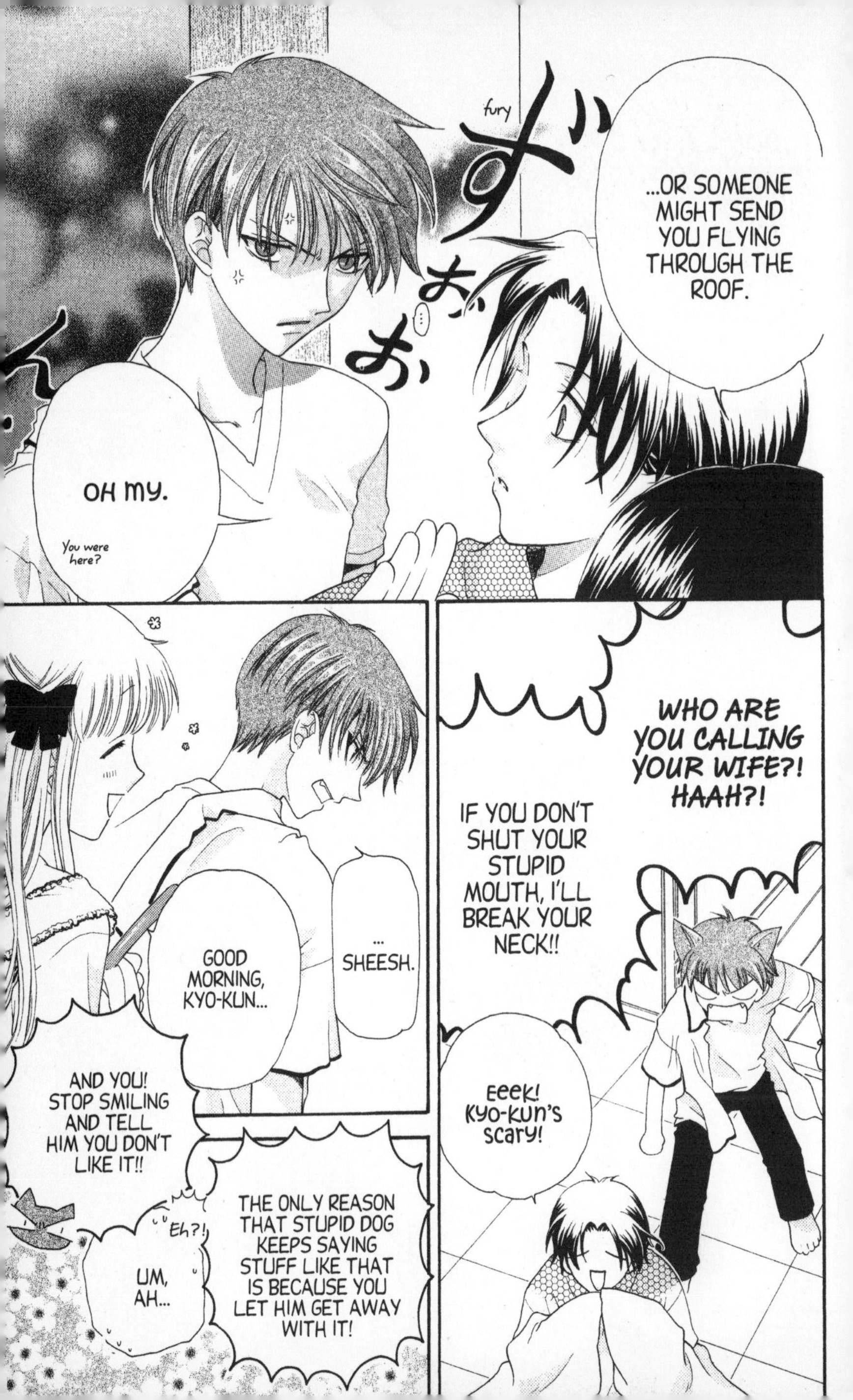
...OR SOMEONE MIGHT SEND YOU FLYING THROUGH THE ROOF.
fury
...
OH MY.
You were here?
WHO ARE YOU CALLING YOUR WIFE?! HAAH?!
IF YOU DON'T SHUT YOUR STUPID MOUTH, I'LL BREAK YOUR NECK!!
Eeek! Kyo-kun's scary!
... SHEESH.
GOOD MORNING, KYO-KUN...
AND YOU! STOP SMILING AND TELL HIM YOU DON'T LIKE IT!!
THE ONLY REASON THAT STUPID DOG KEEPS SAYING STUFF LIKE THAT IS BECAUSE YOU LET HIM GET AWAY WITH IT!
Eh?!
UM, AH...

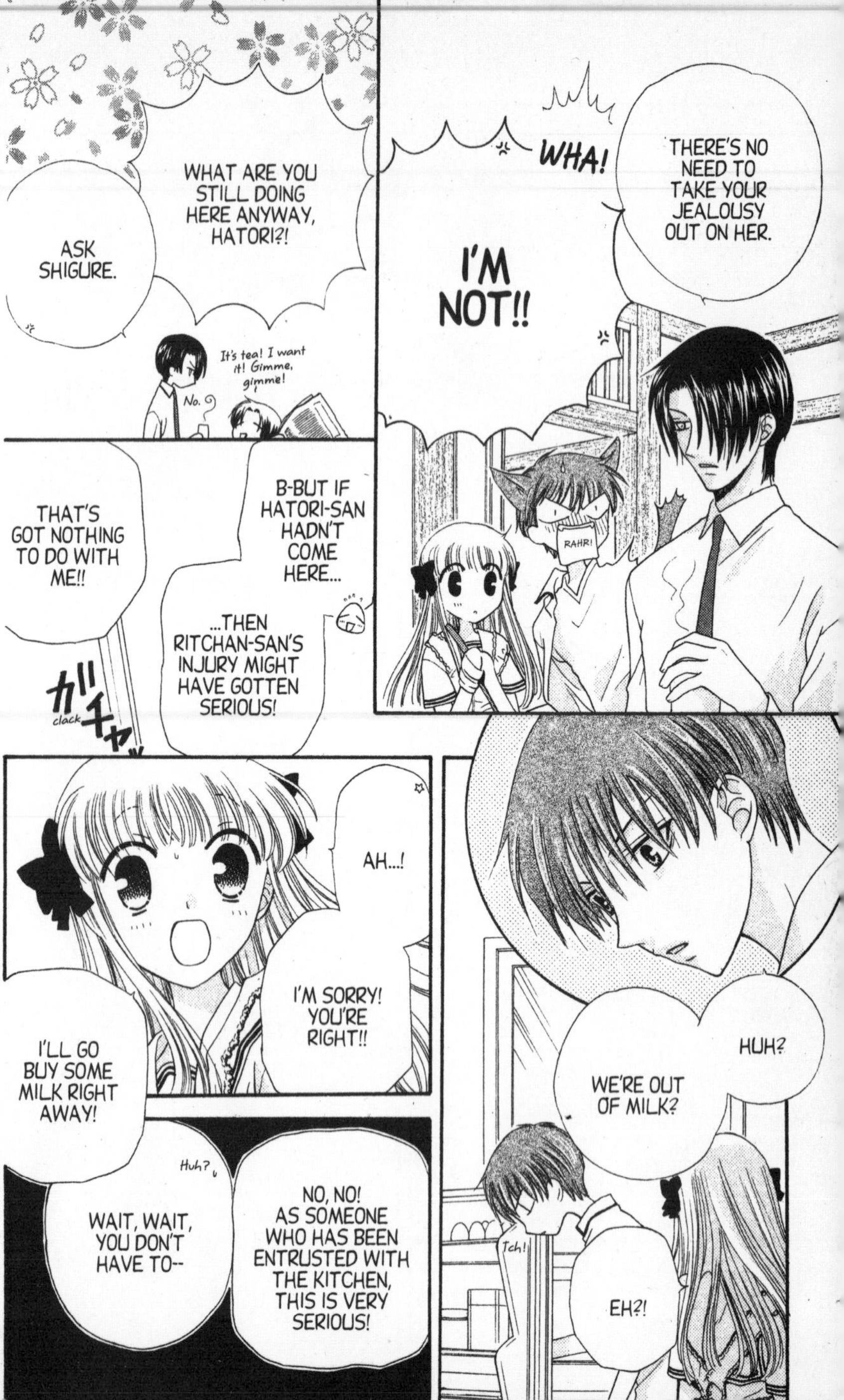
THERE'S NO NEED TO TAKE YOUR JEALOUSY OUT ON HER.
WHA!
I'M NOT!!
WHAT ARE YOU STILL DOING HERE ANYWAY, HATORI?!
ASK SHIGURE.
It's tea! I want it! Gimme, gimme!
No.
B-BUT IF HATORI-SAN HADN'T COME HERE...
...THEN RITCHAN-SAN'S INJURY MIGHT HAVE GOTTEN SERIOUS!
THAT'S GOT NOTHING TO DO WITH ME!!
clack
HUH? WE'RE OUT OF MILK?
Tch!
EH?!
AH...!
I'M SORRY! YOU'RE RIGHT!!
I'LL GO BUY SOME MILK RIGHT AWAY!
NO, NO! AS SOMEONE WHO HAS BEEN ENTRUSTED WITH THE KITCHEN, THIS IS VERY SERIOUS!
Huh?
WAIT, WAIT, YOU DON'T HAVE TO--

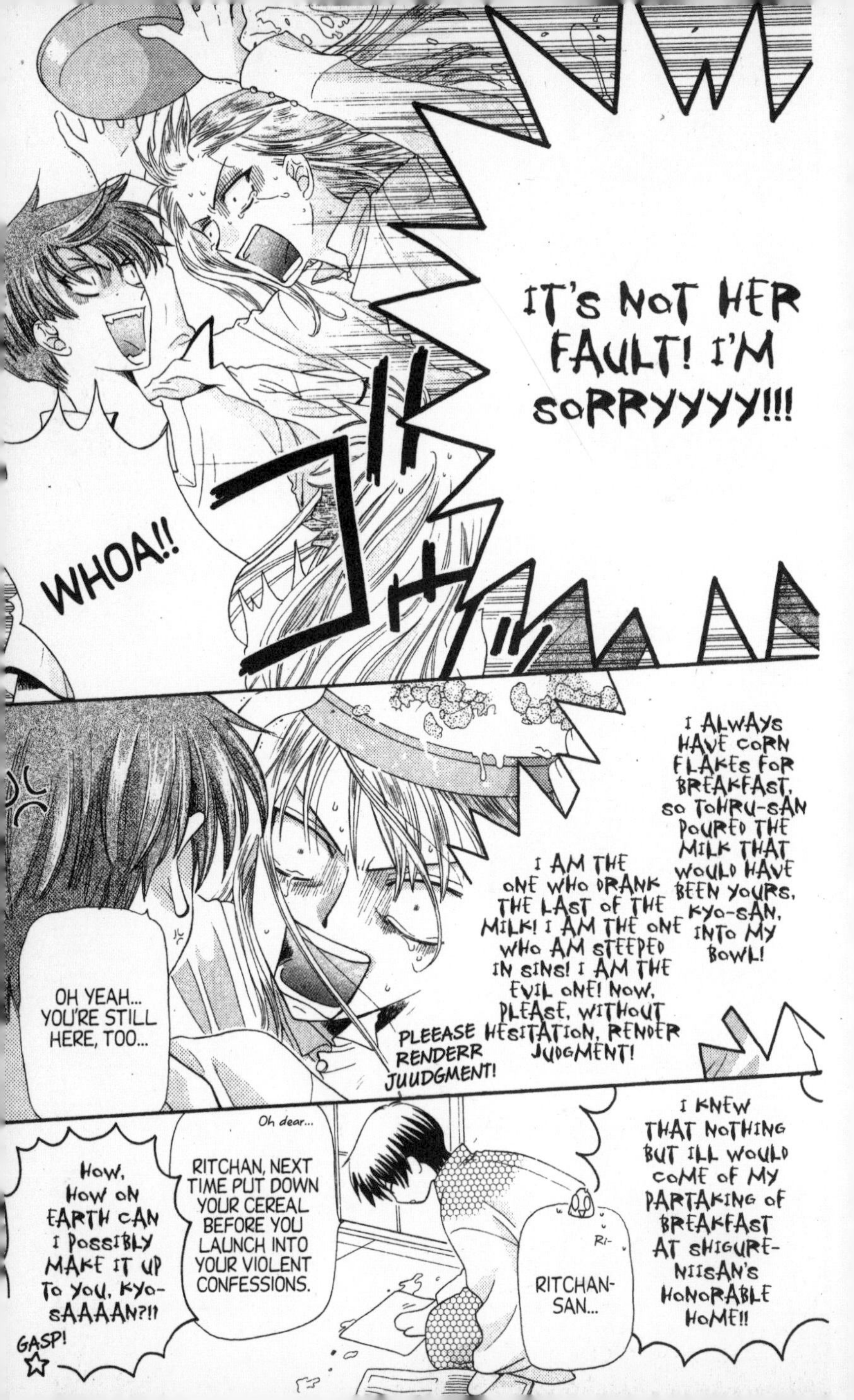
IT'S NOT HER FAULT! I'M SORRYYYY!!!
ゴッ
WHOA!!
I ALWAYS HAVE CORN FLAKES FOR BREAKFAST, SO TOHRU-SAN POURED THE MILK THAT WOULD HAVE BEEN YOURS, KYO-SAN, INTO MY BOWL!
I AM THE ONE WHO DRANK THE LAST OF THE MILK! I AM THE ONE WHO AM STEEPED IN SINS! I AM THE EVIL ONE! NOW, PLEASE, WITHOUT HESITATION, RENDER JUDGMENT!
PLEEASE RENDERR JUUDGMENT!
OH YEAH... YOU'RE STILL HERE, TOO...
I KNEW THAT NOTHING BUT ILL WOULD COME OF MY PARTAKING OF BREAKFAST AT SHIGURE-NIISAN'S HONORABLE HOME!!
Ri-
RITCHAN-SAN...
Oh dear...
RITCHAN, NEXT TIME PUT DOWN YOUR CEREAL BEFORE YOU LAUNCH INTO YOUR VIOLENT CONFESSIONS.
HOW, HOW ON EARTH CAN I POSSIBLY MAKE IT UP TO YOU, KYO-SAAAAN?!!
GASP!

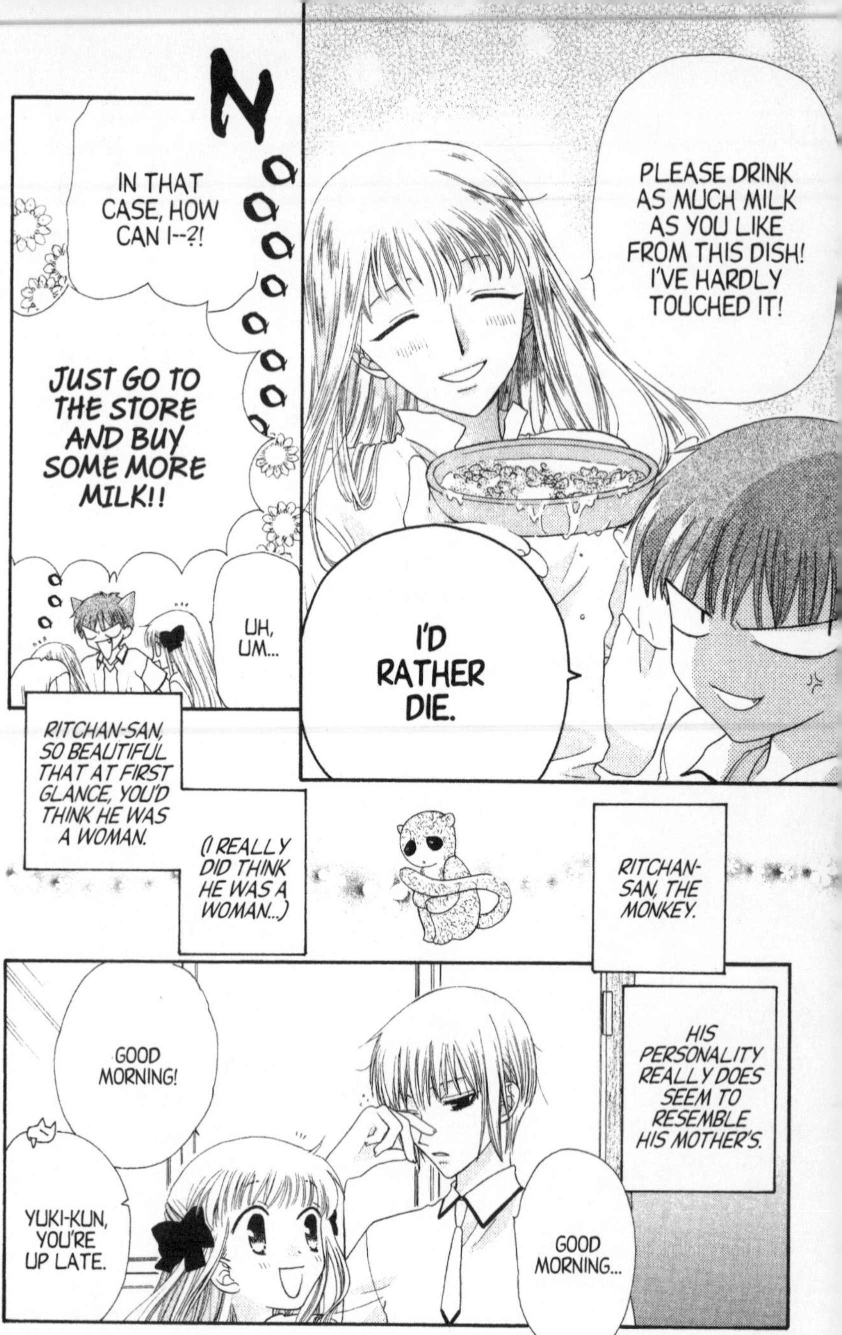
PLEASE DRINK AS MUCH MILK AS YOU LIKE FROM THIS DISH! I'VE HARDLY TOUCHED IT!
I'D RATHER DIE.
IN THAT CASE, HOW CAN I--?!
NOOOOOOOOOO
JUST GO TO THE STORE AND BUY SOME MORE MILK!!
UH, UM...
RITCHAN-SAN, THE MONKEY.
RITCHAN-SAN, SO BEAUTIFUL THAT AT FIRST GLANCE, YOU'D THINK HE WAS A WOMAN.
(I REALLY DID THINK HE WAS A WOMAN...)
HIS PERSONALITY REALLY DOES SEEM TO RESEMBLE HIS MOTHER'S.
GOOD MORNING!
YUKI-KUN, YOU'RE UP LATE.
GOOD MORNING...

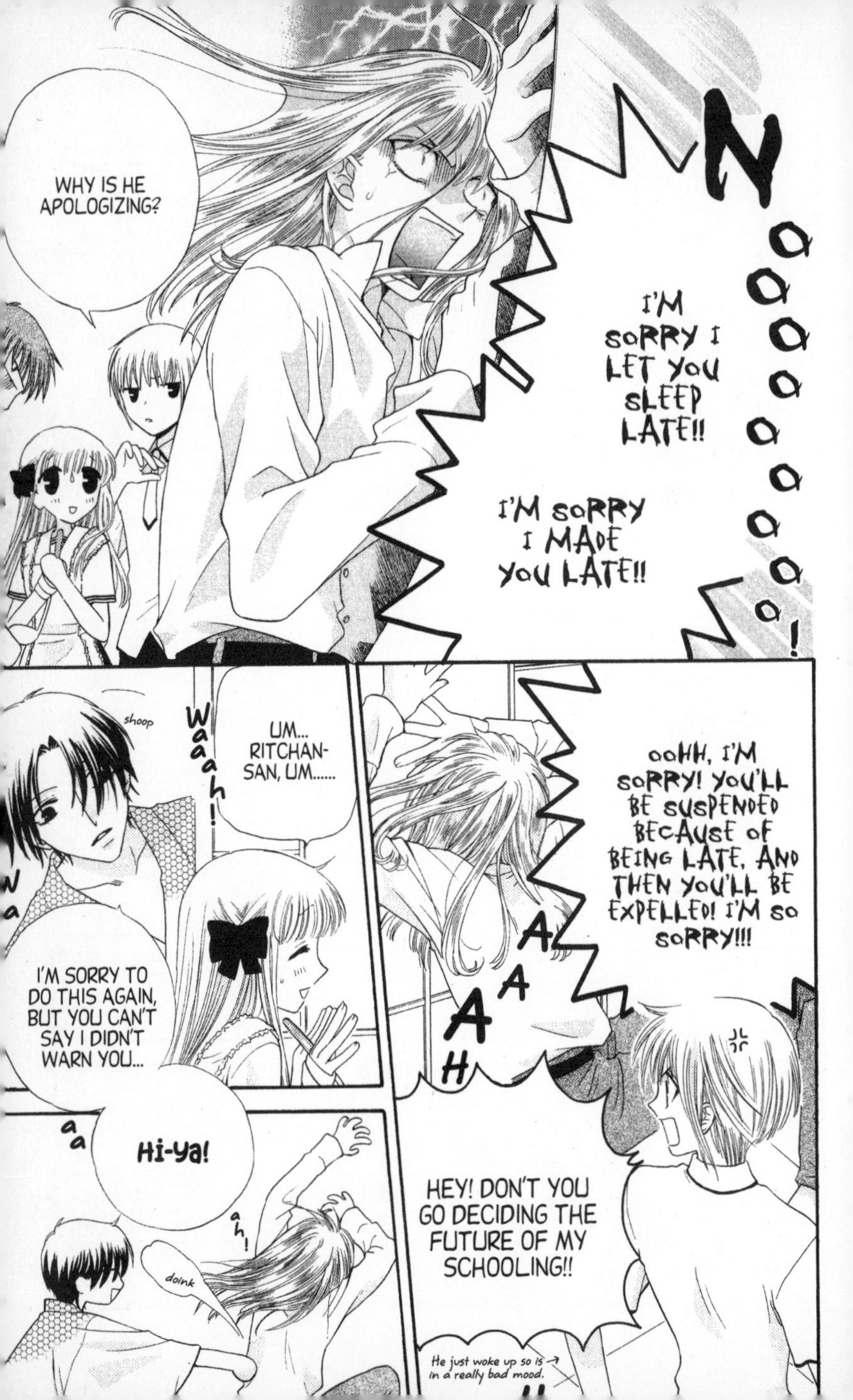
NOOOOOOOOOO!
I'M SORRY I LET YOU SLEEP LATE!!
I'M SORRY I MADE YOU LATE!!
WHY IS HE APOLOGIZING?
OOHH, I'M SORRY! YOU'LL BE SUSPENDED BECAUSE OF BEING LATE, AND THEN YOU'LL BE EXPELLED! I'M SO SORRY!!!
AAAH
HEY! DON'T YOU GO DECIDING THE FUTURE OF MY SCHOOLING!!
He just woke up so is in a really bad mood.
Waaah!
UM... RITCHAN-SAN, UM......
shoop
Wa
I'M SORRY TO DO THIS AGAIN, BUT YOU CAN'T SAY I DIDN'T WARN YOU...
Hi-ya!
aa
ah!
doink

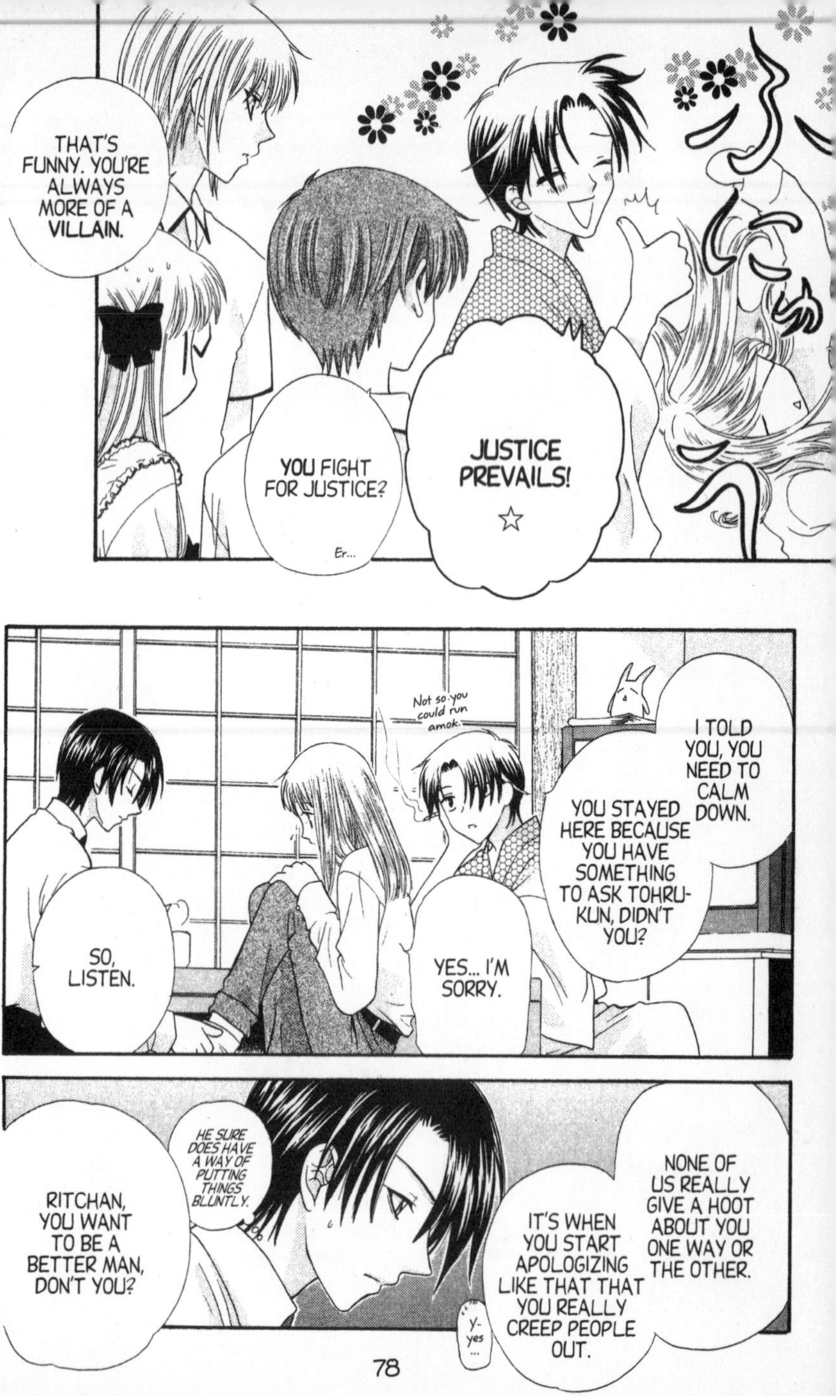
JUSTICE PREVAILS! ☆
YOU FIGHT FOR JUSTICE?
Er...
THAT'S FUNNY. YOU'RE ALWAYS MORE OF A VILLAIN.
I TOLD YOU, YOU NEED TO CALM DOWN.
Not so you could run amok.
YOU STAYED HERE BECAUSE YOU HAVE SOMETHING TO ASK TOHRU-KUN, DIDN'T YOU?
YES... I'M SORRY.
SO, LISTEN.
NONE OF US REALLY GIVE A HOOT ABOUT YOU ONE WAY OR THE OTHER.
IT'S WHEN YOU START APOLOGIZING LIKE THAT THAT YOU REALLY CREEP PEOPLE OUT.
y-yes...
HE SURE DOES HAVE A WAY OF PUTTING THINGS BLUNTLY.
RITCHAN, YOU WANT TO BE A BETTER MAN, DON'T YOU?

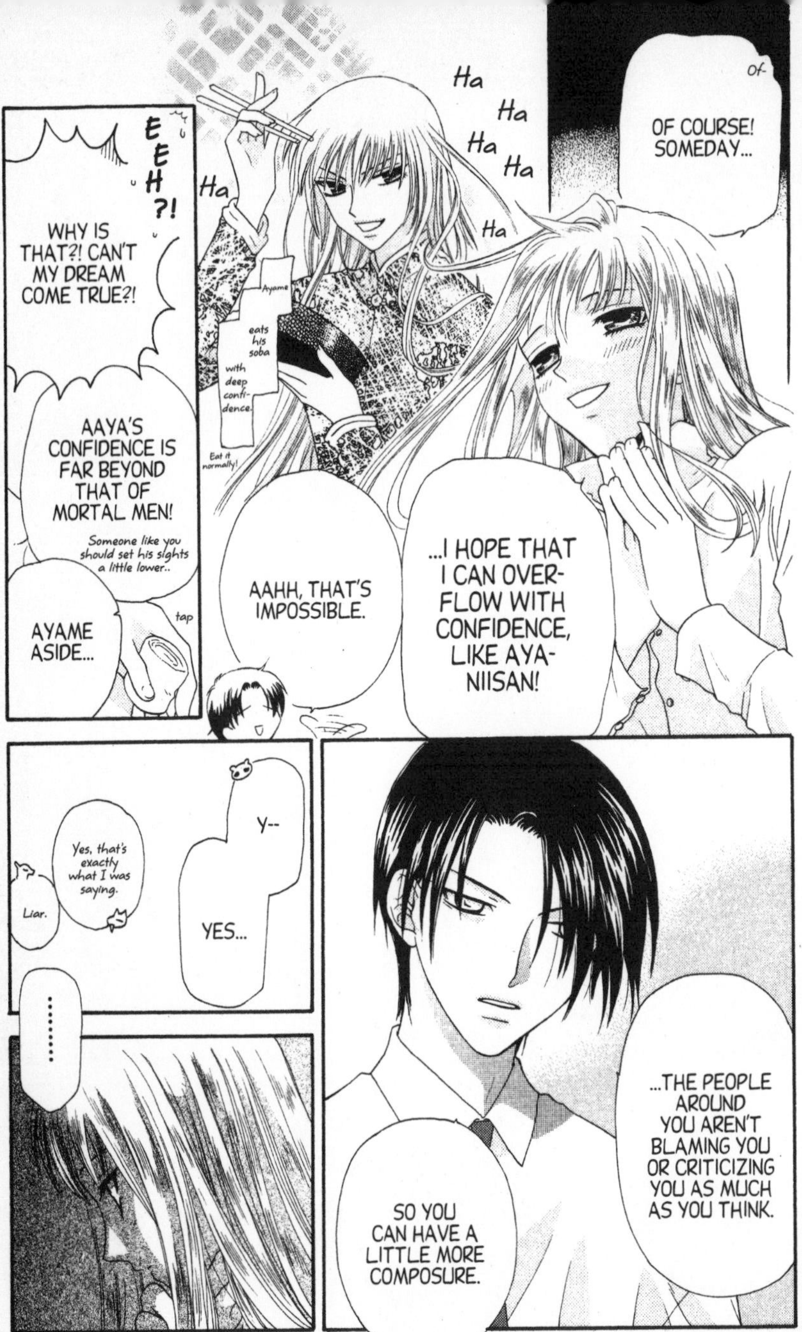
Of-
OF COURSE! SOMEDAY...
Ha Ha Ha Ha Ha Ha Ha
Ayame eats his soba with deep confidence.
Eat it normally!
...I HOPE THAT I CAN OVER-FLOW WITH CONFIDENCE, LIKE AYA-NIISAN!
AAHH, THAT'S IMPOSSIBLE.
EEH?!
WHY IS THAT?! CAN'T MY DREAM COME TRUE?!
AAYA'S CONFIDENCE IS FAR BEYOND THAT OF MORTAL MEN!
Someone like you should set his sights a little lower..
tap
AYAME ASIDE...
...THE PEOPLE AROUND YOU AREN'T BLAMING YOU OR CRITICIZING YOU AS MUCH AS YOU THINK.
SO YOU CAN HAVE A LITTLE MORE COMPOSURE.
Y--
YES...
Yes, that's exactly what I was saying.
Liar.
....

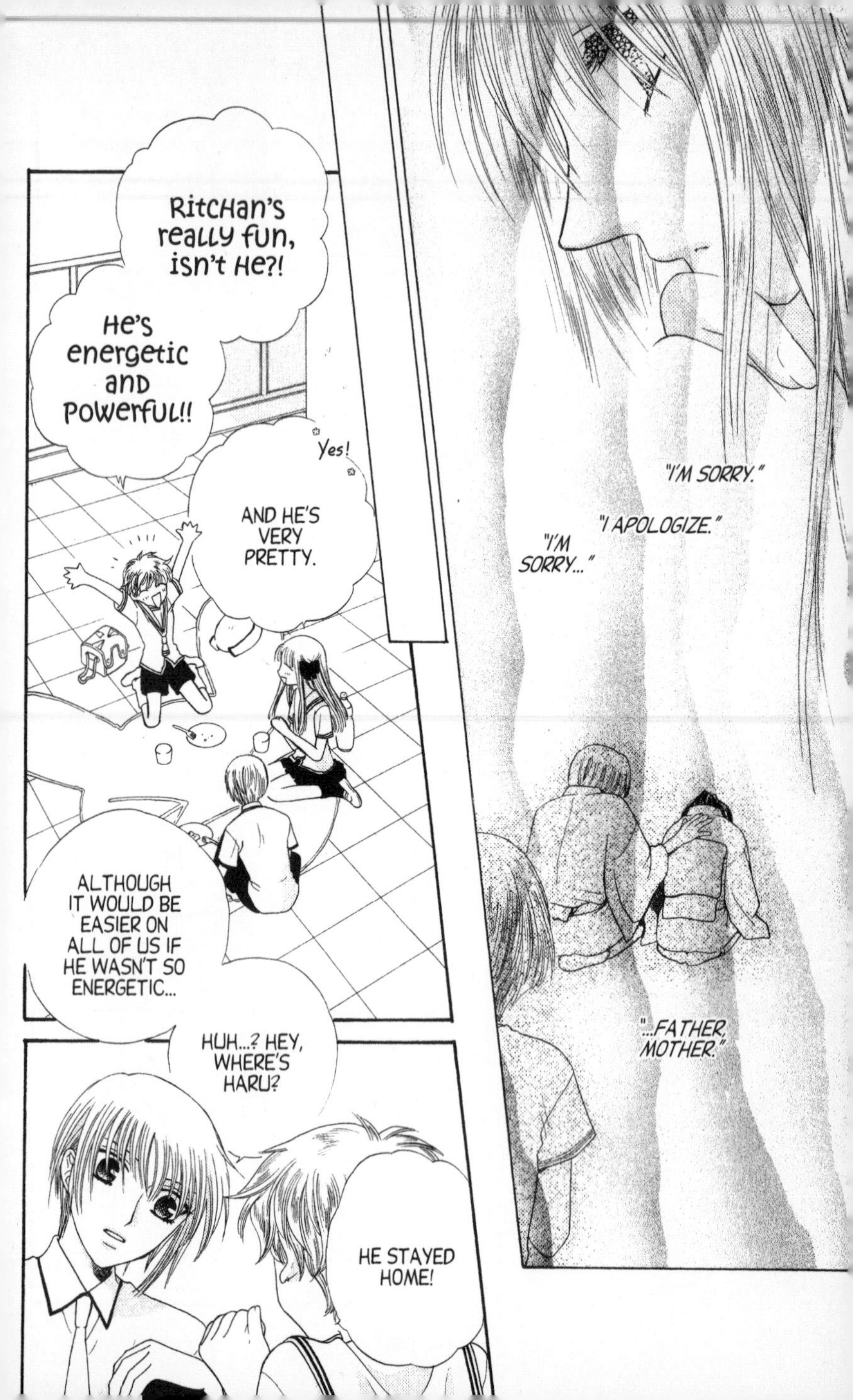
"I'M SORRY."
"I APOLOGIZE."
"I'M SORRY..."
"...FATHER, MOTHER."
Ritchan's really fun, isn't he?!
He's energetic and powerful!!
Yes!
AND HE'S VERY PRETTY.
ALTHOUGH IT WOULD BE EASIER ON ALL OF US IF HE WASN'T SO ENERGETIC...
HUH...? HEY, WHERE'S HARU?
HE STAYED HOME!

Fruits Basket 8: Part 3

So my second Playstation is broken. (The PS2 is fine.) It fizzled out right in the middle of a game. And so, as I sat there and stared (in shock) at the black TV screen, I thought, "Wouldn't it be cool if the titles of all the games I've played and the time I spent playing them scrolled by like credits in a movie?"

You served me well, Playstation-san...Thank you.

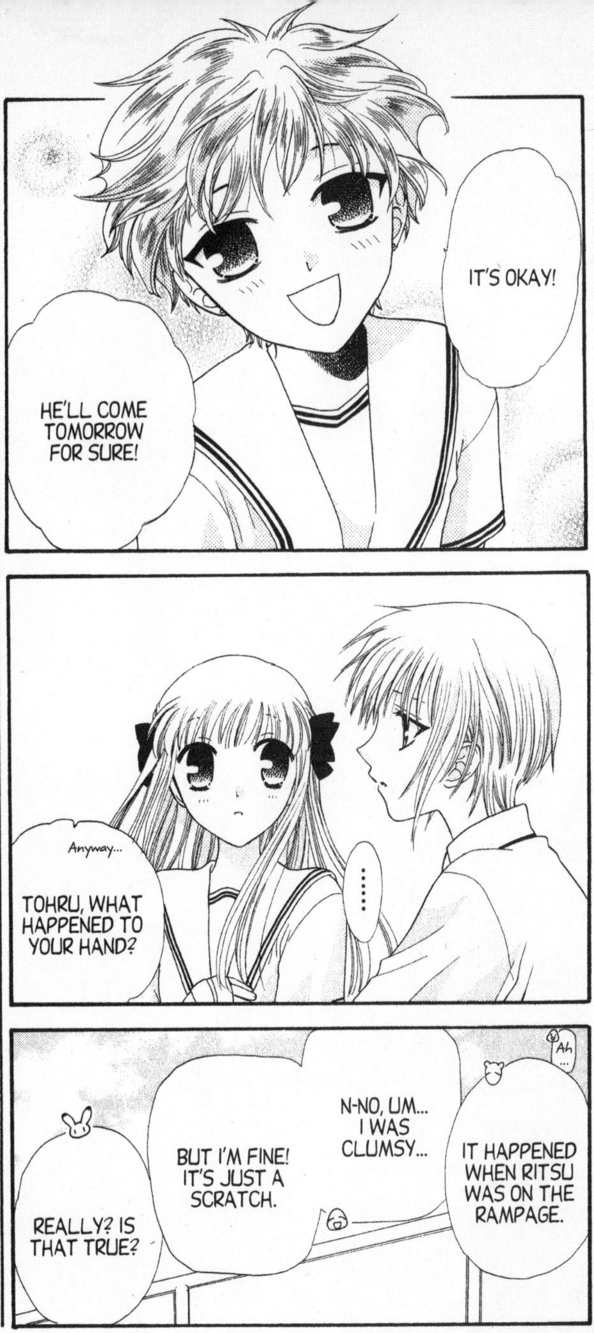

IT'S OKAY!
HE'LL COME TOMORROW FOR SURE!
......
Anyway...
TOHRU, WHAT HAPPENED TO YOUR HAND?
Ah...
IT HAPPENED WHEN RITSU WAS ON THE RAMPAGE.
N-NO, UM... I WAS CLUMSY...
BUT I'M FINE! IT'S JUST A SCRATCH.
REALLY? IS THAT TRUE?

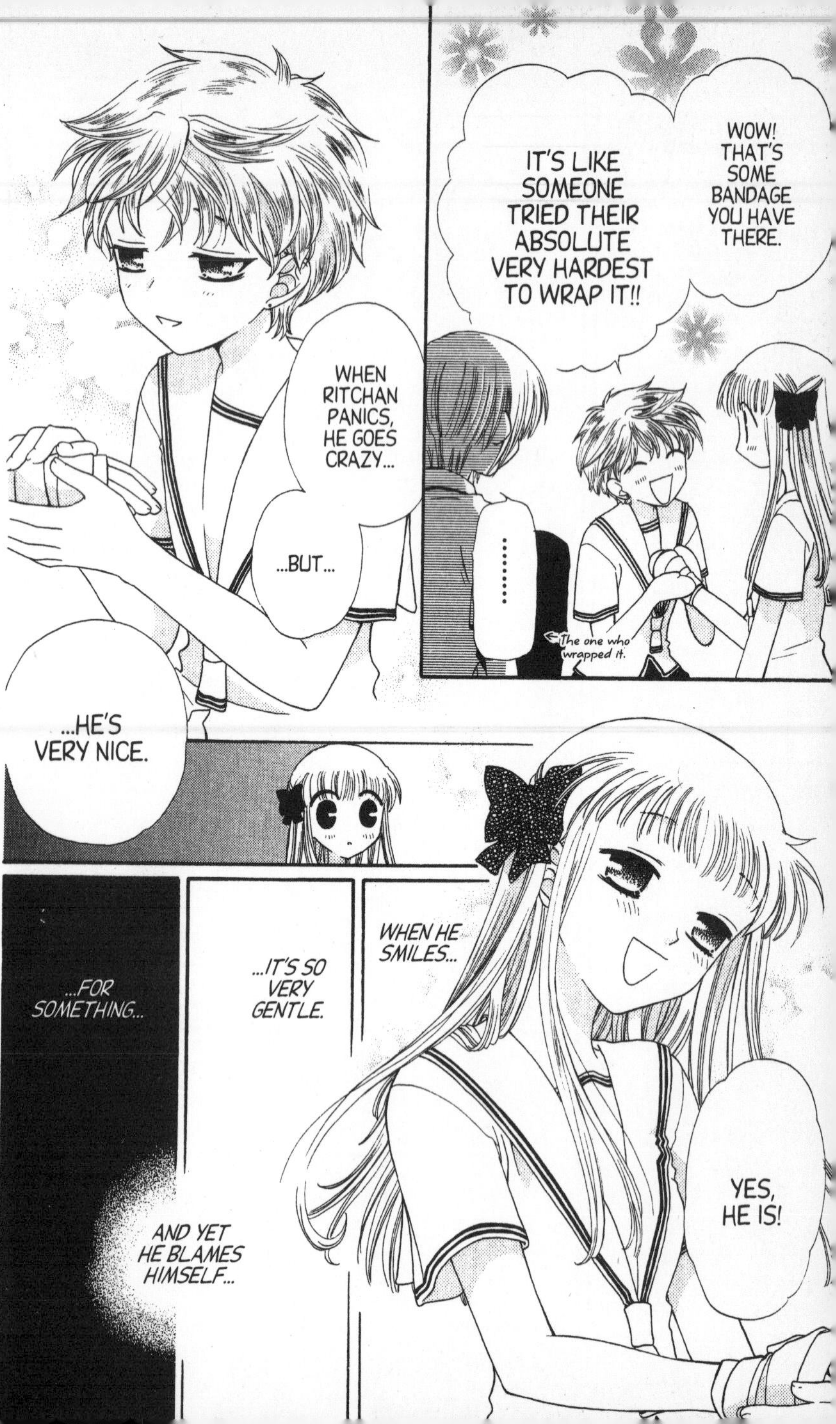

WOW! THAT'S SOME BANDAGE YOU HAVE THERE.
IT'S LIKE SOMEONE TRIED THEIR ABSOLUTE VERY HARDEST TO WRAP IT!!
....
The one who wrapped it.
WHEN RITCHAN PANICS, HE GOES CRAZY...
...BUT...
...HE'S VERY NICE.
YES, HE IS!
WHEN HE SMILES...
...IT'S SO VERY GENTLE.
AND YET HE BLAMES HIMSELF...
...FOR SOMETHING...

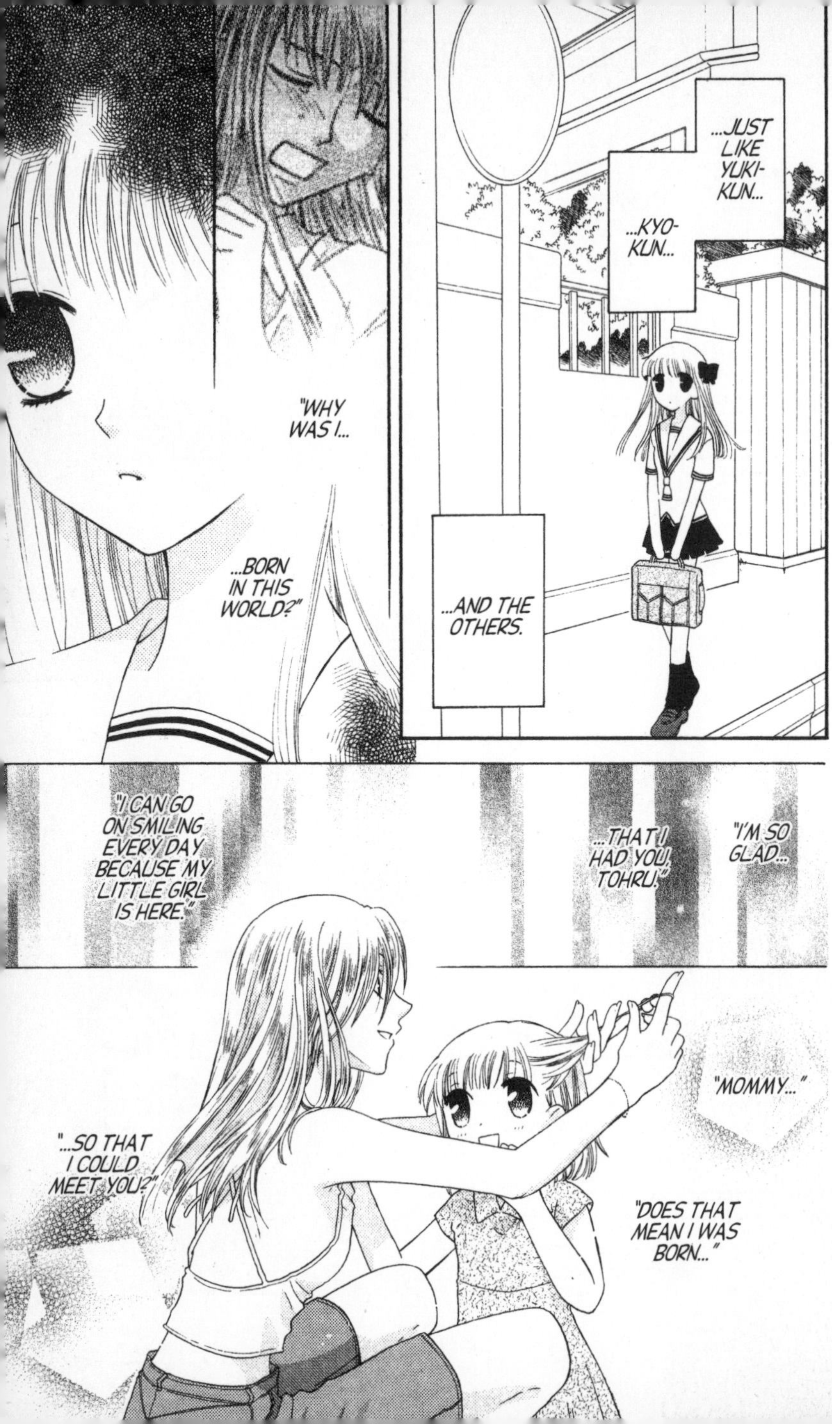
...JUST LIKE YUKI-KUN...
...KYO-KUN...
...AND THE OTHERS.
"WHY WAS I...
...BORN IN THIS WORLD?"
"I'M SO GLAD...
...THAT I HAD YOU, TOHRU."
"I CAN GO ON SMILING EVERY DAY BECAUSE MY LITTLE GIRL IS HERE."
"MOMMY..."
"DOES THAT MEAN I WAS BORN..."
"...SO THAT I COULD MEET YOU?"

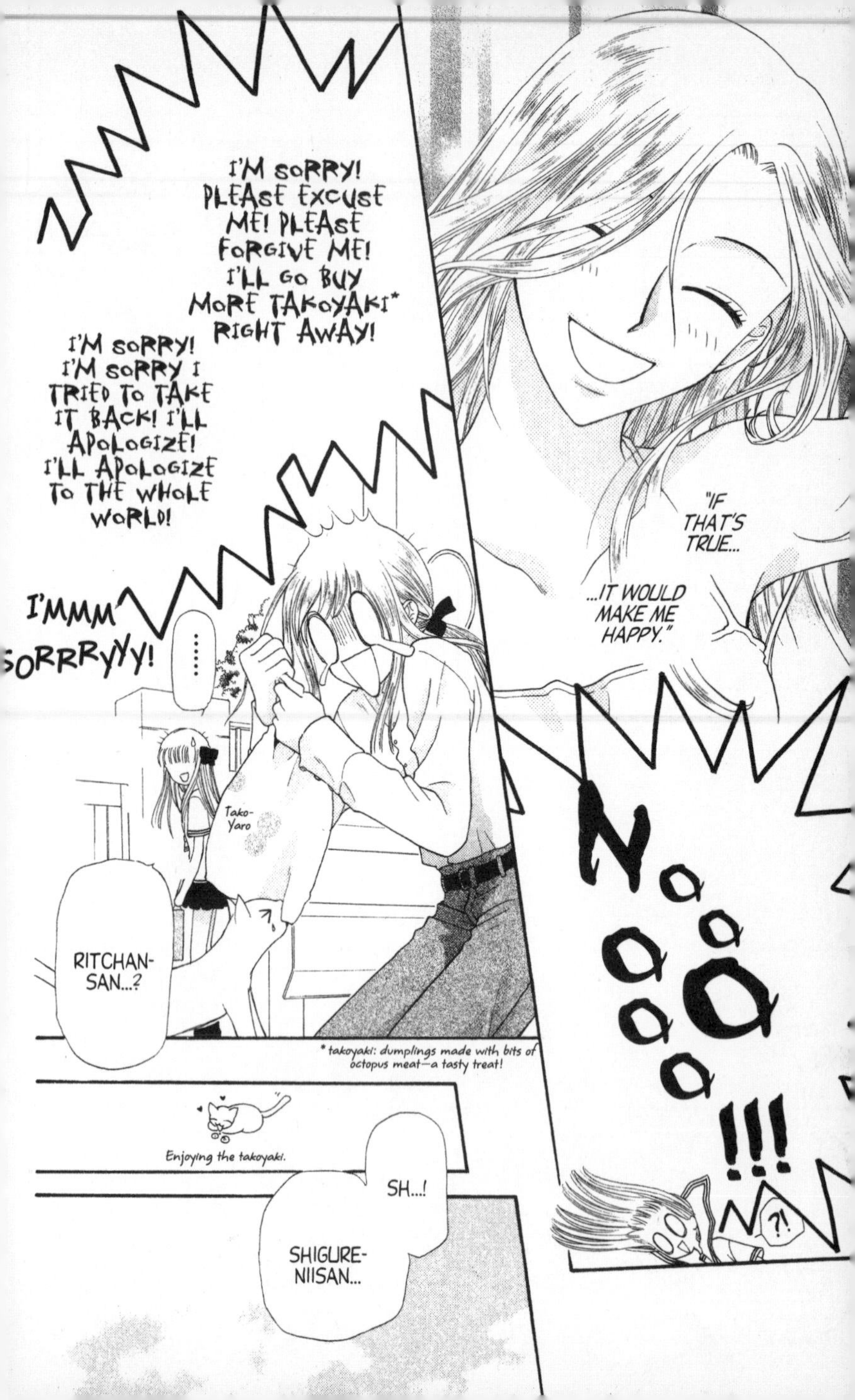
"IF THAT'S TRUE...
...IT WOULD MAKE ME HAPPY."
NAAAAAAA!!!
?!
I'M SORRY! PLEASE EXCUSE ME! PLEASE FORGIVE ME! I'LL GO BUY MORE TAKOYAKI* RIGHT AWAY!
I'M SORRY! I'M SORRY I TRIED TO TAKE IT BACK! I'LL APOLOGIZE! I'LL APOLOGIZE TO THE WHOLE WORLD!
I'MMM SORRRYYY!
......
Tako-Yaro
RITCHAN-SAN...?
Enjoying the takoyaki.
SH...!
SHIGURE-NIISAN...
* takoyaki: dumplings made with bits of octopus meat—a tasty treat!

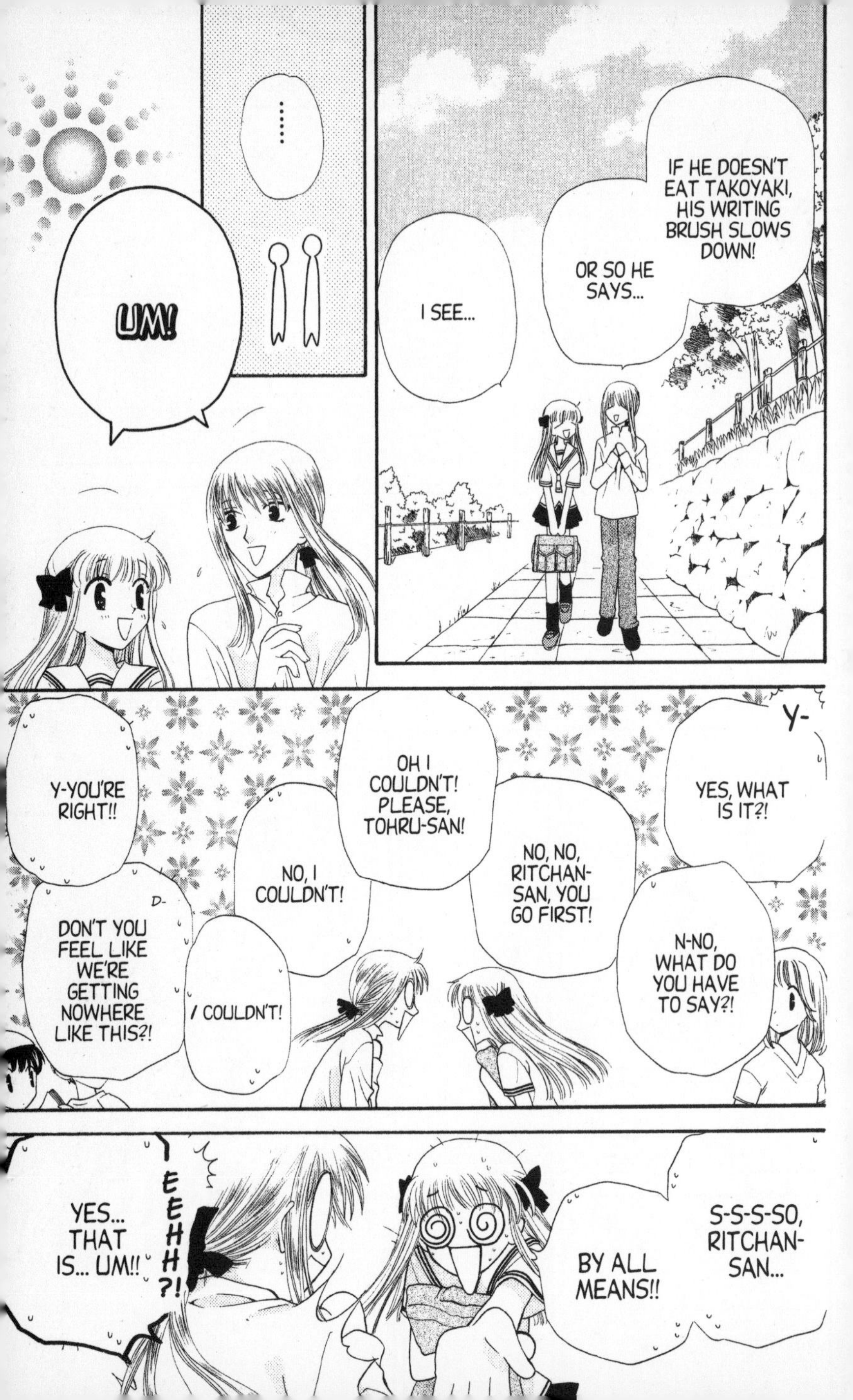
IF HE DOESN'T EAT TAKOYAKI, HIS WRITING BRUSH SLOWS DOWN!
OR SO HE SAYS...
I SEE...
......
UM!
Y-
YES, WHAT IS IT?!
N-NO, WHAT DO YOU HAVE TO SAY?!
NO, NO, RITCHAN-SAN, YOU GO FIRST!
OH I COULDN'T! PLEASE, TOHRU-SAN!
NO, I COULDN'T!
I COULDN'T!
Y-YOU'RE RIGHT!!
D-
DON'T YOU FEEL LIKE WE'RE GETTING NOWHERE LIKE THIS?!
S-S-S-SO, RITCHAN-SAN...
BY ALL MEANS!!
EEHH?!
YES... THAT IS... UM!!

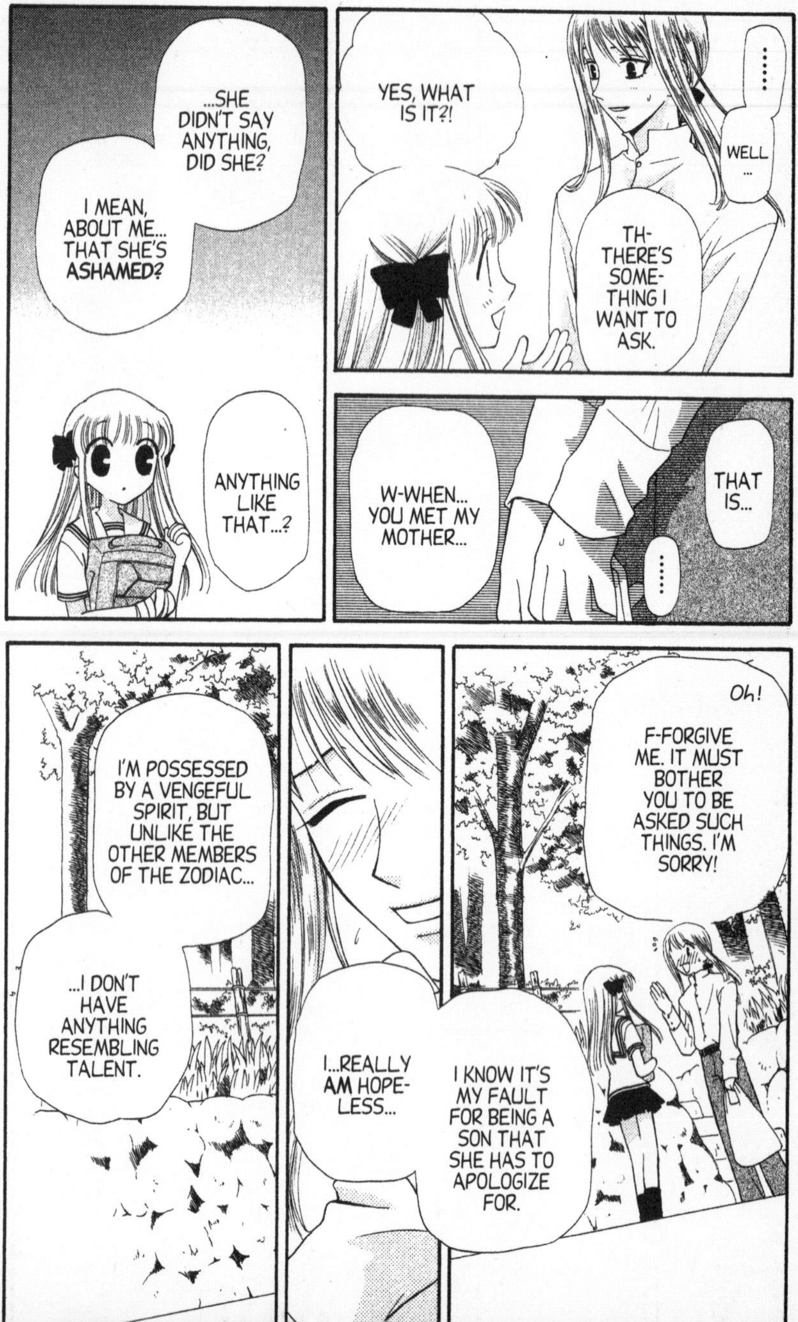
......
WELL ...
TH- THERE'S SOME- THING I WANT TO ASK.
YES, WHAT IS IT?!
THAT IS...
......
W-WHEN... YOU MET MY MOTHER...
...SHE DIDN'T SAY ANYTHING, DID SHE?
I MEAN, ABOUT ME... THAT SHE'S ASHAMED?
ANYTHING LIKE THAT...?
Oh!
F-FORGIVE ME. IT MUST BOTHER YOU TO BE ASKED SUCH THINGS. I'M SORRY!
I KNOW IT'S MY FAULT FOR BEING A SON THAT SHE HAS TO APOLOGIZE FOR.
I...REALLY AM HOPE- LESS...
I'M POSSESSED BY A VENGEFUL SPIRIT, BUT UNLIKE THE OTHER MEMBERS OF THE ZODIAC...
...I DON'T HAVE ANYTHING RESEMBLING TALENT.

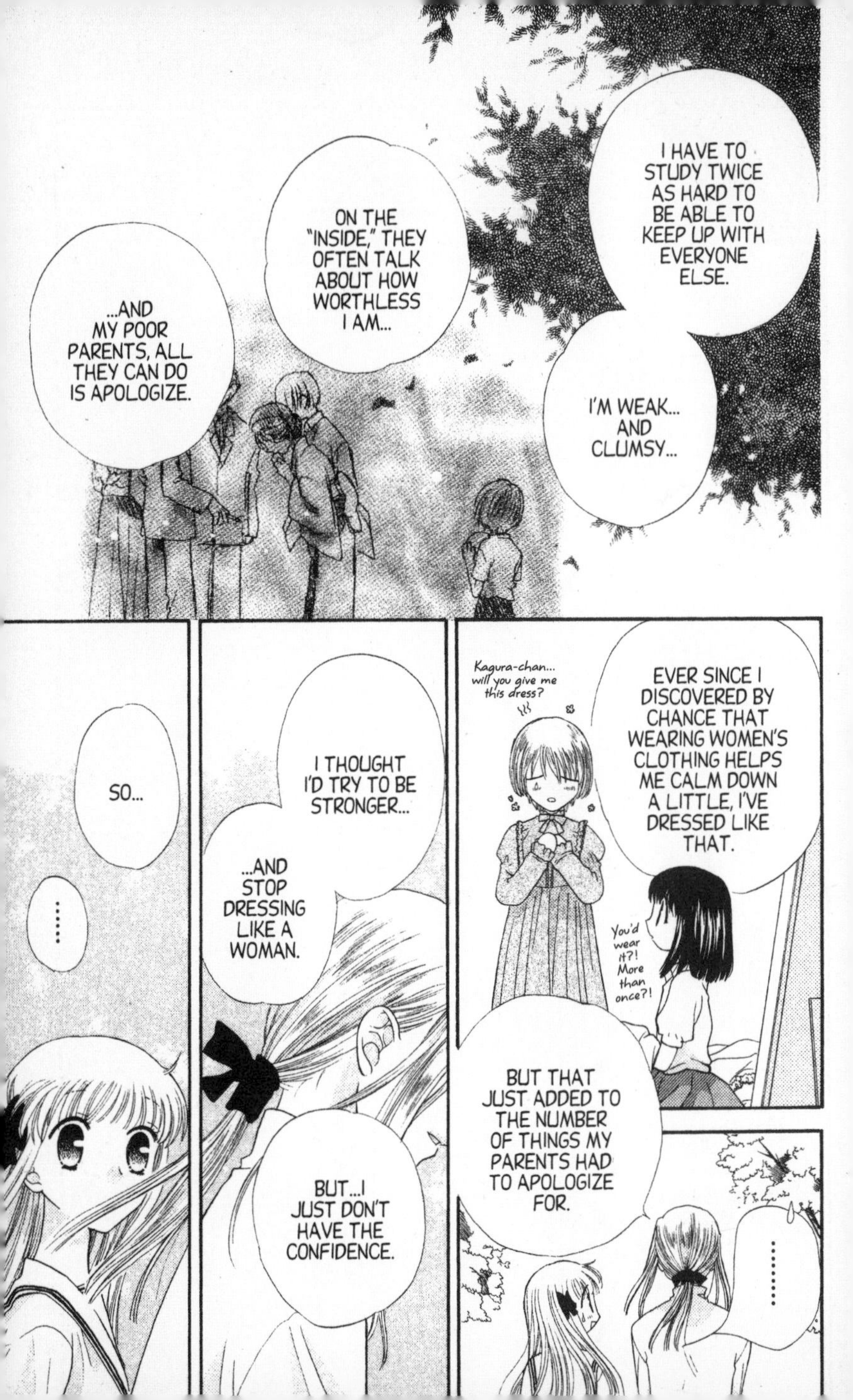
I HAVE TO STUDY TWICE AS HARD TO BE ABLE TO KEEP UP WITH EVERYONE ELSE.
I'M WEAK... AND CLUMSY...
ON THE "INSIDE," THEY OFTEN TALK ABOUT HOW WORTHLESS I AM...
...AND MY POOR PARENTS, ALL THEY CAN DO IS APOLOGIZE.
EVER SINCE I DISCOVERED BY CHANCE THAT WEARING WOMEN'S CLOTHING HELPS ME CALM DOWN A LITTLE, I'VE DRESSED LIKE THAT.
Kagura-chan... will you give me this dress?
You'd wear it?! More than once?!
BUT THAT JUST ADDED TO THE NUMBER OF THINGS MY PARENTS HAD TO APOLOGIZE FOR.
......
I THOUGHT I'D TRY TO BE STRONGER...
...AND STOP DRESSING LIKE A WOMAN.
BUT...I JUST DON'T HAVE THE CONFIDENCE.
SO...
......

THAT'S WHY...
...I'M SO HOPELESS.
MY HEART BROKE.
FATHER AND MOTHER MUST HATE HAVING TO APOLOGIZE FOR ME ALL THE TIME.
SURELY THEY WANTED A SON WHO WOULD MAKE THEM PROUD.
A WORTH-WHILE SON.
I'M SORRY.
I'M SO SORRY.
MAYBE IT WOULD BE BETTER...
...IF I DIDN'T EXIST.

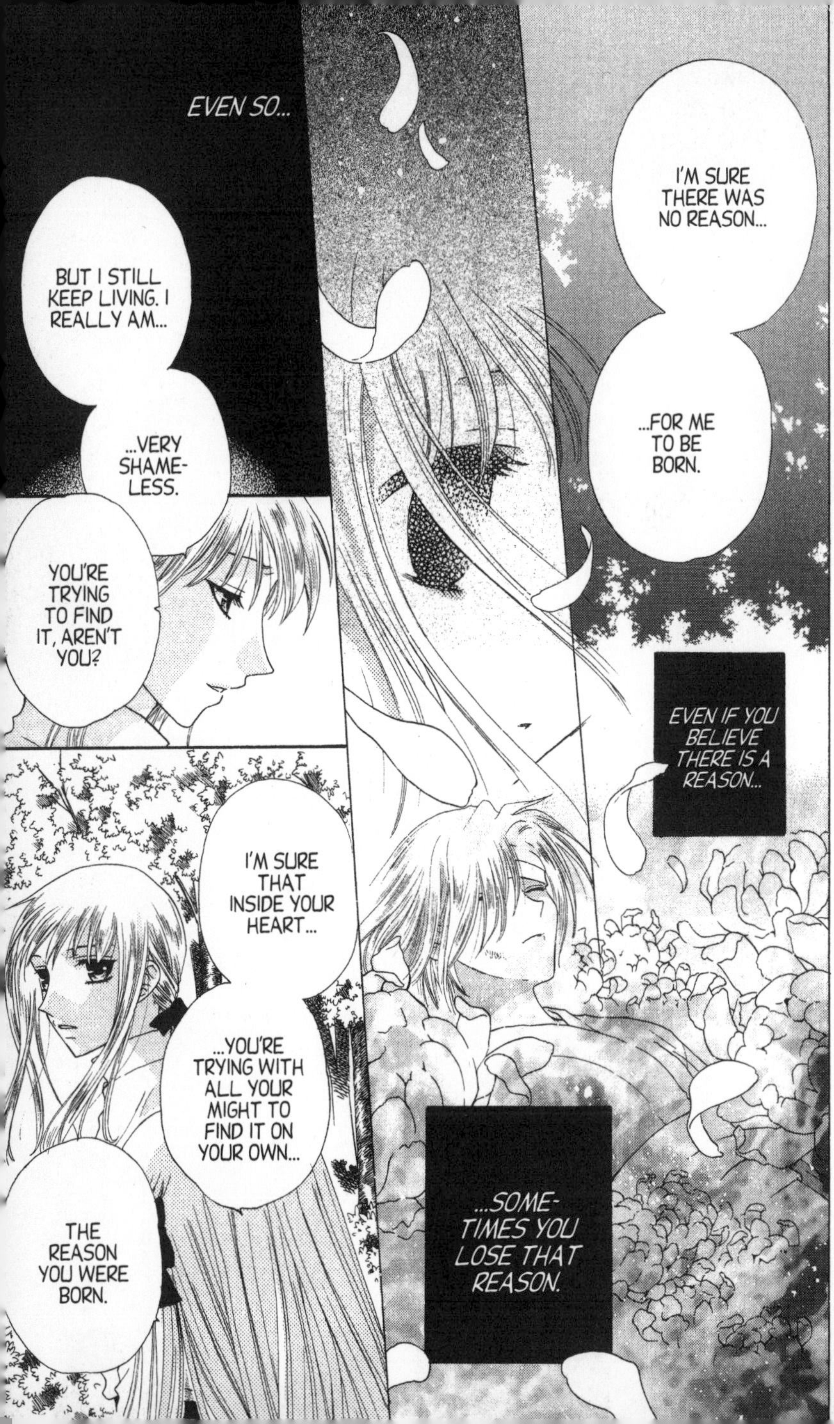
I'M SURE THERE WAS NO REASON...
...FOR ME TO BE BORN.
EVEN SO...
BUT I STILL KEEP LIVING. I REALLY AM...
...VERY SHAMELESS.
YOU'RE TRYING TO FIND IT, AREN'T YOU?
I'M SURE THAT INSIDE YOUR HEART...
...YOU'RE TRYING WITH ALL YOUR MIGHT TO FIND IT ON YOUR OWN...
THE REASON YOU WERE BORN.
EVEN IF YOU BELIEVE THERE IS A REASON...
...SOMETIMES YOU LOSE THAT REASON.

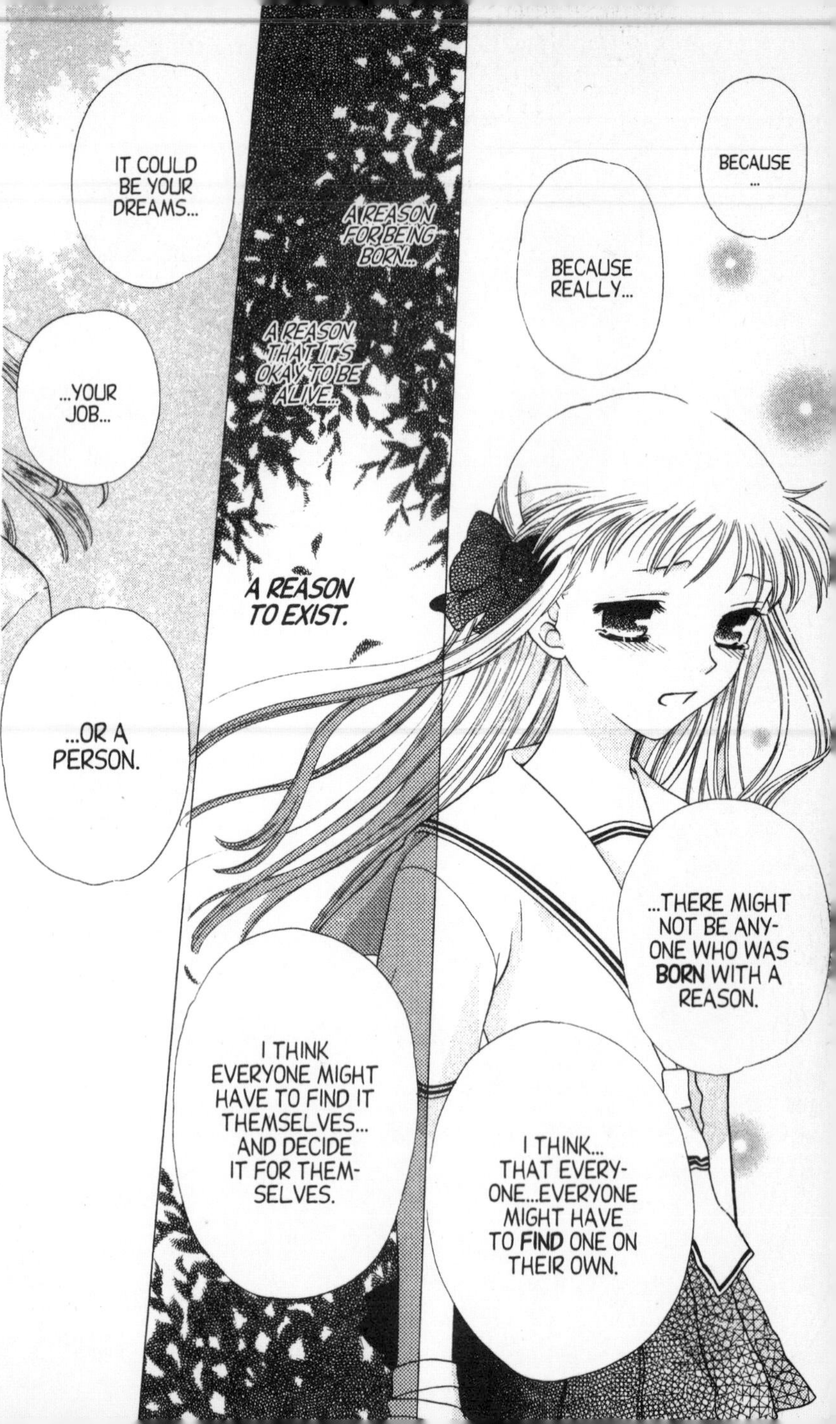
BECAUSE ...
BECAUSE REALLY...
...THERE MIGHT NOT BE ANYONE WHO WAS BORN WITH A REASON.
I THINK... THAT EVERYONE...EVERYONE MIGHT HAVE TO FIND ONE ON THEIR OWN.
A REASON FOR BEING BORN...
A REASON THAT IT'S OKAY TO BE ALIVE...
A REASON TO EXIST.
IT COULD BE YOUR DREAMS...
...YOUR JOB...
...OR A PERSON.
I THINK EVERYONE MIGHT HAVE TO FIND IT THEMSELVES... AND DECIDE IT FOR THEMSELVES.

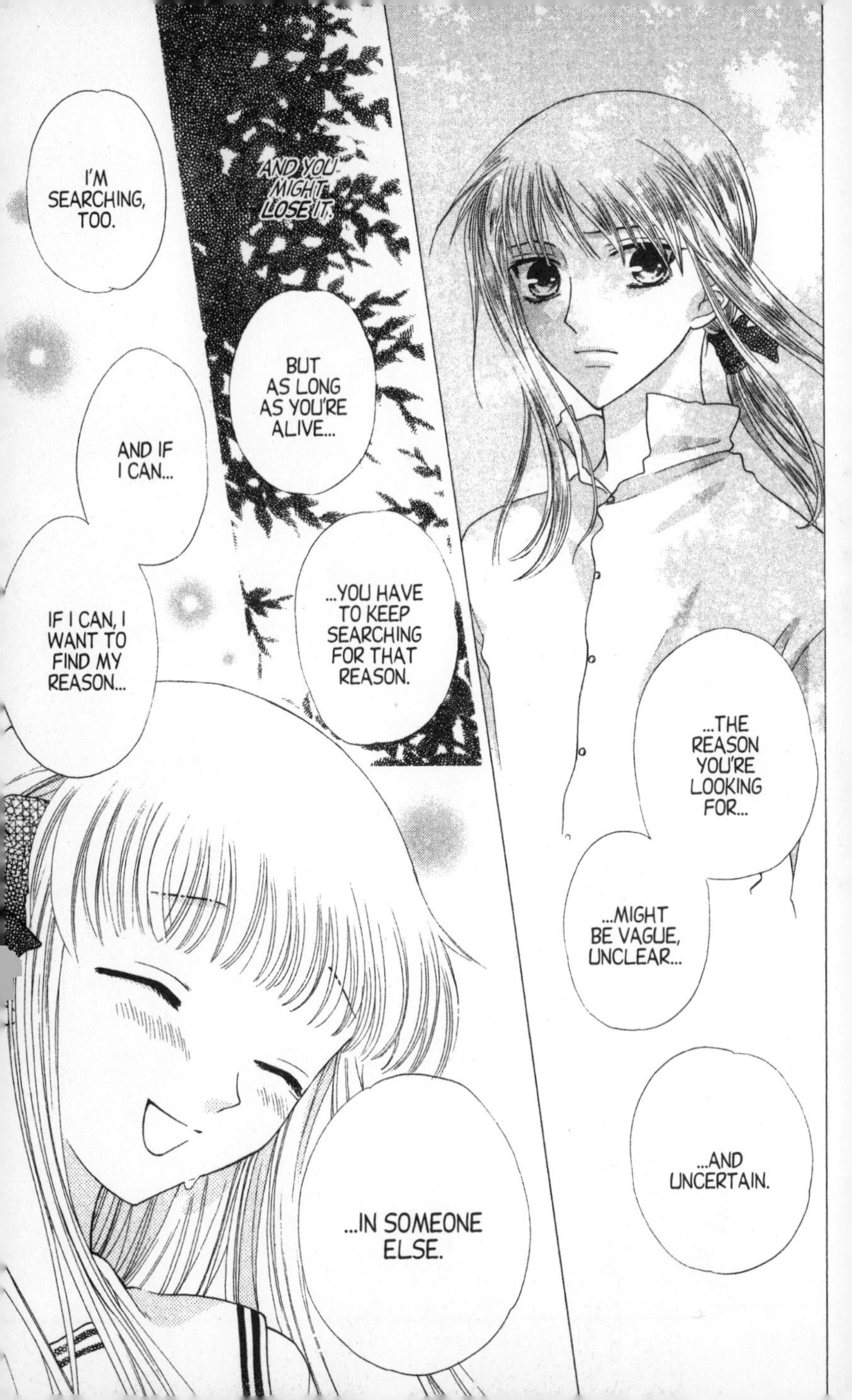
...THE REASON YOU'RE LOOKING FOR...
...MIGHT BE VAGUE, UNCLEAR...
...AND UNCERTAIN.
AND YOU MIGHT LOSE IT.
BUT AS LONG AS YOU'RE ALIVE...
...YOU HAVE TO KEEP SEARCHING FOR THAT REASON.
I'M SEARCHING, TOO.
AND IF I CAN...
IF I CAN, I WANT TO FIND MY REASON...
...IN SOMEONE ELSE.

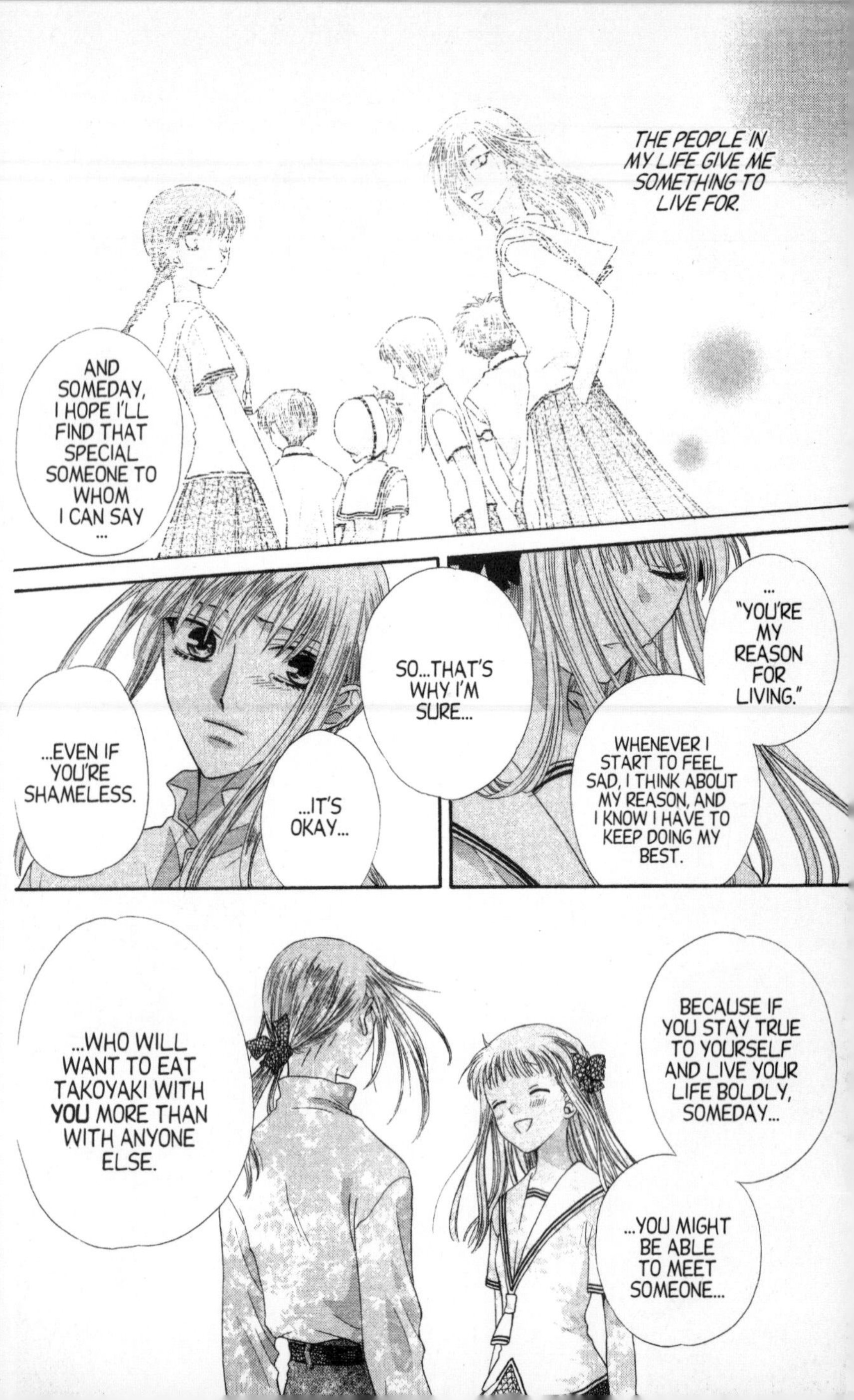
THE PEOPLE IN MY LIFE GIVE ME SOMETHING TO LIVE FOR.
AND SOMEDAY, I HOPE I'LL FIND THAT SPECIAL SOMEONE TO WHOM I CAN SAY ...
... "YOU'RE MY REASON FOR LIVING."
WHENEVER I START TO FEEL SAD, I THINK ABOUT MY REASON, AND I KNOW I HAVE TO KEEP DOING MY BEST.
SO...THAT'S WHY I'M SURE...
...IT'S OKAY...
...EVEN IF YOU'RE SHAMELESS.
BECAUSE IF YOU STAY TRUE TO YOURSELF AND LIVE YOUR LIFE BOLDLY, SOMEDAY...
...YOU MIGHT BE ABLE TO MEET SOMEONE...
...WHO WILL WANT TO EAT TAKOYAKI WITH **YOU** MORE THAN WITH ANYONE ELSE.

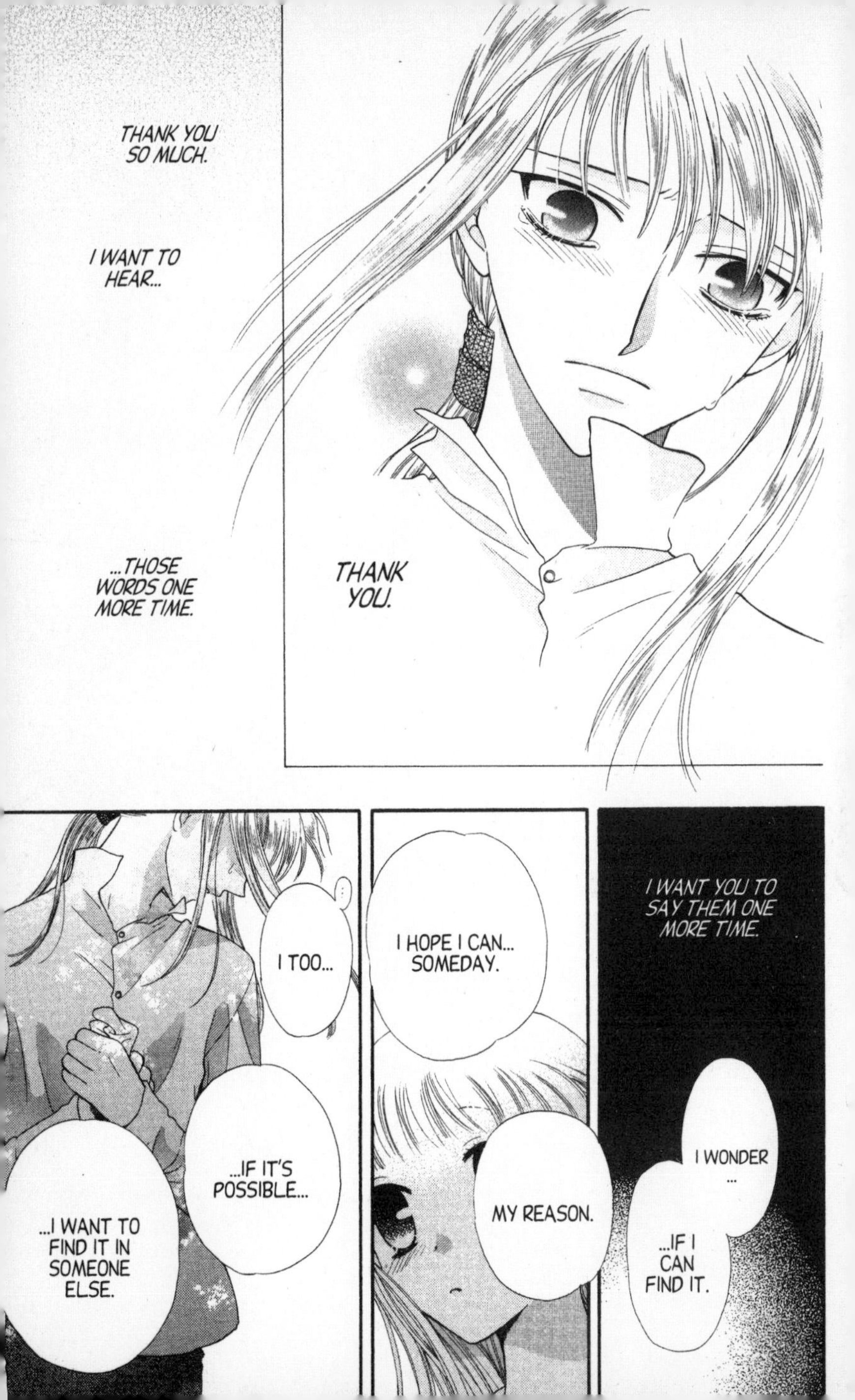
THANK YOU.
THANK YOU SO MUCH.
I WANT TO HEAR...
...THOSE WORDS ONE MORE TIME.
I WANT YOU TO SAY THEM ONE MORE TIME.
I WONDER...
...IF I CAN FIND IT.
I HOPE I CAN... SOMEDAY.
MY REASON.
I TOO...
...IF IT'S POSSIBLE...
...I WANT TO FIND IT IN SOMEONE ELSE.

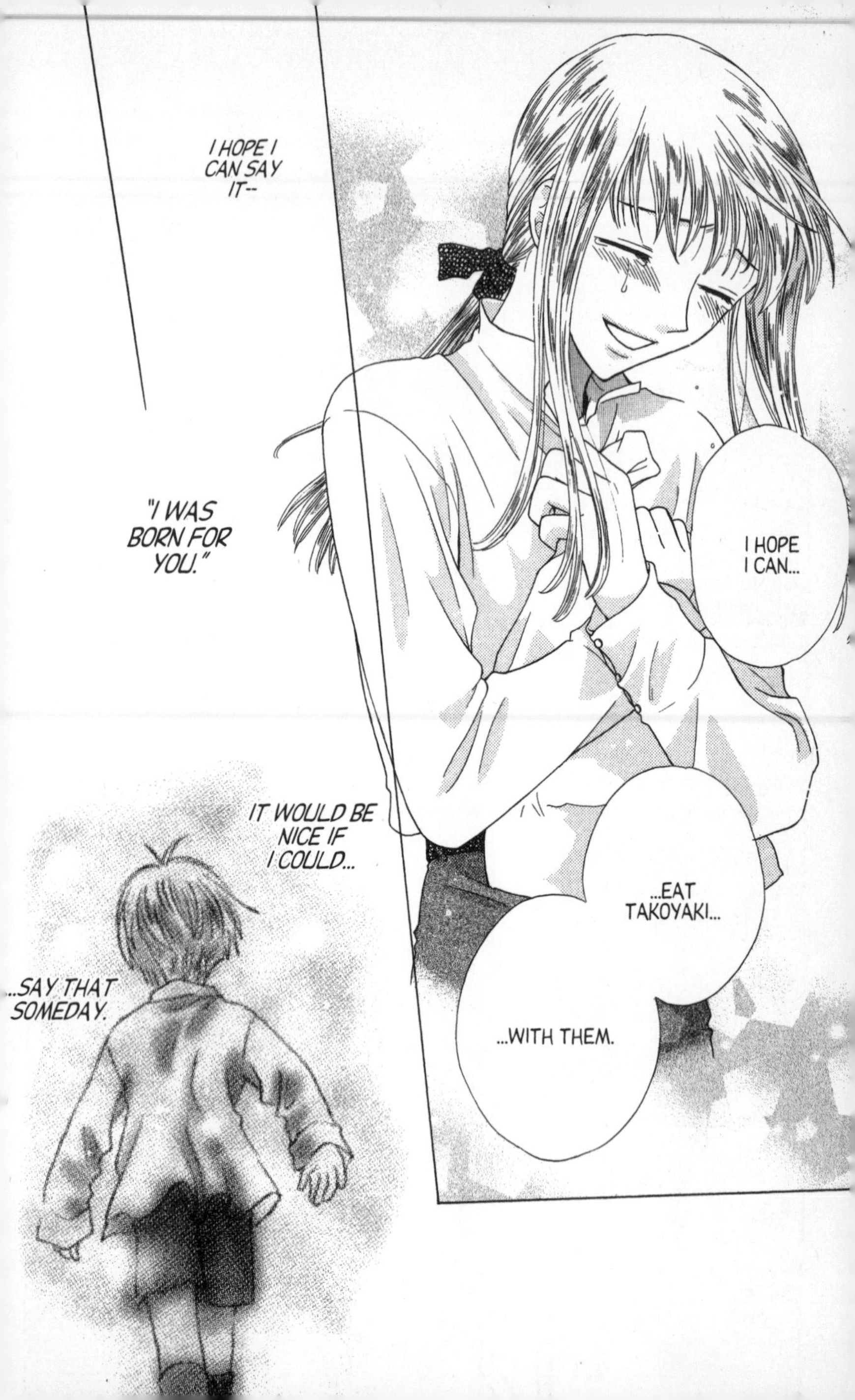
I HOPE I CAN...
...EAT TAKOYAKI...
...WITH THEM.
I HOPE I CAN SAY IT--
"I WAS BORN FOR YOU."
IT WOULD BE NICE IF I COULD...
...SAY THAT SOMEDAY.

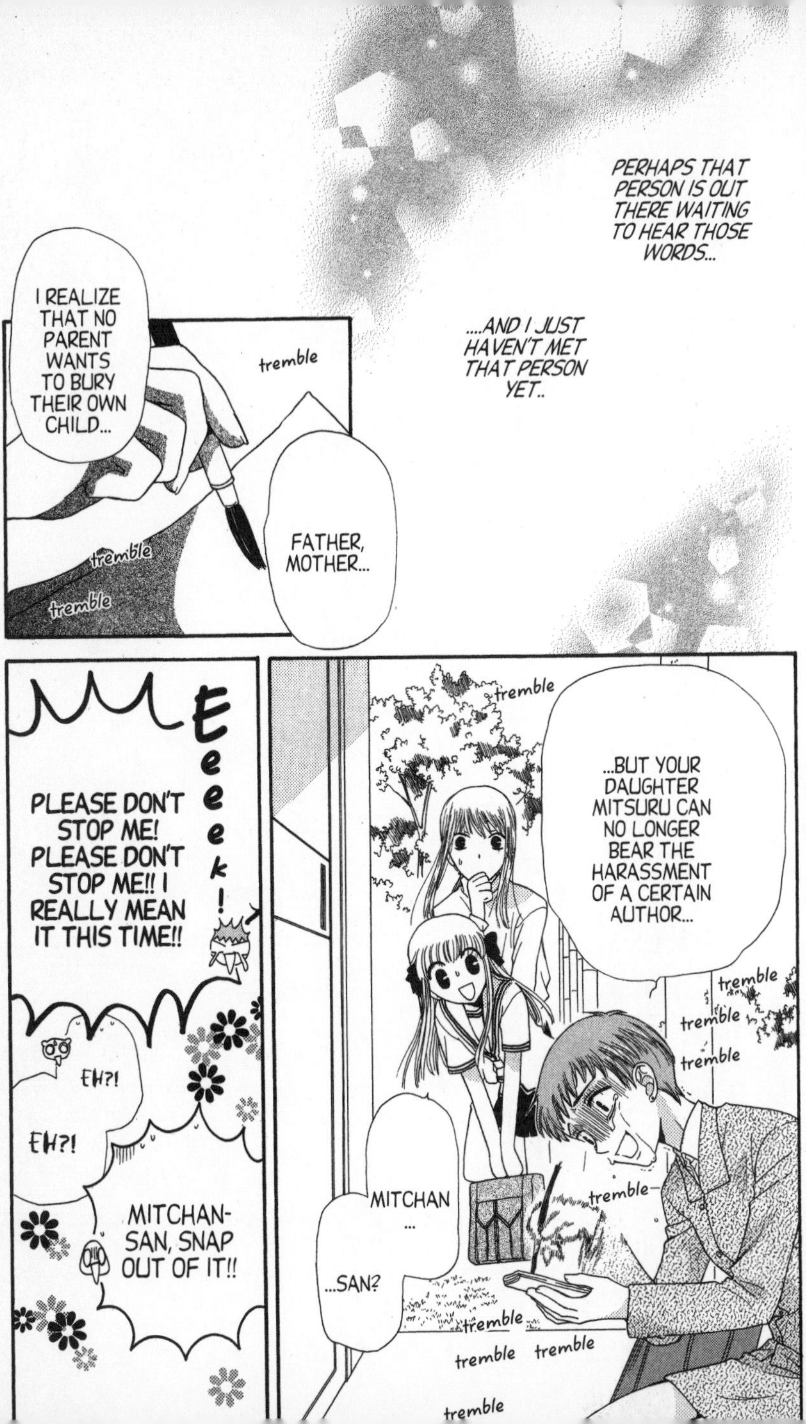
PERHAPS THAT PERSON IS OUT THERE WAITING TO HEAR THOSE WORDS...
....AND I JUST HAVEN'T MET THAT PERSON YET..
tremble
FATHER, MOTHER...
I REALIZE THAT NO PARENT WANTS TO BURY THEIR OWN CHILD...
tremble
tremble
tremble
...BUT YOUR DAUGHTER MITSURU CAN NO LONGER BEAR THE HARASSMENT OF A CERTAIN AUTHOR...
tremble
tremble
tremble
tremble
MITCHAN ...
...SAN?
tremble
tremble
tremble
tremble
Eeeek!
PLEASE DON'T STOP ME! PLEASE DON'T STOP ME!! I REALLY MEAN IT THIS TIME!!
EH?!
EH?!
MITCHAN-SAN, SNAP OUT OF IT!!

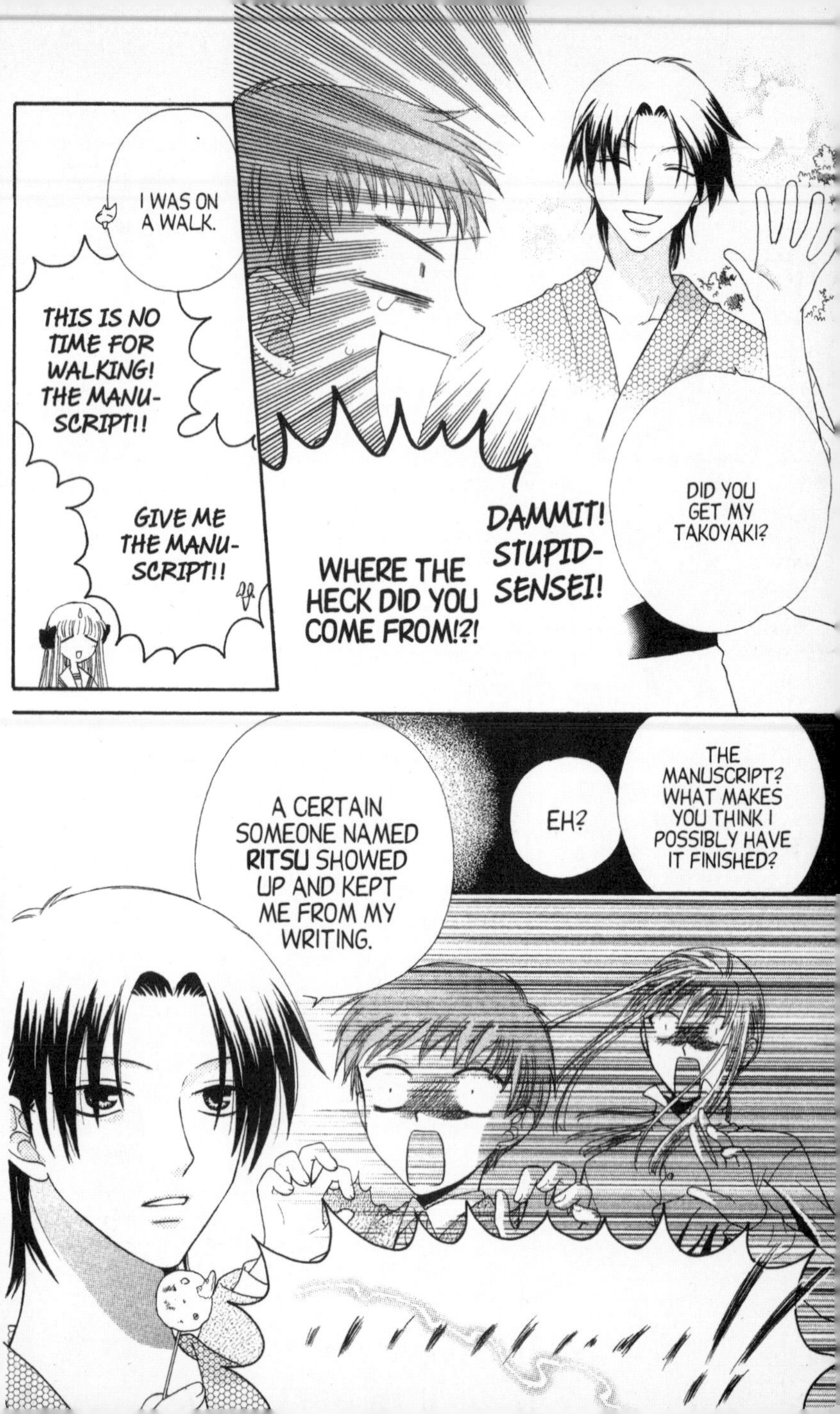
DID YOU GET MY TAKOYAKI?
DAMMIT! STUPID-SENSEI!
WHERE THE HECK DID YOU COME FROM!?!
I WAS ON A WALK.
THIS IS NO TIME FOR WALKING! THE MANU-SCRIPT!!
GIVE ME THE MANU-SCRIPT!!
THE MANUSCRIPT? WHAT MAKES YOU THINK I POSSIBLY HAVE IT FINISHED?
EH?
A CERTAIN SOMEONE NAMED RITSU SHOWED UP AND KEPT ME FROM MY WRITING.

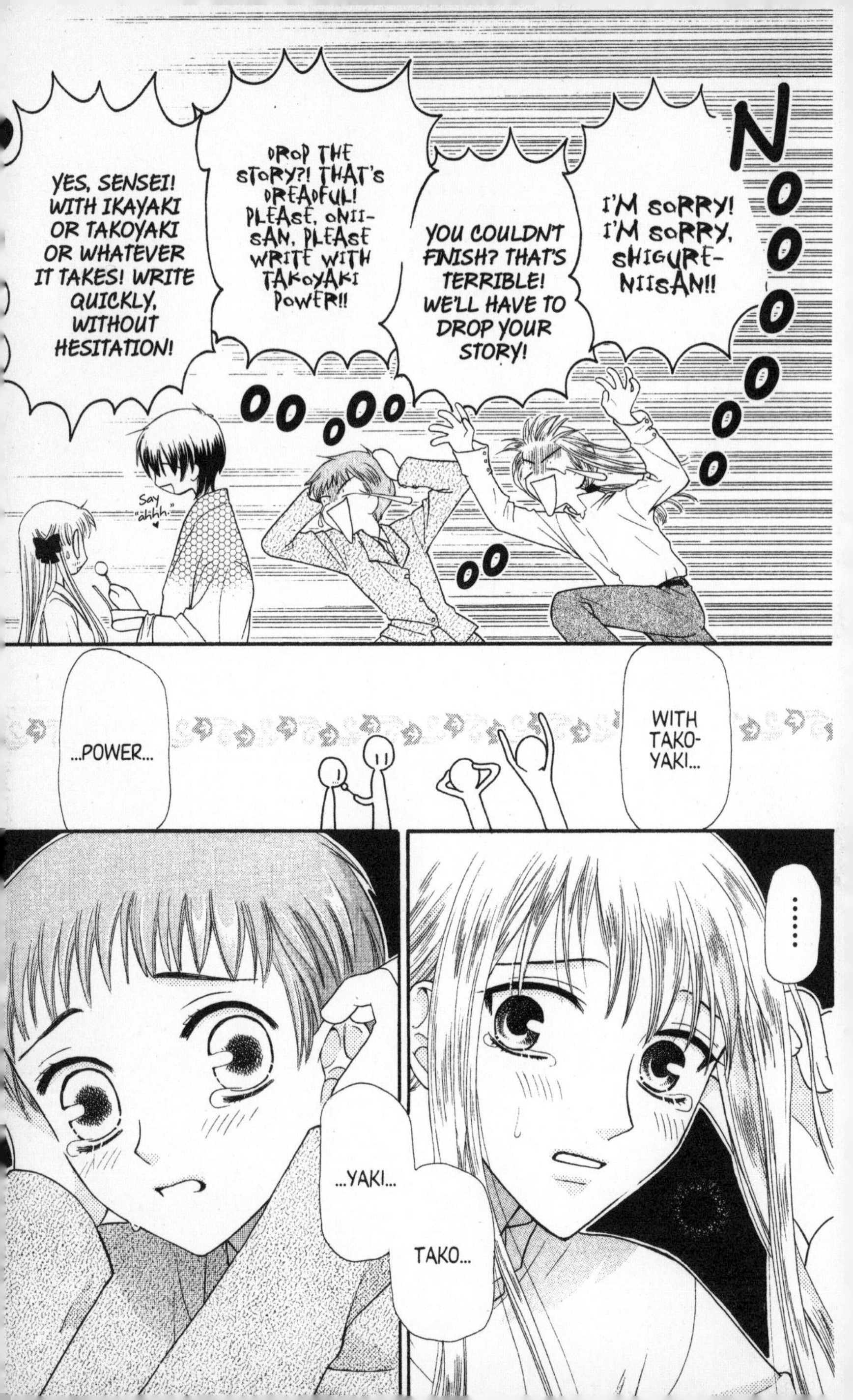
NOOOOOOOOO
I'M SORRY! I'M SORRY, SHIGURE-NIISAN!!
YOU COULDN'T FINISH? THAT'S TERRIBLE! WE'LL HAVE TO DROP YOUR STORY!
DROP THE STORY?! THAT'S DREADFUL! PLEASE, ONII-SAN, PLEASE WRITE WITH TAKOYAKI POWER!!
YES, SENSEI! WITH IKAYAKI OR TAKOYAKI OR WHATEVER IT TAKES! WRITE QUICKLY, WITHOUT HESITATION!
OOOOO
OO
Say "ahhh."
WITH TAKO-YAKI...
...POWER...
......
TAKO...
...YAKI...

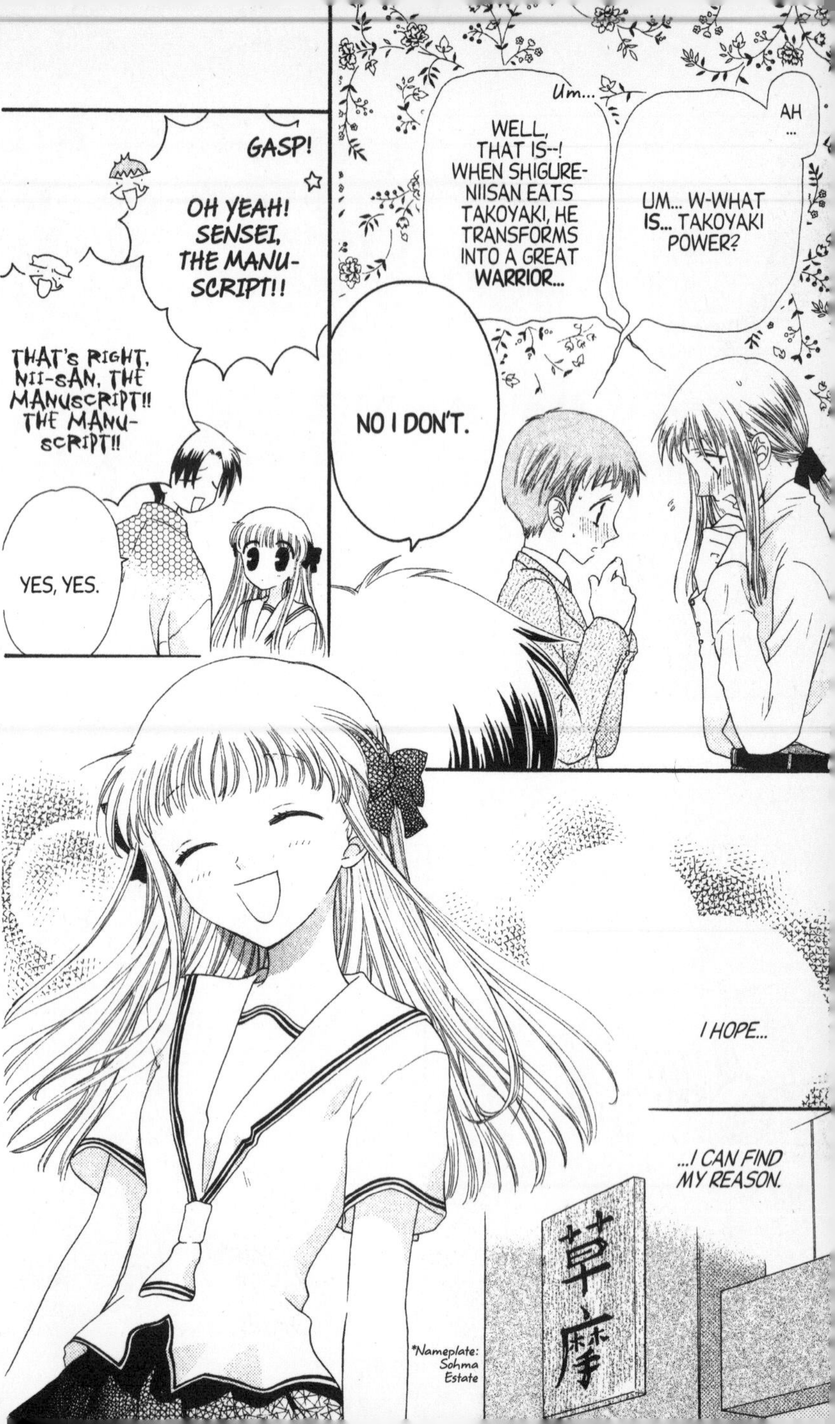
AH...
UM... W-WHAT IS... TAKOYAKI POWER?
Um...
WELL, THAT IS--! WHEN SHIGURE-NIISAN EATS TAKOYAKI, HE TRANSFORMS INTO A GREAT WARRIOR...
NO I DON'T.
GASP!
OH YEAH! SENSEI, THE MANU-SCRIPT!!
THAT'S RIGHT, NII-SAN, THE MANUSCRIPT!! THE MANU-SCRIPT!!
YES, YES.
I HOPE...
...I CAN FIND MY REASON.
草摩
*Nameplate: Sohma Estate

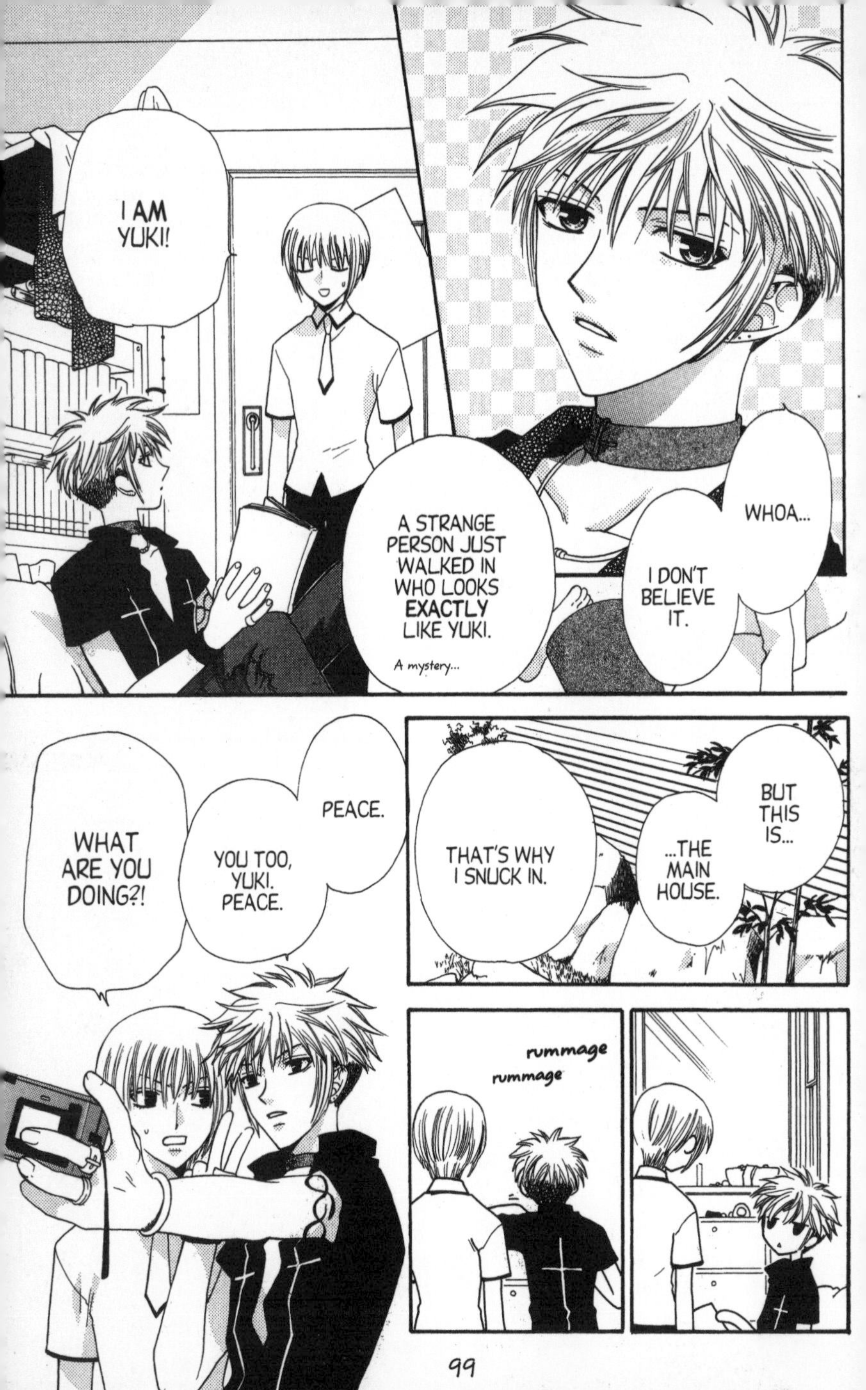
WHOA...
I DON'T BELIEVE IT.
A STRANGE PERSON JUST WALKED IN WHO LOOKS **EXACTLY** LIKE YUKI.
A mystery...
I AM YUKI!
BUT THIS IS...
...THE MAIN HOUSE.
THAT'S WHY I SNUCK IN.
rummage
rummage
PEACE.
YOU TOO, YUKI. PEACE.
WHAT ARE YOU DOING?!

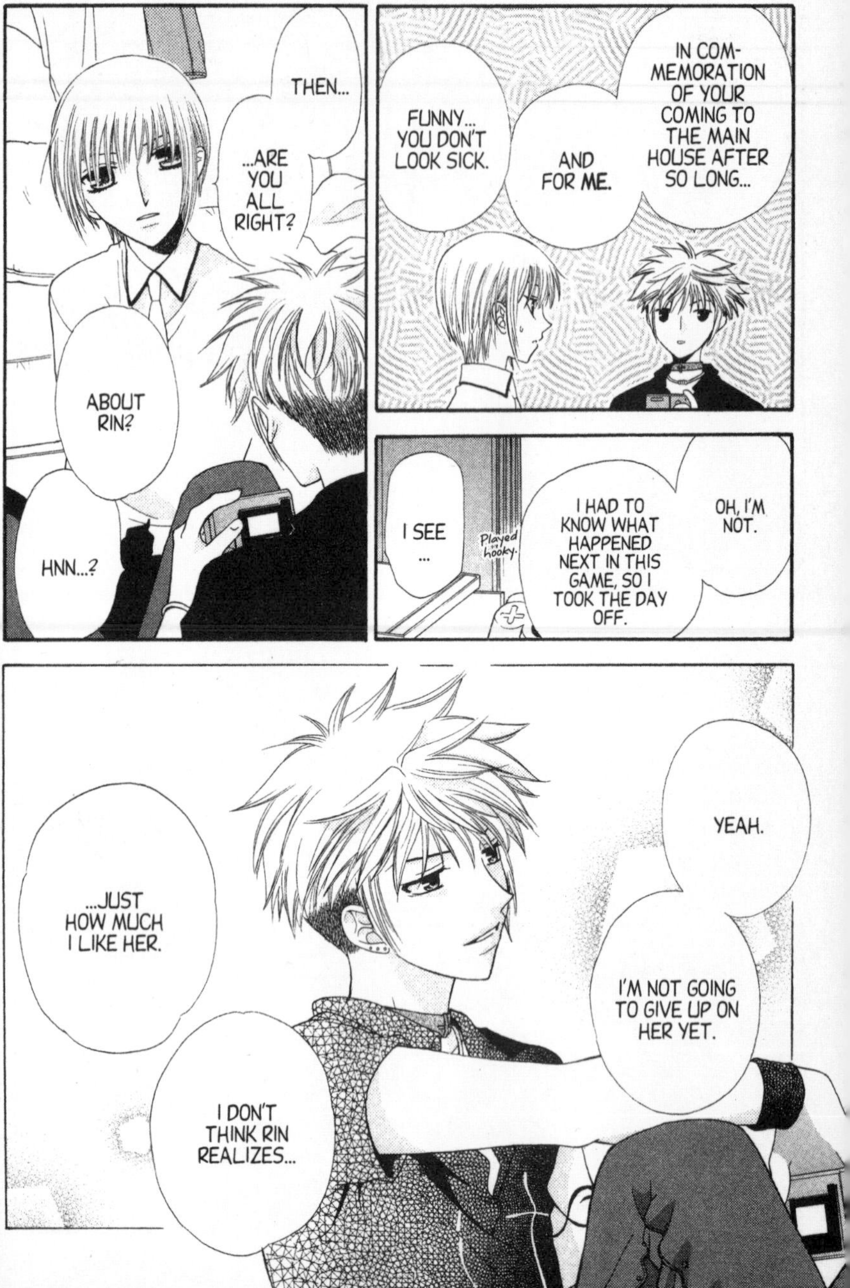
IN COM-MEMORATION OF YOUR COMING TO THE MAIN HOUSE AFTER SO LONG...
AND FOR **ME**.
FUNNY... YOU DON'T LOOK SICK.
OH, I'M NOT.
I HAD TO KNOW WHAT HAPPENED NEXT IN THIS GAME, SO I TOOK THE DAY OFF.
Played hooky.
I SEE ...
THEN...
...ARE YOU ALL RIGHT?
ABOUT RIN?
HNN...?
YEAH.
I'M NOT GOING TO GIVE UP ON HER YET.
I DON'T THINK RIN REALIZES...
...JUST HOW MUCH I LIKE HER.

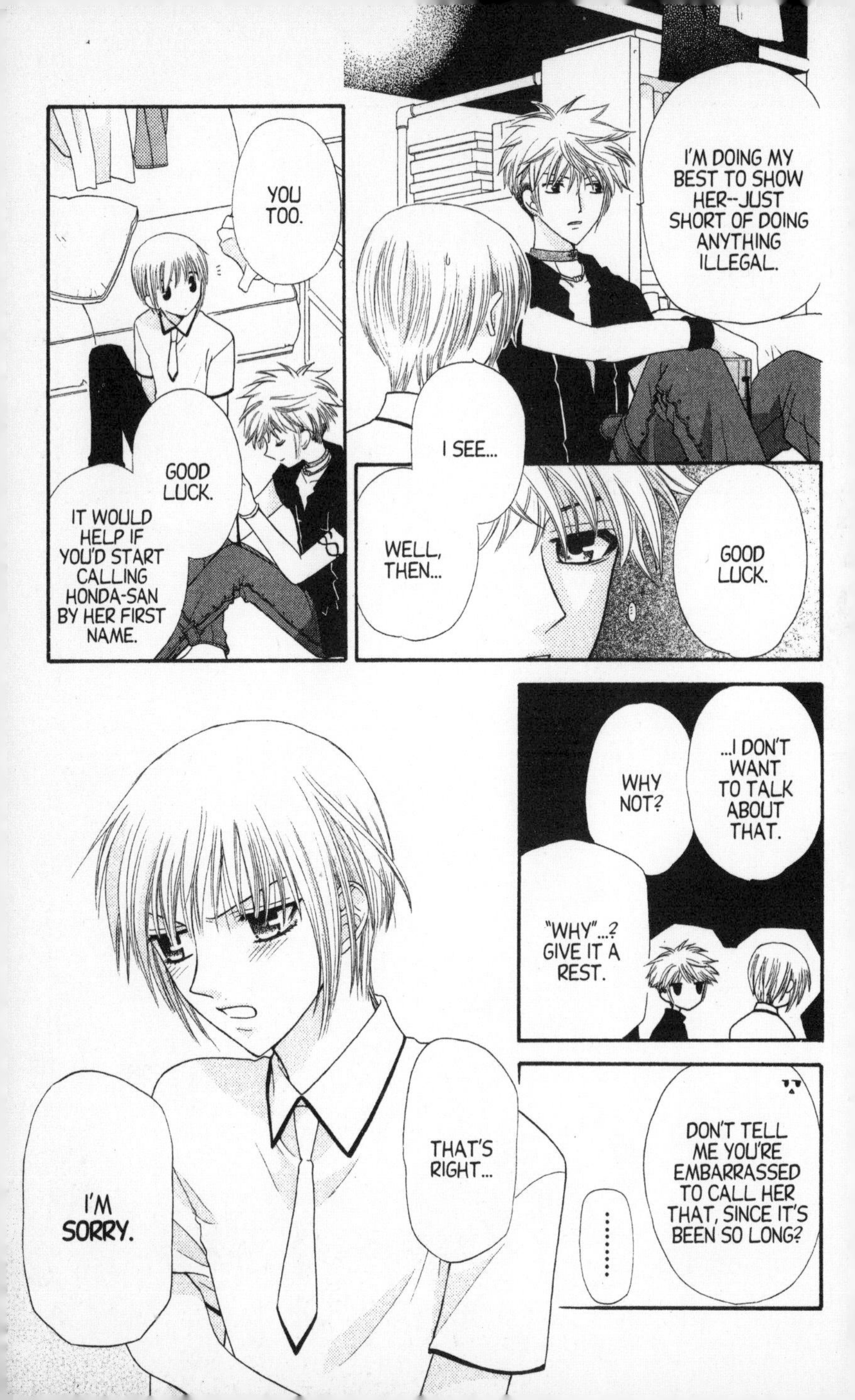
I'M DOING MY BEST TO SHOW HER--JUST SHORT OF DOING ANYTHING ILLEGAL.
I SEE...
GOOD LUCK.
WELL, THEN...
YOU TOO.
GOOD LUCK.
IT WOULD HELP IF YOU'D START CALLING HONDA-SAN BY HER FIRST NAME.
...I DON'T WANT TO TALK ABOUT THAT.
WHY NOT?
"WHY"...? GIVE IT A REST.
DON'T TELL ME YOU'RE EMBARRASSED TO CALL HER THAT, SINCE IT'S BEEN SO LONG?
....
THAT'S RIGHT...
I'M **SORRY.**

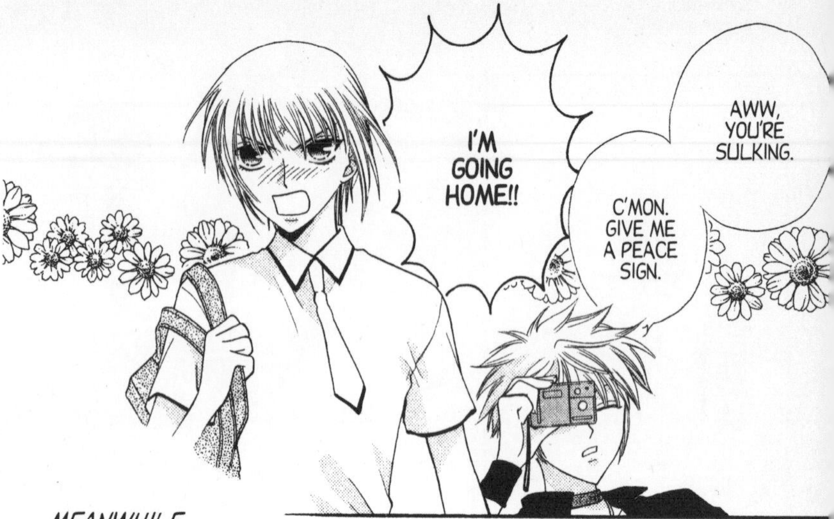
AWW, YOU'RE SULKING.
C'MON. GIVE ME A PEACE SIGN.
I'M GOING HOME!!

MEANWHILE, BACK AT THE HOUSE...

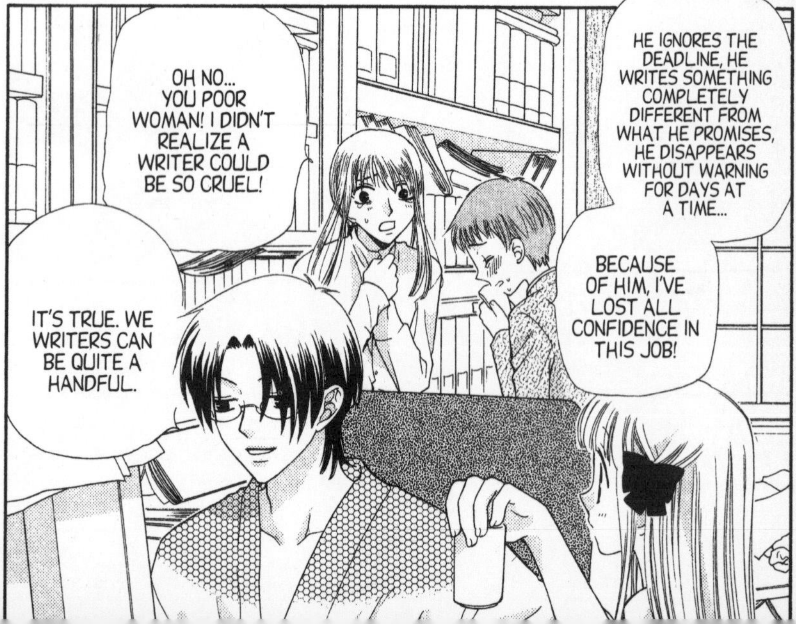
HE IGNORES THE DEADLINE, HE WRITES SOMETHING COMPLETELY DIFFERENT FROM WHAT HE PROMISES, HE DISAPPEARS WITHOUT WARNING FOR DAYS AT A TIME...
BECAUSE OF HIM, I'VE LOST ALL CONFIDENCE IN THIS JOB!
OH NO... YOU POOR WOMAN! I DIDN'T REALIZE A WRITER COULD BE SO CRUEL!
IT'S TRUE. WE WRITERS CAN BE QUITE A HANDFUL.

Filler sketches

Ritchan, having a wonderful dream.

twitch

Monkey-Ritchan, wonderfully frightened.

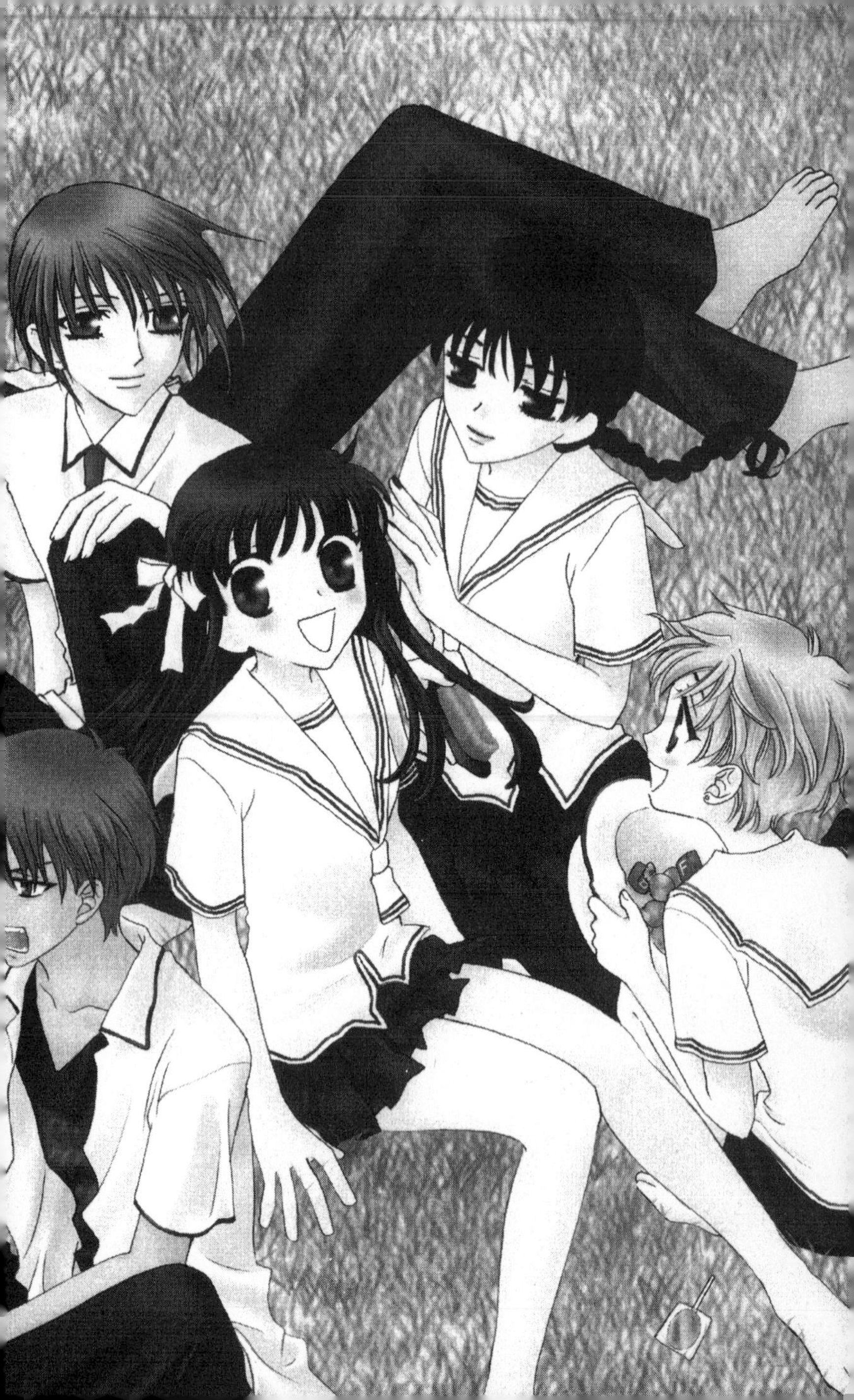

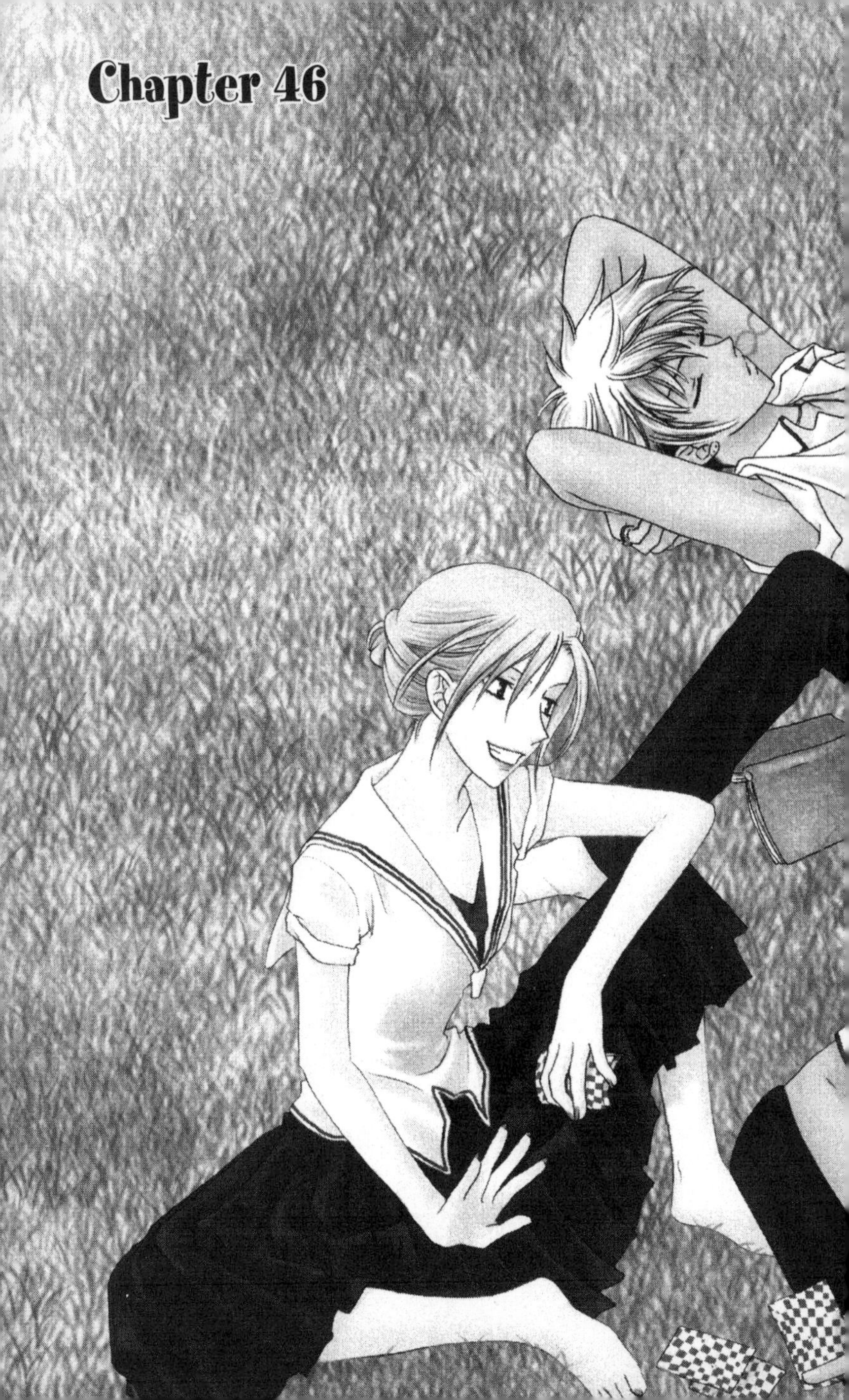
Chapter 46

I feel so grateful!

...she says.

Harada-sama, Araki-sama, Kawaai-sama, mother, father, everyone involved in making the anime, all the voice actors, and everyone who reads this manga...

Thank you for all the letters and presents! And most of all, thank you for the support!

Next up it's His Highness the King's turn. You know who I mean!

—Natsuki Takaya

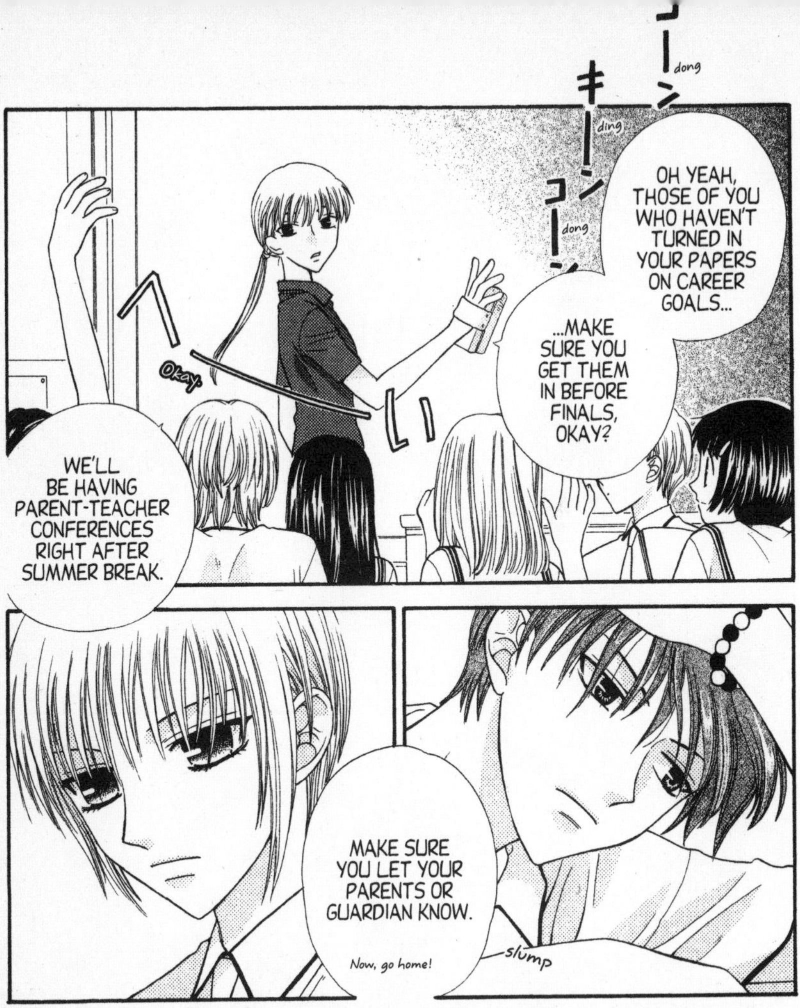
dong
ding
dong
OH YEAH, THOSE OF YOU WHO HAVEN'T TURNED IN YOUR PAPERS ON CAREER GOALS...
...MAKE SURE YOU GET THEM IN BEFORE FINALS, OKAY?
Okay.
WE'LL BE HAVING PARENT-TEACHER CONFERENCES RIGHT AFTER SUMMER BREAK.
slump
MAKE SURE YOU LET YOUR PARENTS OR GUARDIAN KNOW.
Now, go home!

UL-SPE BLAH, BLAH, BLAH. 3

Kyon and Uo are so much alike that they argue a lot, but probably being so much alike is what irritates them the most... something like that.

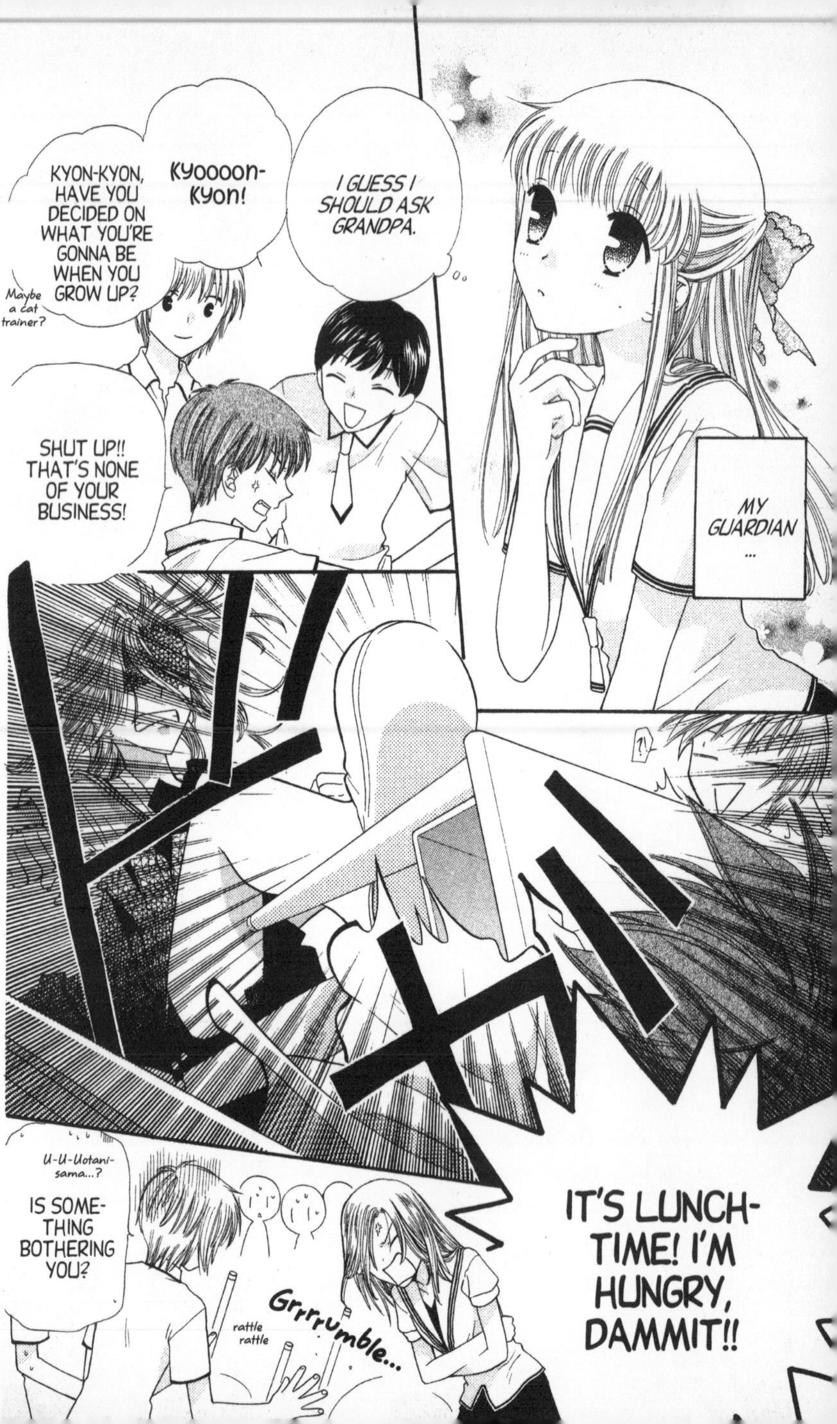
MY GUARDIAN ...
I GUESS I SHOULD ASK GRANDPA.
Kyoooon-Kyon!
KYON-KYON, HAVE YOU DECIDED ON WHAT YOU'RE GONNA BE WHEN YOU GROW UP?
Maybe a cat trainer?
SHUT UP!! THAT'S NONE OF YOUR BUSINESS!
?!
IT'S LUNCH-TIME! I'M HUNGRY, DAMMIT!!
Grrrrumble...
rattle rattle
U-U-Uotani-sama...?
IS SOME-THING BOTHERING YOU?

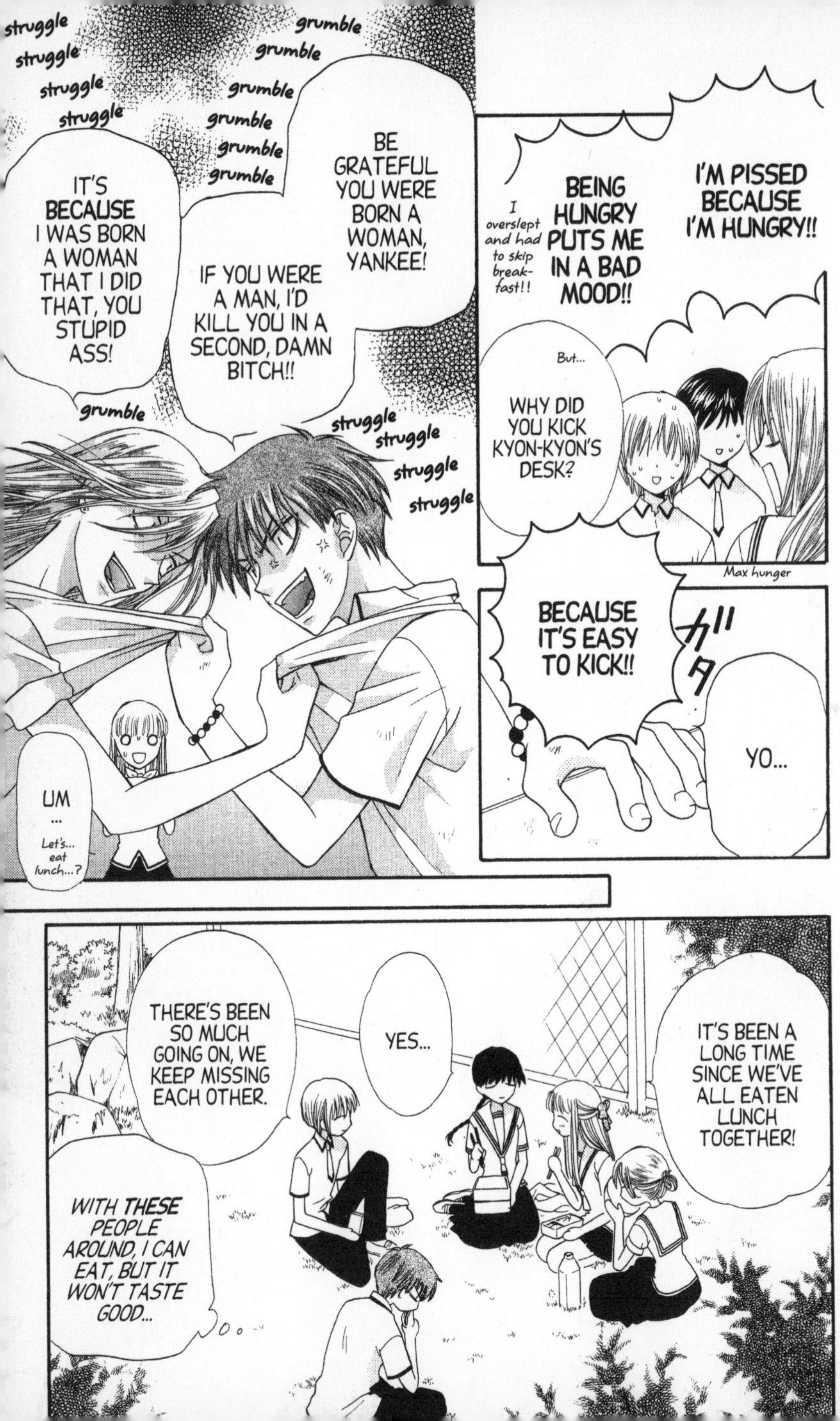
I'M PISSED BECAUSE I'M HUNGRY!!
BEING HUNGRY PUTS ME IN A BAD MOOD!!
I overslept and had to skip break-fast!!
But...
WHY DID YOU KICK KYON-KYON'S DESK?
Max hunger
BECAUSE IT'S EASY TO KICK!!
ガタ
YO...
grumble grumble grumble grumble grumble grumble
struggle struggle struggle struggle
BE GRATEFUL YOU WERE BORN A WOMAN, YANKEE!
IT'S BECAUSE I WAS BORN A WOMAN THAT I DID THAT, YOU STUPID ASS!
IF YOU WERE A MAN, I'D KILL YOU IN A SECOND, DAMN BITCH!!
grumble
struggle struggle struggle struggle
UM ...
Let's... eat lunch...?
IT'S BEEN A LONG TIME SINCE WE'VE ALL EATEN LUNCH TOGETHER!
YES...
THERE'S BEEN SO MUCH GOING ON, WE KEEP MISSING EACH OTHER.
WITH THESE PEOPLE AROUND, I CAN EAT, BUT IT WON'T TASTE GOOD...

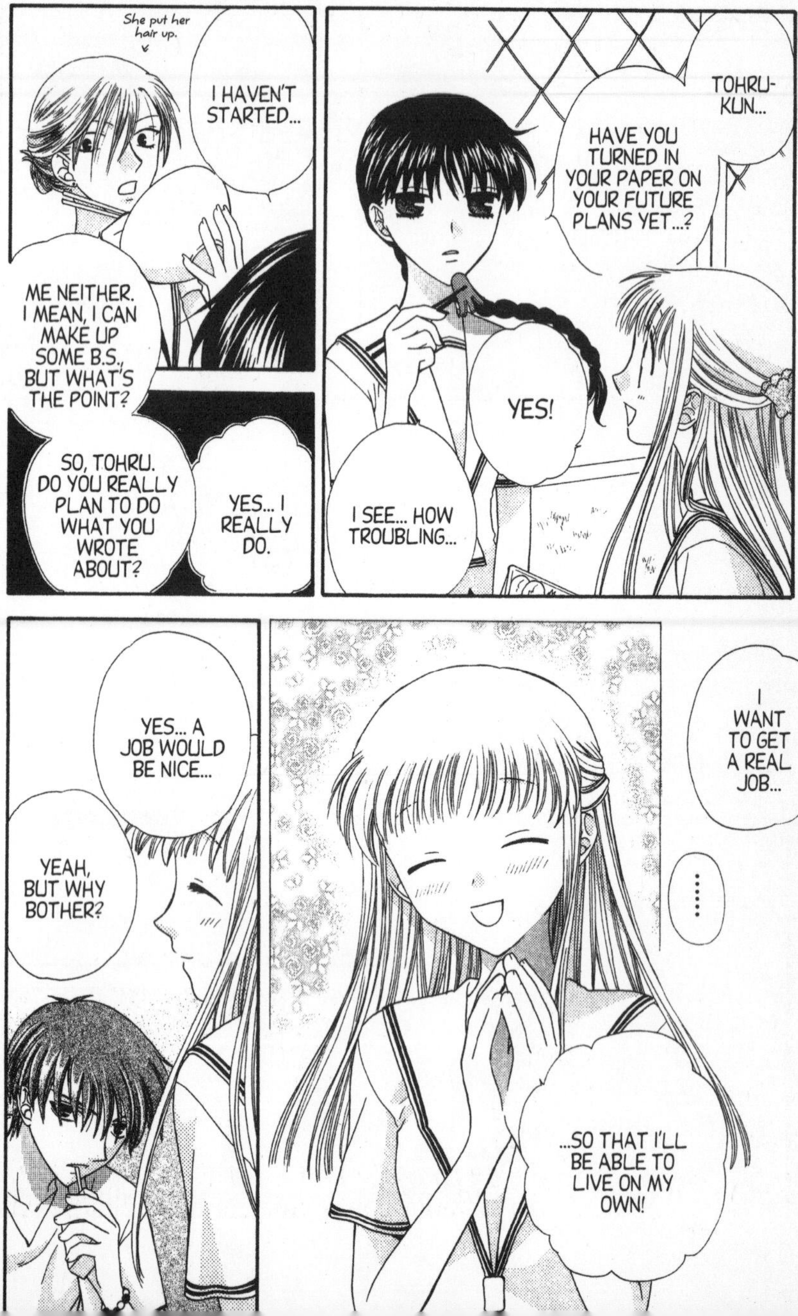
TOHRU-KUN...
HAVE YOU TURNED IN YOUR PAPER ON YOUR FUTURE PLANS YET...?
YES!
I SEE... HOW TROUBLING...
I HAVEN'T STARTED...
She put her hair up.
ME NEITHER. I MEAN, I CAN MAKE UP SOME B.S., BUT WHAT'S THE POINT?
SO, TOHRU. DO YOU REALLY PLAN TO DO WHAT YOU WROTE ABOUT?
YES... I REALLY DO.
I WANT TO GET A REAL JOB...
......
...SO THAT I'LL BE ABLE TO LIVE ON MY OWN!
YES... A JOB WOULD BE NICE...
YEAH, BUT WHY BOTHER?

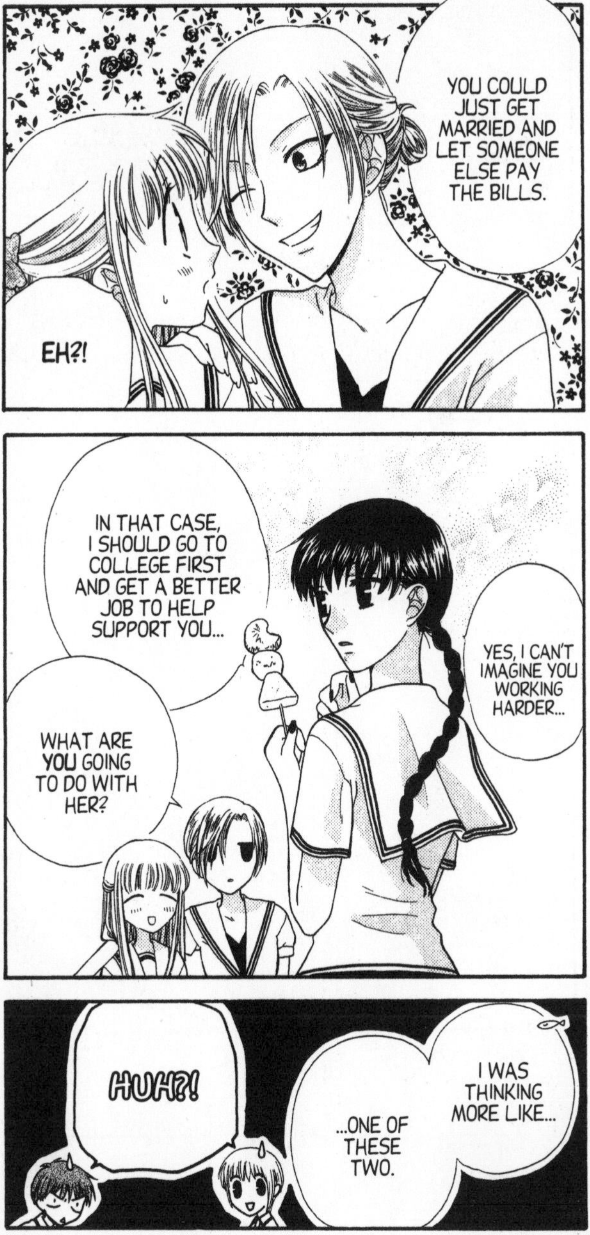
YOU COULD JUST GET MARRIED AND LET SOMEONE ELSE PAY THE BILLS.
EH?!
IN THAT CASE, I SHOULD GO TO COLLEGE FIRST AND GET A BETTER JOB TO HELP SUPPORT YOU...
YES, I CAN'T IMAGINE YOU WORKING HARDER...
WHAT ARE YOU GOING TO DO WITH HER?
I WAS THINKING MORE LIKE...
...ONE OF THESE TWO.
HUH?!

Fruits Basket 8: Part 4

This may be a pretty (really?) old topic, but "Shadow Hearts" for the PS2 was a fun game. For some reason, I kept telling myself, "I like this," and played as if entranced. (I know the reason...) I liked Yuri. I liked how he talked when he got mad and I liked how he moves when battles are over. Because of that, I always tried to have Yuri give the final blow, so I almost died a lot....

To be continued in part 5

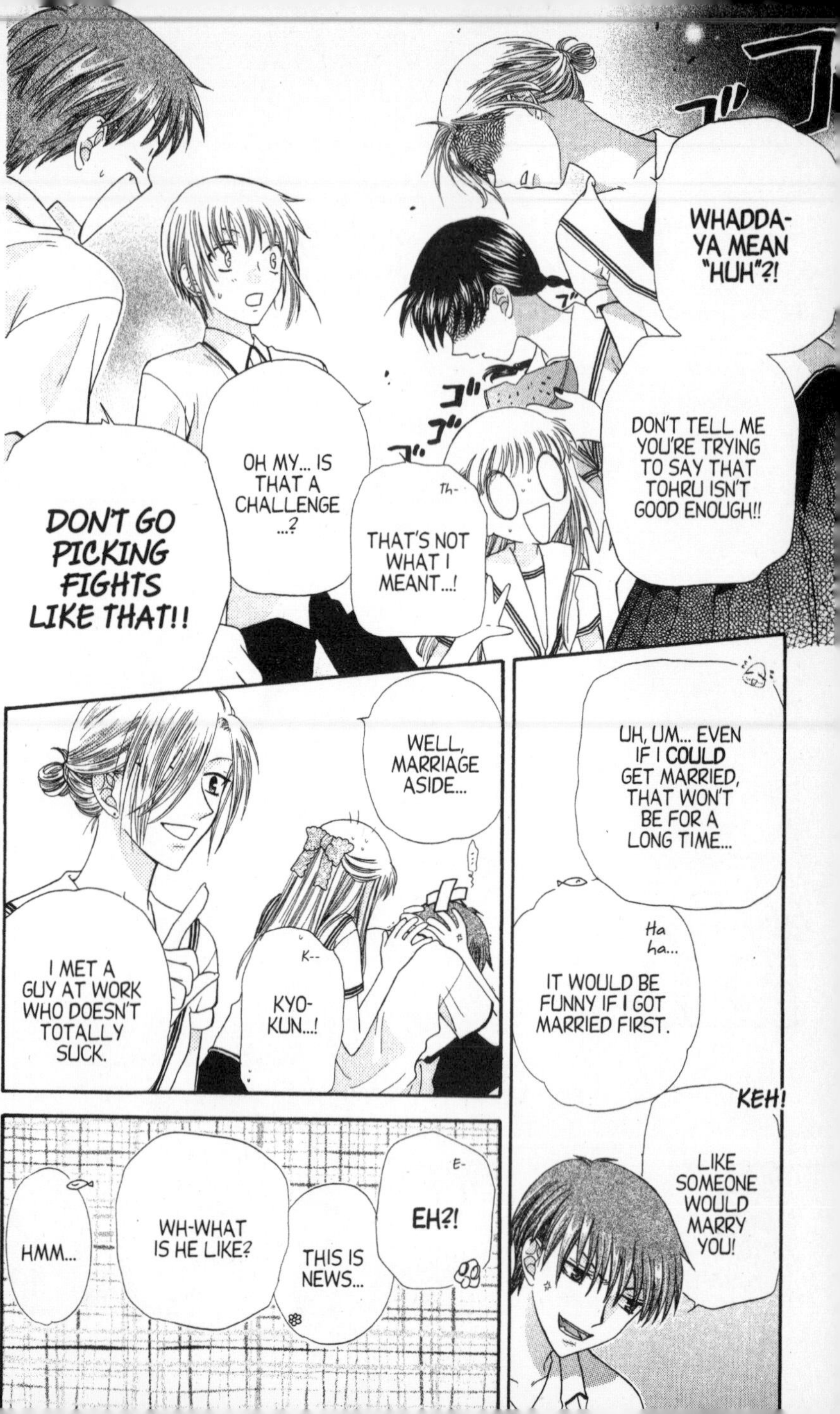
WHADDA-YA MEAN "HUH"?!
DON'T TELL ME YOU'RE TRYING TO SAY THAT TOHRU ISN'T GOOD ENOUGH!!
Th-
THAT'S NOT WHAT I MEANT...!
OH MY... IS THAT A CHALLENGE ...?
DON'T GO PICKING FIGHTS LIKE THAT!!
UH, UM... EVEN IF I COULD GET MARRIED, THAT WON'T BE FOR A LONG TIME...
Ha ha...
IT WOULD BE FUNNY IF I GOT MARRIED FIRST.
KEH!
LIKE SOMEONE WOULD MARRY YOU!
WELL, MARRIAGE ASIDE...
K--
KYO-KUN...!
I MET A GUY AT WORK WHO DOESN'T TOTALLY SUCK.
E-
EH?!
THIS IS NEWS...
WH-WHAT IS HE LIKE?
HMM...

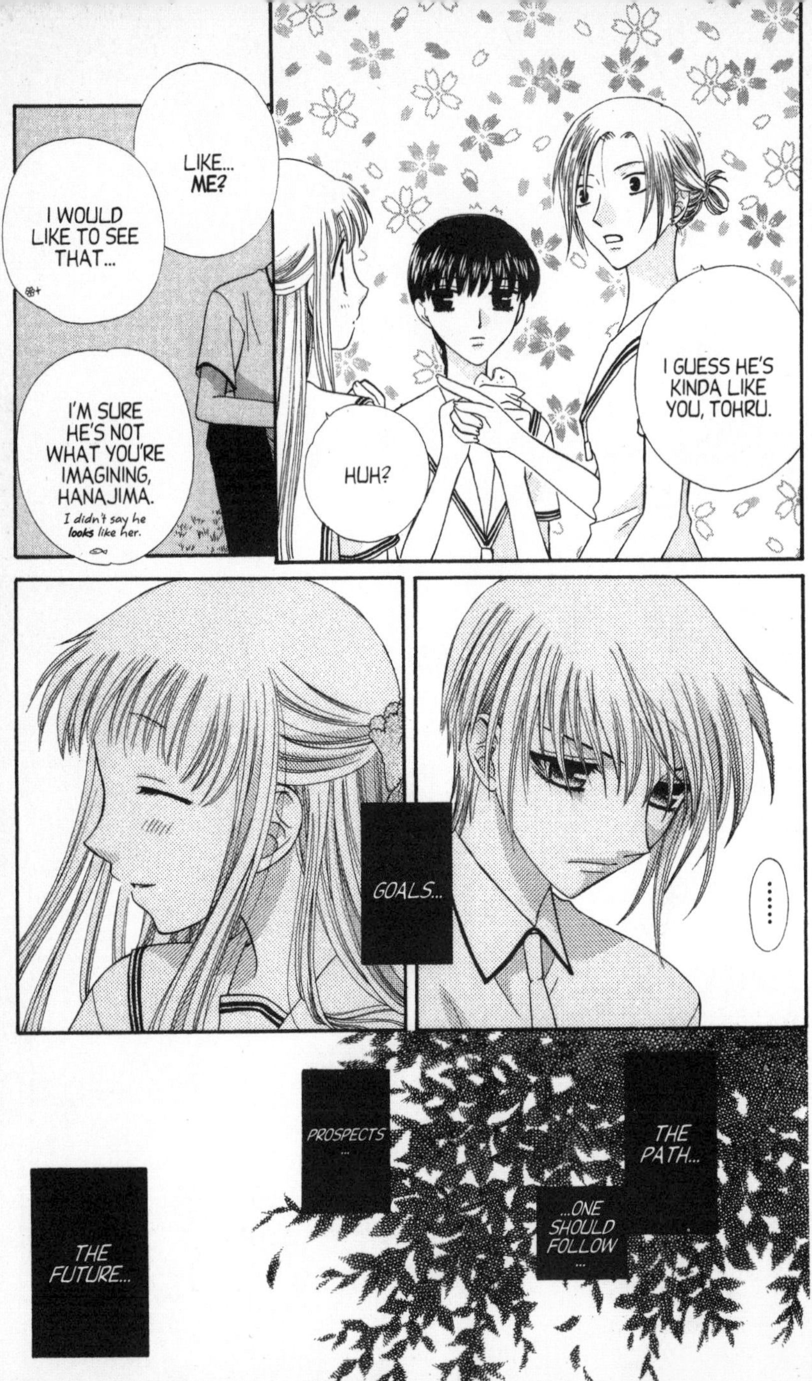
I GUESS HE'S KINDA LIKE YOU, TOHRU.
HUH?
LIKE... ME?
I WOULD LIKE TO SEE THAT...
I'M SURE HE'S NOT WHAT YOU'RE IMAGINING, HANAJIMA.
I didn't say he **looks** like her.
......
GOALS...
THE PATH...
...ONE SHOULD FOLLOW...
PROSPECTS...
THE FUTURE...

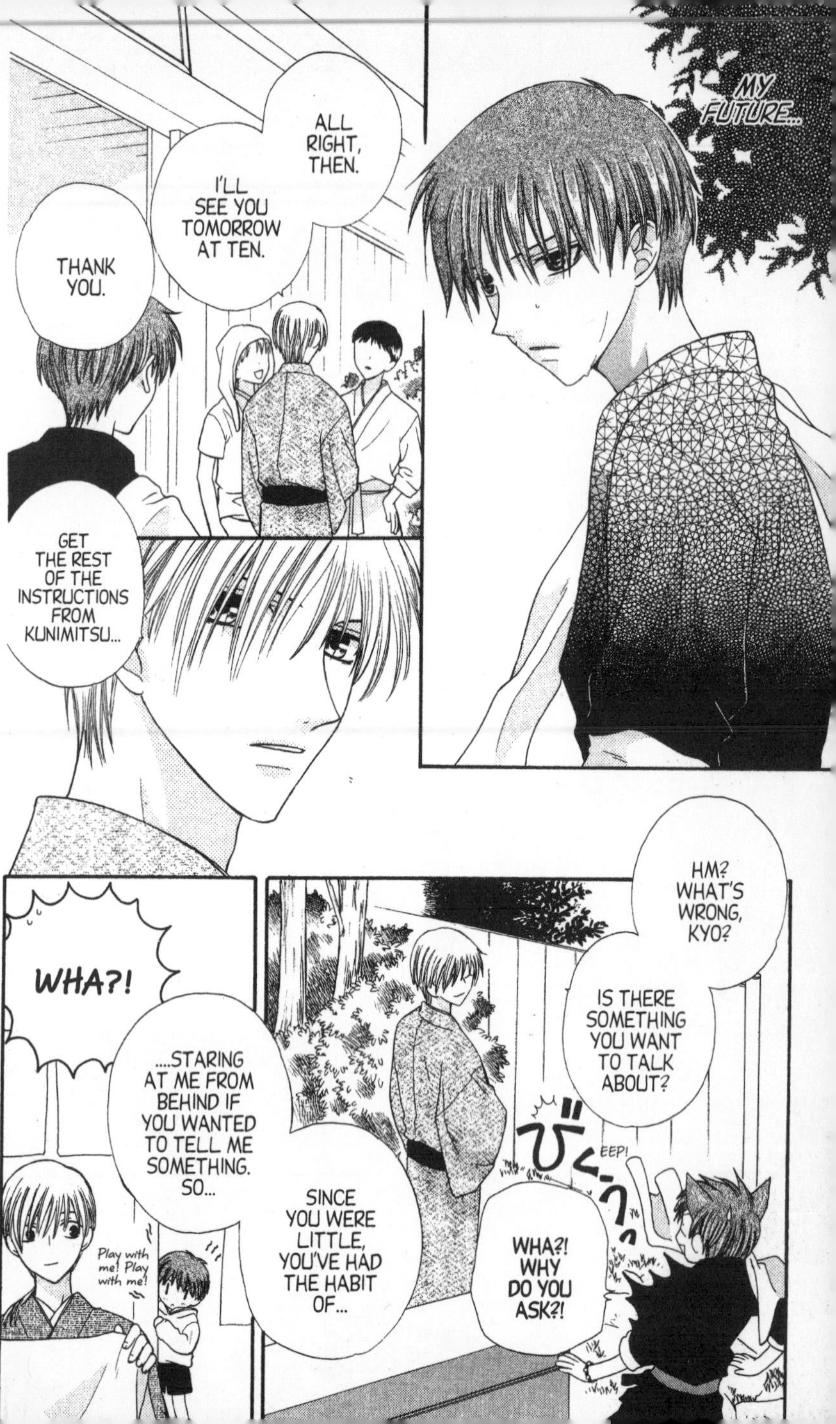
MY FUTURE...
ALL RIGHT, THEN.
I'LL SEE YOU TOMORROW AT TEN.
THANK YOU.
GET THE REST OF THE INSTRUCTIONS FROM KUNIMITSU...
HM? WHAT'S WRONG, KYO?
IS THERE SOMETHING YOU WANT TO TALK ABOUT?
EEP!
WHA?! WHY DO YOU ASK?!
SINCE YOU WERE LITTLE, YOU'VE HAD THE HABIT OF...
....STARING AT ME FROM BEHIND IF YOU WANTED TO TELL ME SOMETHING. SO...
WHA?!
Play with me! Play with me!

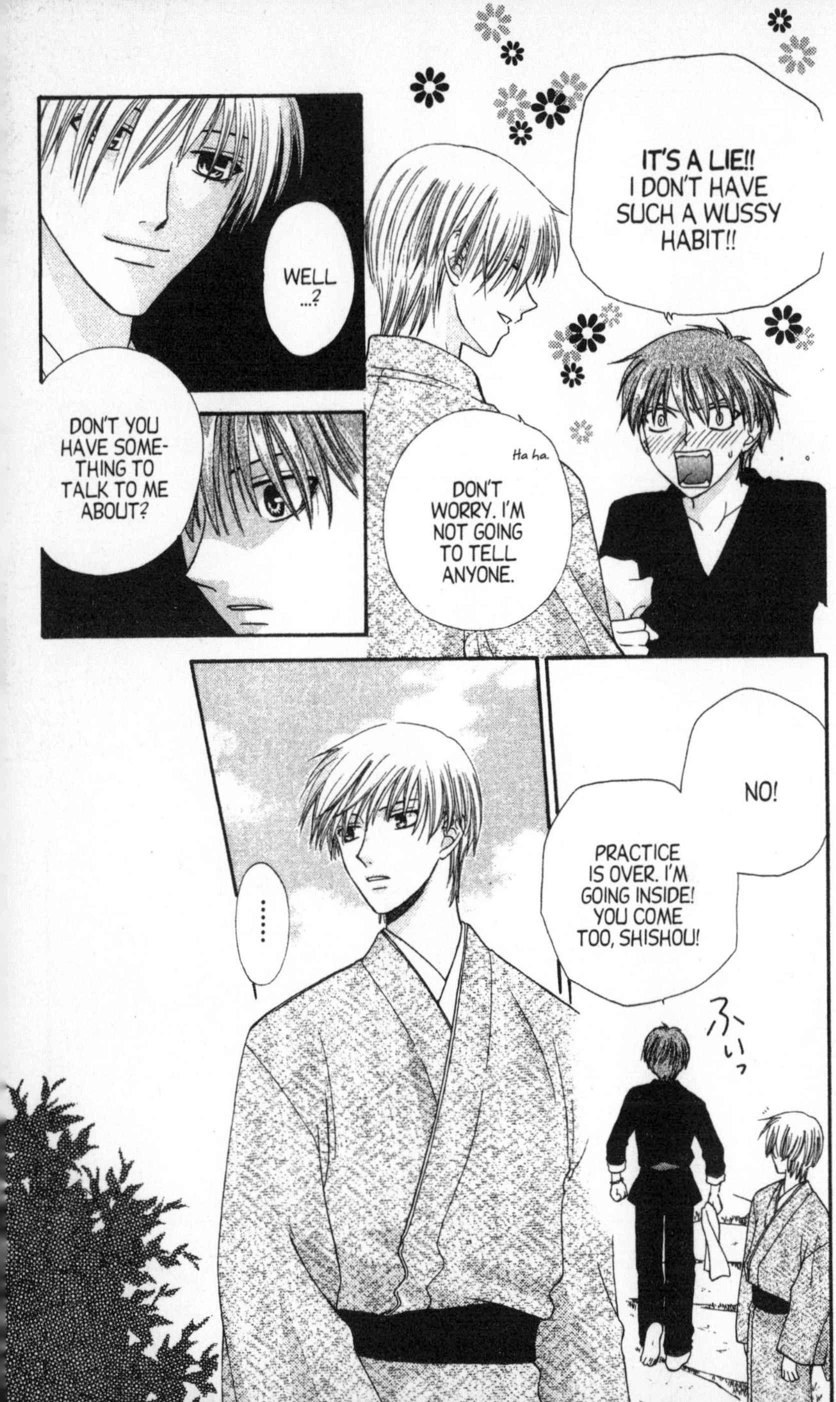

IT'S A LIE!! I DON'T HAVE SUCH A WUSSY HABIT!!
Ha ha.
DON'T WORRY. I'M NOT GOING TO TELL ANYONE.
WELL ...?
DON'T YOU HAVE SOME-THING TO TALK TO ME ABOUT?
NO!
PRACTICE IS OVER. I'M GOING INSIDE! YOU COME TOO, SHISHOU!
ふいっ
......

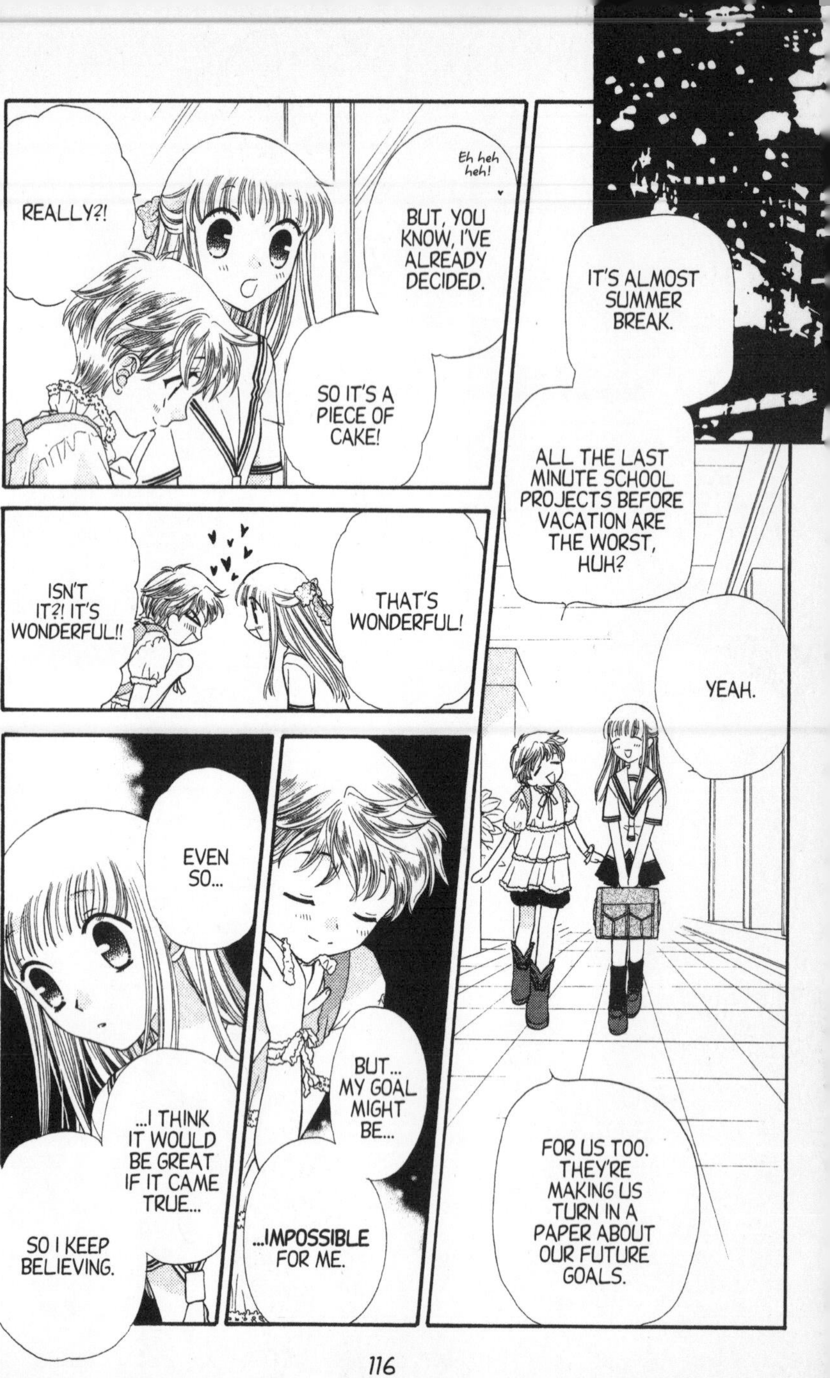
IT'S ALMOST SUMMER BREAK.
ALL THE LAST MINUTE SCHOOL PROJECTS BEFORE VACATION ARE THE WORST, HUH?
YEAH.
FOR US TOO. THEY'RE MAKING US TURN IN A PAPER ABOUT OUR FUTURE GOALS.
Eh heh heh!
BUT, YOU KNOW, I'VE ALREADY DECIDED.
SO IT'S A PIECE OF CAKE!
REALLY?!
THAT'S WONDERFUL!
ISN'T IT?! IT'S WONDERFUL!!
BUT... MY GOAL MIGHT BE...
...IMPOSSIBLE FOR ME.
EVEN SO...
...I THINK IT WOULD BE GREAT IF IT CAME TRUE...
SO I KEEP BELIEVING.

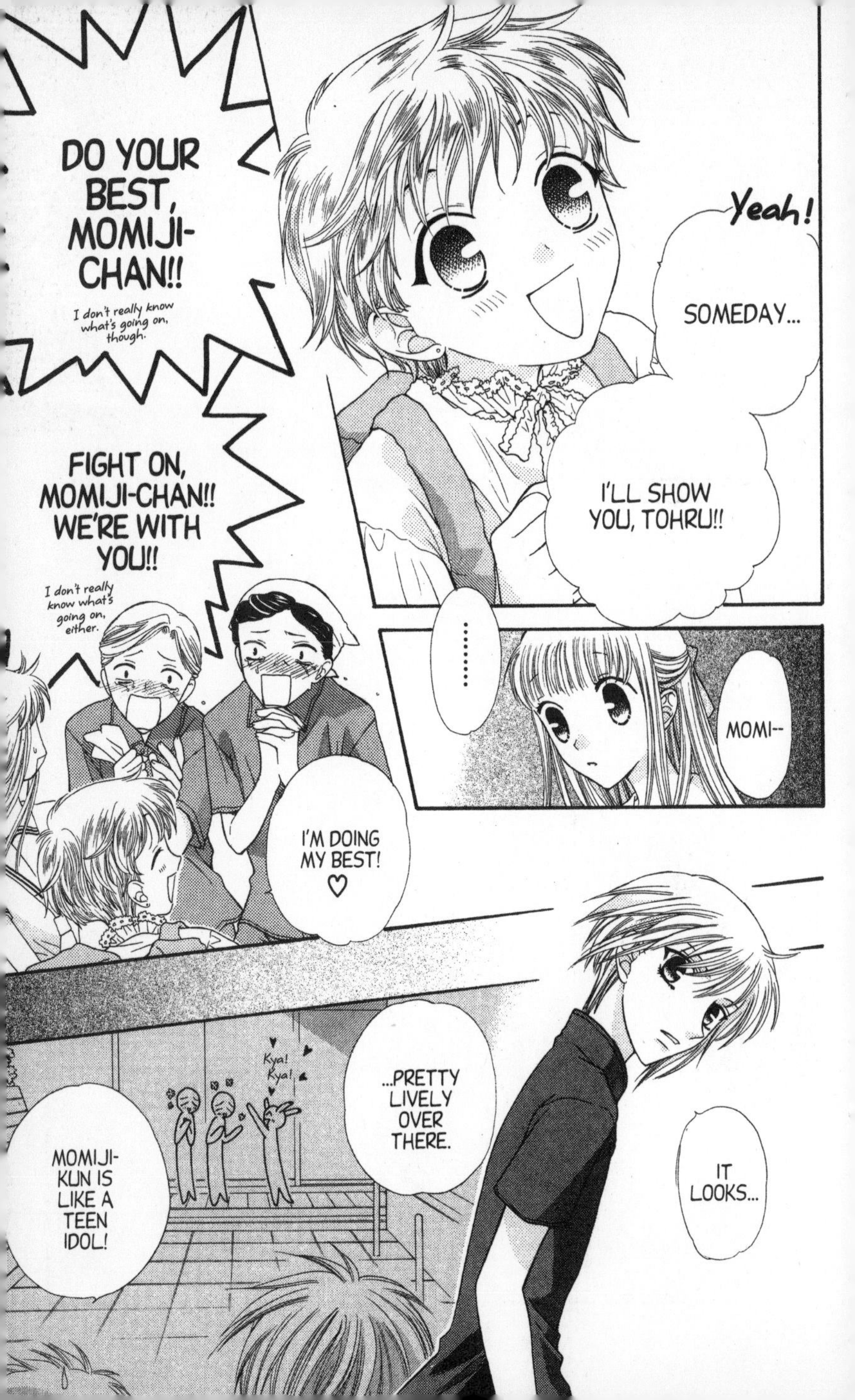

Yeah!
SOMEDAY...
I'LL SHOW YOU, TOHRU!!
......
MOMI--
DO YOUR BEST, MOMIJI-CHAN!!
I don't really know what's going on, though.
FIGHT ON, MOMIJI-CHAN!! WE'RE WITH YOU!!
I don't really know what's going on, either.
I'M DOING MY BEST! ♡
IT LOOKS...
...PRETTY LIVELY OVER THERE.
Kya! Kya!
MOMIJI-KUN IS LIKE A TEEN IDOL!

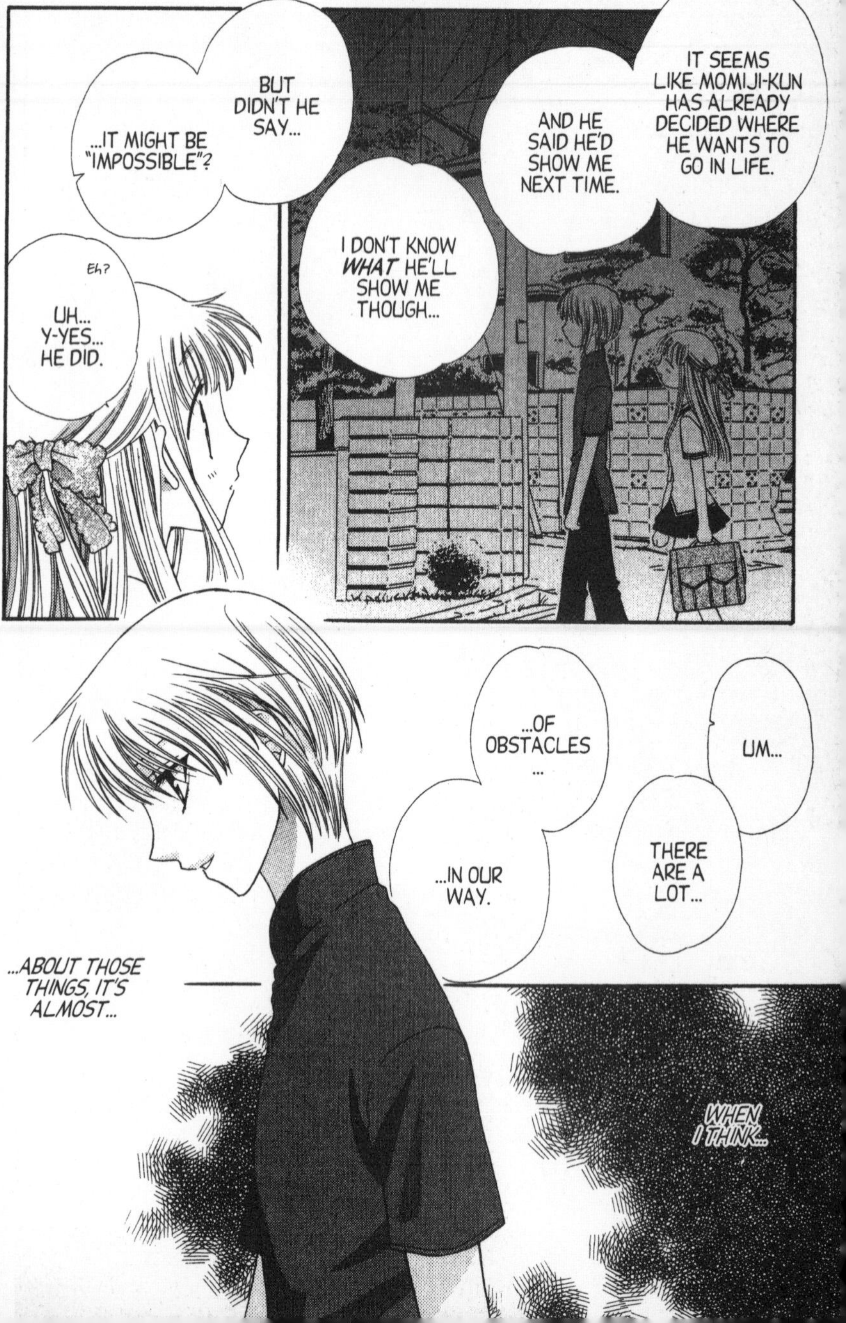
IT SEEMS LIKE MOMIJI-KUN HAS ALREADY DECIDED WHERE HE WANTS TO GO IN LIFE.
AND HE SAID HE'D SHOW ME NEXT TIME.
I DON'T KNOW *WHAT* HE'LL SHOW ME THOUGH...
BUT DIDN'T HE SAY...
...IT MIGHT BE "IMPOSSIBLE"?
Eh?
UH... Y-YES... HE DID.
UM...
THERE ARE A LOT...
...OF OBSTACLES ...
...IN OUR WAY.
WHEN I THINK...
...ABOUT THOSE THINGS, IT'S ALMOST...

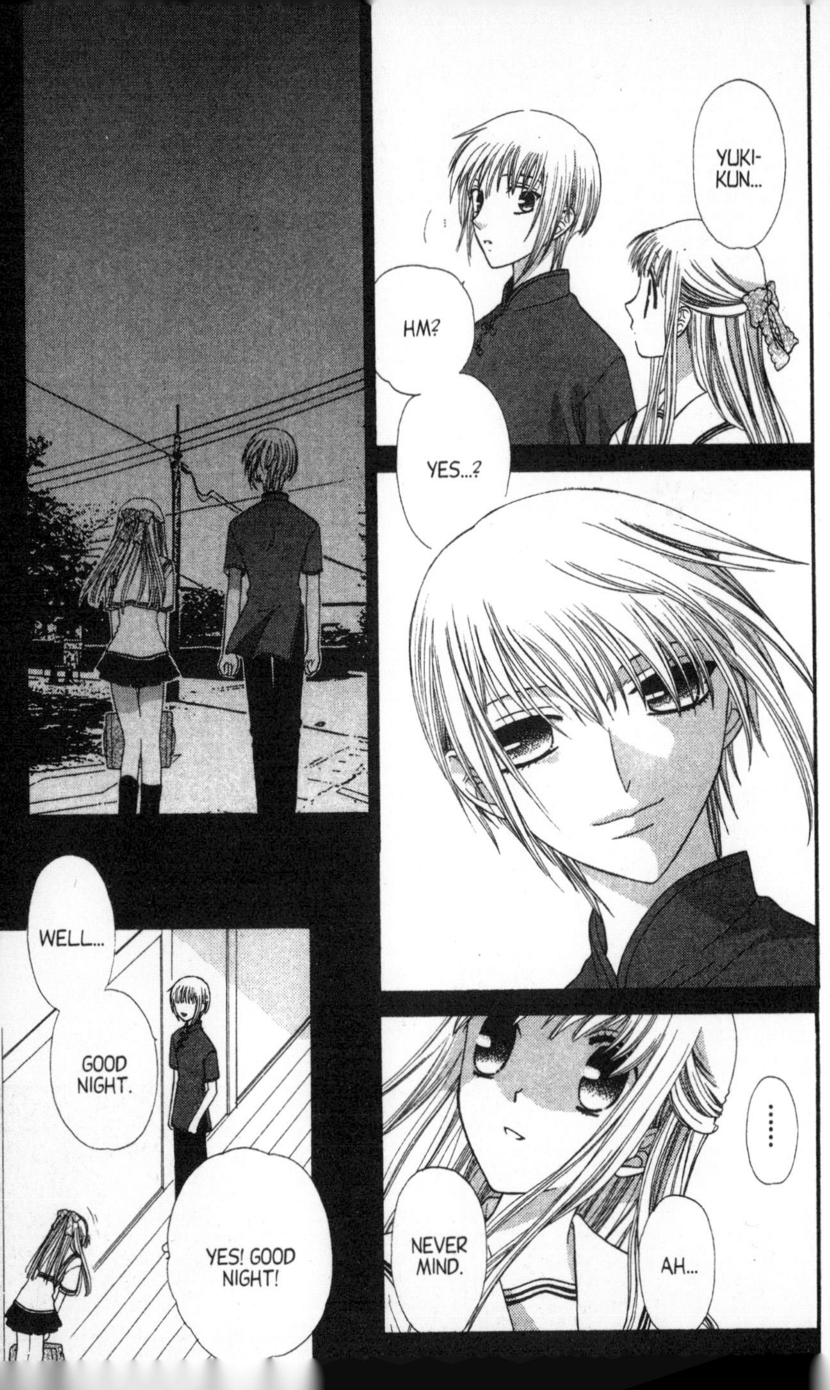
YUKI-KUN...
HM?
YES...?
......
AH...
NEVER MIND.
WELL...
GOOD NIGHT.
YES! GOOD NIGHT!

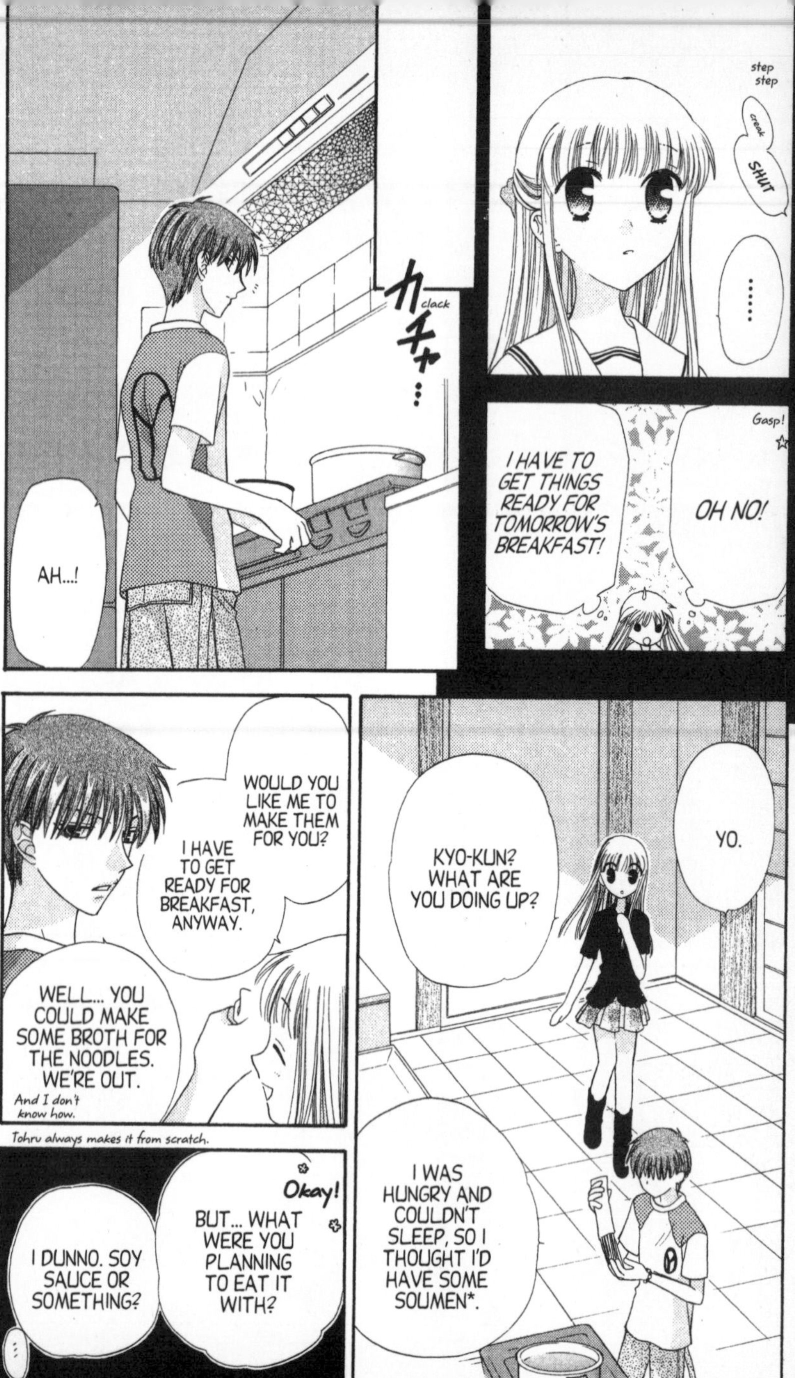
step step
creak
SHUT
......
Gasp!
OH NO!
I HAVE TO GET THINGS READY FOR TOMORROW'S BREAKFAST!
カチャ…
clack
AH...!
YO.
KYO-KUN? WHAT ARE YOU DOING UP?
I WAS HUNGRY AND COULDN'T SLEEP, SO I THOUGHT I'D HAVE SOME SOUMEN*.
*soumen: noodles
WOULD YOU LIKE ME TO MAKE THEM FOR YOU?
I HAVE TO GET READY FOR BREAKFAST, ANYWAY.
WELL... YOU COULD MAKE SOME BROTH FOR THE NOODLES. WE'RE OUT.
And I don't know how.
Tohru always makes it from scratch.
Okay!
BUT... WHAT WERE YOU PLANNING TO EAT IT WITH?
I DUNNO. SOY SAUCE OR SOMETHING?
...

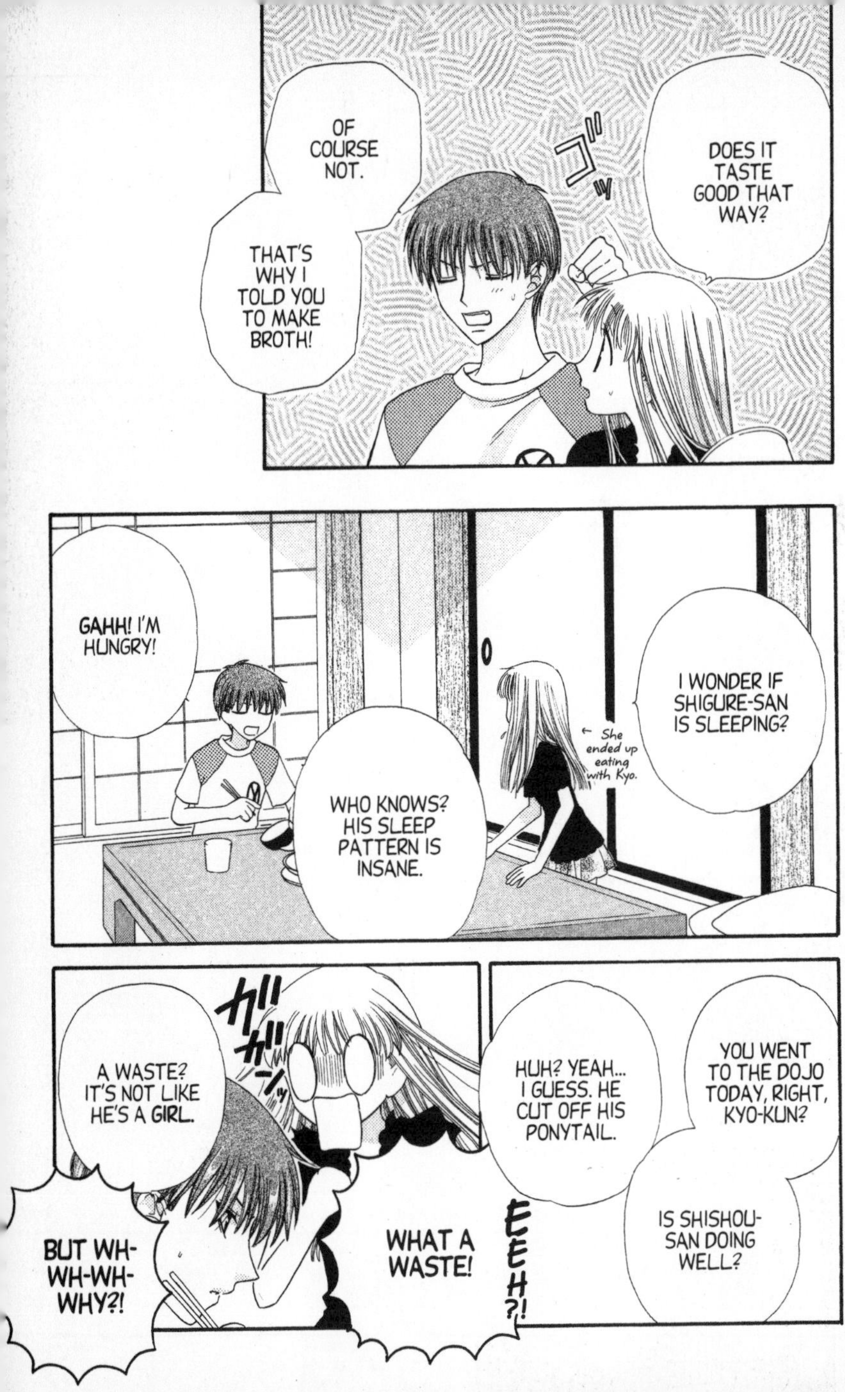
DOES IT TASTE GOOD THAT WAY?
ゴッ
OF COURSE NOT.
THAT'S WHY I TOLD YOU TO MAKE BROTH!
I WONDER IF SHIGURE-SAN IS SLEEPING?
← She ended up eating with Kyo.
WHO KNOWS? HIS SLEEP PATTERN IS INSANE.
GAHH! I'M HUNGRY!
YOU WENT TO THE DOJO TODAY, RIGHT, KYO-KUN?
HUH? YEAH... I GUESS. HE CUT OFF HIS PONYTAIL.
IS SHISHOU-SAN DOING WELL?
EEEH?!
WHAT A WASTE!
ガガーンッ
A WASTE? IT'S NOT LIKE HE'S A GIRL.
BUT WH-WH-WH-WHY?!

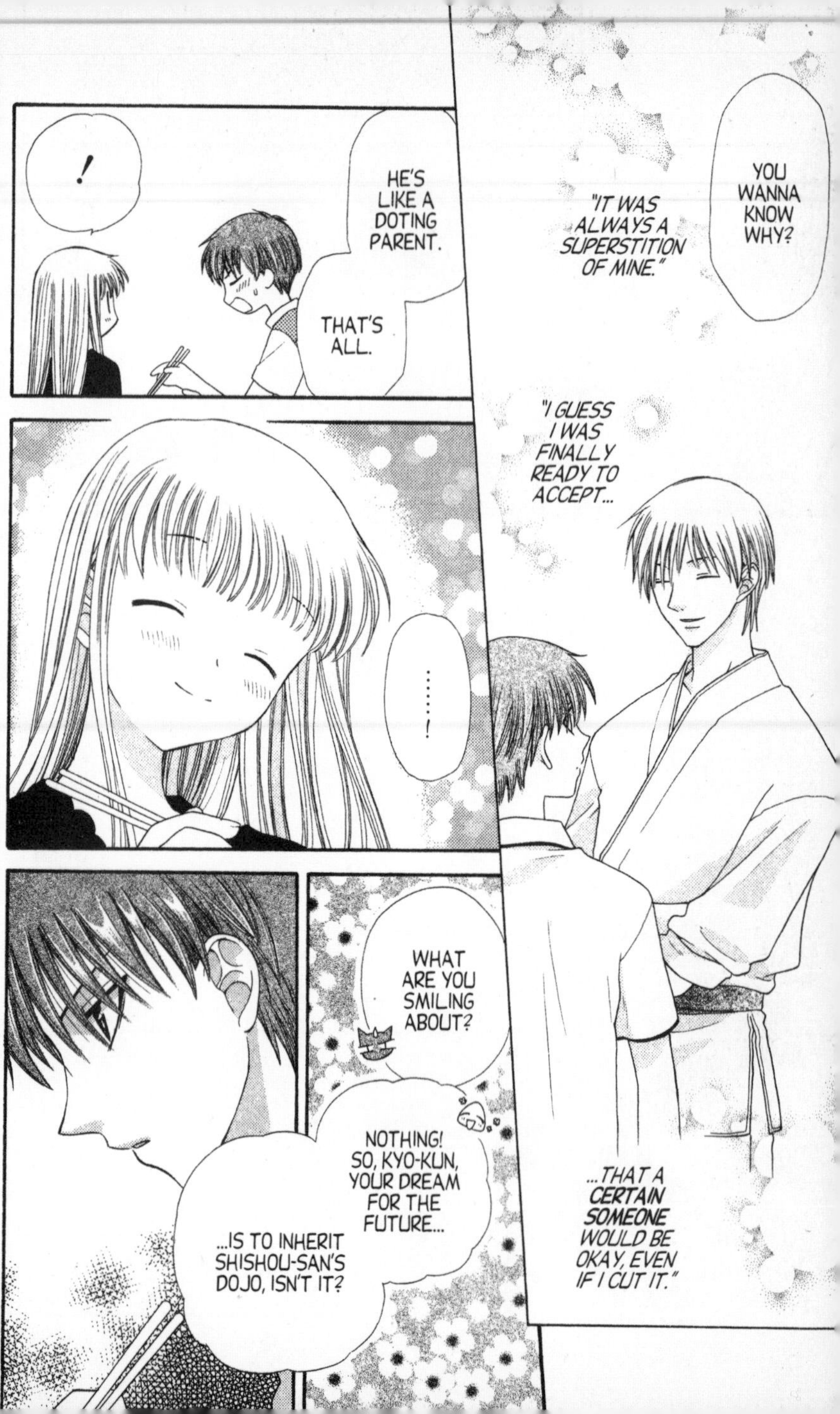
YOU WANNA KNOW WHY?
"IT WAS ALWAYS A SUPERSTITION OF MINE."
"I GUESS I WAS FINALLY READY TO ACCEPT...
...THAT A *CERTAIN SOMEONE* WOULD BE OKAY, EVEN IF I CUT IT."
HE'S LIKE A DOTING PARENT.
THAT'S ALL.
!
......!
WHAT ARE YOU SMILING ABOUT?
NOTHING! SO, KYO-KUN, YOUR DREAM FOR THE FUTURE...
...IS TO INHERIT SHISHOU-SAN'S DOJO, ISN'T IT?

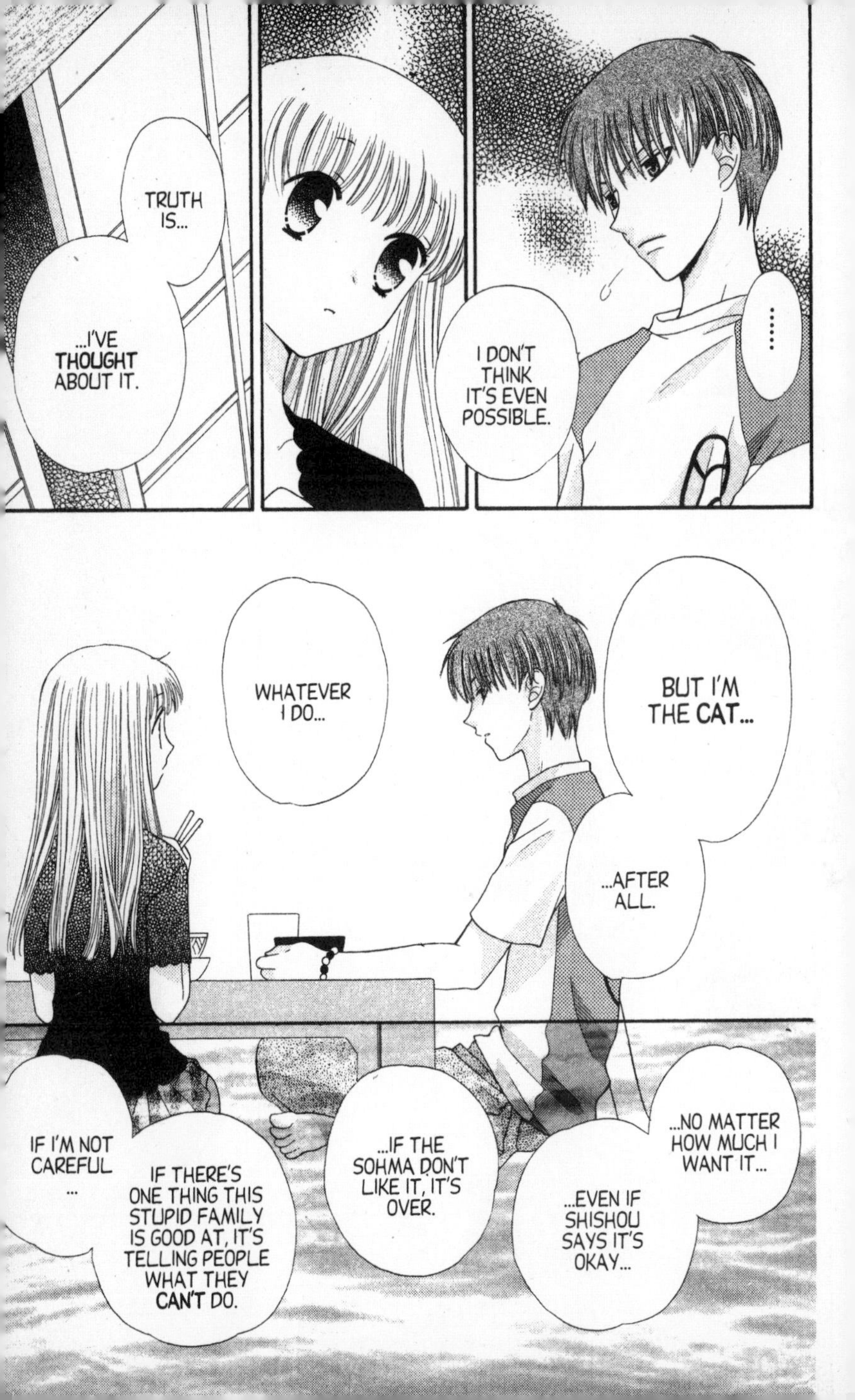
......
I DON'T THINK IT'S EVEN POSSIBLE.
TRUTH IS...
...I'VE **THOUGHT** ABOUT IT.
BUT I'M THE **CAT**...
...AFTER ALL.
WHATEVER I DO...
...NO MATTER HOW MUCH I WANT IT...
...EVEN IF SHISHOU SAYS IT'S OKAY...
...IF THE SOHMA DON'T LIKE IT, IT'S OVER.
IF THERE'S ONE THING THIS STUPID FAMILY IS GOOD AT, IT'S TELLING PEOPLE WHAT THEY **CAN'T** DO.
IF I'M NOT CAREFUL ...

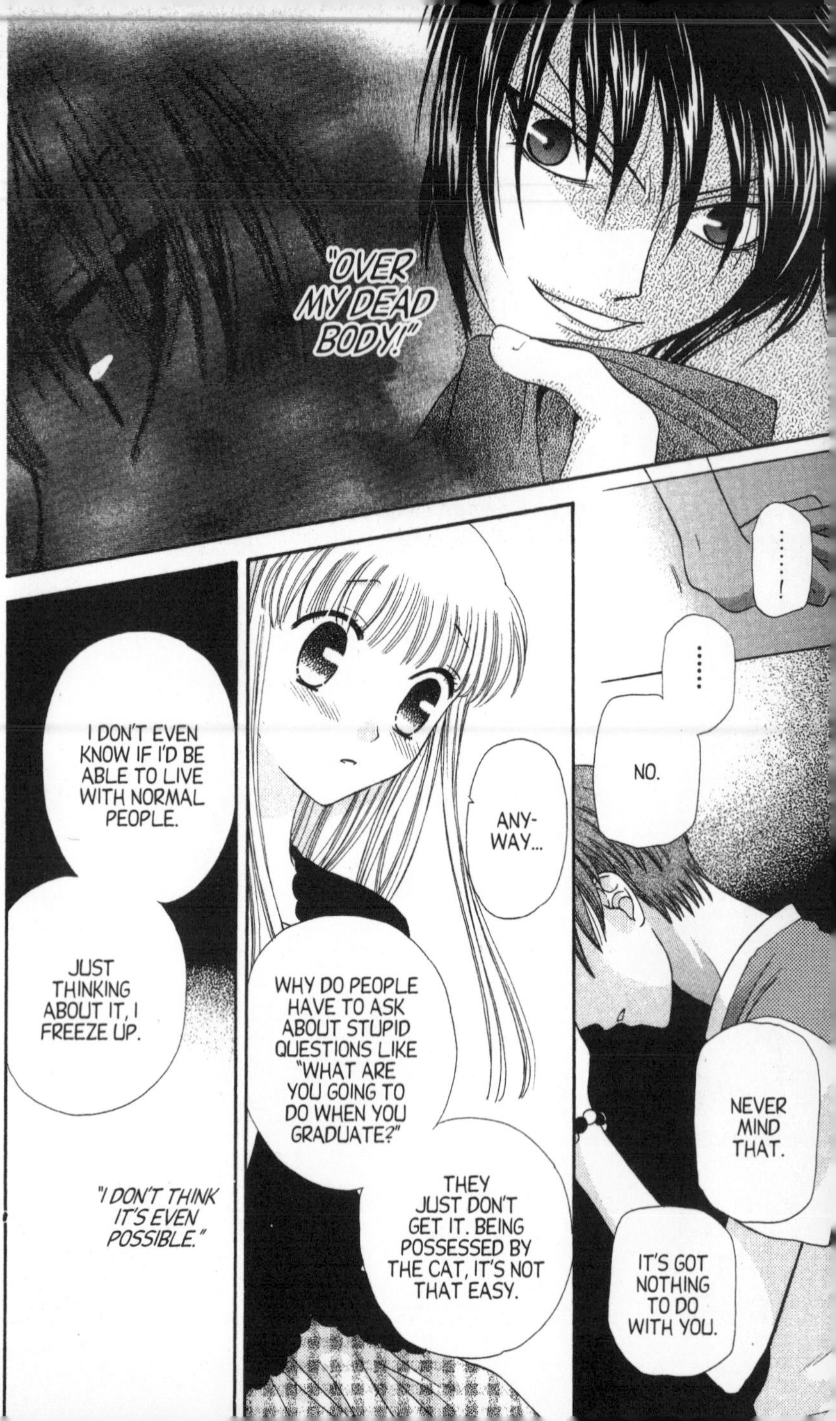
"OVER MY DEAD BODY!"
......!
......
NO.
NEVER MIND THAT.
IT'S GOT NOTHING TO DO WITH YOU.
ANY-WAY...
WHY DO PEOPLE HAVE TO ASK ABOUT STUPID QUESTIONS LIKE "WHAT ARE YOU GOING TO DO WHEN YOU GRADUATE?"
THEY JUST DON'T GET IT. BEING POSSESSED BY THE CAT, IT'S NOT THAT EASY.
I DON'T EVEN KNOW IF I'D BE ABLE TO LIVE WITH NORMAL PEOPLE.
JUST THINKING ABOUT IT, I FREEZE UP.
"I DON'T THINK IT'S EVEN POSSIBLE."

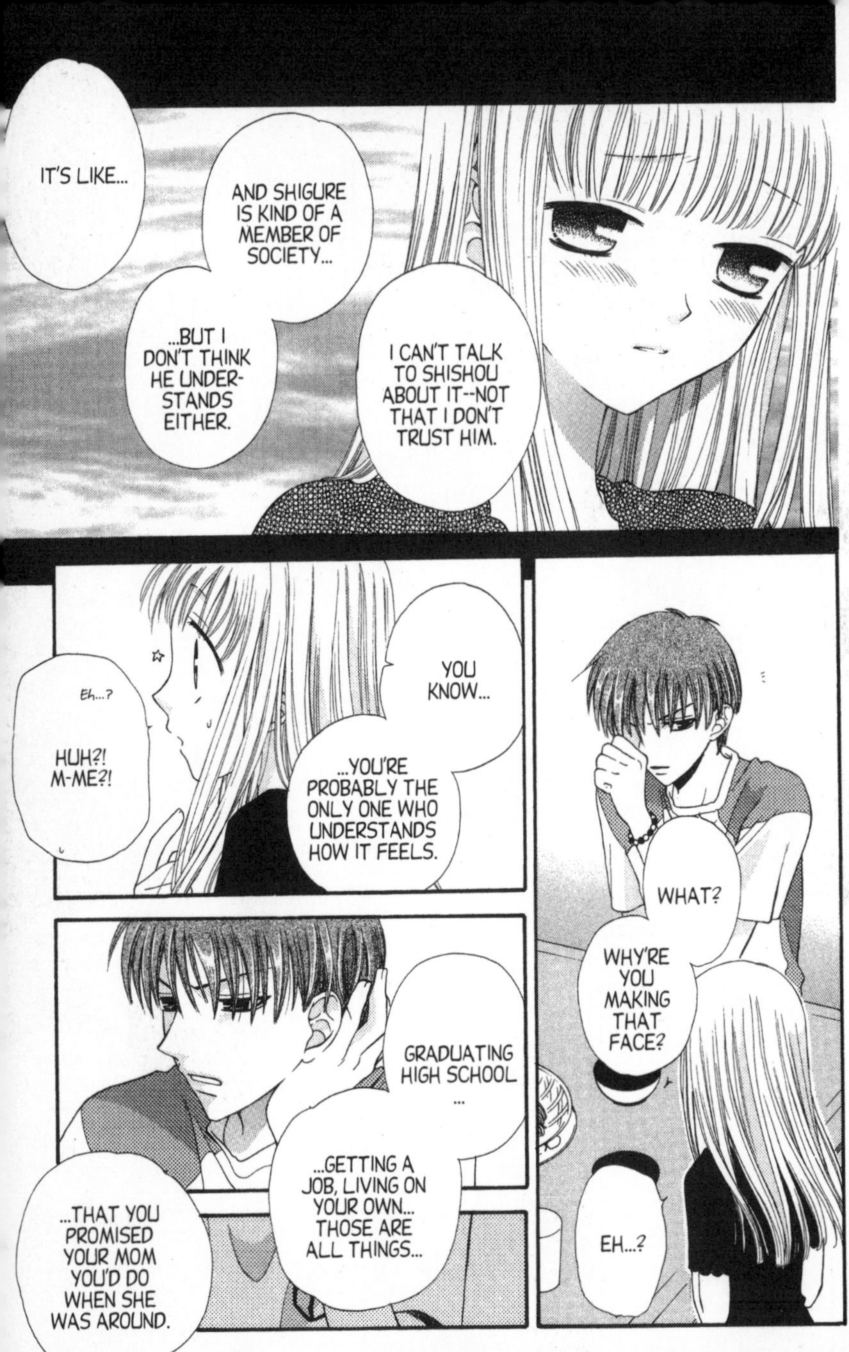
I CAN'T TALK TO SHISHOU ABOUT IT--NOT THAT I DON'T TRUST HIM.
AND SHIGURE IS KIND OF A MEMBER OF SOCIETY...
...BUT I DON'T THINK HE UNDER-STANDS EITHER.
IT'S LIKE...
WHAT?
WHY'RE YOU MAKING THAT FACE?
EH...?
YOU KNOW...
...YOU'RE PROBABLY THE ONLY ONE WHO UNDERSTANDS HOW IT FEELS.
Eh...?
HUH?! M-ME?!
GRADUATING HIGH SCHOOL ...
...GETTING A JOB, LIVING ON YOUR OWN... THOSE ARE ALL THINGS...
...THAT YOU PROMISED YOUR MOM YOU'D DO WHEN SHE WAS AROUND.

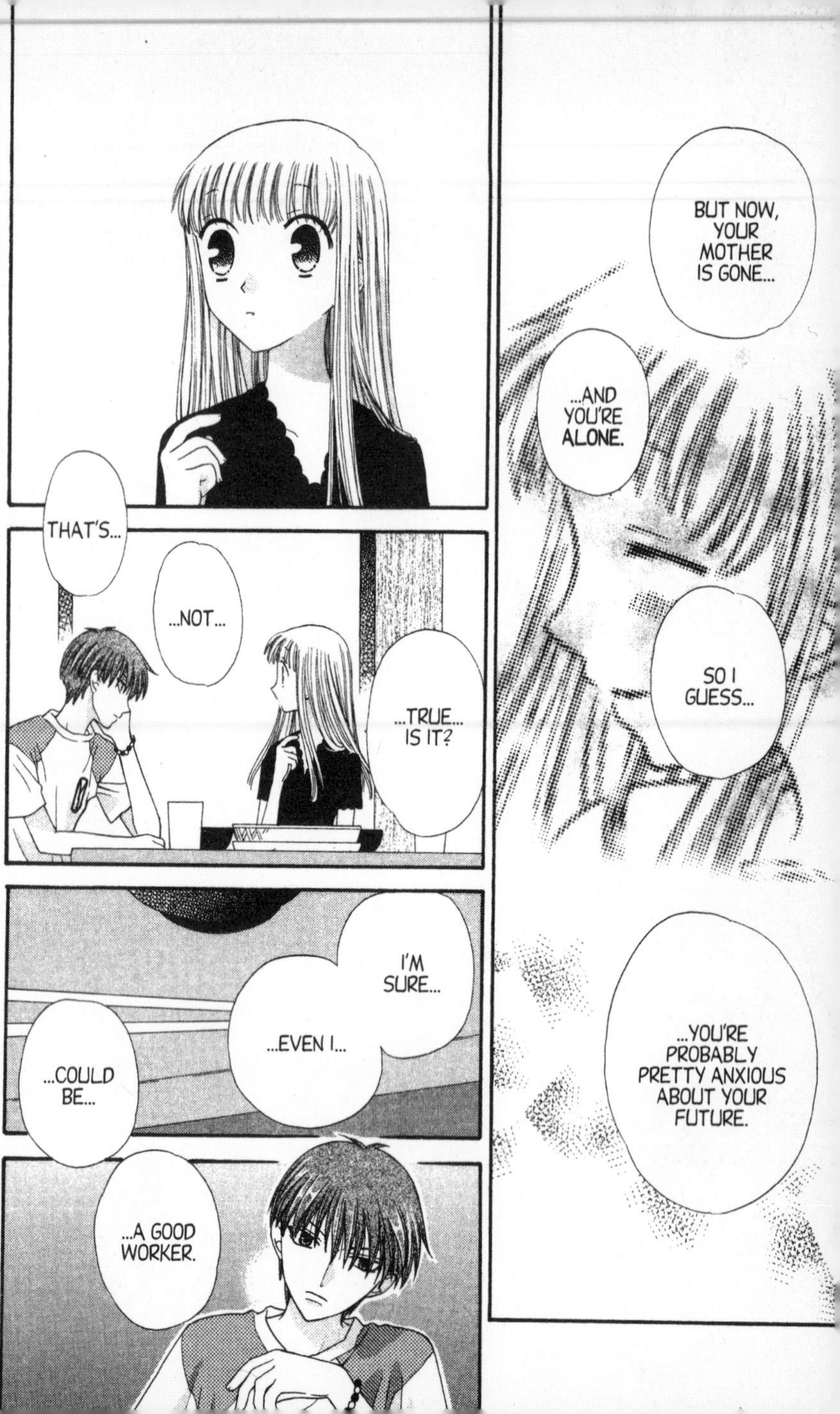
BUT NOW, YOUR MOTHER IS GONE...
...AND YOU'RE ALONE.
SO I GUESS...
...YOU'RE PROBABLY PRETTY ANXIOUS ABOUT YOUR FUTURE.
THAT'S...
...NOT...
...TRUE... IS IT?
I'M SURE...
...EVEN I...
...COULD BE...
...A GOOD WORKER.

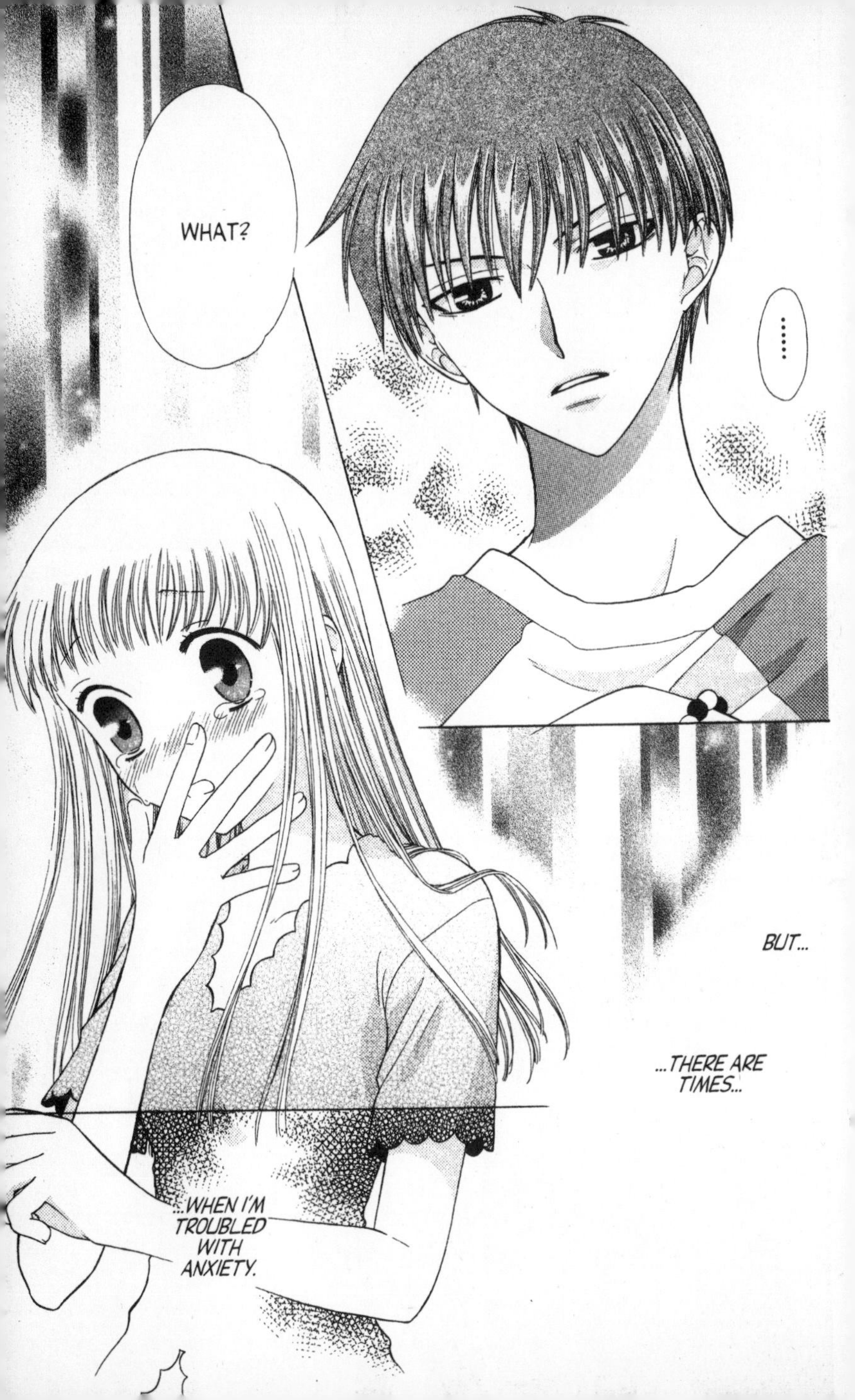
......
WHAT?
BUT...
...THERE ARE TIMES...
...WHEN I'M TROUBLED WITH ANXIETY.

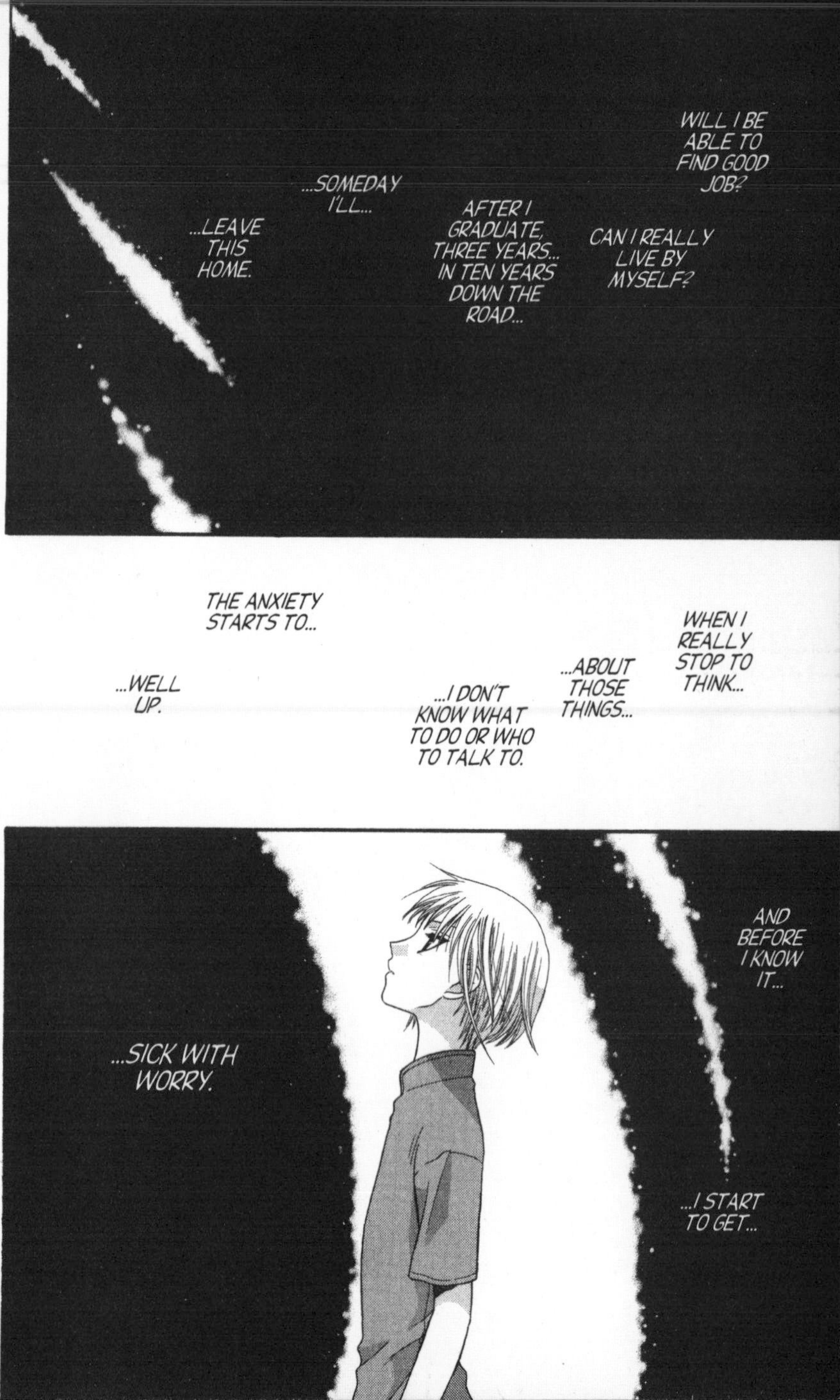
WILL I BE ABLE TO FIND GOOD JOB?
CAN I REALLY LIVE BY MYSELF?
AFTER I GRADUATE, THREE YEARS... IN TEN YEARS DOWN THE ROAD...
...SOMEDAY I'LL...
...LEAVE THIS HOME.
WHEN I REALLY STOP TO THINK...
...ABOUT THOSE THINGS...
...I DON'T KNOW WHAT TO DO OR WHO TO TALK TO.
THE ANXIETY STARTS TO...
...WELL UP.
AND BEFORE I KNOW IT...
...I START TO GET...
...SICK WITH WORRY.

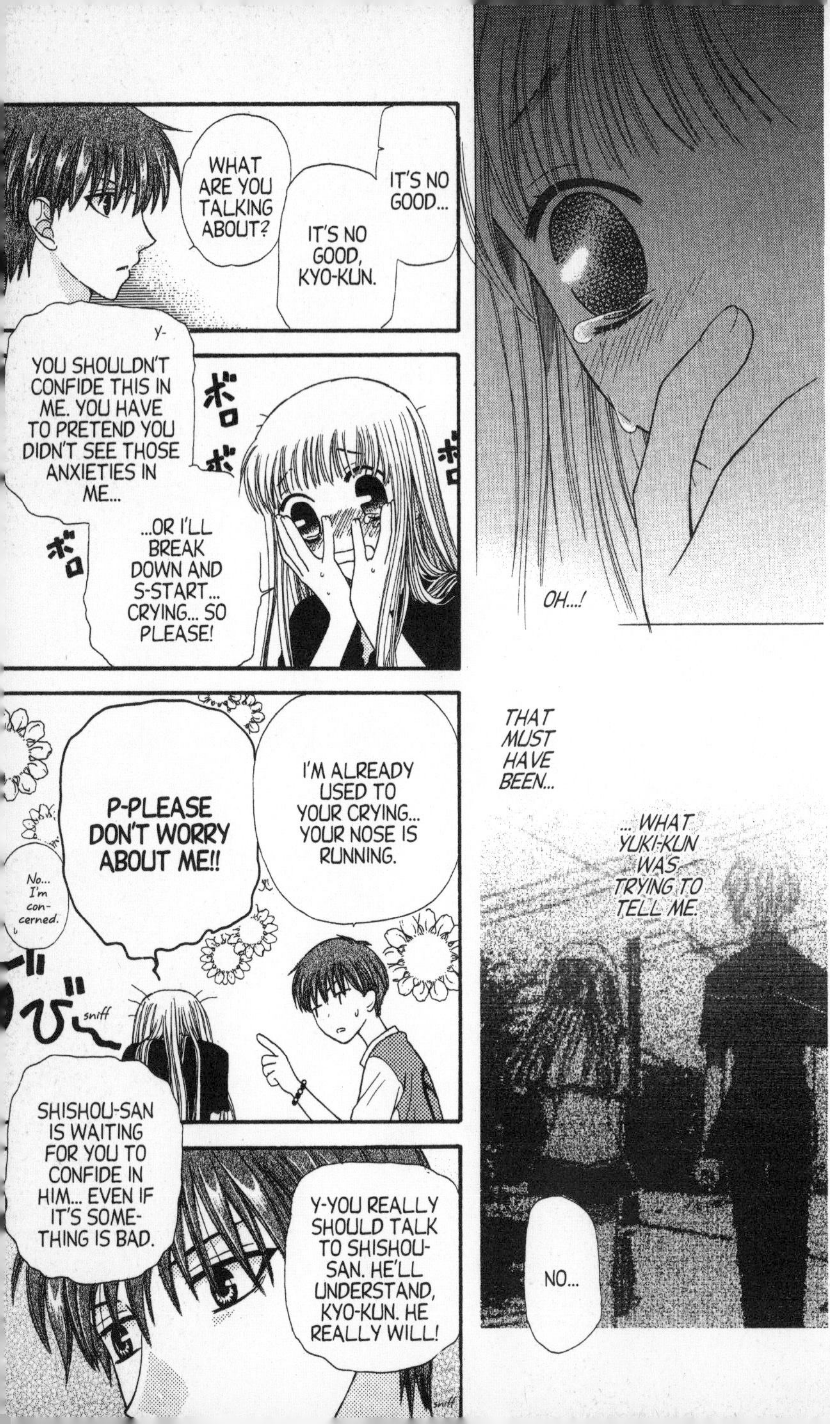
OH...!
IT'S NO GOOD...
IT'S NO GOOD, KYO-KUN.
WHAT ARE YOU TALKING ABOUT?
ボロ
ボロ
ボロ
Y-
YOU SHOULDN'T CONFIDE THIS IN ME. YOU HAVE TO PRETEND YOU DIDN'T SEE THOSE ANXIETIES IN ME...
...OR I'LL BREAK DOWN AND S-START... CRYING... SO PLEASE!
THAT MUST HAVE BEEN...
...WHAT YUKI-KUN WAS TRYING TO TELL ME.
NO...
I'M ALREADY USED TO YOUR CRYING... YOUR NOSE IS RUNNING.
P-PLEASE DON'T WORRY ABOUT ME!!
No... I'm concerned.
びー
sniff
Y-YOU REALLY SHOULD TALK TO SHISHOU-SAN. HE'LL UNDERSTAND, KYO-KUN. HE REALLY WILL!
SHISHOU-SAN IS WAITING FOR YOU TO CONFIDE IN HIM... EVEN IF IT'S SOME-THING IS BAD.
sniff

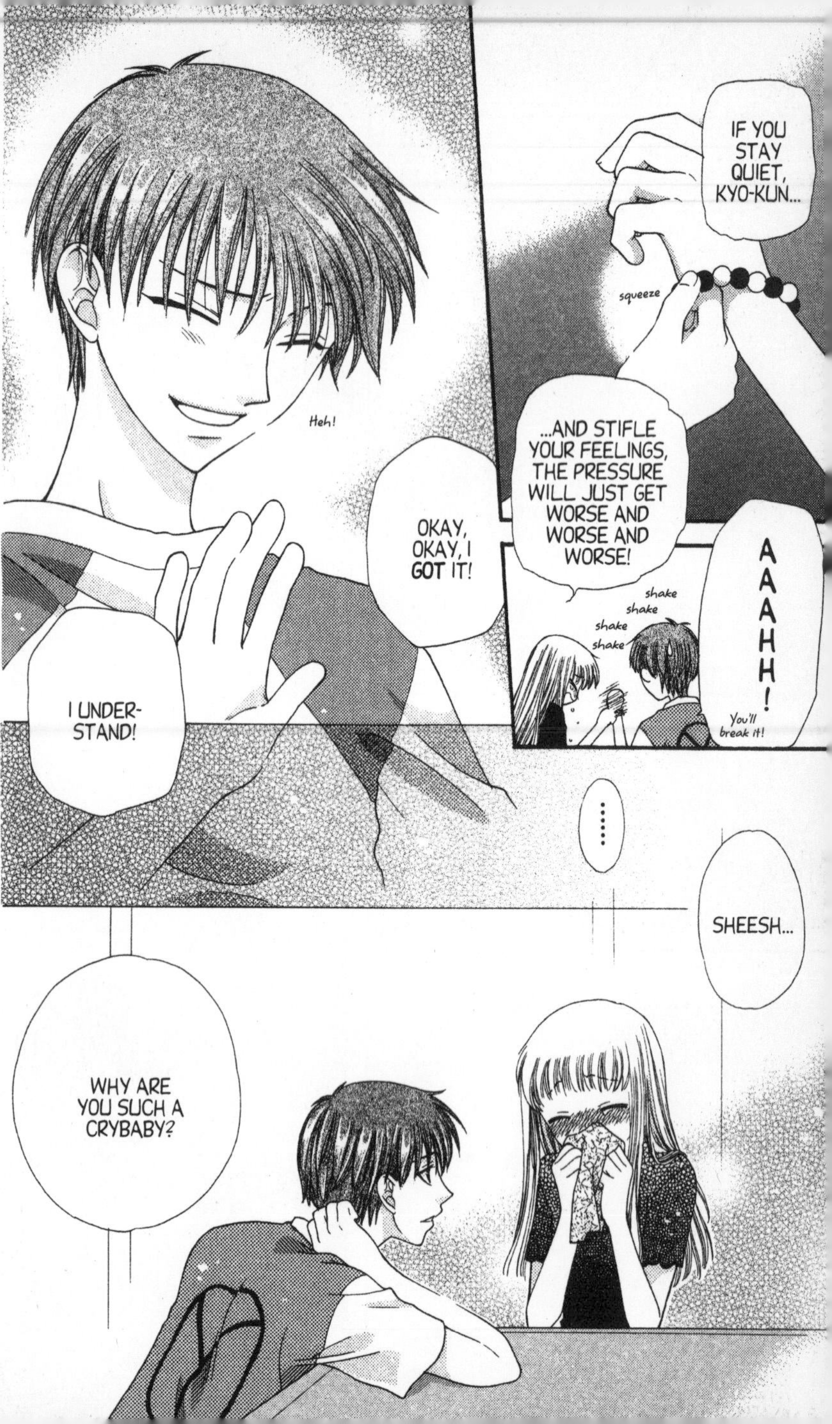
IF YOU STAY QUIET, KYO-KUN...
squeeze
...AND STIFLE YOUR FEELINGS, THE PRESSURE WILL JUST GET WORSE AND WORSE AND WORSE!
shake
shake
shake
shake
AAAHH!
You'll break it!
Heh!
OKAY, OKAY, I GOT IT!
I UNDER-STAND!
......
SHEESH...
WHY ARE YOU SUCH A CRYBABY?

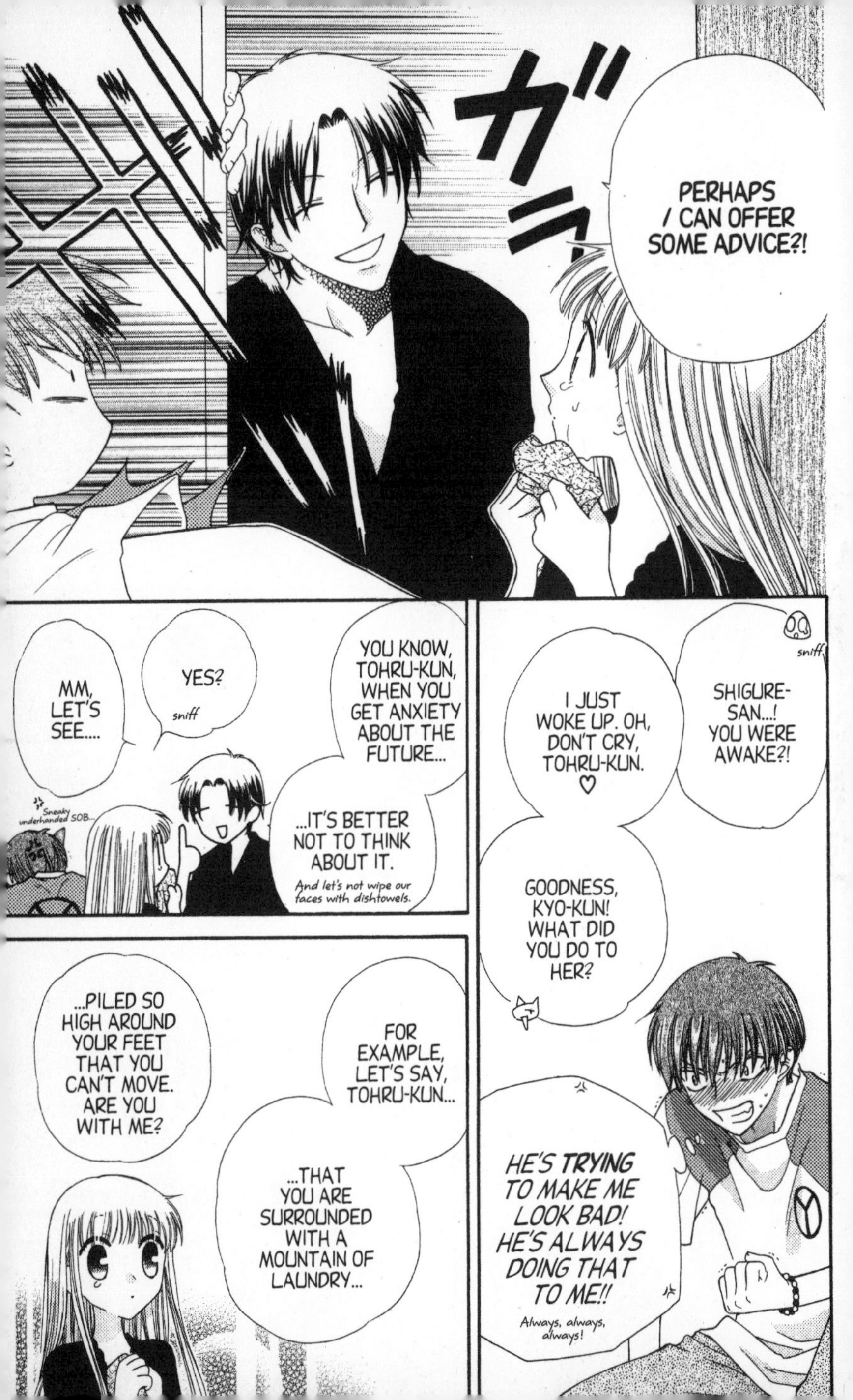
ガラ
PERHAPS I CAN OFFER SOME ADVICE?!
sniff
SHIGURE-SAN...! YOU WERE AWAKE?!
I JUST WOKE UP. OH, DON'T CRY, TOHRU-KUN. ♡
GOODNESS, KYO-KUN! WHAT DID YOU DO TO HER?
HE'S TRYING TO MAKE ME LOOK BAD! HE'S ALWAYS DOING THAT TO ME!!
Always, always, always!
YOU KNOW, TOHRU-KUN, WHEN YOU GET ANXIETY ABOUT THE FUTURE...
YES?
sniff
MM, LET'S SEE....
...IT'S BETTER NOT TO THINK ABOUT IT.
And let's not wipe our faces with dishtowels.
Sneaky underhanded SOB...
FOR EXAMPLE, LET'S SAY, TOHRU-KUN...
...THAT YOU ARE SURROUNDED WITH A MOUNTAIN OF LAUNDRY...
...PILED SO HIGH AROUND YOUR FEET THAT YOU CAN'T MOVE. ARE YOU WITH ME?

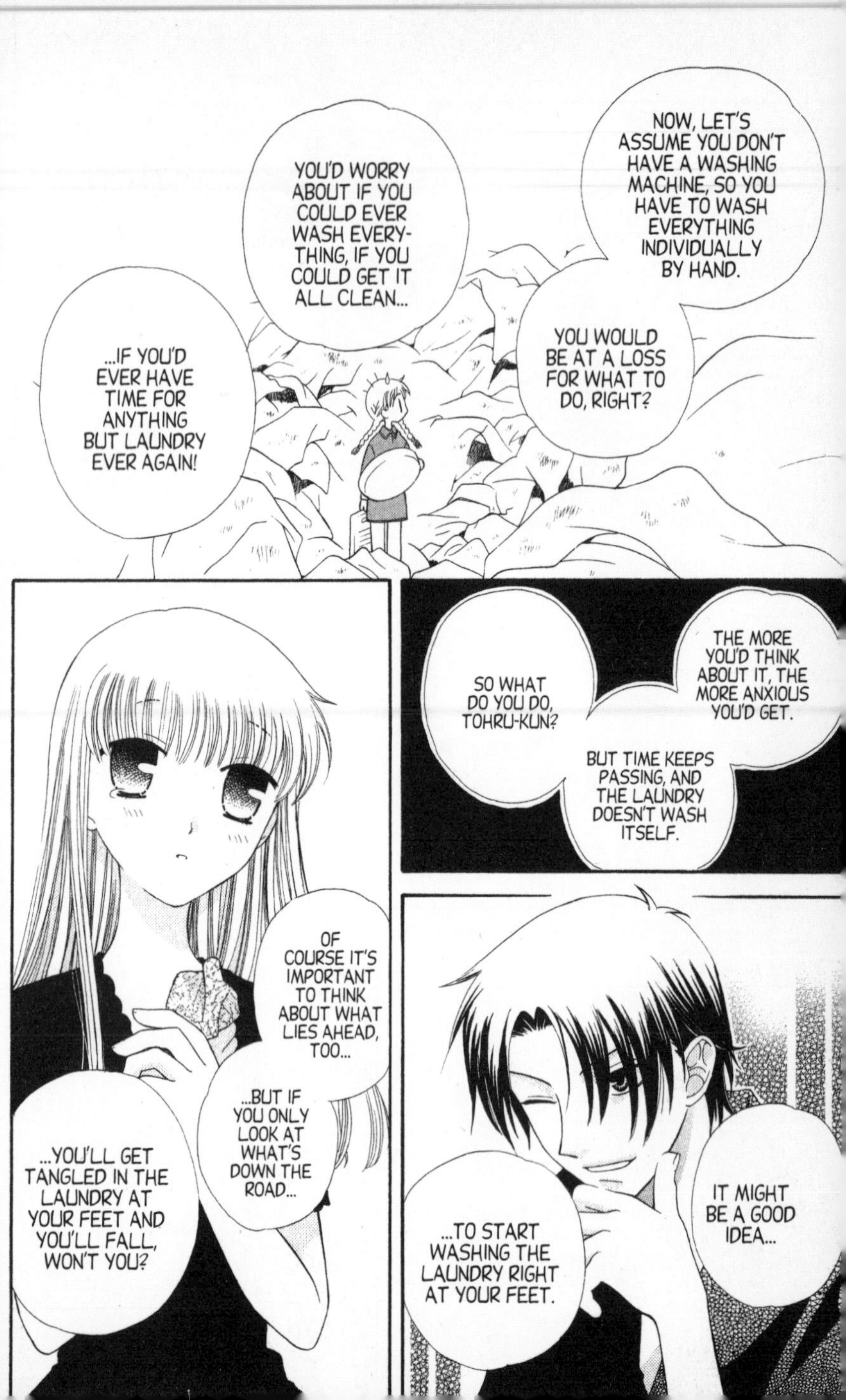
NOW, LET'S ASSUME YOU DON'T HAVE A WASHING MACHINE, SO YOU HAVE TO WASH EVERYTHING INDIVIDUALLY BY HAND.
YOU WOULD BE AT A LOSS FOR WHAT TO DO, RIGHT?
YOU'D WORRY ABOUT IF YOU COULD EVER WASH EVERY-THING, IF YOU COULD GET IT ALL CLEAN...
...IF YOU'D EVER HAVE TIME FOR ANYTHING BUT LAUNDRY EVER AGAIN!
THE MORE YOU'D THINK ABOUT IT, THE MORE ANXIOUS YOU'D GET.
BUT TIME KEEPS PASSING, AND THE LAUNDRY DOESN'T WASH ITSELF.
SO WHAT DO YOU DO, TOHRU-KUN?
IT MIGHT BE A GOOD IDEA...
...TO START WASHING THE LAUNDRY RIGHT AT YOUR FEET.
OF COURSE IT'S IMPORTANT TO THINK ABOUT WHAT LIES AHEAD, TOO...
...BUT IF YOU ONLY LOOK AT WHAT'S DOWN THE ROAD...
...YOU'LL GET TANGLED IN THE LAUNDRY AT YOUR FEET AND YOU'LL FALL, WON'T YOU?

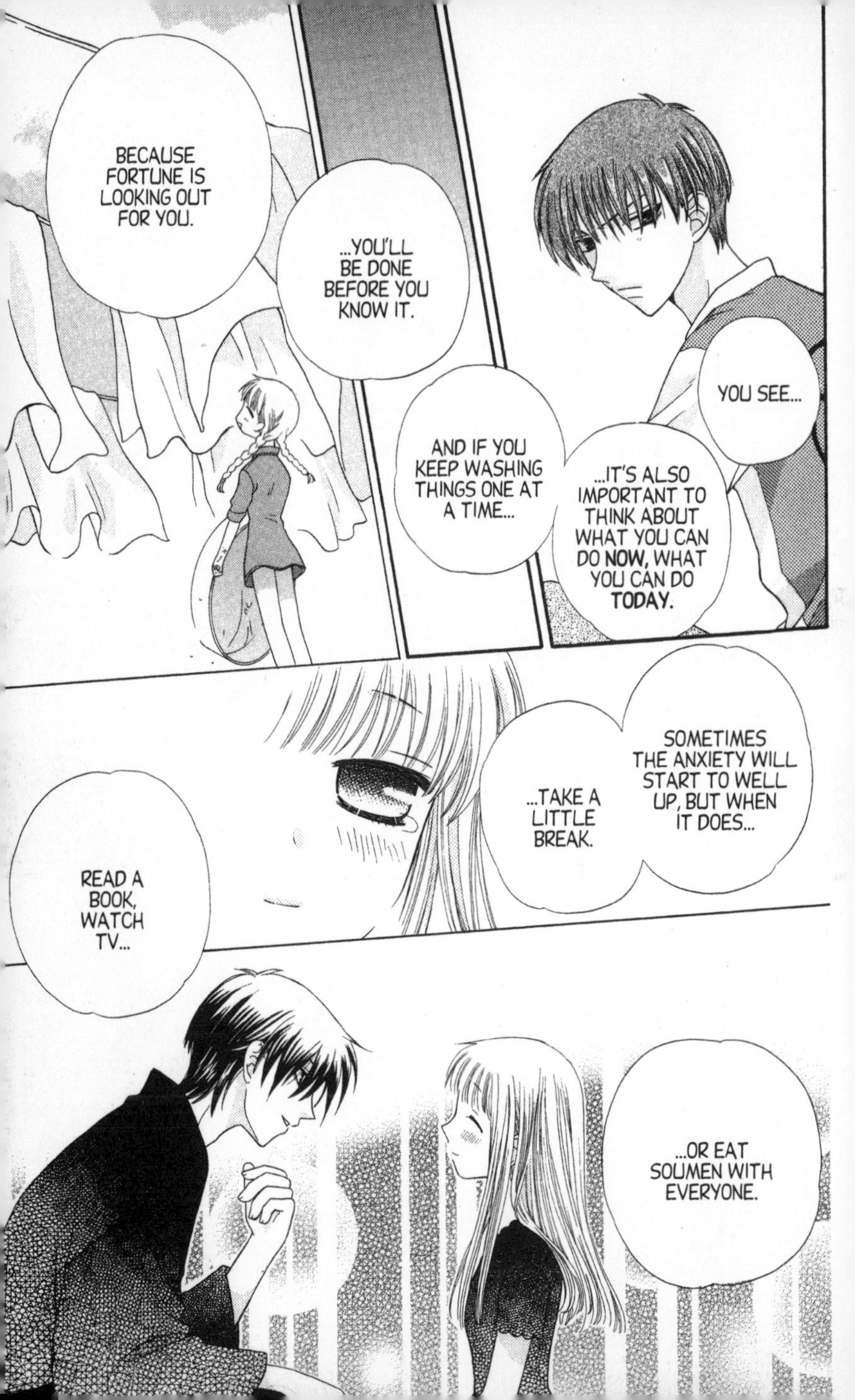
YOU SEE...
...IT'S ALSO IMPORTANT TO THINK ABOUT WHAT YOU CAN DO **NOW**, WHAT YOU CAN DO **TODAY**.
AND IF YOU KEEP WASHING THINGS ONE AT A TIME...
...YOU'LL BE DONE BEFORE YOU KNOW IT.
BECAUSE FORTUNE IS LOOKING OUT FOR YOU.
SOMETIMES THE ANXIETY WILL START TO WELL UP, BUT WHEN IT DOES...
...TAKE A LITTLE BREAK.
READ A BOOK, WATCH TV...
...OR EAT SOUMEN WITH EVERYONE.

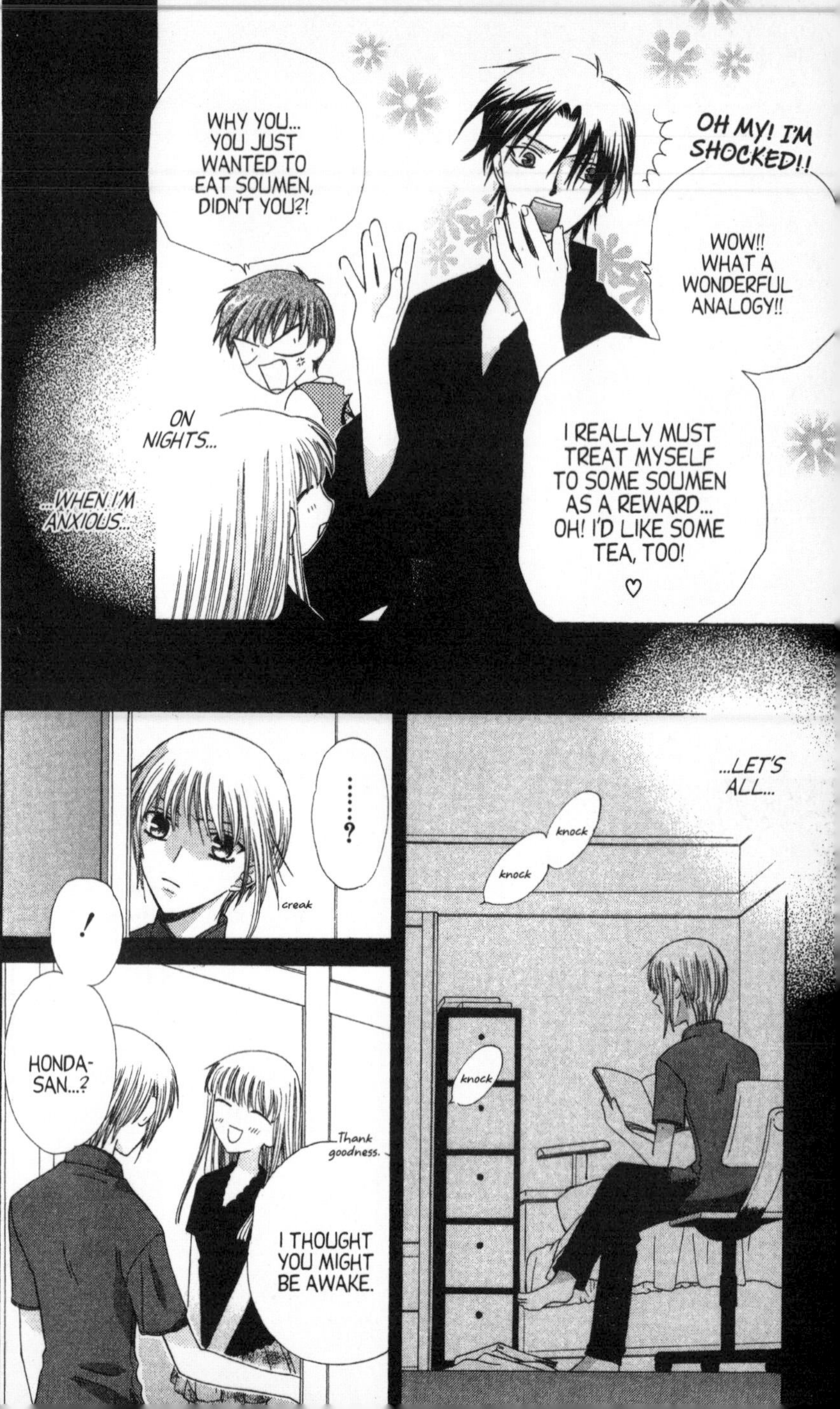
OH MY! I'M SHOCKED!!
WOW!! WHAT A WONDERFUL ANALOGY!!
I REALLY MUST TREAT MYSELF TO SOME SOUMEN AS A REWARD... OH! I'D LIKE SOME TEA, TOO! ♡
WHY YOU... YOU JUST WANTED TO EAT SOUMEN, DIDN'T YOU?!
ON NIGHTS...
...WHEN I'M ANXIOUS...
...LET'S ALL...
knock
knock
knock
......?
creak
!
HONDA-SAN...?
Thank goodness.
I THOUGHT YOU MIGHT BE AWAKE.

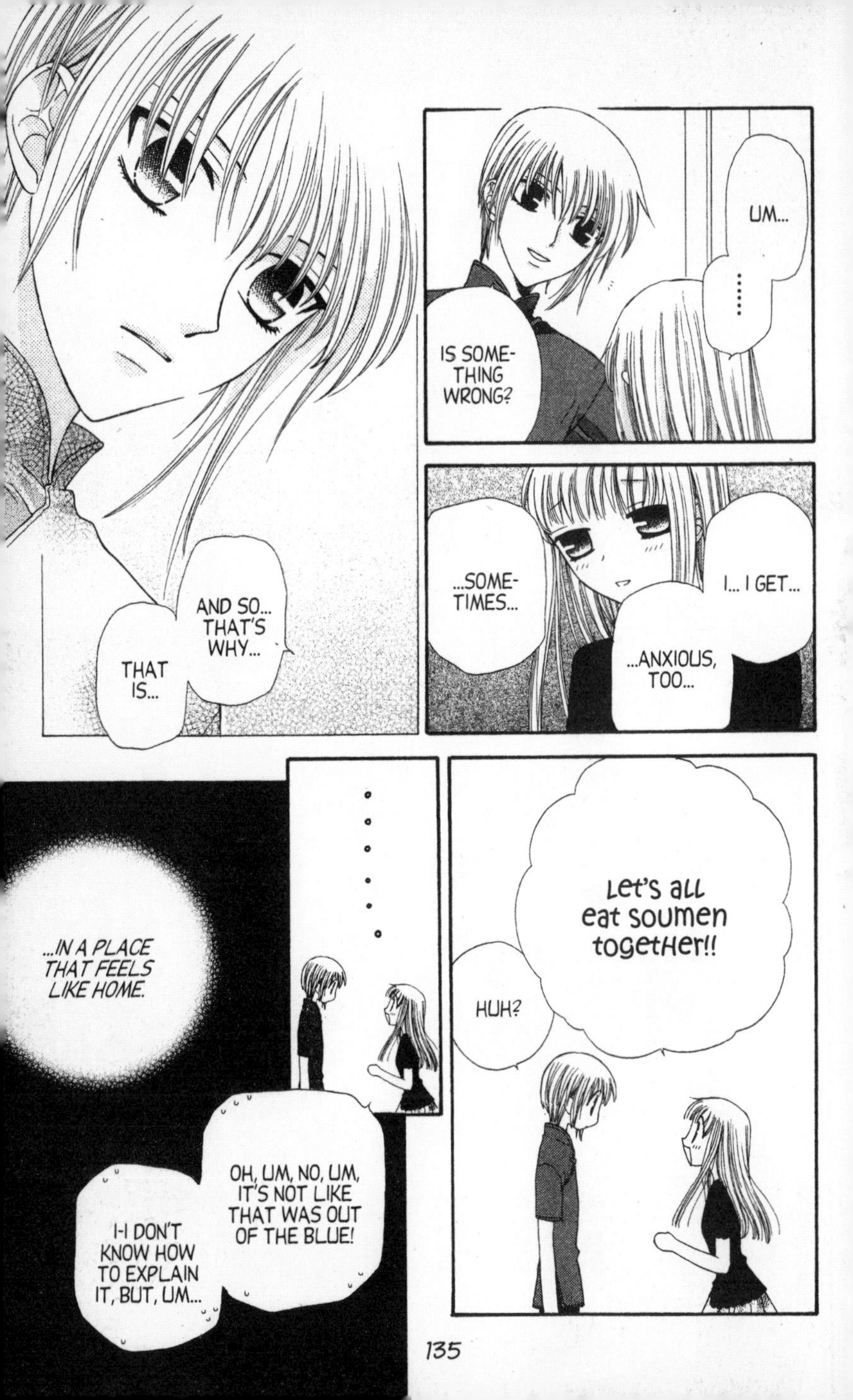
UM...
......
IS SOME-THING WRONG?
I... I GET...
...ANXIOUS, TOO...
...SOME-TIMES...
AND SO... THAT'S WHY...
THAT IS...
Let's all eat soumen together!!
HUH?
......
...IN A PLACE THAT FEELS LIKE HOME.
OH, UM, NO, UM, IT'S NOT LIKE THAT WAS OUT OF THE BLUE!
I-I DON'T KNOW HOW TO EXPLAIN IT, BUT, UM...

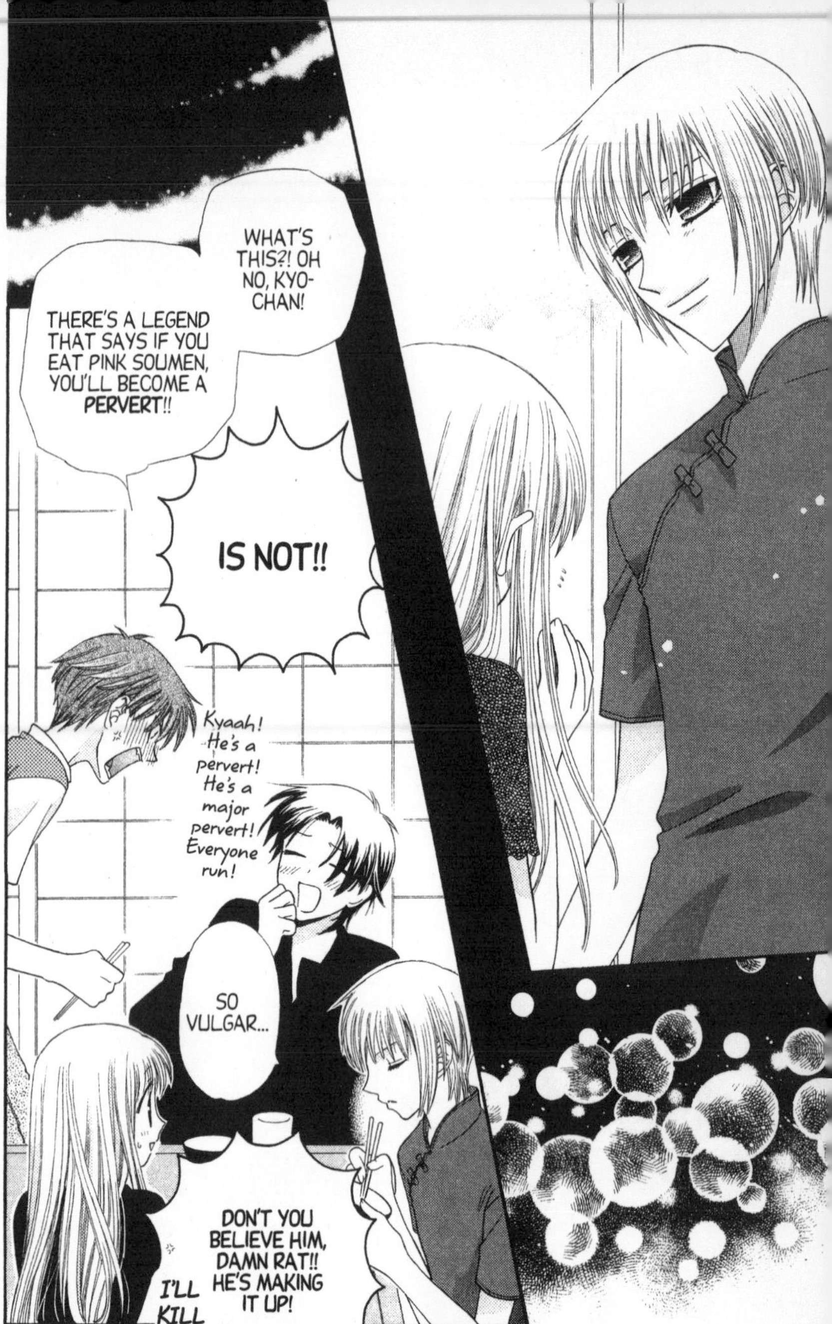

WHAT'S THIS?! OH NO, KYO-CHAN!
THERE'S A LEGEND THAT SAYS IF YOU EAT PINK SOUMEN, YOU'LL BECOME A **PERVERT**!!
IS NOT!!
Kyaah! He's a pervert! He's a major pervert! Everyone run!
SO VULGAR...
DON'T YOU BELIEVE HIM, DAMN RAT!! HE'S MAKING IT UP!
I'LL KILL YOU!!

Chapter 47

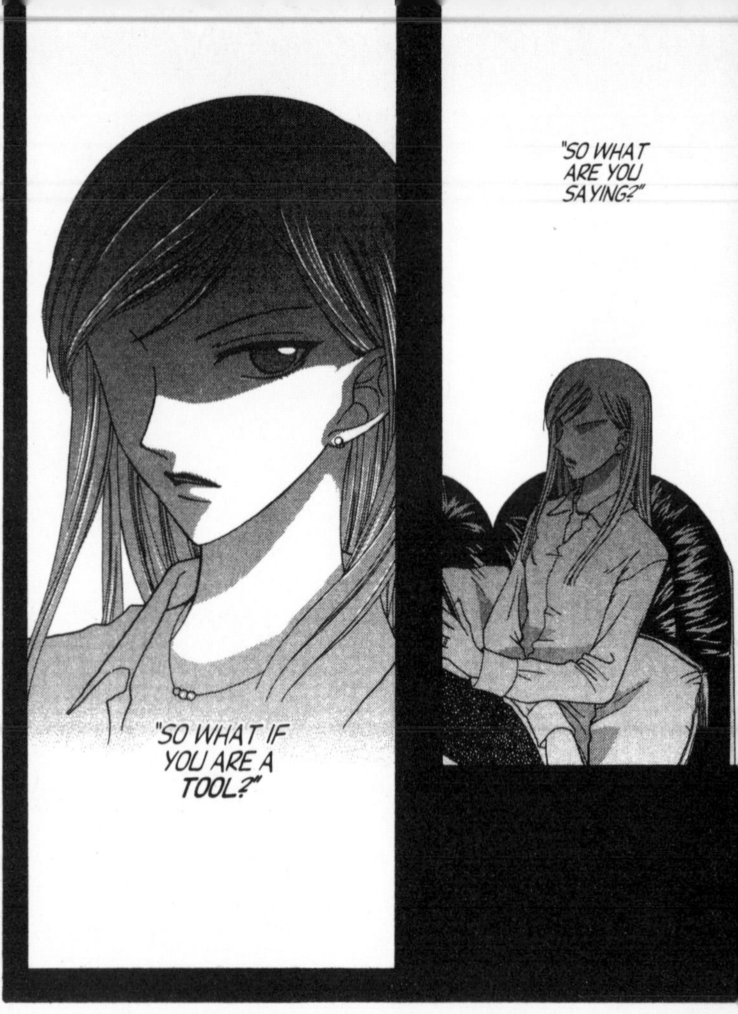
"SO WHAT ARE YOU SAYING?"
"SO WHAT IF YOU ARE A TOOL?"

UL-SPE BLAH, BLAH, BLAH 4

The reason Aaya is wearing long sleeves is to protect against sunburn. He's the type that sunburns easily. Hatori's probably the same way.

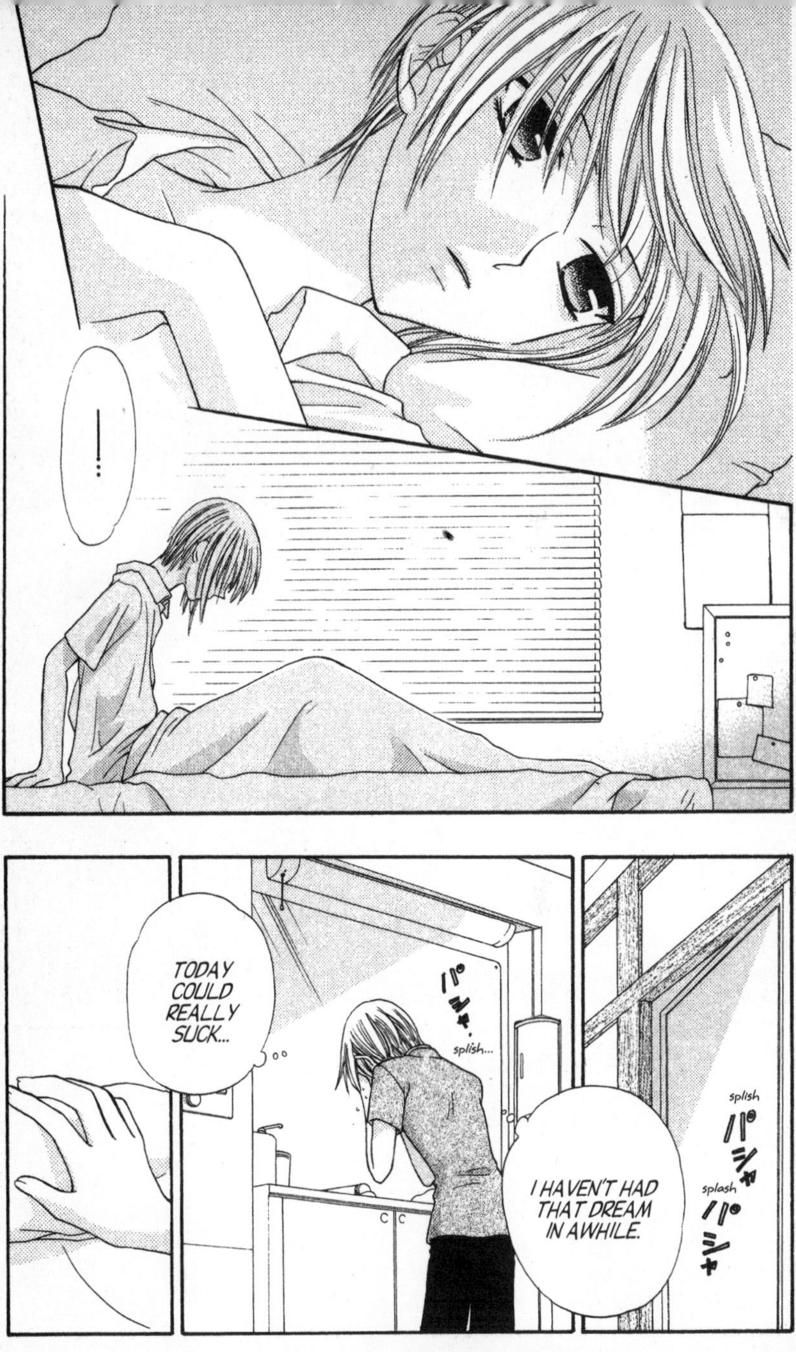
!...
splish
パシャ
splash
パシャ
I HAVEN'T HAD THAT DREAM IN AWHILE.
パシャ.
splish...
TODAY COULD REALLY SUCK...

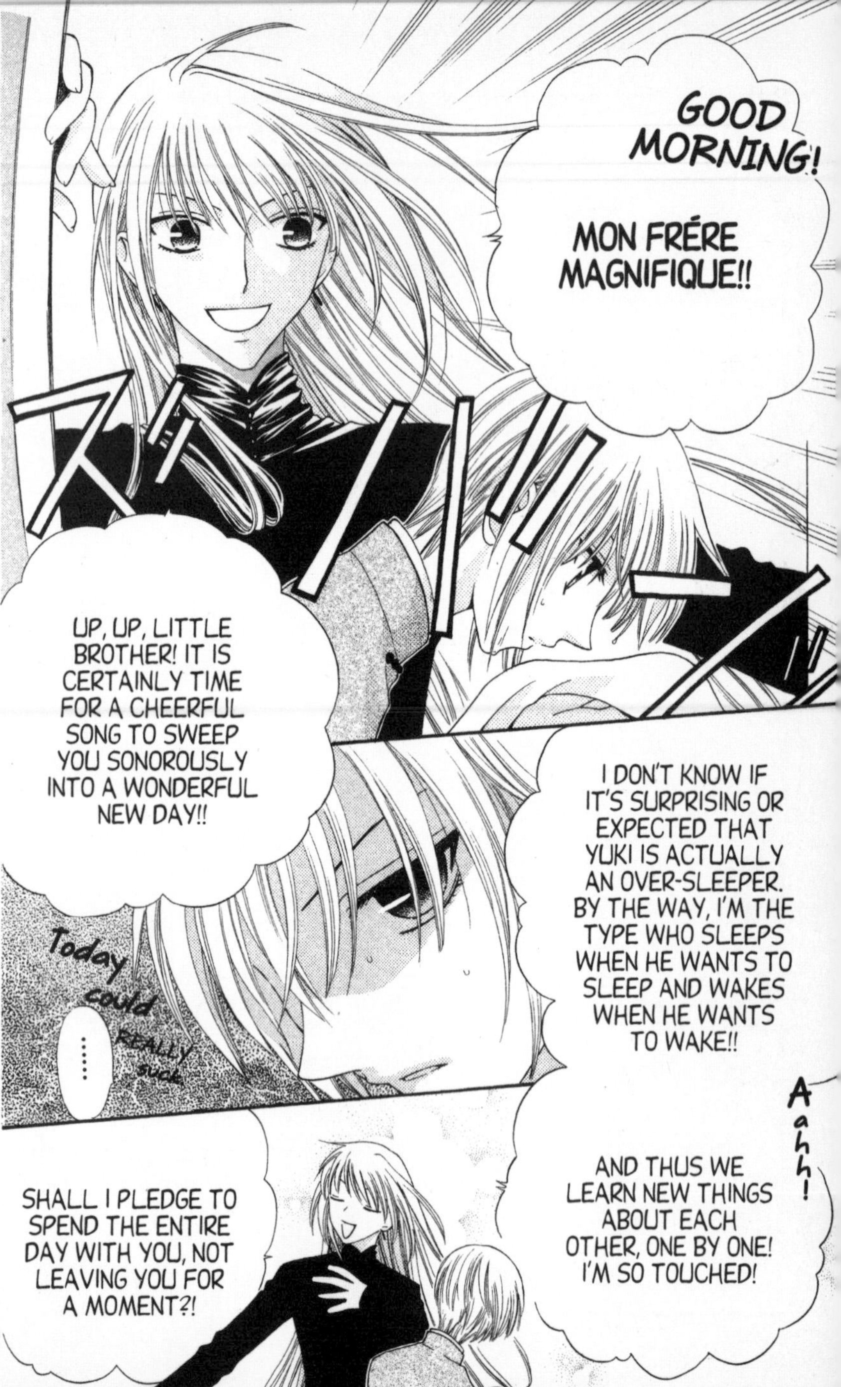
GOOD MORNING!
MON FRÉRE MAGNIFIQUE!!
UP, UP, LITTLE BROTHER! IT IS CERTAINLY TIME FOR A CHEERFUL SONG TO SWEEP YOU SONOROUSLY INTO A WONDERFUL NEW DAY!!
I DON'T KNOW IF IT'S SURPRISING OR EXPECTED THAT YUKI IS ACTUALLY AN OVER-SLEEPER. BY THE WAY, I'M THE TYPE WHO SLEEPS WHEN HE WANTS TO SLEEP AND WAKES WHEN HE WANTS TO WAKE!!
Today could REALLY suck
......
Aahh!
AND THUS WE LEARN NEW THINGS ABOUT EACH OTHER, ONE BY ONE! I'M SO TOUCHED!
SHALL I PLEDGE TO SPEND THE ENTIRE DAY WITH YOU, NOT LEAVING YOU FOR A MOMENT?!

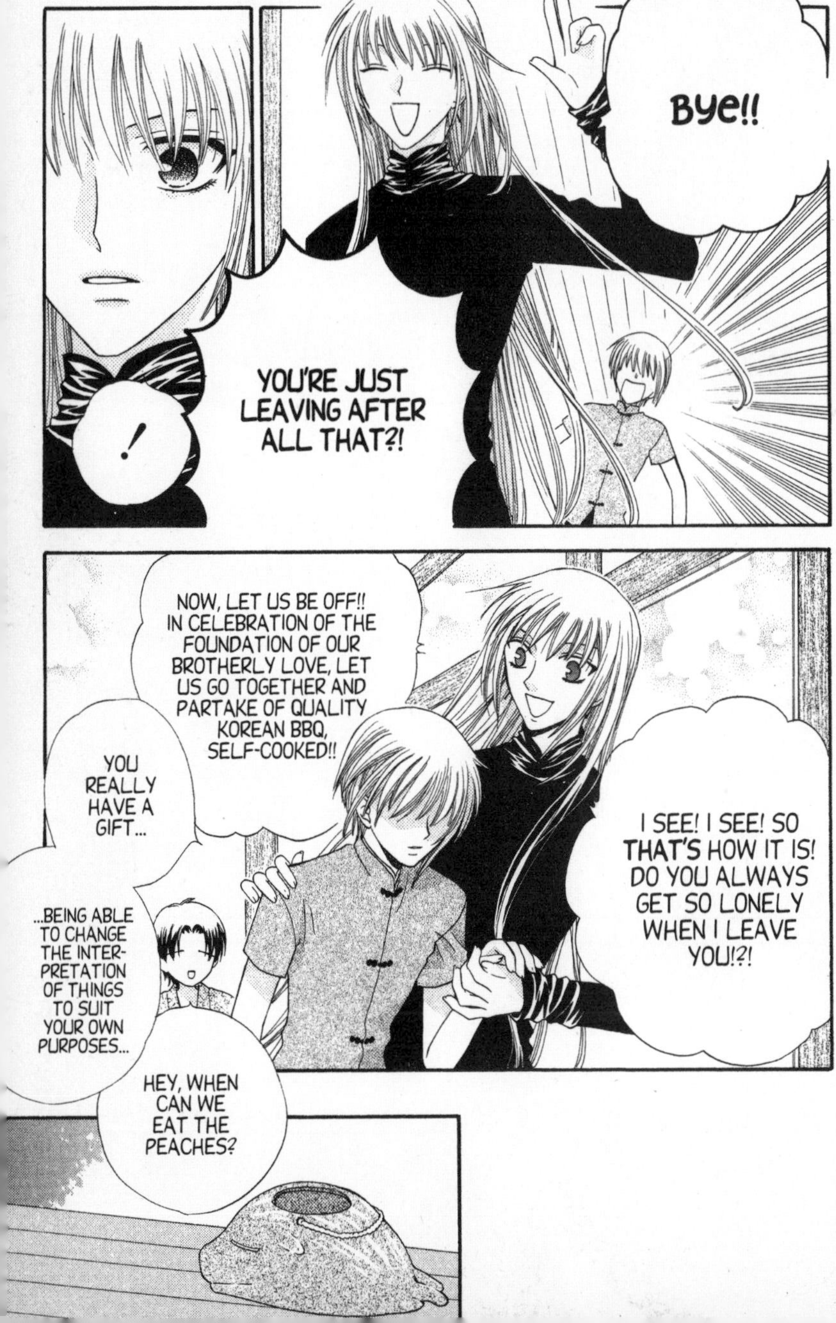
BYE!!
YOU'RE JUST LEAVING AFTER ALL THAT?!
!
I SEE! I SEE! SO THAT'S HOW IT IS! DO YOU ALWAYS GET SO LONELY WHEN I LEAVE YOU!?!
NOW, LET US BE OFF!! IN CELEBRATION OF THE FOUNDATION OF OUR BROTHERLY LOVE, LET US GO TOGETHER AND PARTAKE OF QUALITY KOREAN BBQ, SELF-COOKED!!
YOU REALLY HAVE A GIFT...
...BEING ABLE TO CHANGE THE INTER-PRETATION OF THINGS TO SUIT YOUR OWN PURPOSES...
HEY, WHEN CAN WE EAT THE PEACHES?

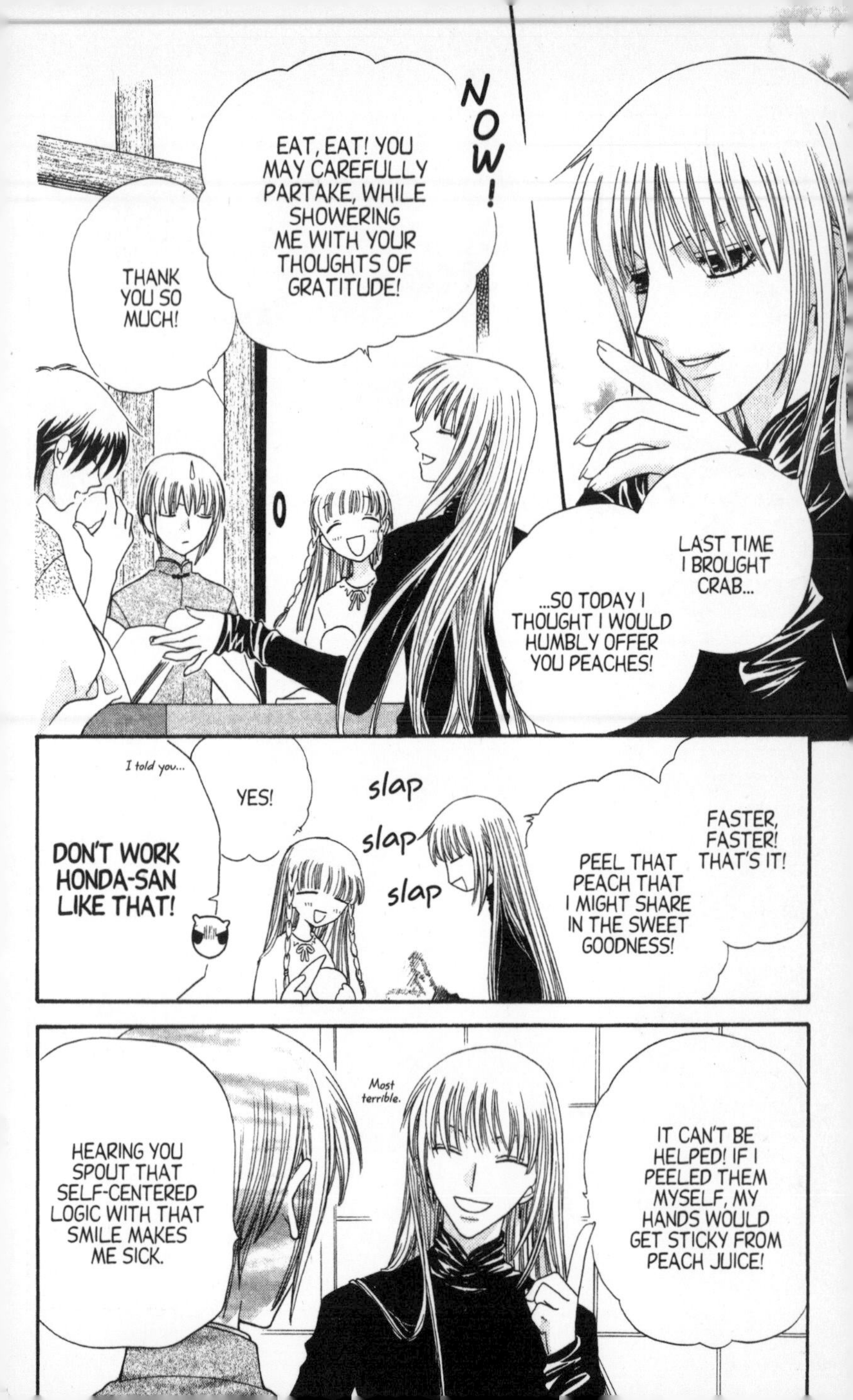
LAST TIME I BROUGHT CRAB...
...SO TODAY I THOUGHT I WOULD HUMBLY OFFER YOU PEACHES!
NOW!
EAT, EAT! YOU MAY CAREFULLY PARTAKE, WHILE SHOWERING ME WITH YOUR THOUGHTS OF GRATITUDE!
THANK YOU SO MUCH!
FASTER, FASTER! THAT'S IT!
PEEL THAT PEACH THAT I MIGHT SHARE IN THE SWEET GOODNESS!
slap
slap
slap
YES!
I told you...
DON'T WORK HONDA-SAN LIKE THAT!
IT CAN'T BE HELPED! IF I PEELED THEM MYSELF, MY HANDS WOULD GET STICKY FROM PEACH JUICE!
Most terrible.
HEARING YOU SPOUT THAT SELF-CENTERED LOGIC WITH THAT SMILE MAKES ME SICK.

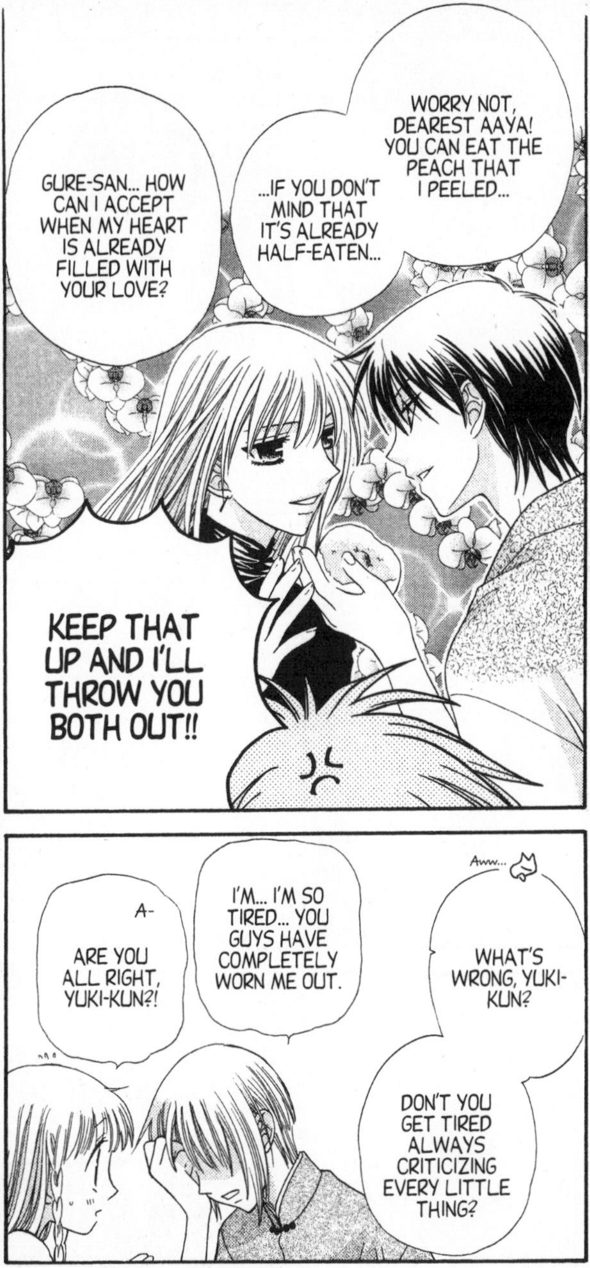
WORRY NOT, DEAREST AAYA! YOU CAN EAT THE PEACH THAT I PEELED...
...IF YOU DON'T MIND THAT IT'S ALREADY HALF-EATEN...
GURE-SAN... HOW CAN I ACCEPT WHEN MY HEART IS ALREADY FILLED WITH YOUR LOVE?
KEEP THAT UP AND I'LL THROW YOU BOTH OUT!!
Aww...
WHAT'S WRONG, YUKI-KUN?
DON'T YOU GET TIRED ALWAYS CRITICIZING EVERY LITTLE THING?
I'M... I'M SO TIRED... YOU GUYS HAVE COMPLETELY WORN ME OUT.
A-
ARE YOU ALL RIGHT, YUKI-KUN?!

Fruits Basket 8: Part 5

Continued...

I really liked the "Shadow Hearts" music, so I bought the soundtrack, too. (I know why...) I especially like the battle music. Now I even listen to it while I'm working. But, oh... that Judgment Ring theme goes around and around inside my head...

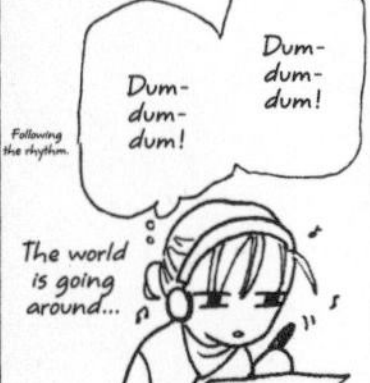
Dum-dum-dum!
Dum-dum-dum!
Following the rhythm.
The world is going around...

I was relieved when I beat Atman. I'm playing the sequel, too.

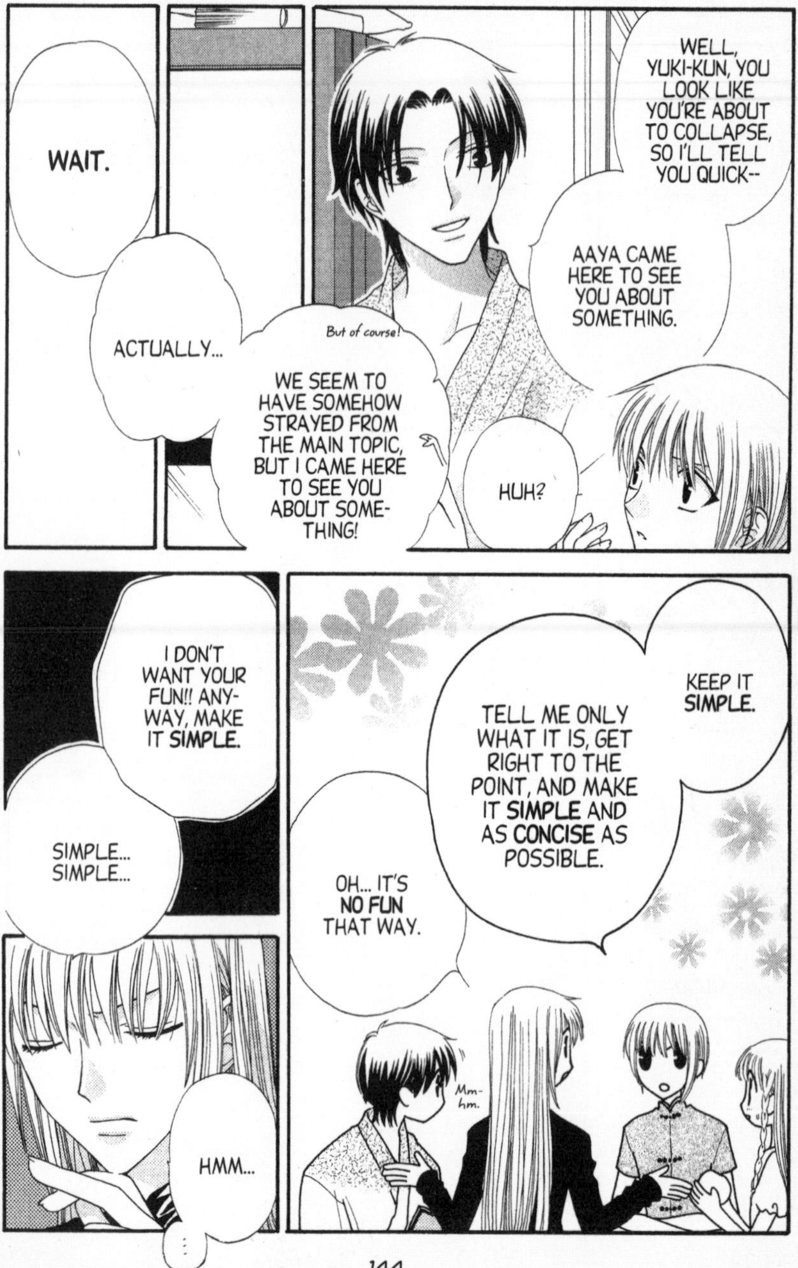
WELL, YUKI-KUN, YOU LOOK LIKE YOU'RE ABOUT TO COLLAPSE, SO I'LL TELL YOU QUICK--
AAYA CAME HERE TO SEE YOU ABOUT SOMETHING.
HUH?
But of course!
WE SEEM TO HAVE SOMEHOW STRAYED FROM THE MAIN TOPIC, BUT I CAME HERE TO SEE YOU ABOUT SOME-THING!
ACTUALLY...
WAIT.
KEEP IT SIMPLE.
TELL ME ONLY WHAT IT IS, GET RIGHT TO THE POINT, AND MAKE IT SIMPLE AND AS CONCISE AS POSSIBLE.
OH... IT'S NO FUN THAT WAY.
Mm-hm.
I DON'T WANT YOUR FUN!! ANY-WAY, MAKE IT SIMPLE.
SIMPLE... SIMPLE...
HMM...
...

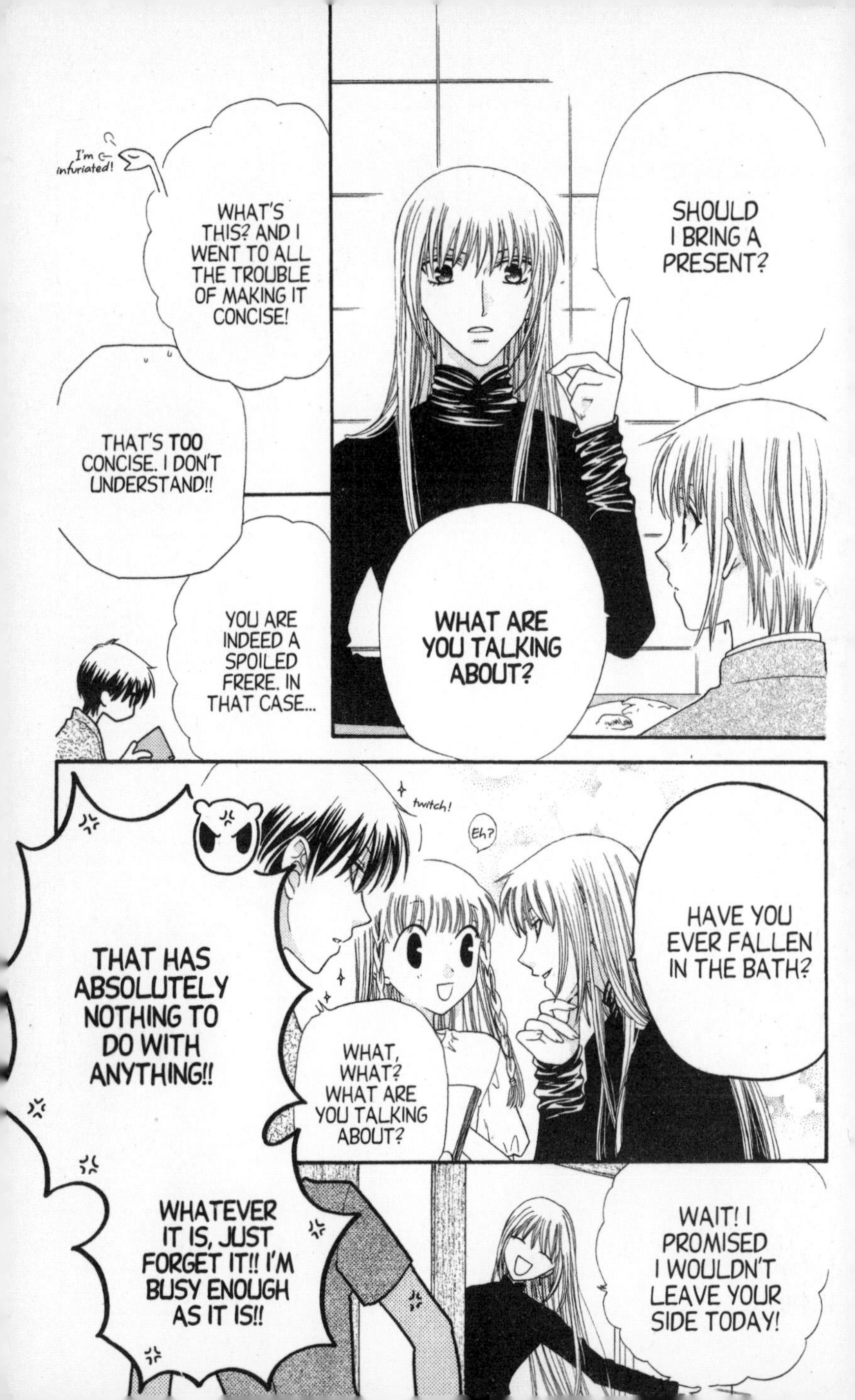

SHOULD I BRING A PRESENT?
WHAT ARE YOU TALKING ABOUT?
I'm infuriated!
WHAT'S THIS? AND I WENT TO ALL THE TROUBLE OF MAKING IT CONCISE!
THAT'S TOO CONCISE. I DON'T UNDERSTAND!!
YOU ARE INDEED A SPOILED FRERE. IN THAT CASE...
HAVE YOU EVER FALLEN IN THE BATH?
Eh?
WHAT, WHAT? WHAT ARE YOU TALKING ABOUT?
twitch!
THAT HAS ABSOLUTELY NOTHING TO DO WITH ANYTHING!!
WHATEVER IT IS, JUST FORGET IT!! I'M BUSY ENOUGH AS IT IS!!
WAIT! I PROMISED I WOULDN'T LEAVE YOUR SIDE TODAY!

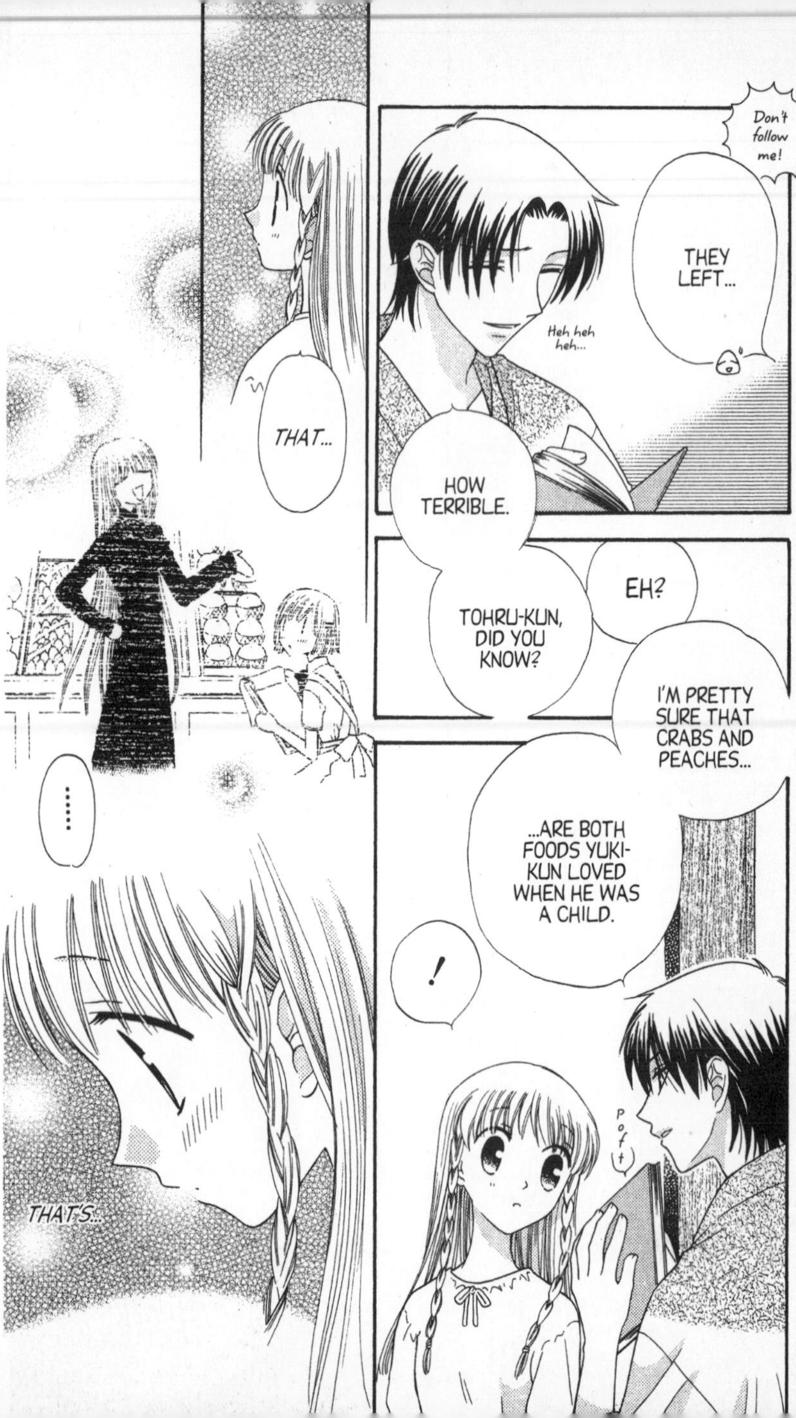
Don't follow me!
THEY LEFT...
Heh heh heh...
THAT...
HOW TERRIBLE.
EH?
TOHRU-KUN, DID YOU KNOW?
......
I'M PRETTY SURE THAT CRABS AND PEACHES...
...ARE BOTH FOODS YUKI-KUN LOVED WHEN HE WAS A CHILD.
!
Poft
THAT'S...

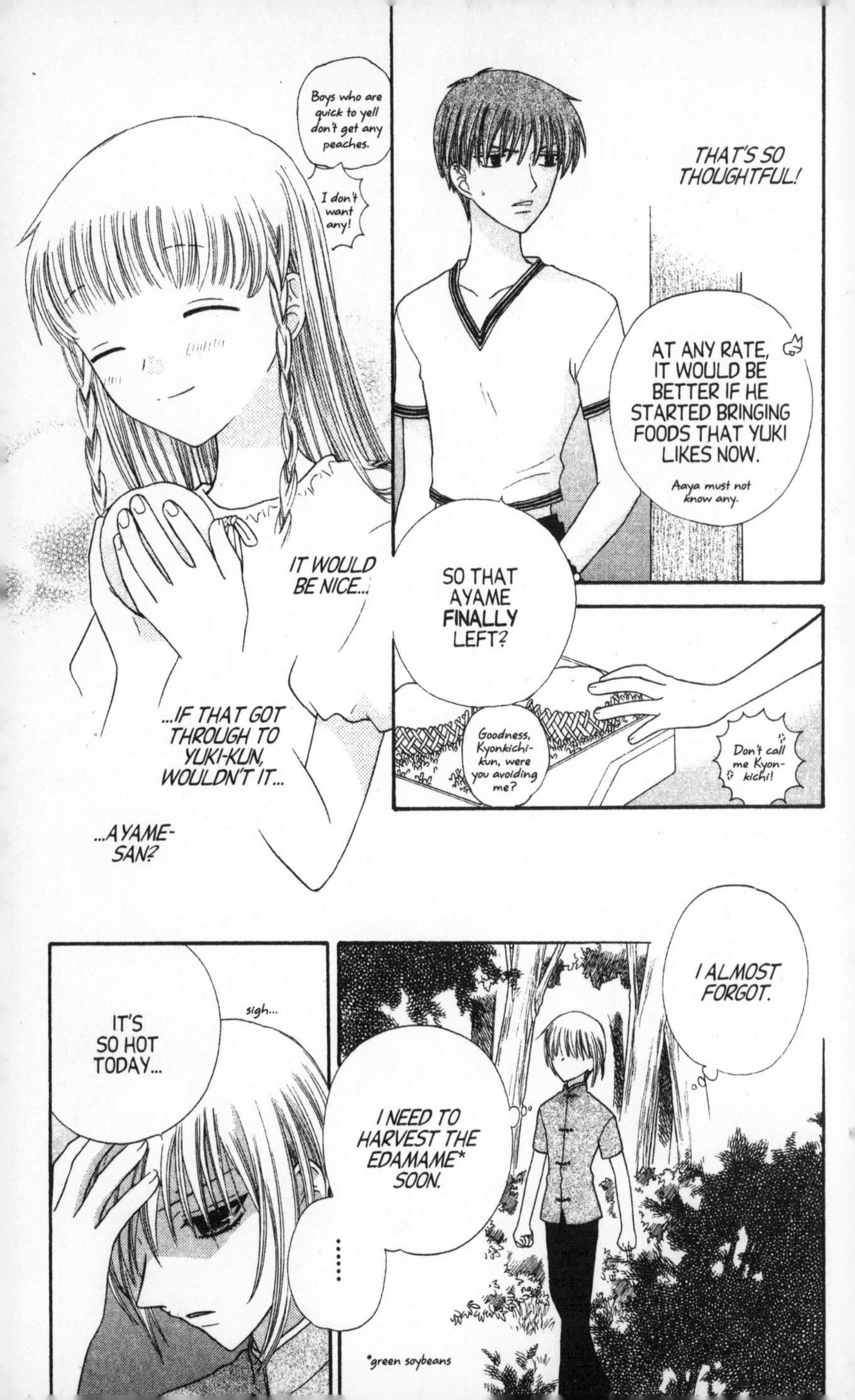
THAT'S SO THOUGHTFUL!
AT ANY RATE, IT WOULD BE BETTER IF HE STARTED BRINGING FOODS THAT YUKI LIKES NOW.
Aaya must not know any.
SO THAT AYAME FINALLY LEFT?
Don't call me Kyon-kichi!
Goodness, Kyonkichi-kun, were you avoiding me?
Boys who are quick to yell don't get any peaches.
I don't want any!
IT WOULD BE NICE...
...IF THAT GOT THROUGH TO YUKI-KUN, WOULDN'T IT...
...AYAME-SAN?
I ALMOST FORGOT.
I NEED TO HARVEST THE EDAMAME* SOON.
......
IT'S SO HOT TODAY...
sigh...
*green soybeans

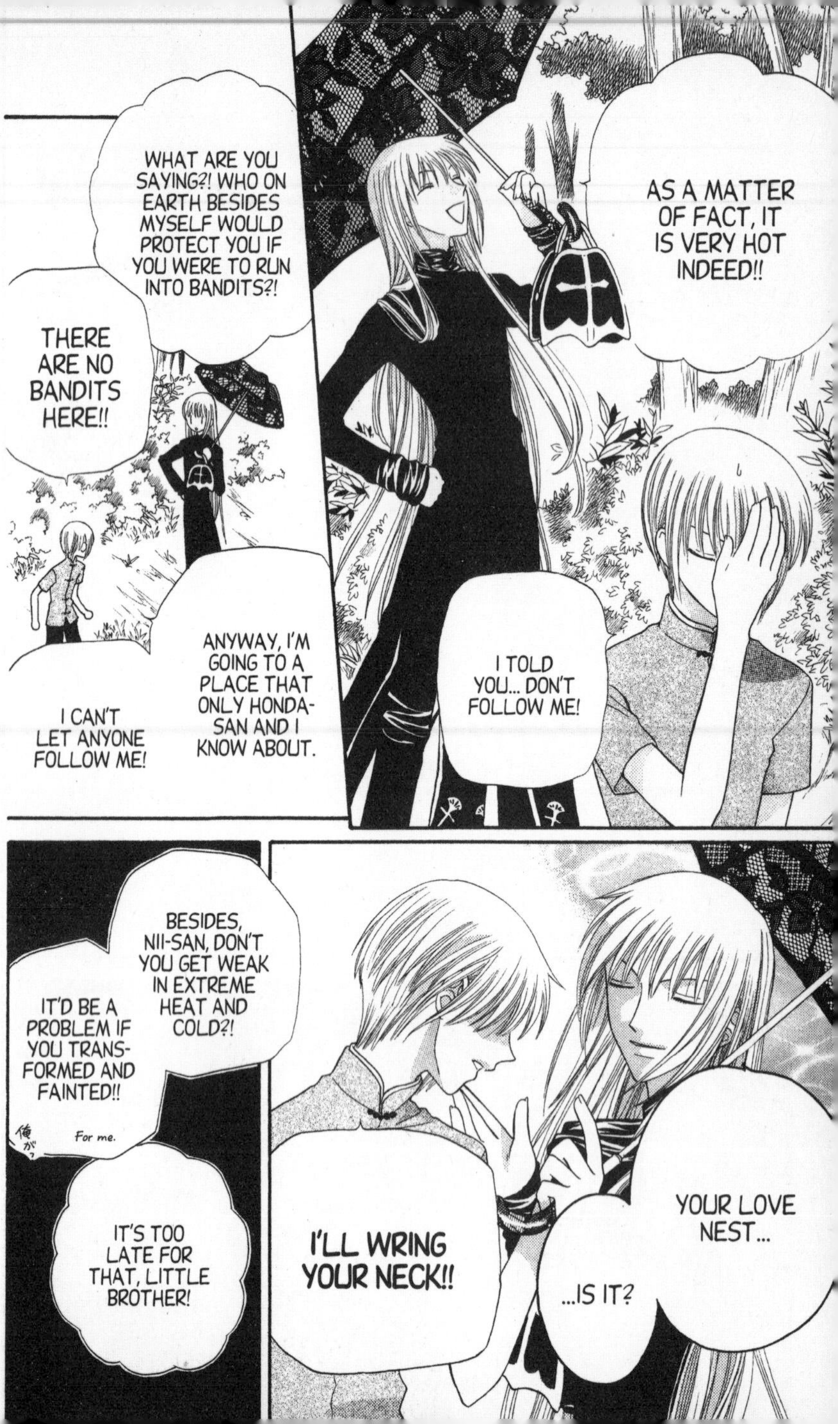
AS A MATTER OF FACT, IT IS VERY HOT INDEED!!
I TOLD YOU... DON'T FOLLOW ME!
WHAT ARE YOU SAYING?! WHO ON EARTH BESIDES MYSELF WOULD PROTECT YOU IF YOU WERE TO RUN INTO BANDITS?!
THERE ARE NO BANDITS HERE!!
ANYWAY, I'M GOING TO A PLACE THAT ONLY HONDA-SAN AND I KNOW ABOUT.
I CAN'T LET ANYONE FOLLOW ME!
YOUR LOVE NEST...
...IS IT?
I'LL WRING YOUR NECK!!
BESIDES, NII-SAN, DON'T YOU GET WEAK IN EXTREME HEAT AND COLD?!
IT'D BE A PROBLEM IF YOU TRANS-FORMED AND FAINTED!!
俺が
For me.
IT'S TOO LATE FOR THAT, LITTLE BROTHER!

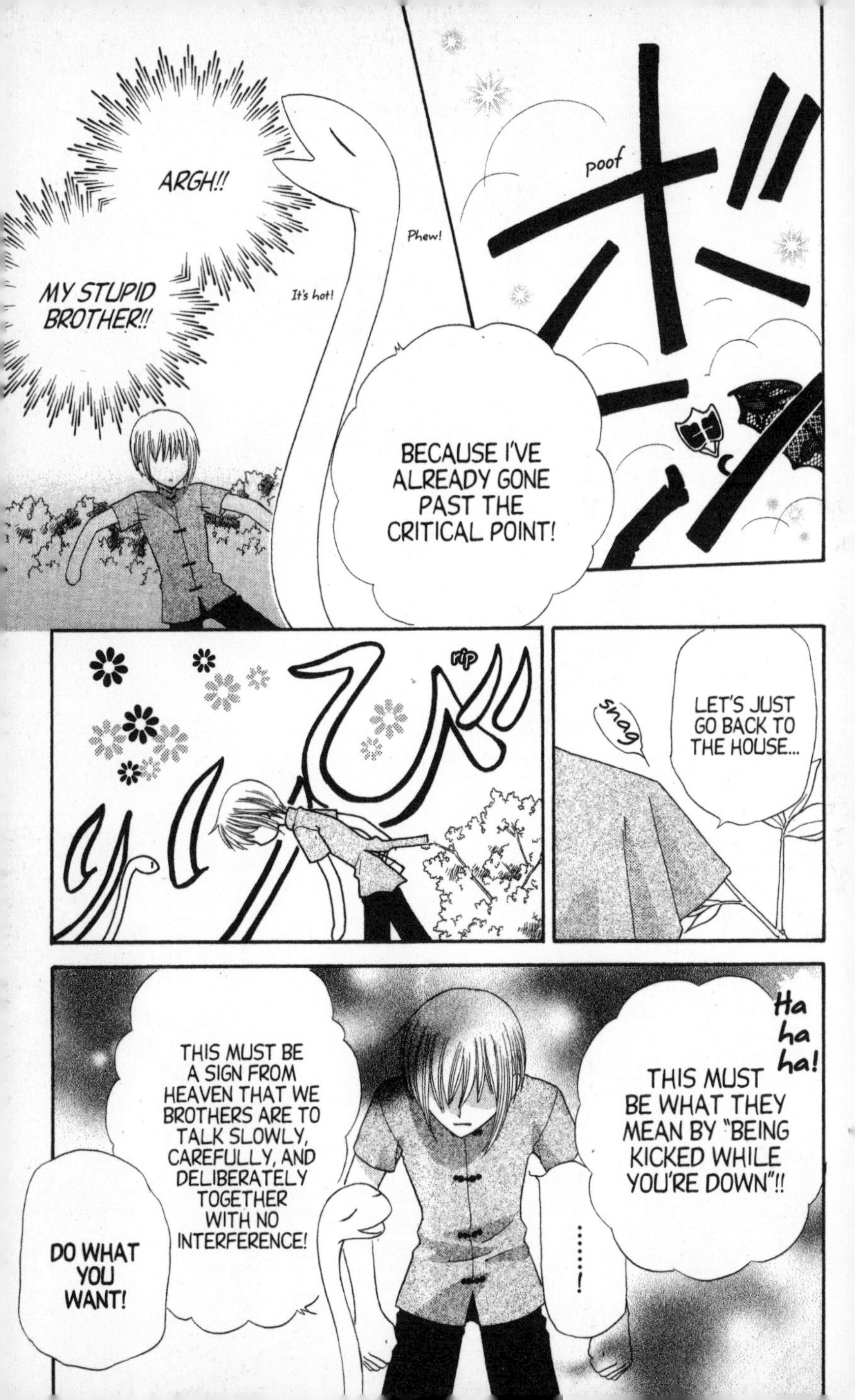
poof
BECAUSE I'VE ALREADY GONE PAST THE CRITICAL POINT!
Phew!
It's hot!
ARGH!!
MY STUPID BROTHER!!
snag
LET'S JUST GO BACK TO THE HOUSE...
rip
Ha ha ha!
THIS MUST BE WHAT THEY MEAN BY "BEING KICKED WHILE YOU'RE DOWN"!!
......!
THIS MUST BE A SIGN FROM HEAVEN THAT WE BROTHERS ARE TO TALK SLOWLY, CAREFULLY, AND DELIBERATELY TOGETHER WITH NO INTERFERENCE!
DO WHAT YOU WANT!

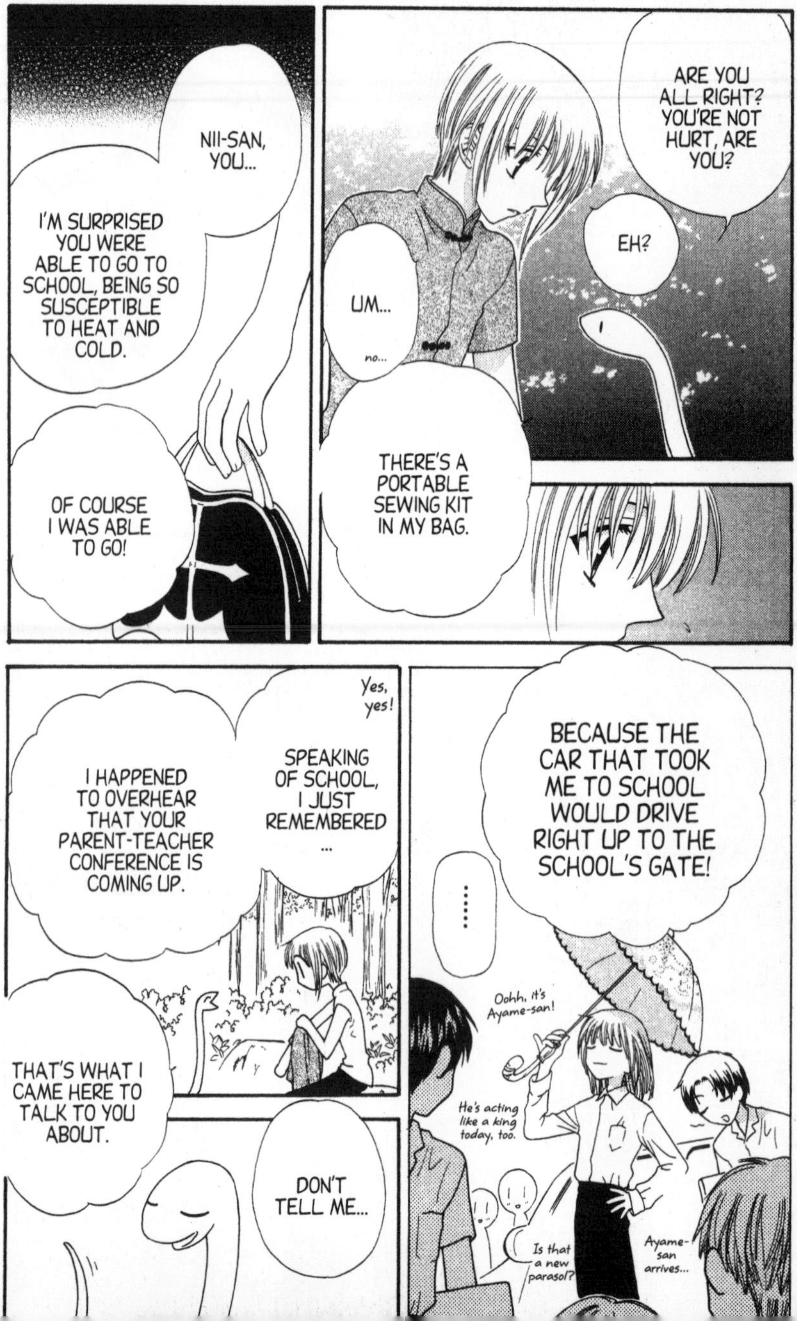
ARE YOU ALL RIGHT? YOU'RE NOT HURT, ARE YOU?
EH?
UM...
no...
THERE'S A PORTABLE SEWING KIT IN MY BAG.
NII-SAN, YOU...
I'M SURPRISED YOU WERE ABLE TO GO TO SCHOOL, BEING SO SUSCEPTIBLE TO HEAT AND COLD.
OF COURSE I WAS ABLE TO GO!
BECAUSE THE CAR THAT TOOK ME TO SCHOOL WOULD DRIVE RIGHT UP TO THE SCHOOL'S GATE!
......
Oohh, it's Ayame-san!
He's acting like a king today, too.
Ayame-san arrives...
Is that a new parasol?
Yes, yes!
SPEAKING OF SCHOOL, I JUST REMEMBERED ...
I HAPPENED TO OVERHEAR THAT YOUR PARENT-TEACHER CONFERENCE IS COMING UP.
THAT'S WHAT I CAME HERE TO TALK TO YOU ABOUT.
DON'T TELL ME...

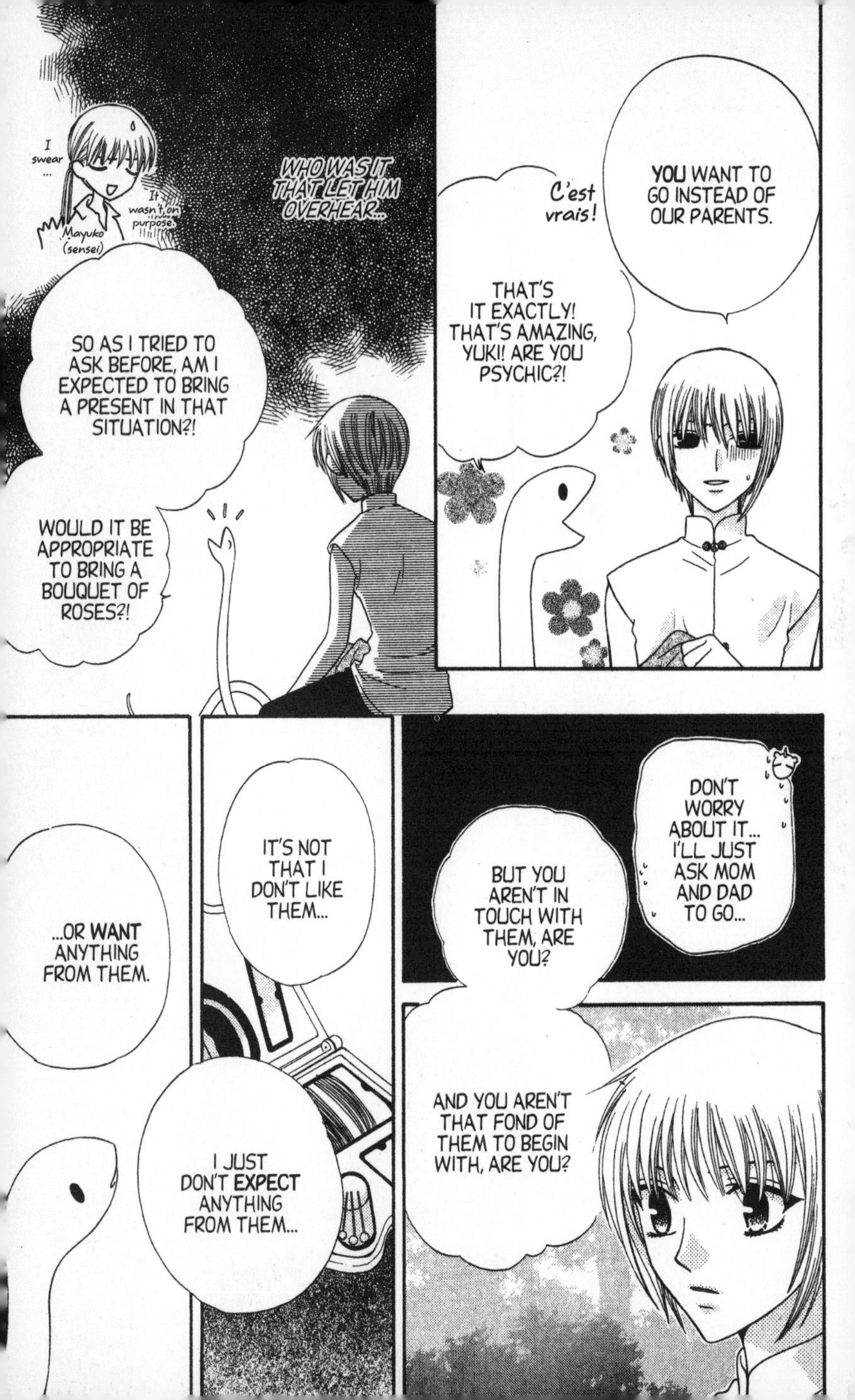
YOU WANT TO GO INSTEAD OF OUR PARENTS.
C'est vrais!
THAT'S IT EXACTLY! THAT'S AMAZING, YUKI! ARE YOU PSYCHIC?!
WHO WAS IT THAT LET HIM OVERHEAR...
I swear...
It wasn't on purpose.
Mayuko (sensei)
SO AS I TRIED TO ASK BEFORE, AM I EXPECTED TO BRING A PRESENT IN THAT SITUATION?!
WOULD IT BE APPROPRIATE TO BRING A BOUQUET OF ROSES?!
DON'T WORRY ABOUT IT... I'LL JUST ASK MOM AND DAD TO GO...
BUT YOU AREN'T IN TOUCH WITH THEM, ARE YOU?
AND YOU AREN'T THAT FOND OF THEM TO BEGIN WITH, ARE YOU?
IT'S NOT THAT I DON'T LIKE THEM...
I JUST DON'T EXPECT ANYTHING FROM THEM...
...OR WANT ANYTHING FROM THEM.

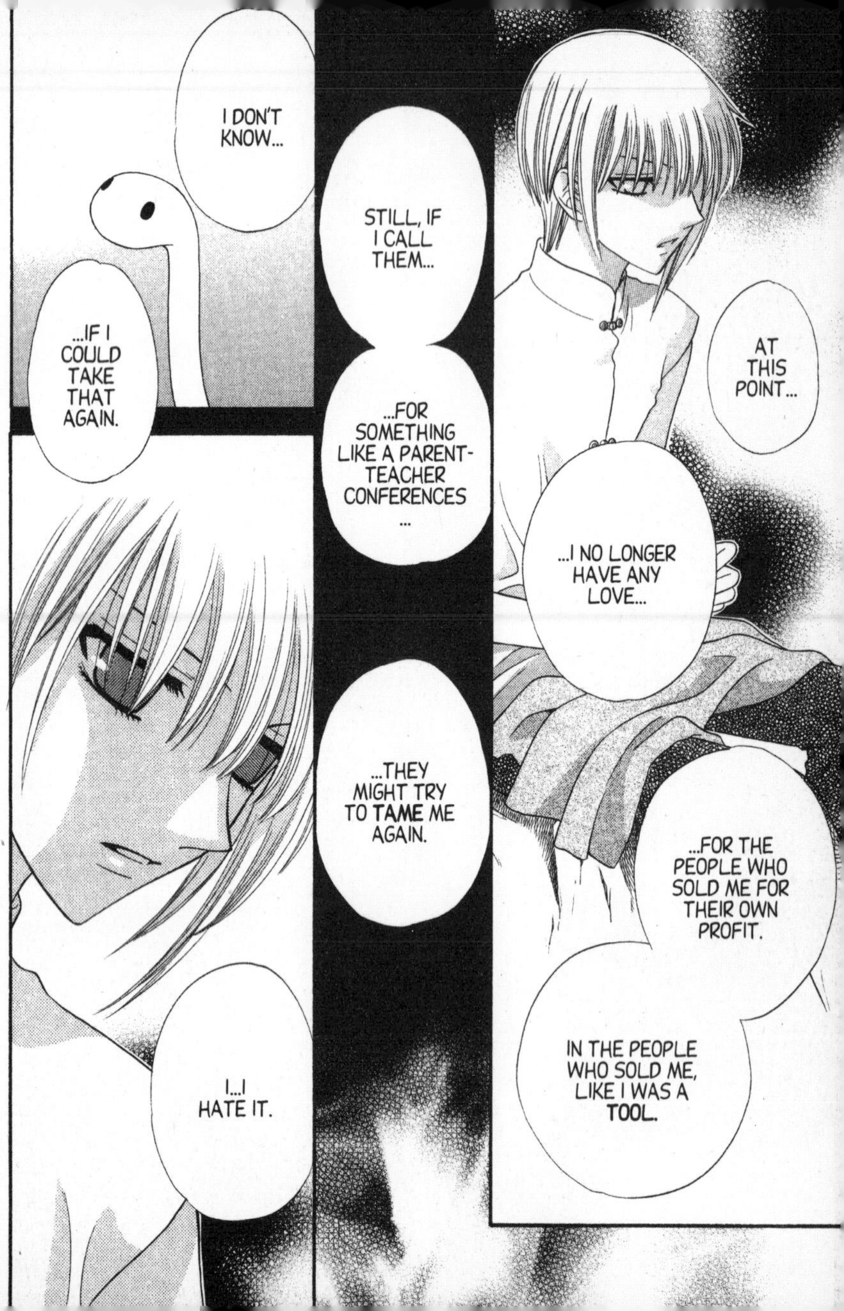
AT THIS POINT...
...I NO LONGER HAVE ANY LOVE...
...FOR THE PEOPLE WHO SOLD ME FOR THEIR OWN PROFIT.
IN THE PEOPLE WHO SOLD ME, LIKE I WAS A **TOOL.**
STILL, IF I CALL THEM...
...FOR SOMETHING LIKE A PARENT-TEACHER CONFERENCES ...
...THEY MIGHT TRY TO **TAME** ME AGAIN.
I DON'T KNOW...
...IF I COULD TAKE THAT AGAIN.
I...I HATE IT.

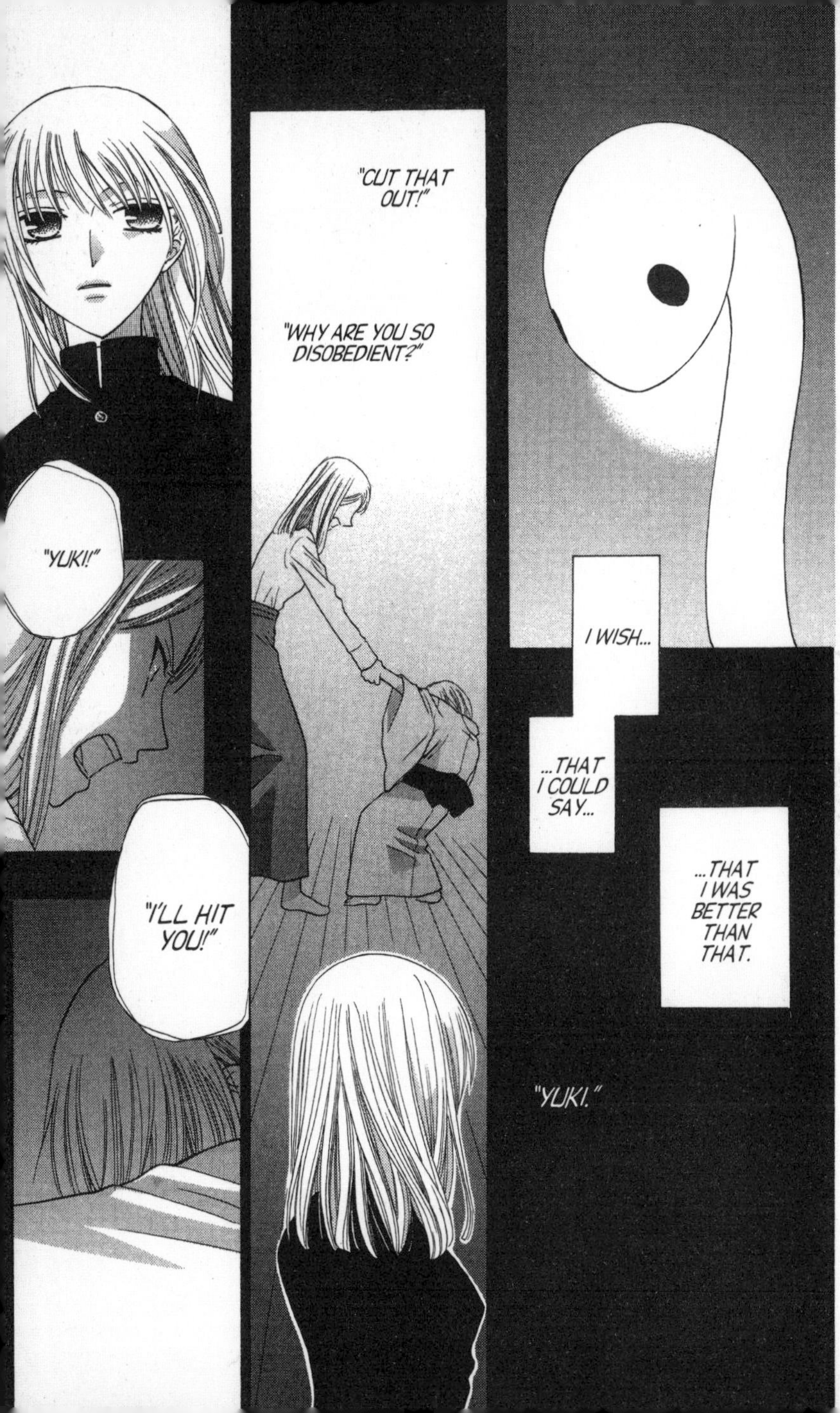
I WISH...
...THAT I COULD SAY...
...THAT I WAS BETTER THAN THAT.
"YUKI."
"CUT THAT OUT!"
"WHY ARE YOU SO DISOBEDIENT?"
"YUKI!"
"I'LL HIT YOU!"

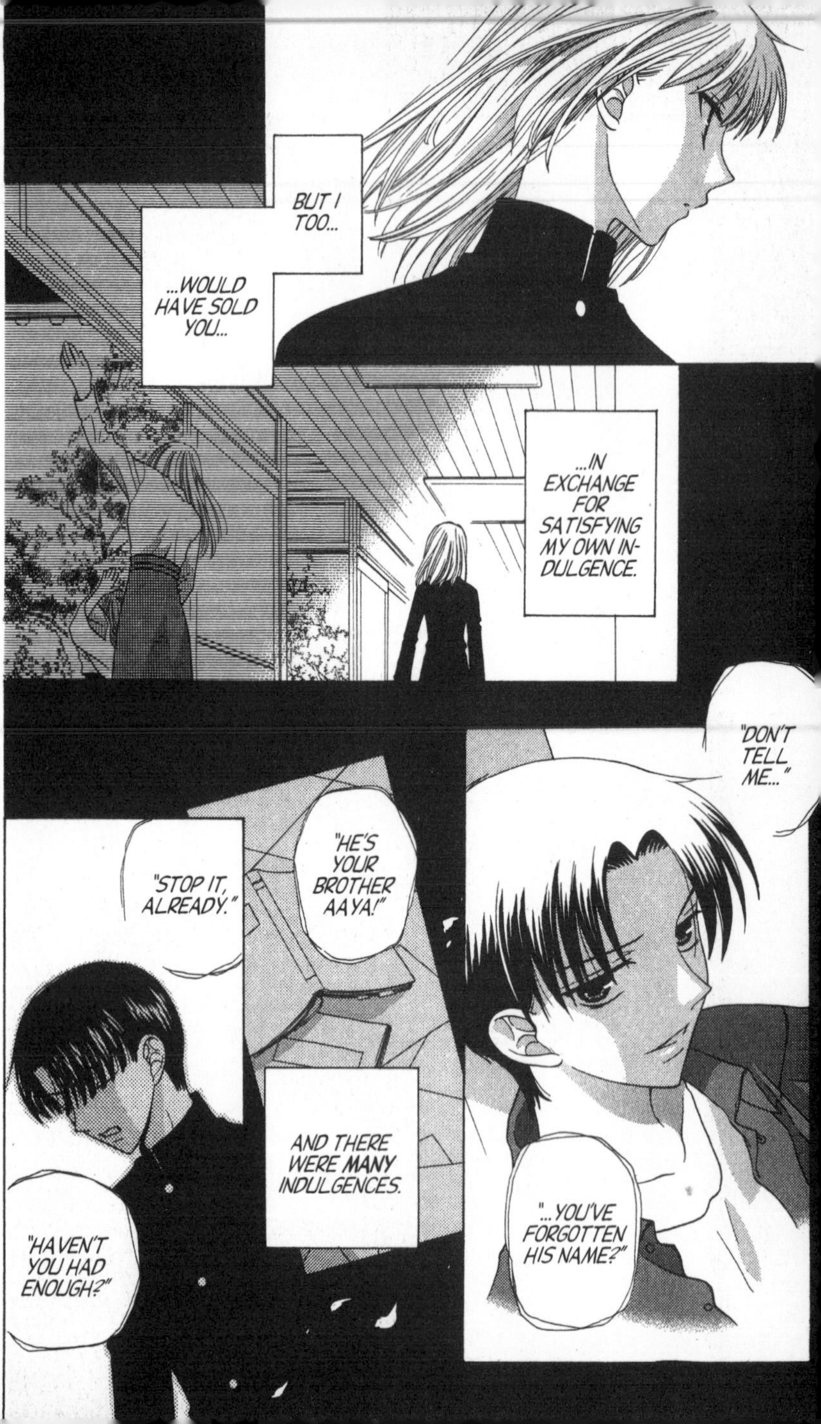
BUT I TOO...
...WOULD HAVE SOLD YOU...
...IN EXCHANGE FOR SATISFYING MY OWN IN-DULGENCE.
"DON'T TELL ME..."
"...YOU'VE FORGOTTEN HIS NAME?"
"HE'S YOUR BROTHER AAYA!"
AND THERE WERE MANY INDULGENCES.
"STOP IT, ALREADY."
"HAVEN'T YOU HAD ENOUGH?"

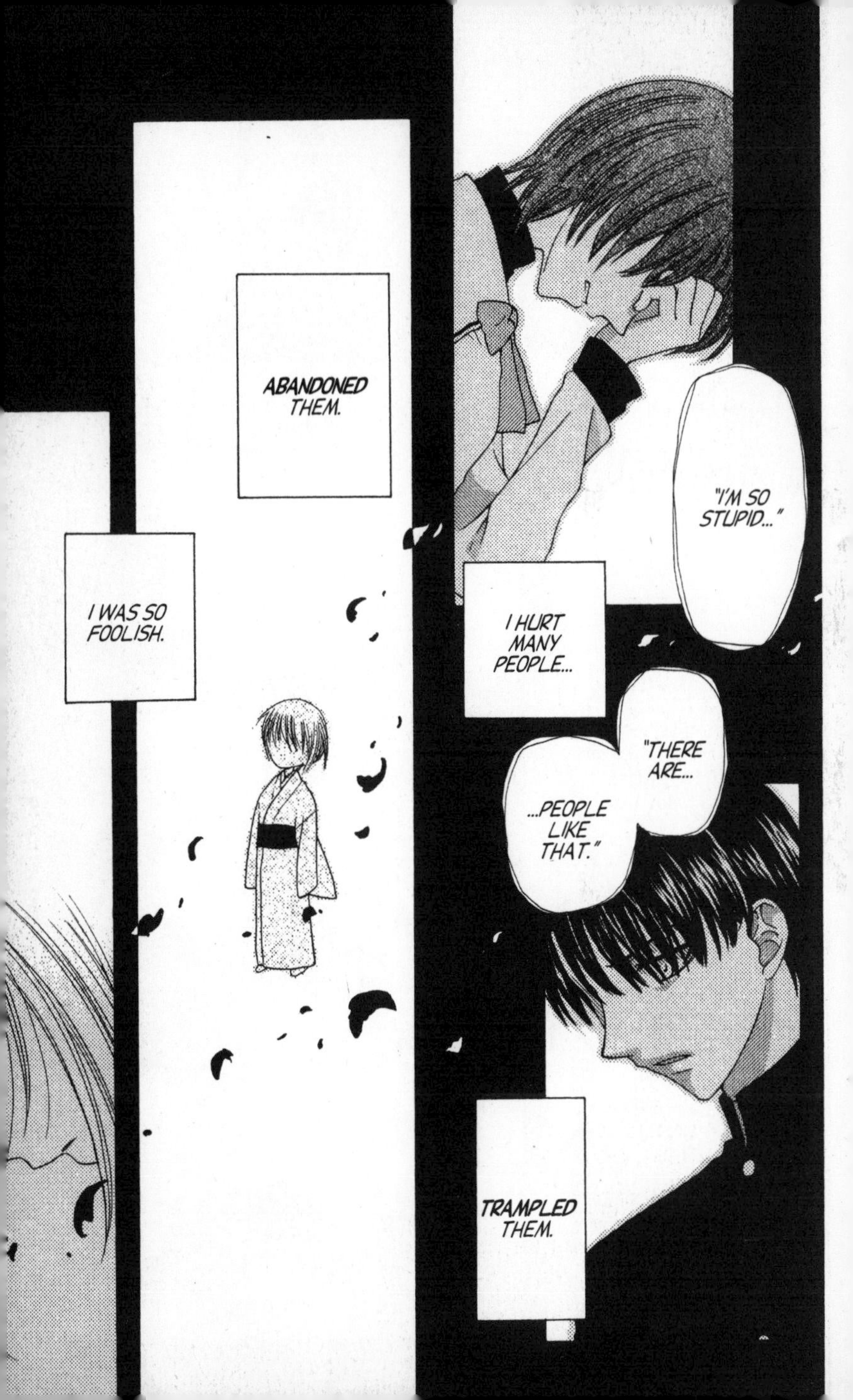
"I'M SO STUPID..."
I HURT MANY PEOPLE...
"THERE ARE...
...PEOPLE LIKE THAT."
TRAMPLED THEM.
ABANDONED THEM.
I WAS SO FOOLISH.

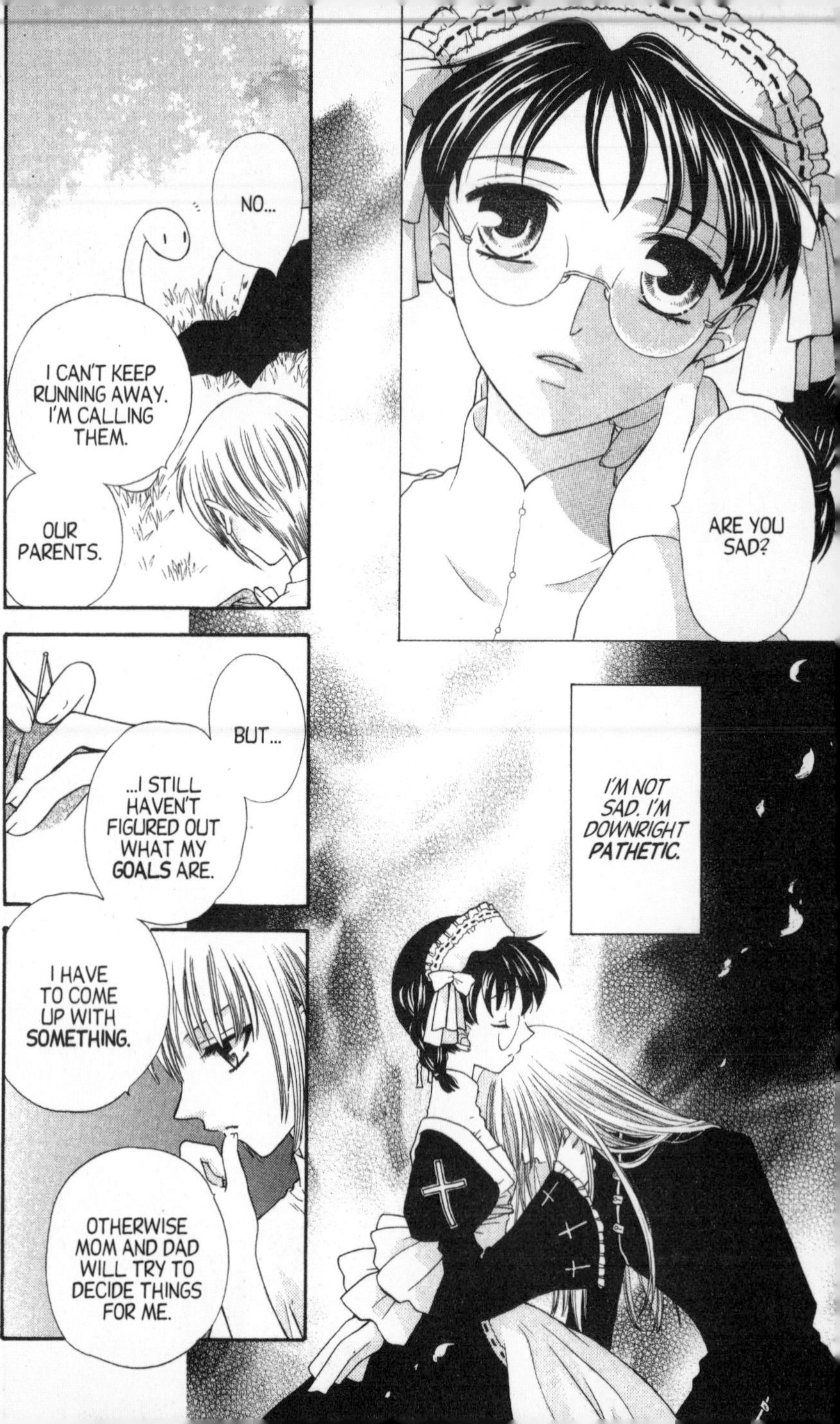
ARE YOU SAD?
NO...
I CAN'T KEEP RUNNING AWAY. I'M CALLING THEM.
OUR PARENTS.
I'M NOT SAD. I'M DOWNRIGHT **PATHETIC.**
BUT...
...I STILL HAVEN'T FIGURED OUT WHAT MY **GOALS** ARE.
I HAVE TO COME UP WITH **SOMETHING.**
OTHERWISE MOM AND DAD WILL TRY TO DECIDE THINGS FOR ME.

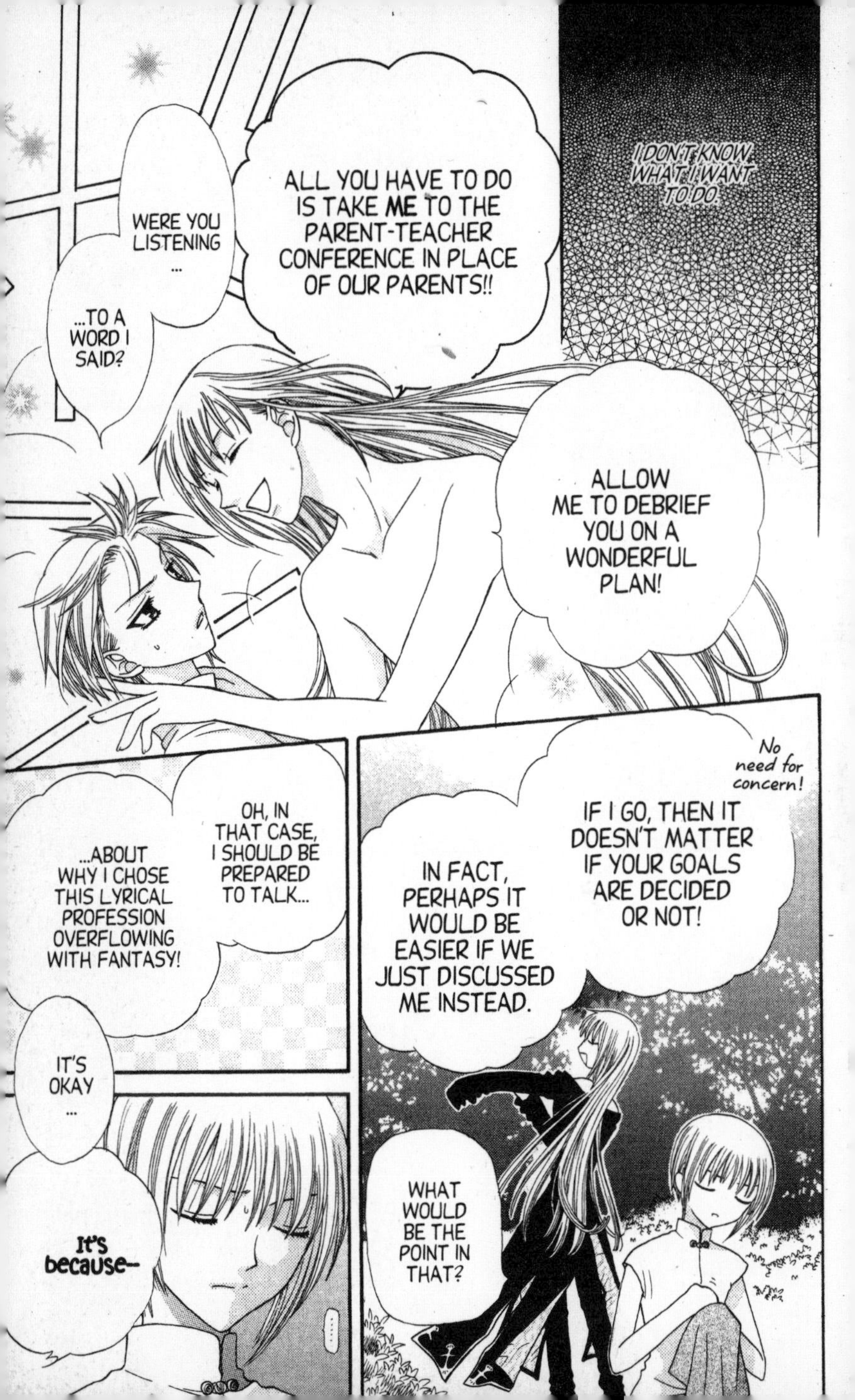
I DON'T KNOW WHAT I WANT TO DO.
ALL YOU HAVE TO DO IS TAKE ME TO THE PARENT-TEACHER CONFERENCE IN PLACE OF OUR PARENTS!!
WERE YOU LISTENING ...
...TO A WORD I SAID?
ALLOW ME TO DEBRIEF YOU ON A WONDERFUL PLAN!
No need for concern!
IF I GO, THEN IT DOESN'T MATTER IF YOUR GOALS ARE DECIDED OR NOT!
IN FACT, PERHAPS IT WOULD BE EASIER IF WE JUST DISCUSSED ME INSTEAD.
WHAT WOULD BE THE POINT IN THAT?
OH, IN THAT CASE, I SHOULD BE PREPARED TO TALK...
...ABOUT WHY I CHOSE THIS LYRICAL PROFESSION OVERFLOWING WITH FANTASY!
IT'S OKAY ...
It's because--
......

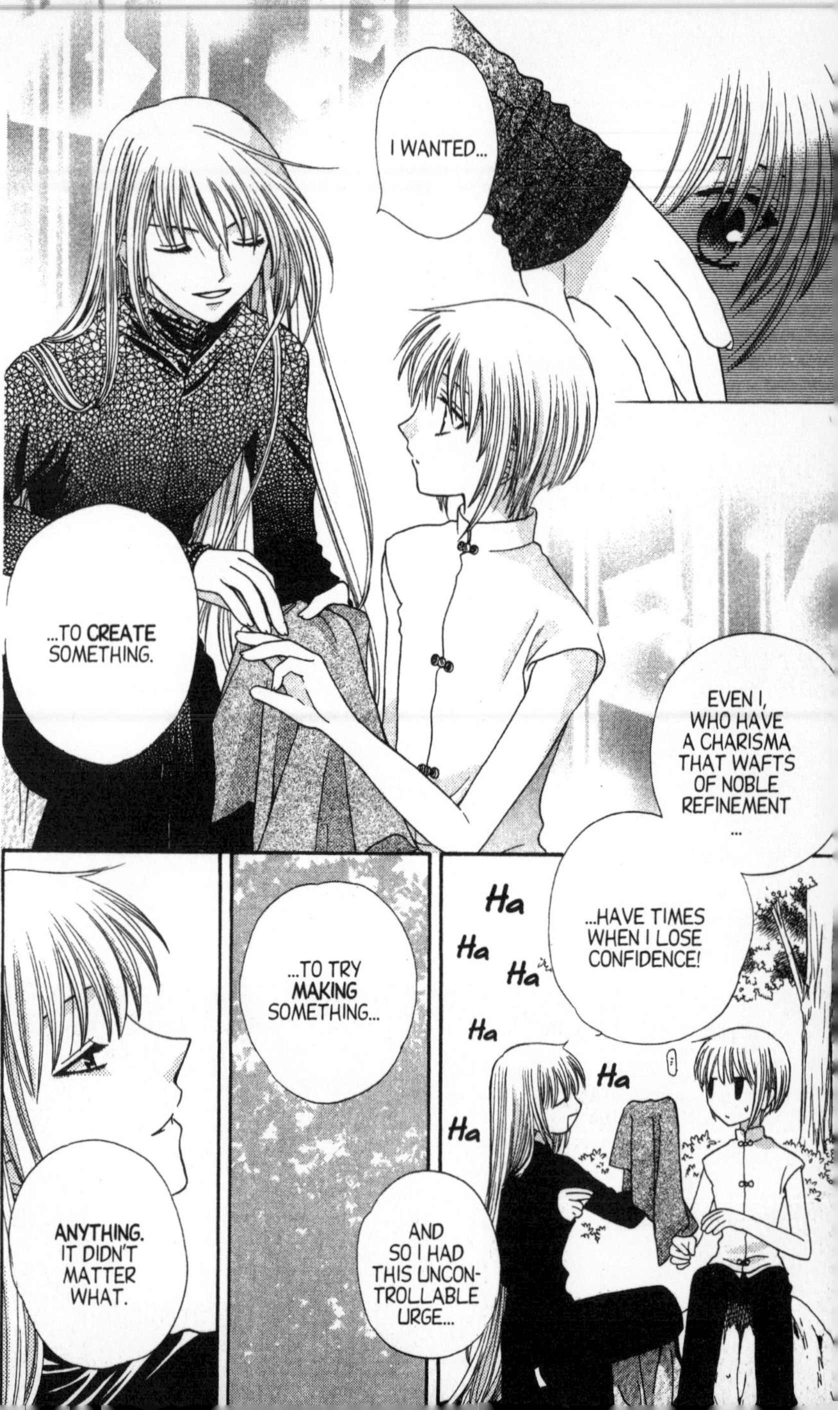
I WANTED...
...TO CREATE SOMETHING.
EVEN I, WHO HAVE A CHARISMA THAT WAFTS OF NOBLE REFINEMENT ...
...HAVE TIMES WHEN I LOSE CONFIDENCE!
Ha Ha Ha Ha Ha Ha
AND SO I HAD THIS UNCON-TROLLABLE URGE...
...TO TRY MAKING SOMETHING...
ANYTHING. IT DIDN'T MATTER WHAT.

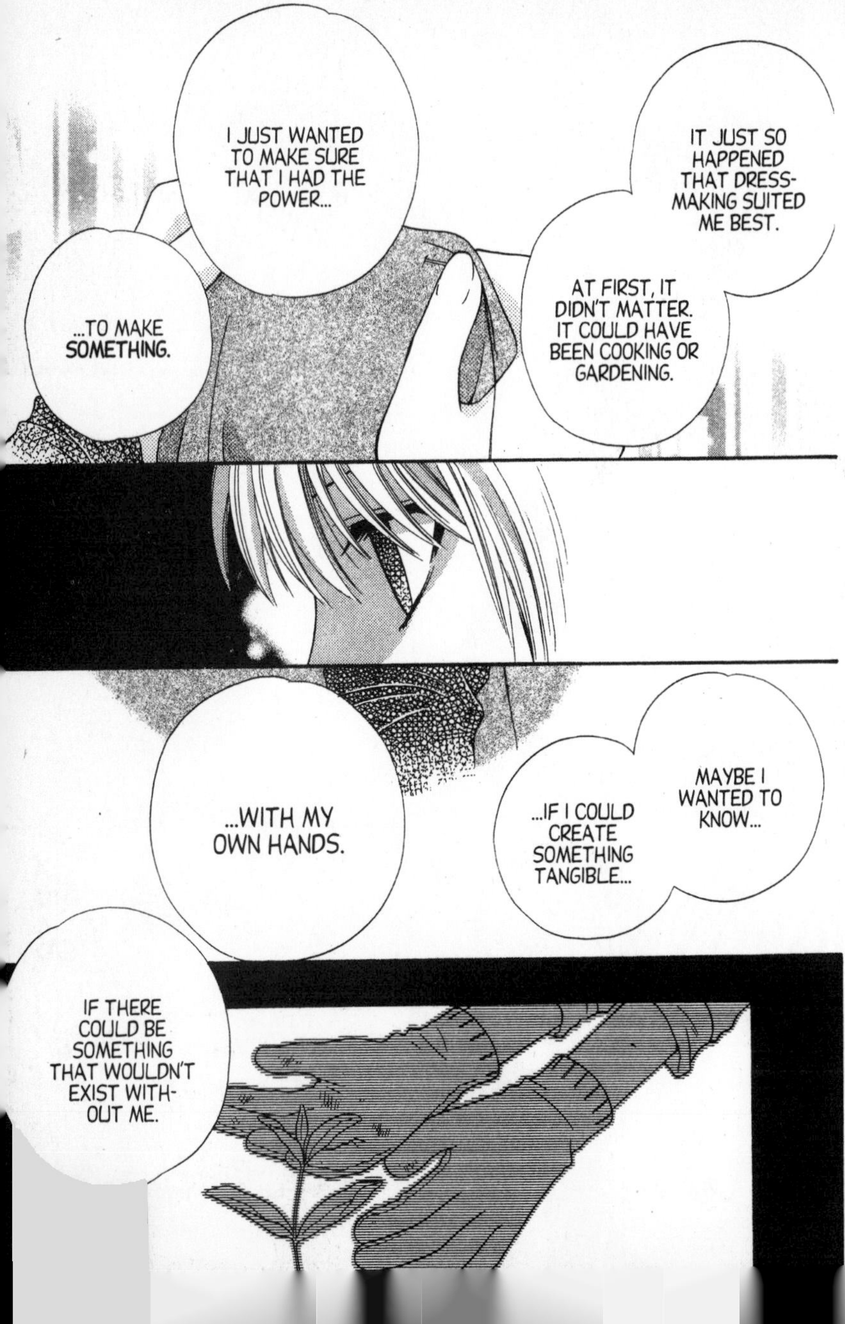
IT JUST SO HAPPENED THAT DRESS-MAKING SUITED ME BEST.
AT FIRST, IT DIDN'T MATTER. IT COULD HAVE BEEN COOKING OR GARDENING.
I JUST WANTED TO MAKE SURE THAT I HAD THE POWER...
...TO MAKE SOMETHING.
MAYBE I WANTED TO KNOW...
...IF I COULD CREATE SOMETHING TANGIBLE...
...WITH MY OWN HANDS.
IF THERE COULD BE SOMETHING THAT WOULDN'T EXIST WITH-OUT ME.

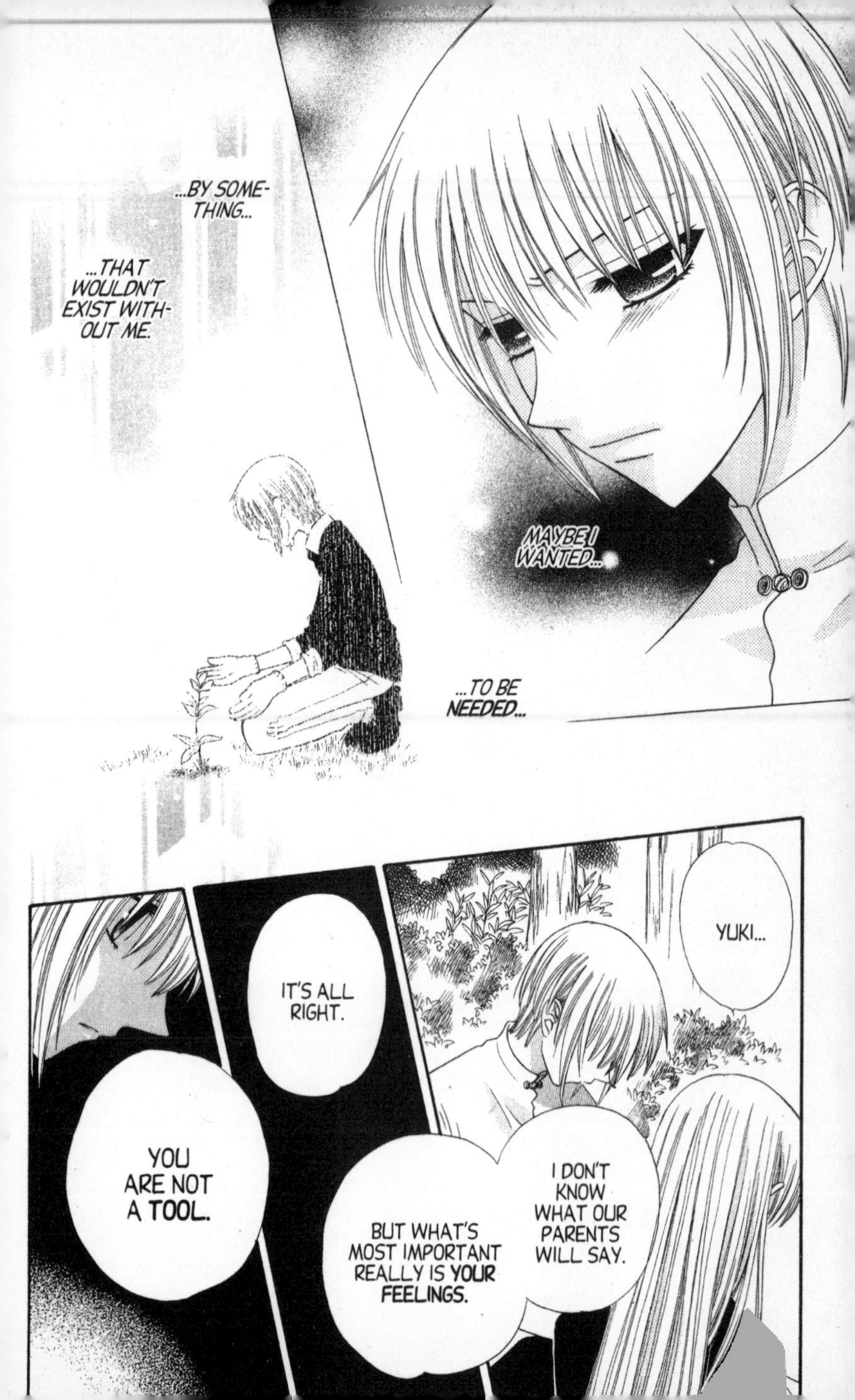
MAYBE I WANTED...
...TO BE NEEDED...
...BY SOME-THING...
...THAT WOULDN'T EXIST WITH-OUT ME.
YUKI...
I DON'T KNOW WHAT OUR PARENTS WILL SAY.
BUT WHAT'S MOST IMPORTANT REALLY IS **YOUR** FEELINGS.
IT'S ALL RIGHT.
YOU ARE NOT A **TOOL**.

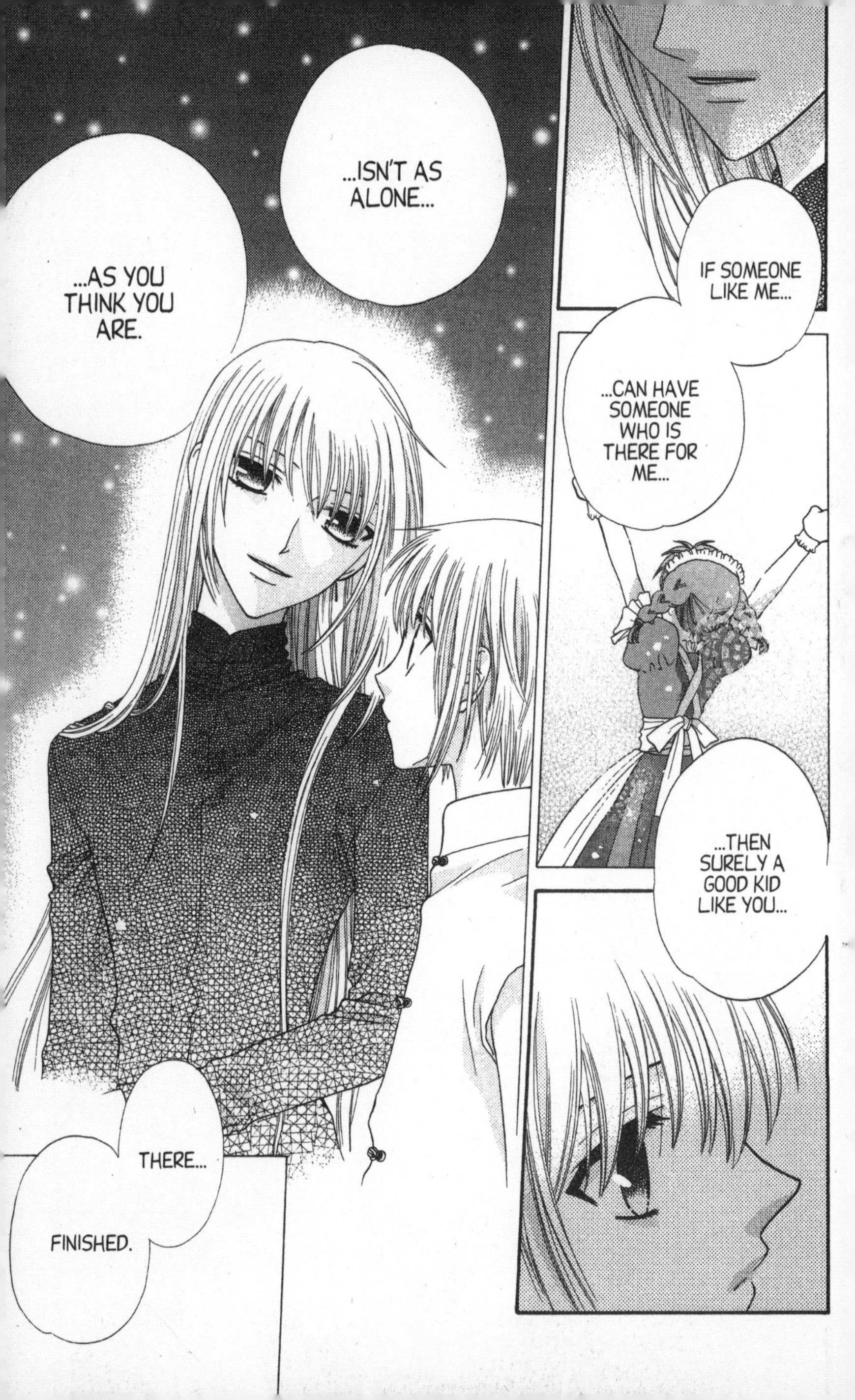
IF SOMEONE LIKE ME...
...CAN HAVE SOMEONE WHO IS THERE FOR ME...
...THEN SURELY A GOOD KID LIKE YOU...
...ISN'T AS ALONE...
...AS YOU THINK YOU ARE.
THERE...
FINISHED.

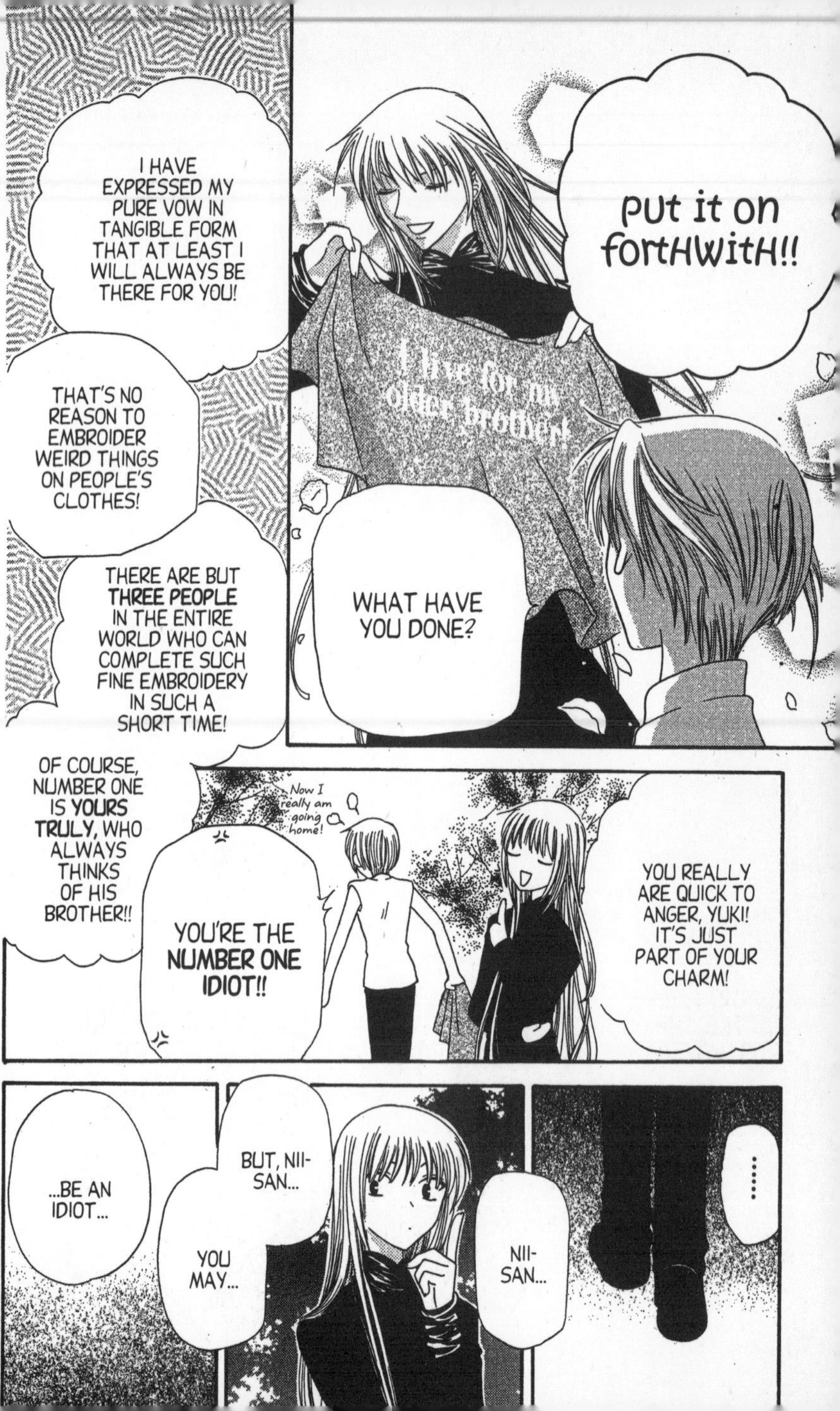
PUT IT ON FORTHWITH!!
I live for my older brother!
WHAT HAVE YOU DONE?
I HAVE EXPRESSED MY PURE VOW IN TANGIBLE FORM THAT AT LEAST I WILL ALWAYS BE THERE FOR YOU!
THAT'S NO REASON TO EMBROIDER WEIRD THINGS ON PEOPLE'S CLOTHES!
THERE ARE BUT **THREE PEOPLE** IN THE ENTIRE WORLD WHO CAN COMPLETE SUCH FINE EMBROIDERY IN SUCH A SHORT TIME!
OF COURSE, NUMBER ONE IS **YOURS TRULY,** WHO ALWAYS THINKS OF HIS BROTHER!!
YOU'RE THE **NUMBER ONE IDIOT!!**
YOU REALLY ARE QUICK TO ANGER, YUKI! IT'S JUST PART OF YOUR CHARM!
Now I really am going home!
......
NII-SAN...
BUT, NII-SAN...
YOU MAY...
...BE AN IDIOT...

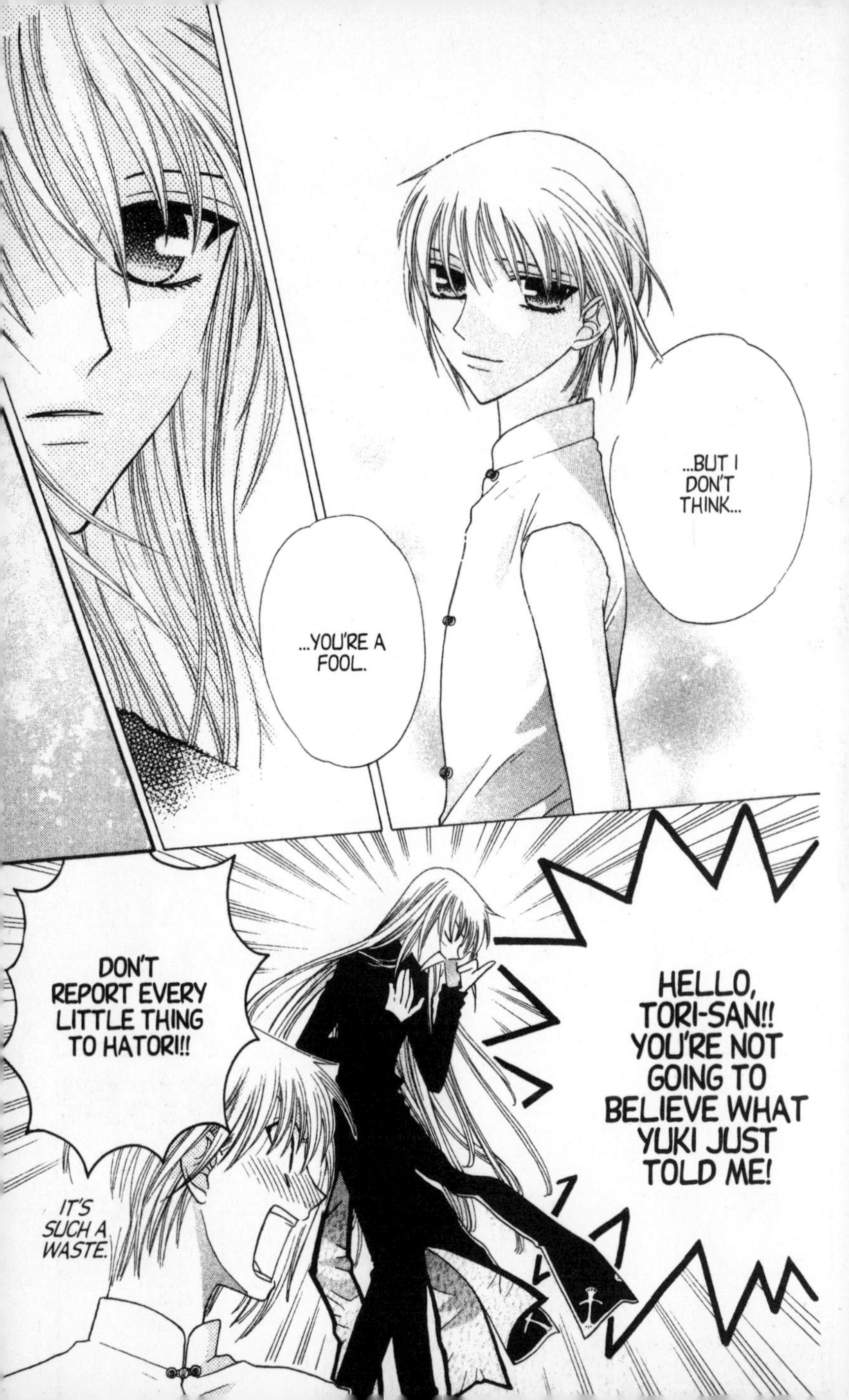
...BUT I DON'T THINK...
...YOU'RE A FOOL.
HELLO, TORI-SAN!! YOU'RE NOT GOING TO BELIEVE WHAT YUKI JUST TOLD ME!
DON'T REPORT EVERY LITTLE THING TO HATORI!!
IT'S SUCH A WASTE.

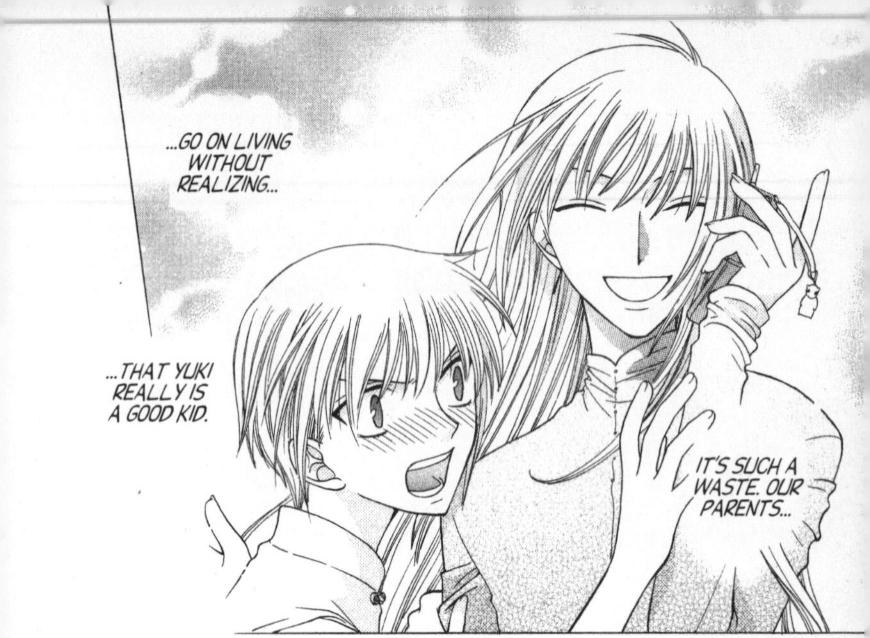
IT'S SUCH A WASTE. OUR PARENTS...
...GO ON LIVING WITHOUT REALIZING...
...THAT YUKI REALLY IS A GOOD KID.

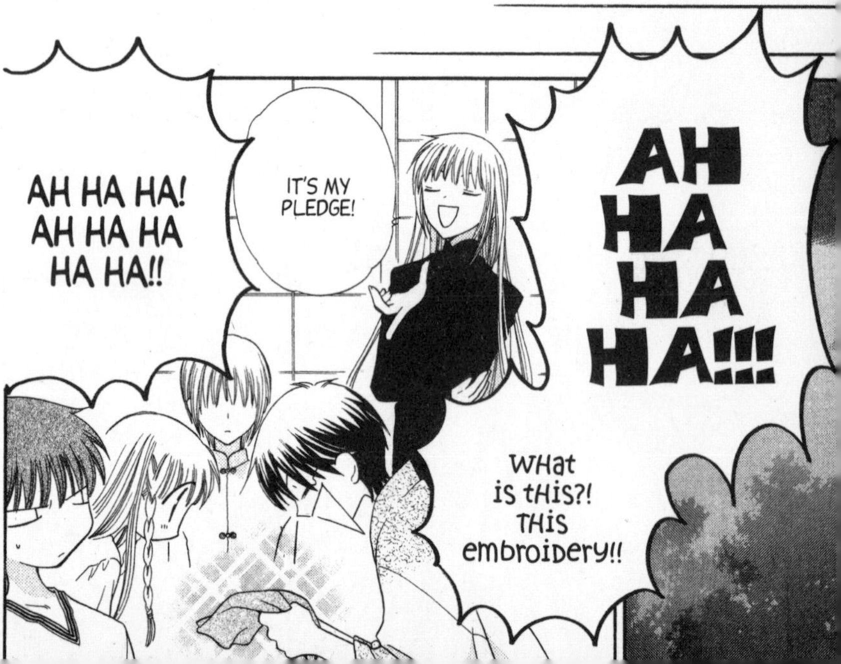
AH HA HA HA HA!!!
IT'S MY PLEDGE!
AH HA HA! AH HA HA HA HA!!
WHAT IS THIS?! THIS EMBROIDERY!!

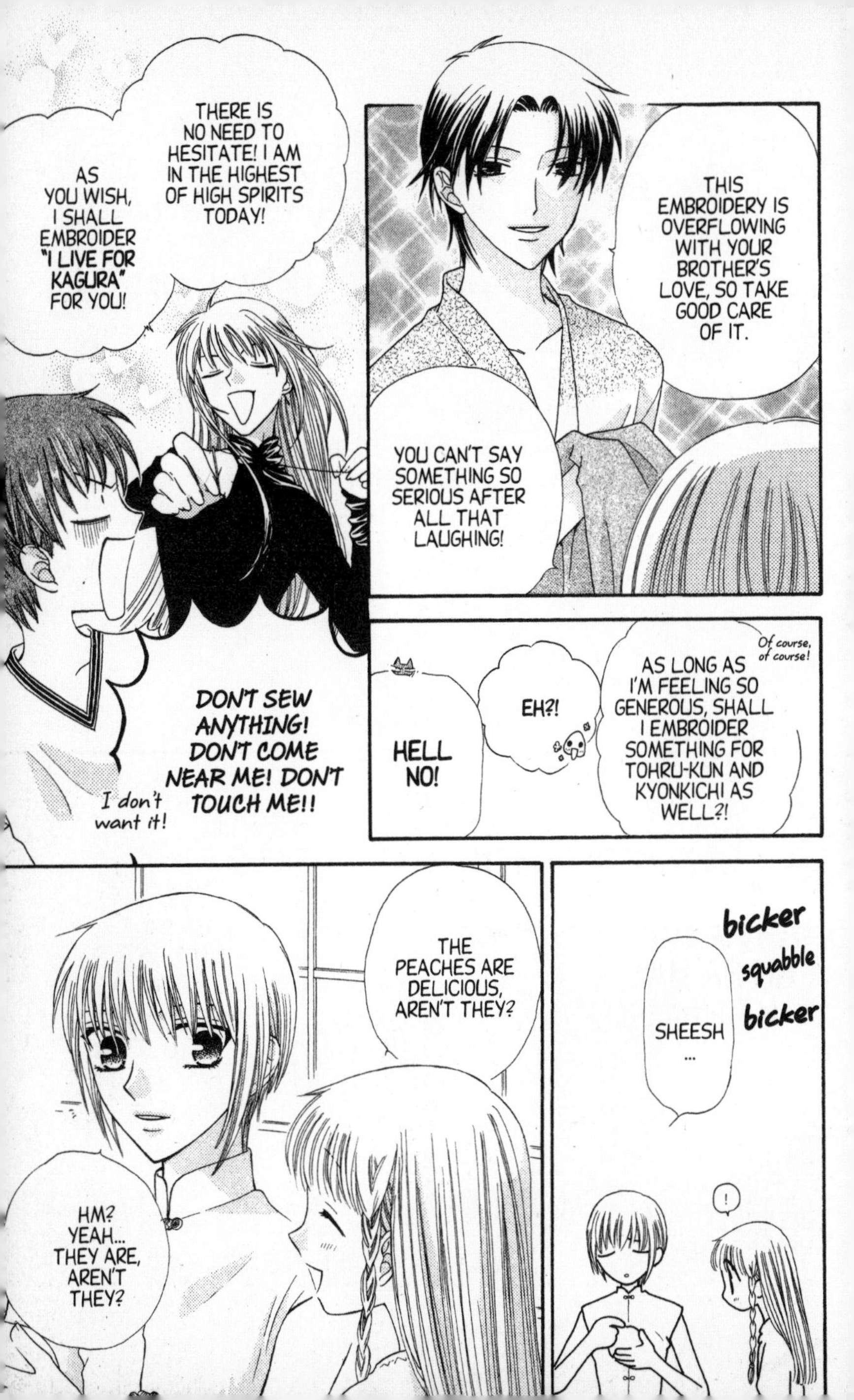
THIS EMBROIDERY IS OVERFLOWING WITH YOUR BROTHER'S LOVE, SO TAKE GOOD CARE OF IT.
YOU CAN'T SAY SOMETHING SO SERIOUS AFTER ALL THAT LAUGHING!
Of course, of course!
AS LONG AS I'M FEELING SO GENEROUS, SHALL I EMBROIDER SOMETHING FOR TOHRU-KUN AND KYONKICHI AS WELL?!
EH?!
HELL NO!
THERE IS NO NEED TO HESITATE! I AM IN THE HIGHEST OF HIGH SPIRITS TODAY!
AS YOU WISH, I SHALL EMBROIDER "I LIVE FOR KAGURA" FOR YOU!
DON'T SEW ANYTHING! DON'T COME NEAR ME! DON'T TOUCH ME!!
I don't want it!
bicker
squabble
bicker
SHEESH...
!
THE PEACHES ARE DELICIOUS, AREN'T THEY?
HM? YEAH... THEY ARE, AREN'T THEY?

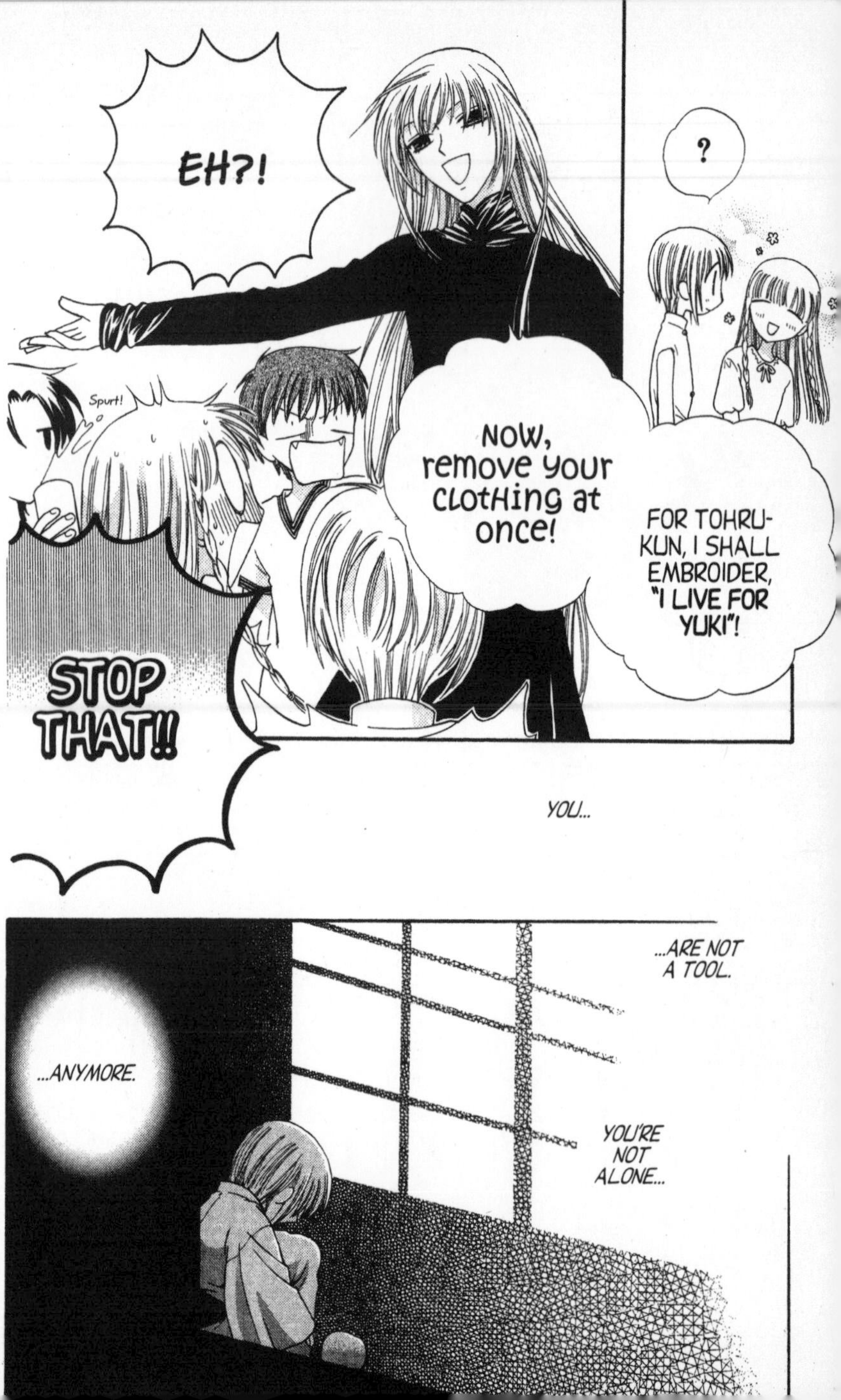
?
NOW, remove your clothing at once!
FOR TOHRU-KUN, I SHALL EMBROIDER, "I LIVE FOR YUKI"!
EH?!
Spurt!
STOP THAT!!
YOU...
...ARE NOT A TOOL.
YOU'RE NOT ALONE...
...ANYMORE.

Chapter 48

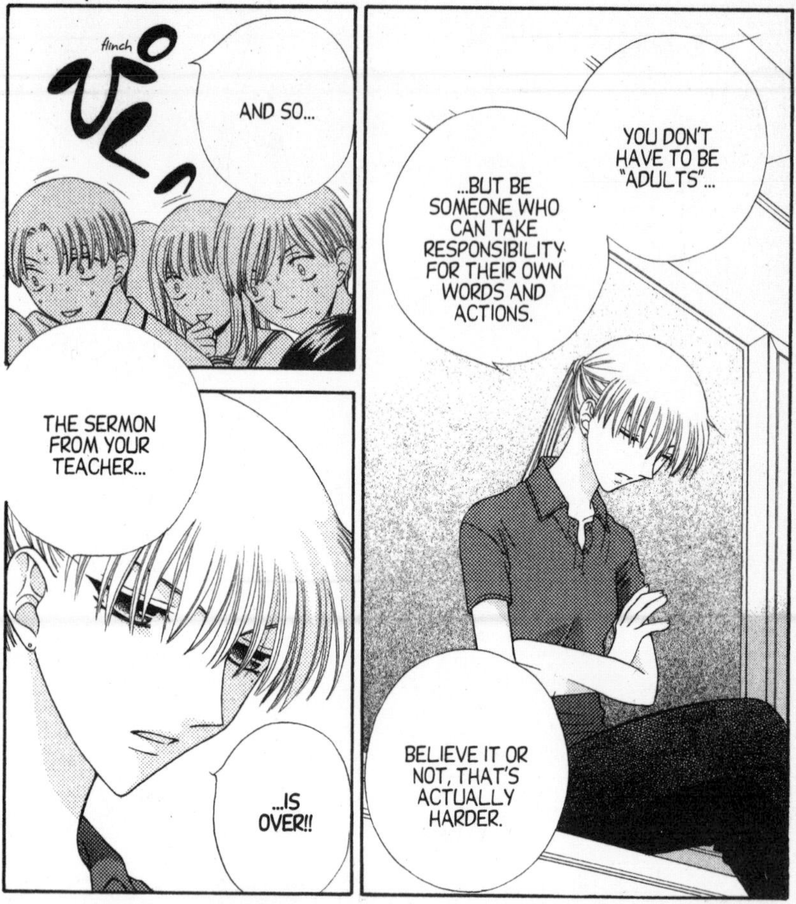
YOU DON'T HAVE TO BE "ADULTS"...
...BUT BE SOMEONE WHO CAN TAKE RESPONSIBILITY FOR THEIR OWN WORDS AND ACTIONS.
BELIEVE IT OR NOT, THAT'S ACTUALLY HARDER.
flinch
AND SO...
THE SERMON FROM YOUR TEACHER...
...IS OVER!!

UL-SPE BLAH, BLAH, BLAH 5

While I drew Kyo saying, "Why are you so scared?" I kept thinking, "Why aren't **you** scared?" Haunted houses are **really scary!** They're no good. I can't stand them.

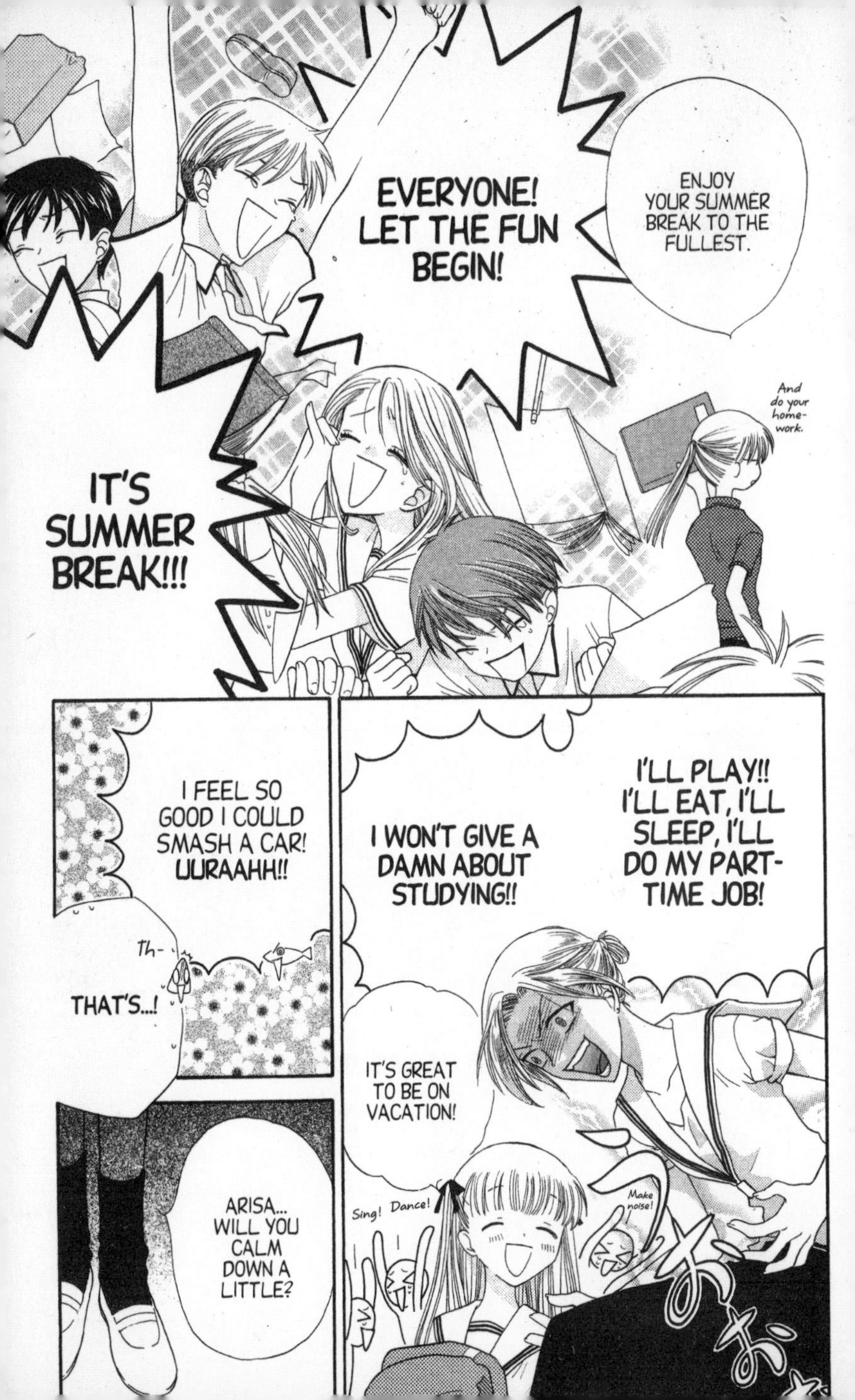

ENJOY YOUR SUMMER BREAK TO THE FULLEST.
EVERYONE! LET THE FUN BEGIN!
And do your home-work.
IT'S SUMMER BREAK!!!
I'LL PLAY!! I'LL EAT, I'LL SLEEP, I'LL DO MY PART-TIME JOB!
I WON'T GIVE A DAMN ABOUT STUDYING!!
IT'S GREAT TO BE ON VACATION!
Make noise!
Dance!
Sing!
I FEEL SO GOOD I COULD SMASH A CAR! UURAAHH!!
Th-
THAT'S...!
ARISA... WILL YOU CALM DOWN A LITTLE?

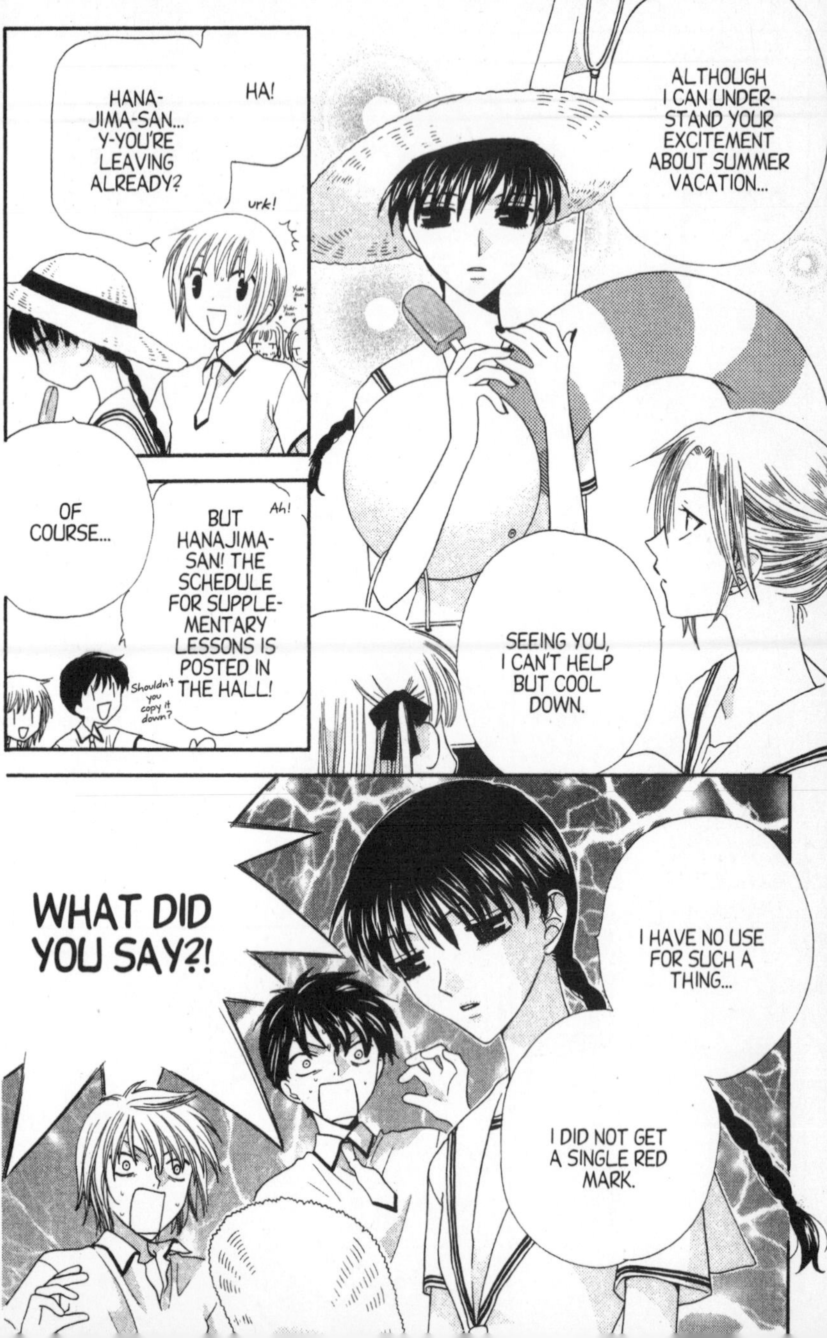
ALTHOUGH I CAN UNDER-STAND YOUR EXCITEMENT ABOUT SUMMER VACATION...
SEEING YOU, I CAN'T HELP BUT COOL DOWN.
HA!
HANA-JIMA-SAN... Y-YOU'RE LEAVING ALREADY?
urk!
OF COURSE...
Ah!
BUT HANAJIMA-SAN! THE SCHEDULE FOR SUPPLE-MENTARY LESSONS IS POSTED IN THE HALL!
Shouldn't you copy it down?
I HAVE NO USE FOR SUCH A THING...
I DID NOT GET A SINGLE RED MARK.
WHAT DID YOU SAY?!

Fruits Basket 8: Part 6

"Sakura Wars 3" was fun. (Is this a late topic too?) I was obsessed with Erica. She's so cute with her good morning dance! Paris is great too. The "Sakura" series always has mini-games; this time there were lots of hard ones, and the hardest one was Erica's. (Of all things...) It would be nice if I could be better at mini-games and other action stuff. Why am I so bad at them...? (I don't know.)

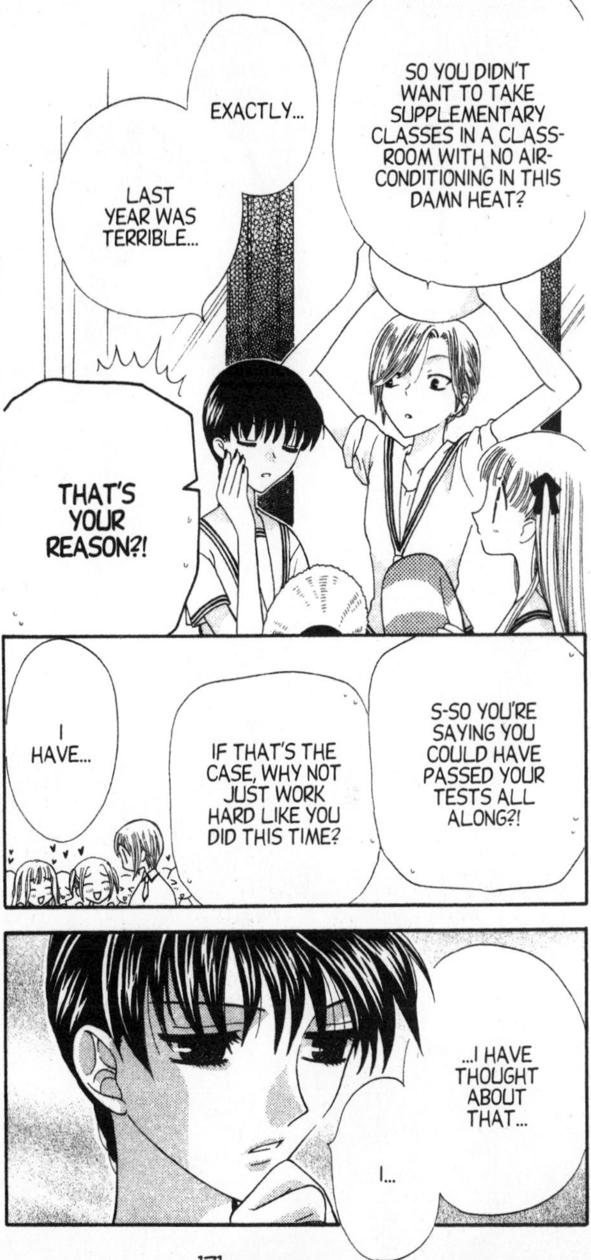

SO YOU DIDN'T WANT TO TAKE SUPPLEMENTARY CLASSES IN A CLASSROOM WITH NO AIR-CONDITIONING IN THIS DAMN HEAT?
EXACTLY...
LAST YEAR WAS TERRIBLE...
THAT'S YOUR REASON?!
S-SO YOU'RE SAYING YOU COULD HAVE PASSED YOUR TESTS ALL ALONG?!
IF THAT'S THE CASE, WHY NOT JUST WORK HARD LIKE YOU DID THIS TIME?
I HAVE...
...I HAVE THOUGHT ABOUT THAT...
I...

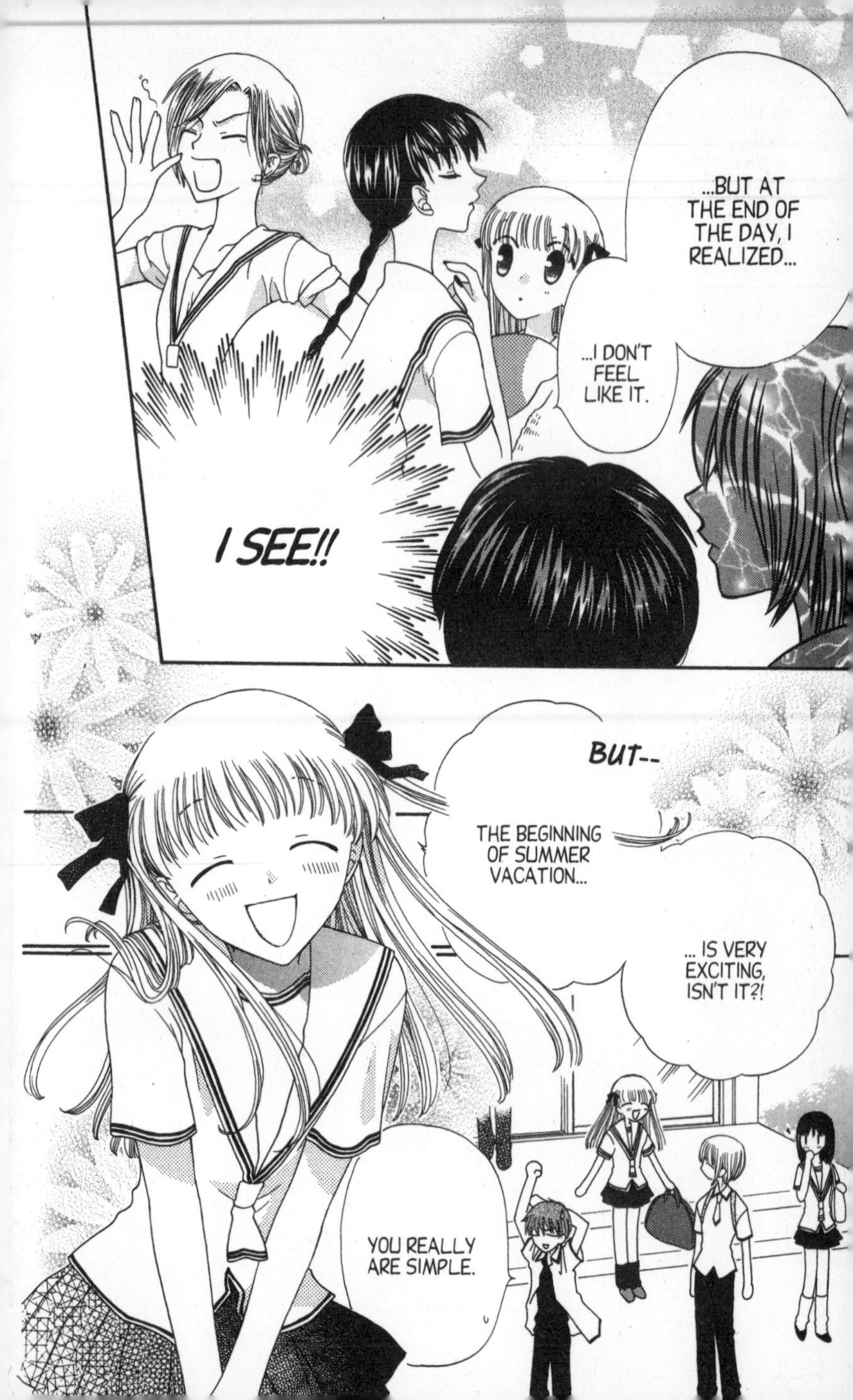
...BUT AT THE END OF THE DAY, I REALIZED...
...I DON'T FEEL LIKE IT.
I SEE!!
BUT--
THE BEGINNING OF SUMMER VACATION...
... IS VERY EXCITING, ISN'T IT?!
YOU REALLY ARE SIMPLE.

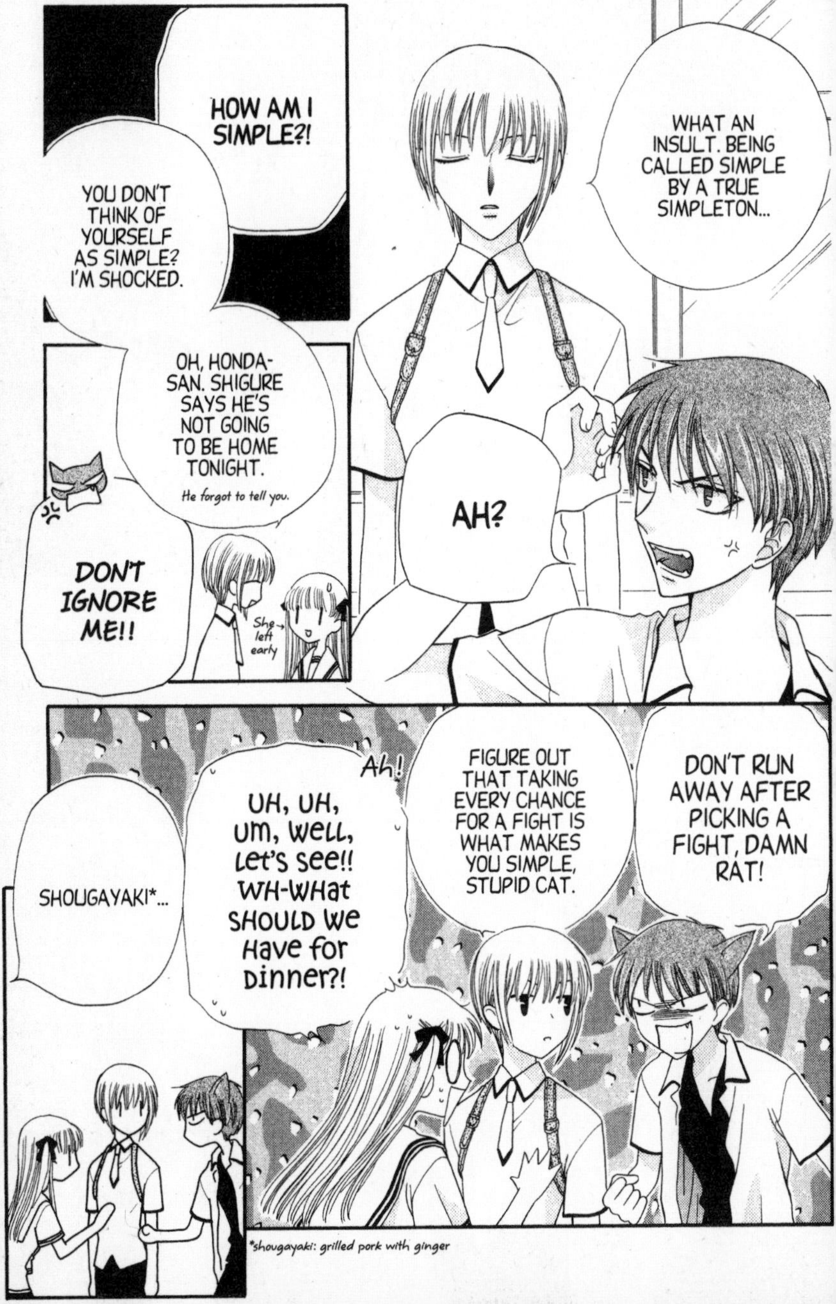
WHAT AN INSULT. BEING CALLED SIMPLE BY A TRUE SIMPLETON...
AH?
HOW AM I SIMPLE?!
YOU DON'T THINK OF YOURSELF AS SIMPLE? I'M SHOCKED.
OH, HONDA-SAN. SHIGURE SAYS HE'S NOT GOING TO BE HOME TONIGHT.
He forgot to tell you.
DON'T IGNORE ME!!
She left early
DON'T RUN AWAY AFTER PICKING A FIGHT, DAMN RAT!
FIGURE OUT THAT TAKING EVERY CHANCE FOR A FIGHT IS WHAT MAKES YOU SIMPLE, STUPID CAT.
Ah!
UH, UH, UM, WELL, LET'S SEE!! WH-WHAT SHOULD WE HAVE FOR DINNER?!
SHOUGAYAKI*...

*shougayaki: grilled pork with ginger

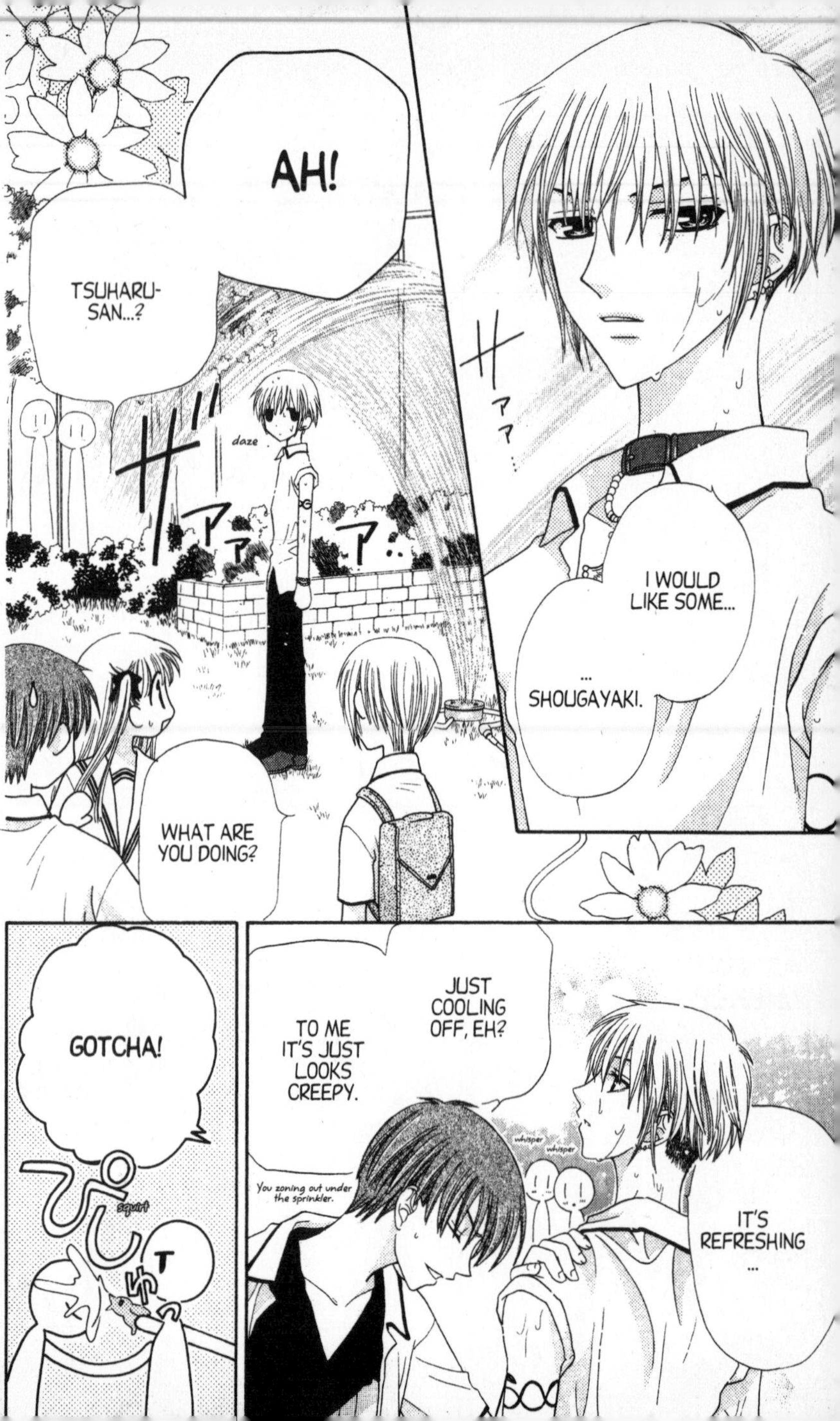
ザァァ…
I WOULD LIKE SOME...
... SHOUGAYAKI.
AH!
TSUHARU-SAN...?
daze
ザァァア…
WHAT ARE YOU DOING?
IT'S REFRESHING ...
JUST COOLING OFF, EH?
TO ME IT'S JUST LOOKS CREEPY.
You zoning out under the sprinkler.
whisper
whisper
GOTCHA!
squirt
T

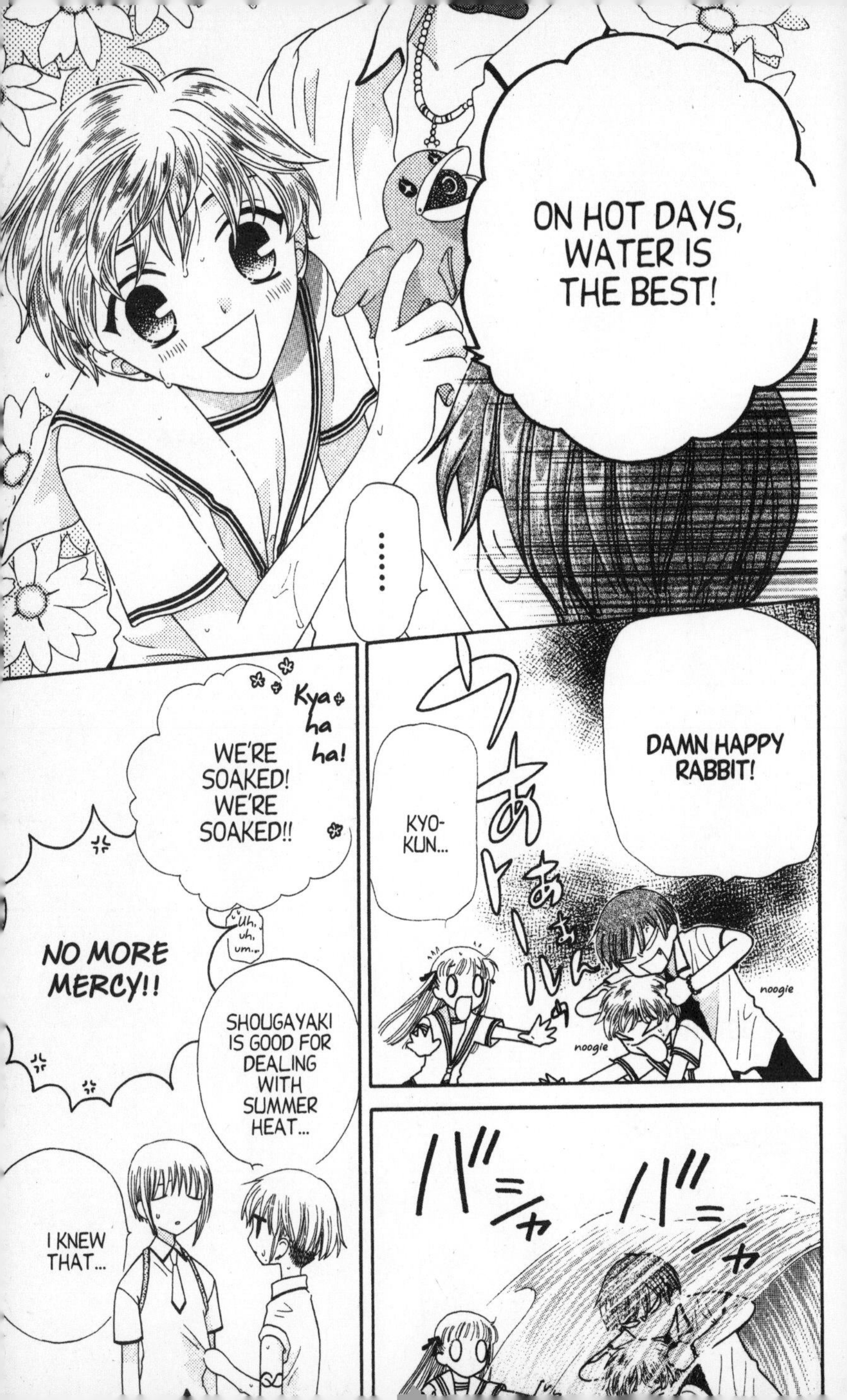
ON HOT DAYS, WATER IS THE BEST!
......
DAMN HAPPY RABBIT!
KYO-KUN...
noogie
noogie
バシャ
バシャ
Kya ha ha!
WE'RE SOAKED! WE'RE SOAKED!!
NO MORE MERCY!!
Uh, uh, um...
SHOUGAYAKI IS GOOD FOR DEALING WITH SUMMER HEAT...
I KNEW THAT...

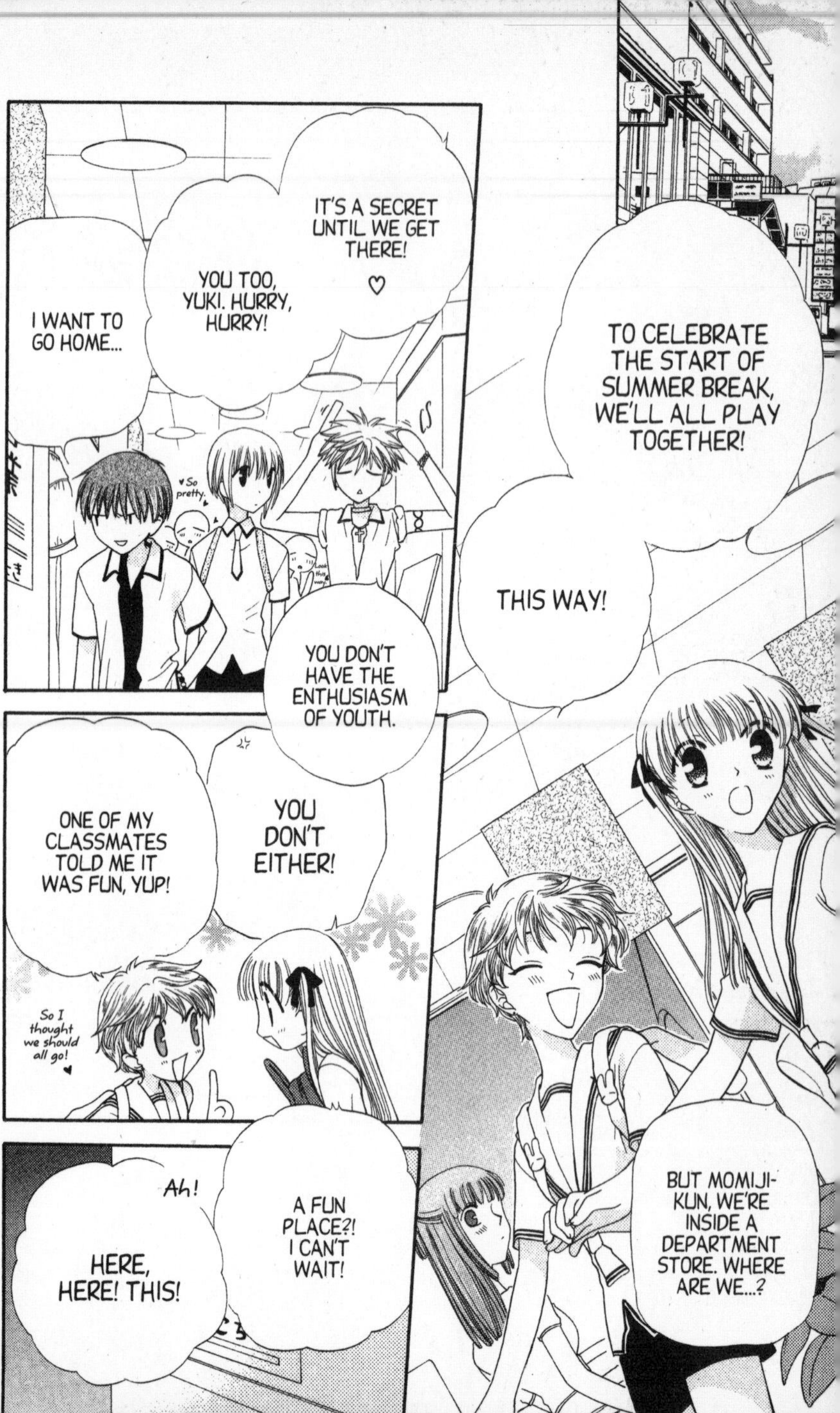

TO CELEBRATE THE START OF SUMMER BREAK, WE'LL ALL PLAY TOGETHER!
THIS WAY!
BUT MOMIJI-KUN, WE'RE INSIDE A DEPARTMENT STORE. WHERE ARE WE...?
IT'S A SECRET UNTIL WE GET THERE! ♡
YOU TOO, YUKI. HURRY, HURRY!
I WANT TO GO HOME...
♥So pretty.♥
Look this way
YOU DON'T HAVE THE ENTHUSIASM OF YOUTH.
YOU DON'T EITHER!
ONE OF MY CLASSMATES TOLD ME IT WAS FUN, YUP!
So I thought we should all go! ♥
A FUN PLACE?! I CAN'T WAIT!
Ah!
HERE, HERE! THIS!

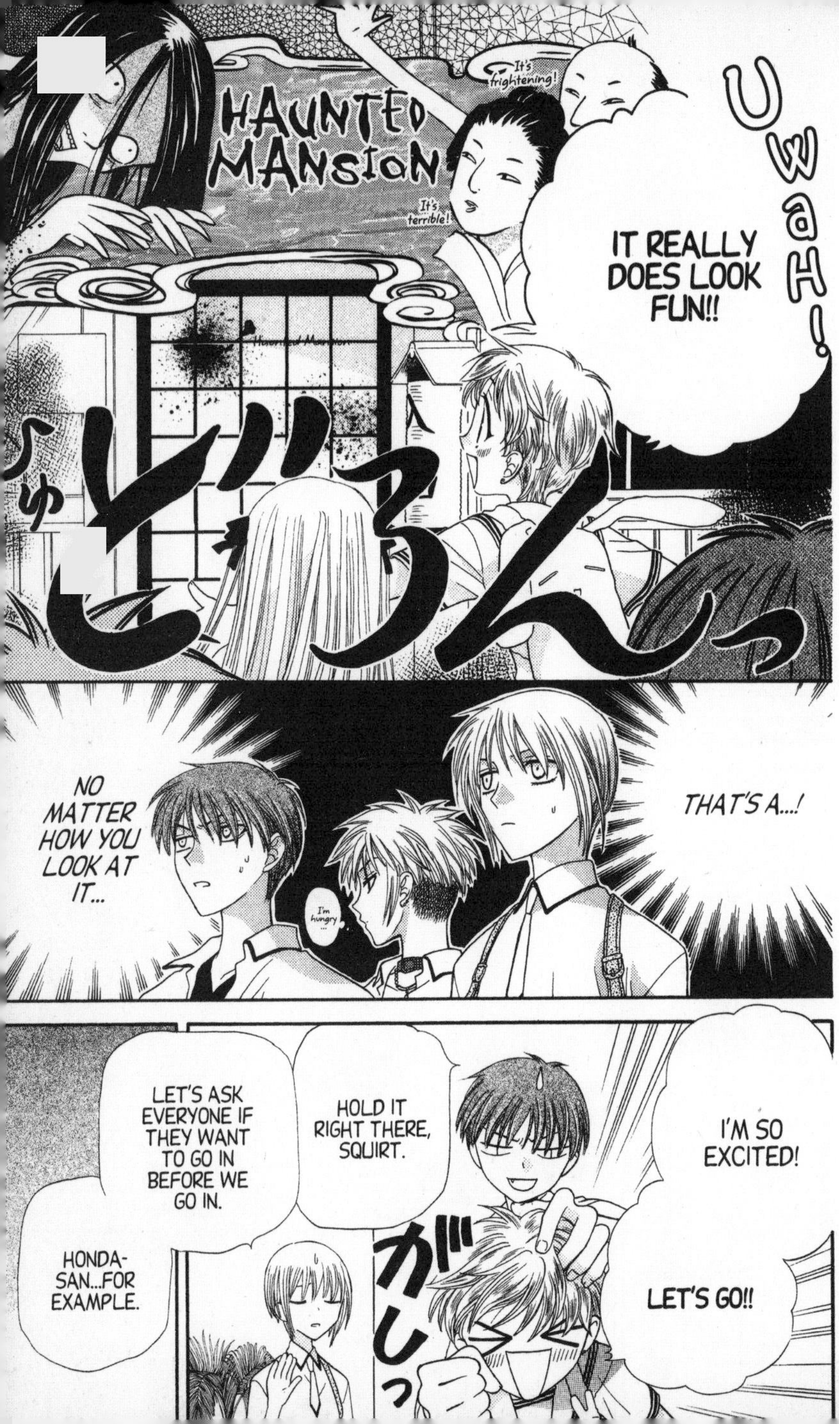
Uwah!
IT REALLY DOES LOOK FUN!!
It's frightening!
HAUNTED MANSION
It's terrible!
どろん
ひゅ
THAT'S A...!
I'm hungry...
NO MATTER HOW YOU LOOK AT IT...
I'M SO EXCITED!
LET'S GO!!
HOLD IT RIGHT THERE, SQUIRT.
がしっ
LET'S ASK EVERYONE IF THEY WANT TO GO IN BEFORE WE GO IN.
HONDA-SAN...FOR EXAMPLE.

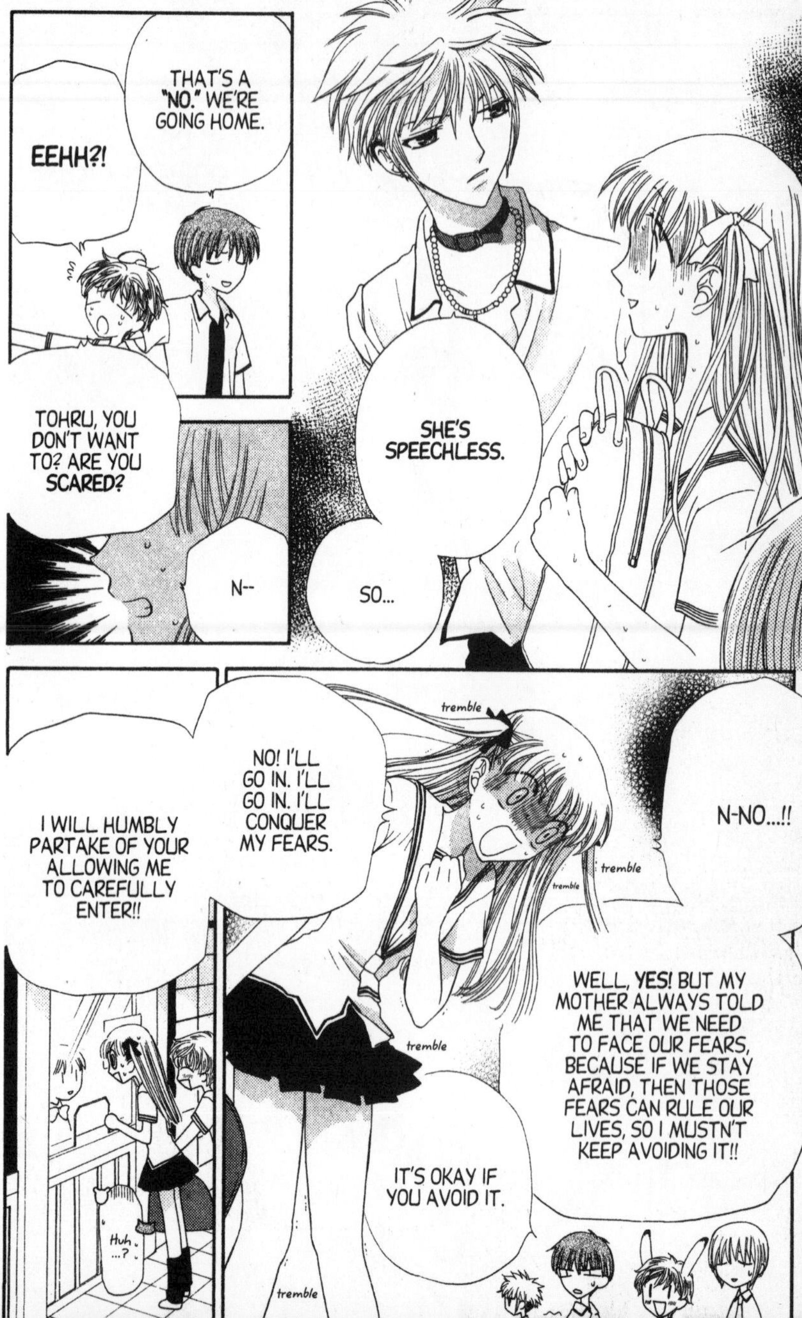
SHE'S SPEECHLESS.
SO...
THAT'S A "NO." WE'RE GOING HOME.
EEHH?!
TOHRU, YOU DON'T WANT TO? ARE YOU SCARED?
N--
N-NO...!!
tremble
tremble
tremble
WELL, YES! BUT MY MOTHER ALWAYS TOLD ME THAT WE NEED TO FACE OUR FEARS, BECAUSE IF WE STAY AFRAID, THEN THOSE FEARS CAN RULE OUR LIVES, SO I MUSTN'T KEEP AVOIDING IT!!
tremble
IT'S OKAY IF YOU AVOID IT.
tremble
NO! I'LL GO IN. I'LL GO IN. I'LL CONQUER MY FEARS.
I WILL HUMBLY PARTAKE OF YOUR ALLOWING ME TO CAREFULLY ENTER!!
Huh...?

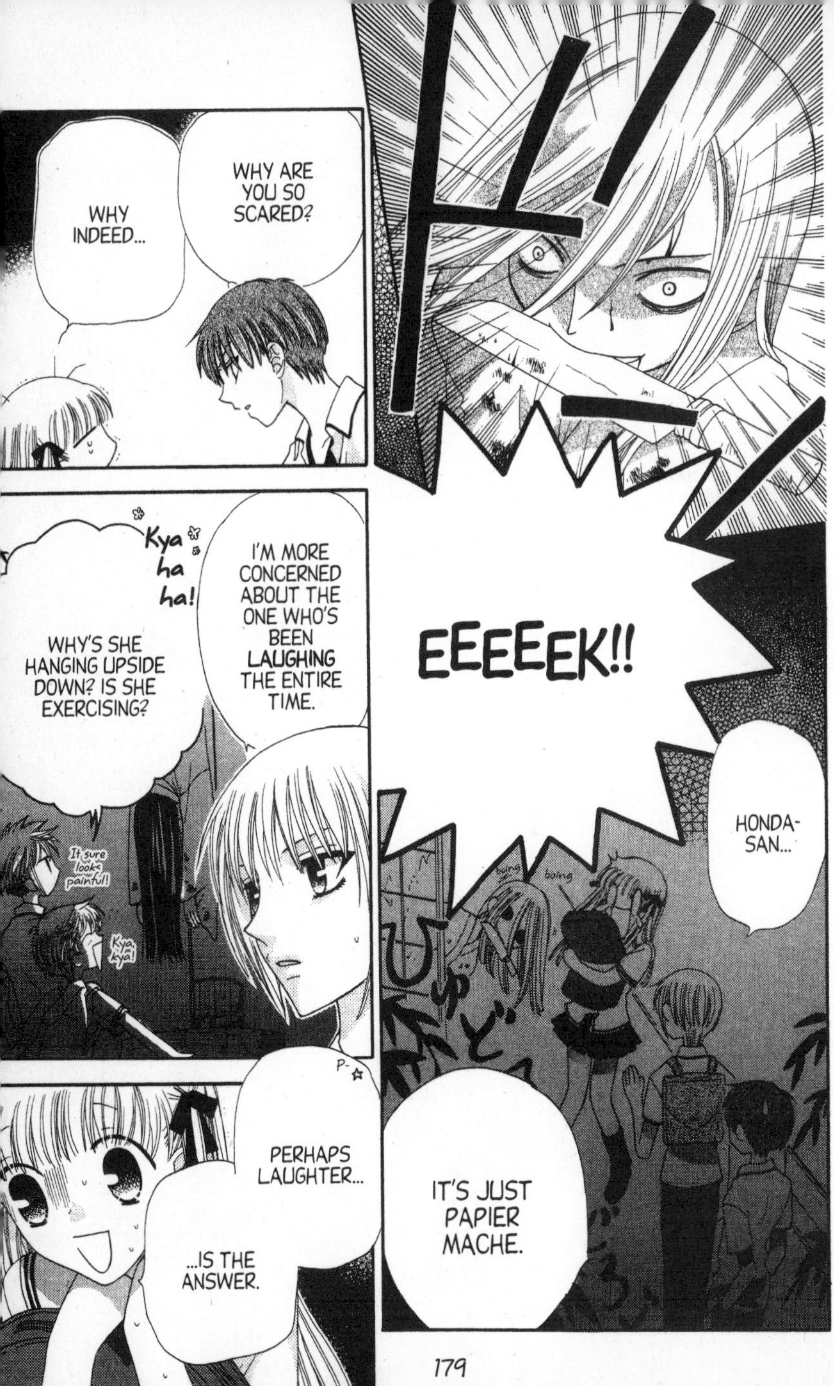
EEEEEK!!
HONDA-SAN...
boing
boing
IT'S JUST PAPIER MACHE.
WHY ARE YOU SO SCARED?
WHY INDEED...
I'M MORE CONCERNED ABOUT THE ONE WHO'S BEEN LAUGHING THE ENTIRE TIME.
Kya ha ha!
WHY'S SHE HANGING UPSIDE DOWN? IS SHE EXERCISING?
It sure looks painful!
Kya, kya!
P-
PERHAPS LAUGHTER...
...IS THE ANSWER.

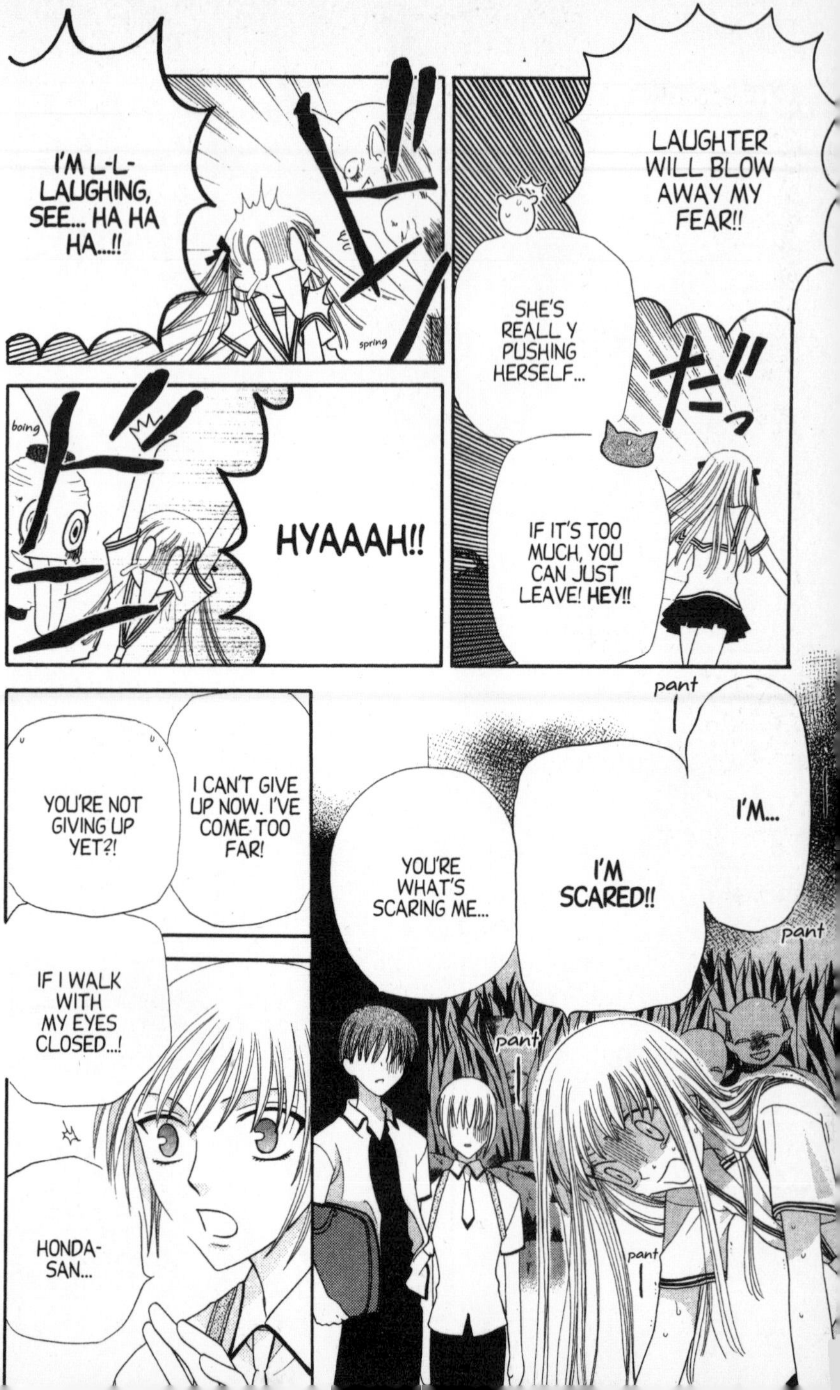
LAUGHTER WILL BLOW AWAY MY FEAR!!
SHE'S REALL Y PUSHING HERSELF...
IF IT'S TOO MUCH, YOU CAN JUST LEAVE! HEY!!
I'M L-L-LAUGHING, SEE... HA HA HA...!!
spring
boing
HYAAAH!!
pant
I'M...
I'M SCARED!!
YOU'RE WHAT'S SCARING ME...
pant
pant
pant
I CAN'T GIVE UP NOW. I'VE COME TOO FAR!
YOU'RE NOT GIVING UP YET?!
IF I WALK WITH MY EYES CLOSED...!
HONDA-SAN...

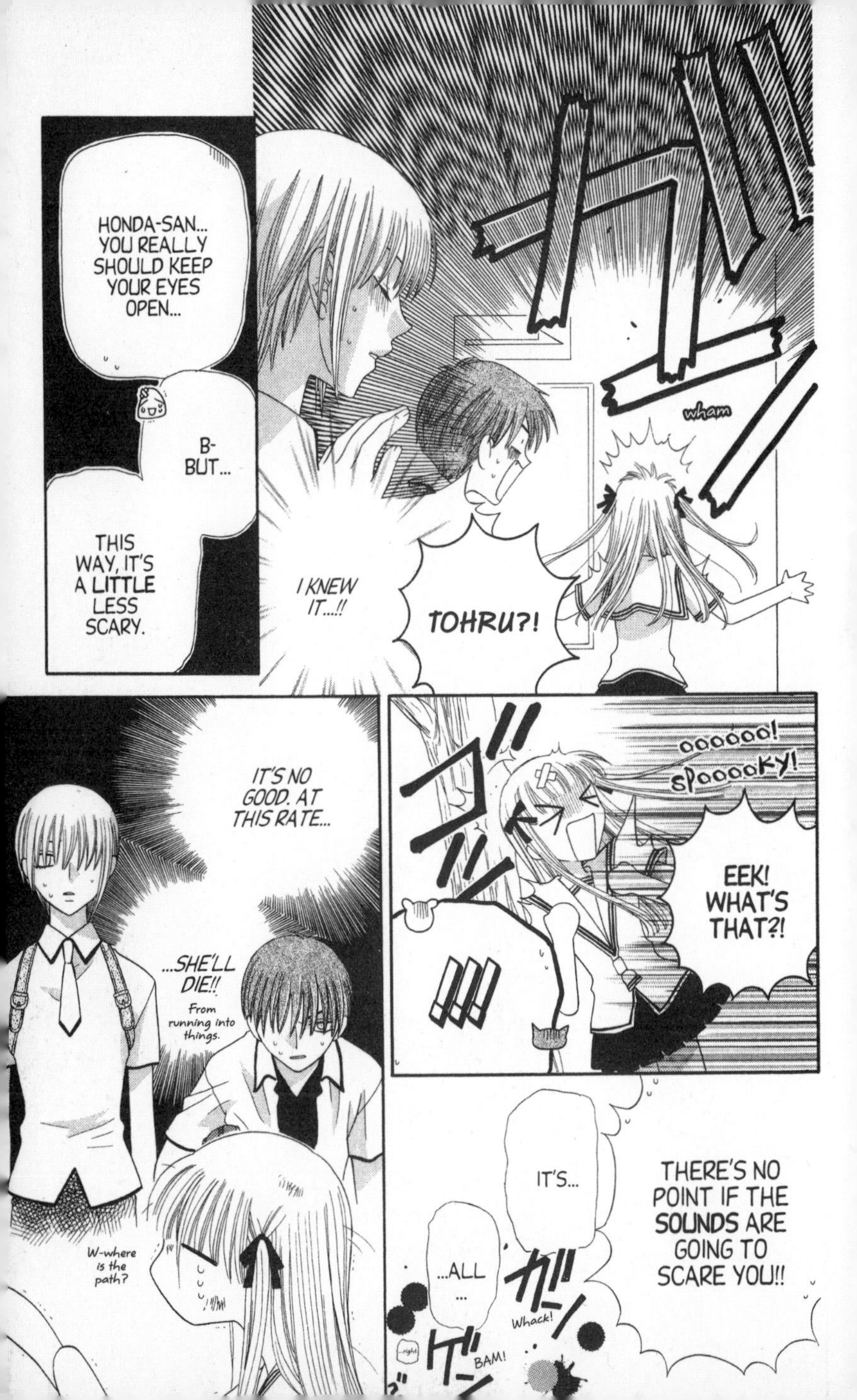
wham
TOHRU?!
I KNEW IT...!!
HONDA-SAN... YOU REALLY SHOULD KEEP YOUR EYES OPEN...
B-BUT...
THIS WAY, IT'S A LITTLE LESS SCARY.
oooooo! spoooooKY!
EEK! WHAT'S THAT?!
THERE'S NO POINT IF THE SOUNDS ARE GOING TO SCARE YOU!!
IT'S...
...ALL ...
Whack!
...right
BAM!
IT'S NO GOOD. AT THIS RATE...
...SHE'LL DIE!!
From running into things.
W-where is the path?

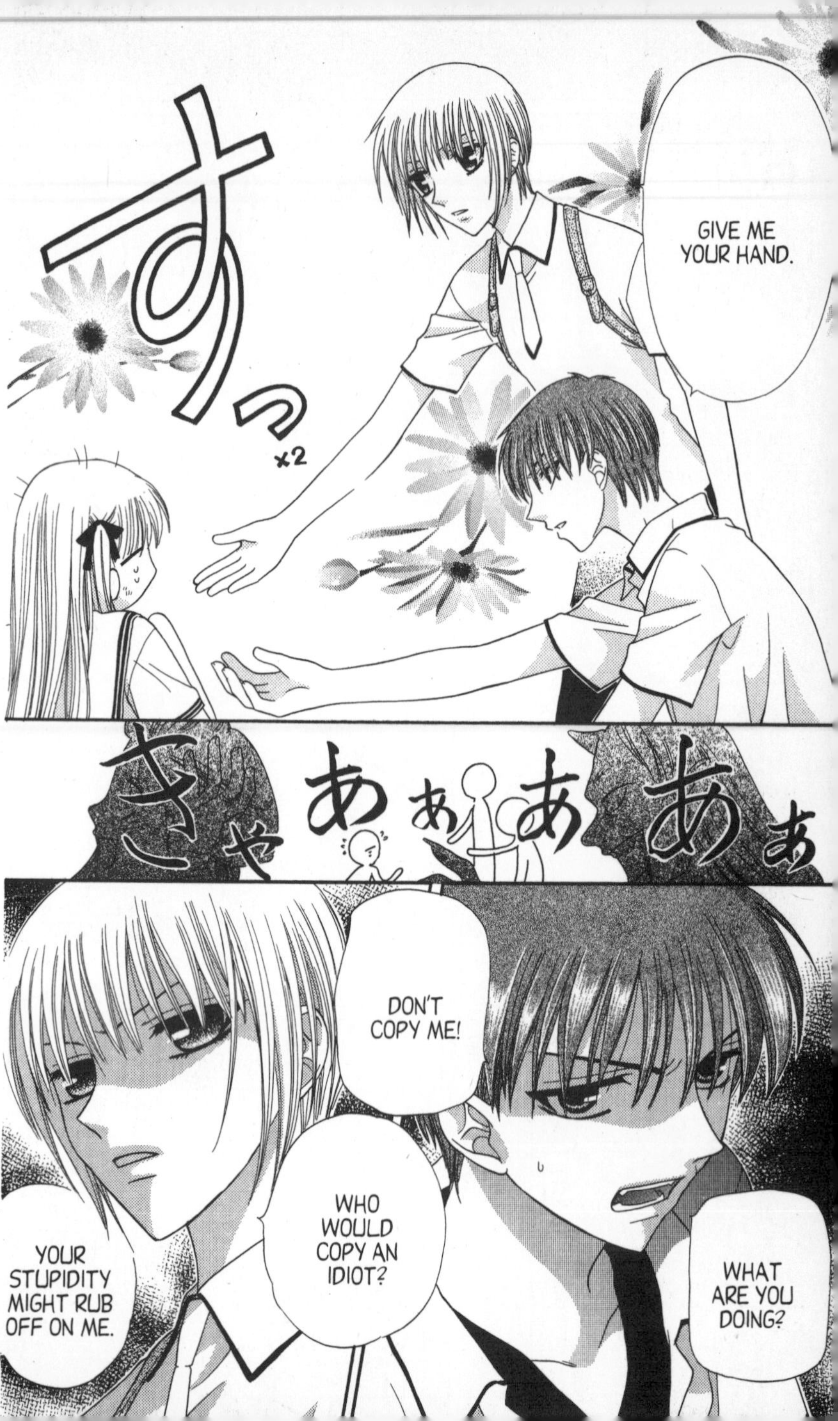
GIVE ME YOUR HAND.
すっ ×2
きゃあぁああぁ
WHAT ARE YOU DOING?
DON'T COPY ME!
WHO WOULD COPY AN IDIOT?
YOUR STUPIDITY MIGHT RUB OFF ON ME.

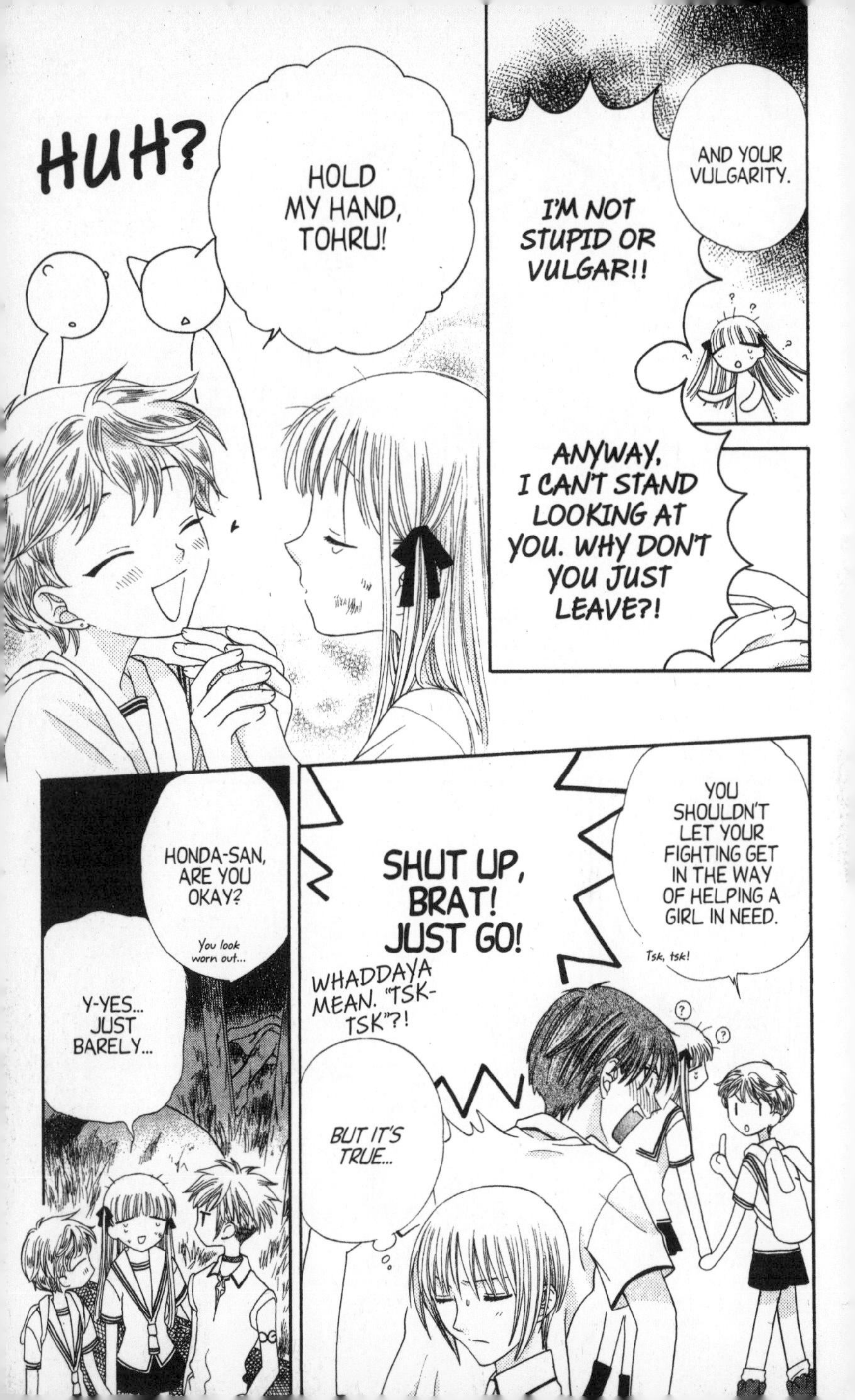
AND YOUR VULGARITY.
I'M NOT STUPID OR VULGAR!!
ANYWAY, I CAN'T STAND LOOKING AT YOU. WHY DON'T YOU JUST LEAVE?!
HOLD MY HAND, TOHRU!
HUH?
YOU SHOULDN'T LET YOUR FIGHTING GET IN THE WAY OF HELPING A GIRL IN NEED.
Tsk, tsk!
SHUT UP, BRAT! JUST GO!
WHADDAYA MEAN. "TSK-TSK"?!
BUT IT'S TRUE...
HONDA-SAN, ARE YOU OKAY?
You look worn out...
Y-YES... JUST BARELY...

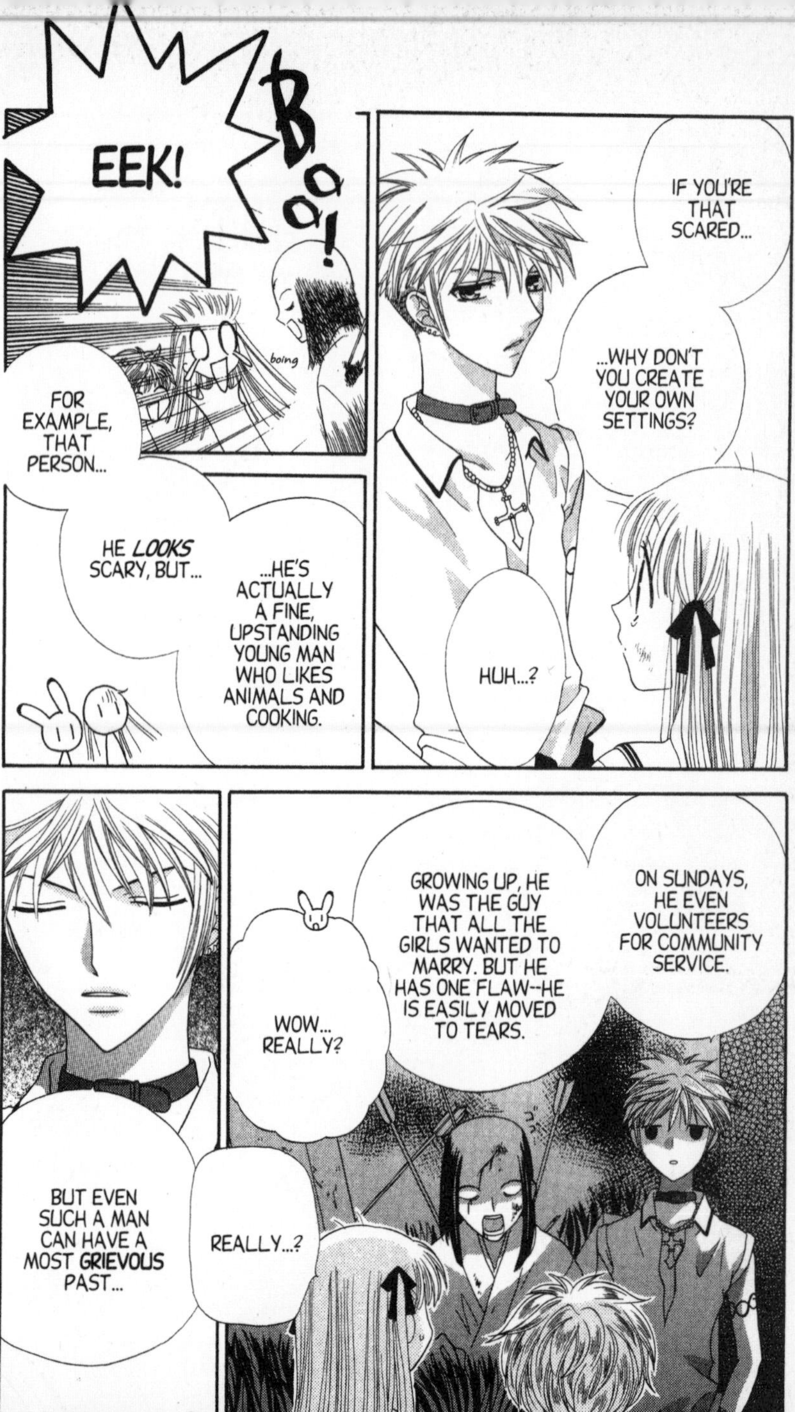
IF YOU'RE THAT SCARED...
...WHY DON'T YOU CREATE YOUR OWN SETTINGS?
HUH...?
EEK!
Baa!
boing
FOR EXAMPLE, THAT PERSON...
HE *LOOKS* SCARY, BUT...
...HE'S ACTUALLY A FINE, UPSTANDING YOUNG MAN WHO LIKES ANIMALS AND COOKING.
ON SUNDAYS, HE EVEN VOLUNTEERS FOR COMMUNITY SERVICE.
GROWING UP, HE WAS THE GUY THAT ALL THE GIRLS WANTED TO MARRY. BUT HE HAS ONE FLAW--HE IS EASILY MOVED TO TEARS.
WOW... REALLY?
BUT EVEN SUCH A MAN CAN HAVE A MOST **GRIEVOUS** PAST...
REALLY...?

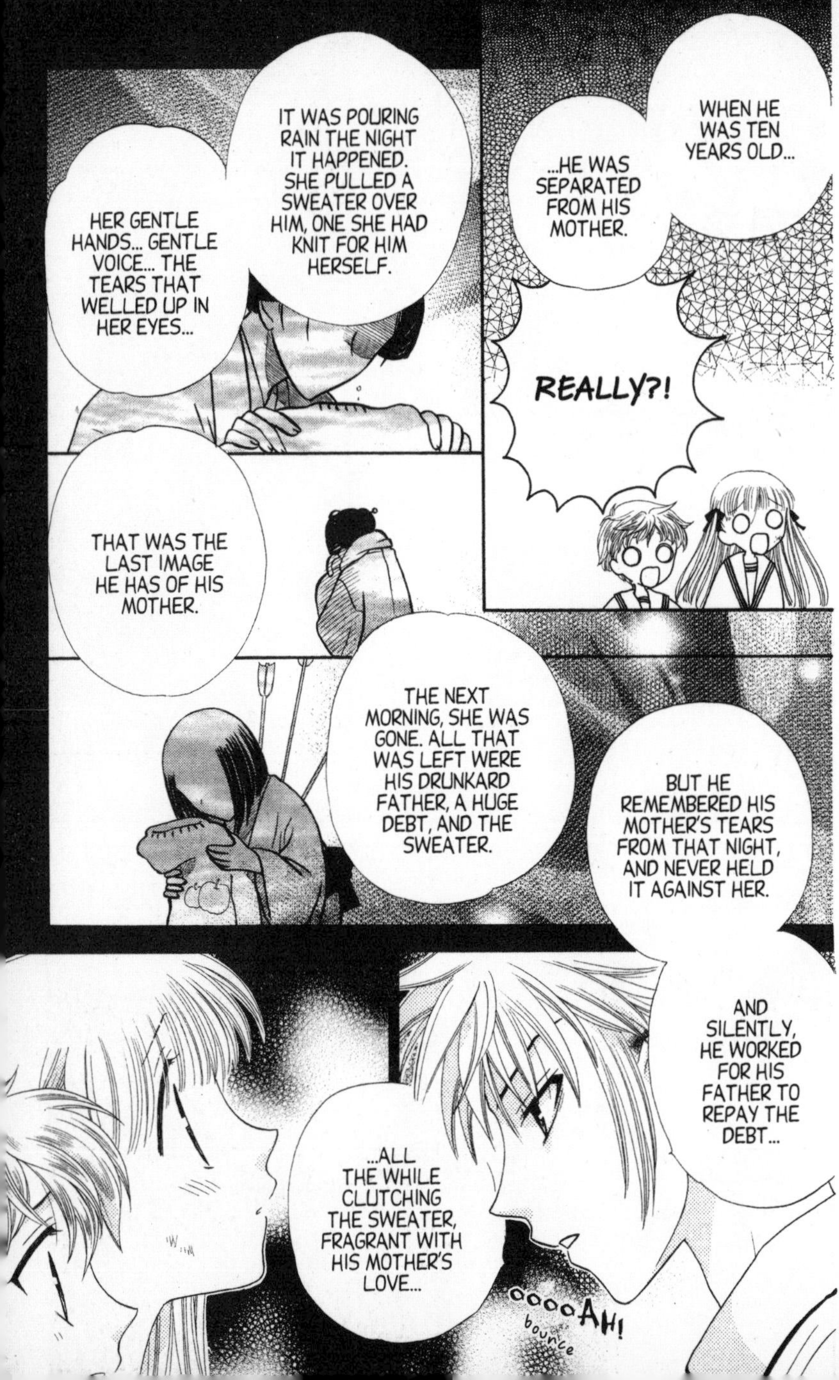
WHEN HE WAS TEN YEARS OLD...
...HE WAS SEPARATED FROM HIS MOTHER.
REALLY?!
IT WAS POURING RAIN THE NIGHT IT HAPPENED. SHE PULLED A SWEATER OVER HIM, ONE SHE HAD KNIT FOR HIM HERSELF.
HER GENTLE HANDS... GENTLE VOICE... THE TEARS THAT WELLED UP IN HER EYES...
THAT WAS THE LAST IMAGE HE HAS OF HIS MOTHER.
THE NEXT MORNING, SHE WAS GONE. ALL THAT WAS LEFT WERE HIS DRUNKARD FATHER, A HUGE DEBT, AND THE SWEATER.
BUT HE REMEMBERED HIS MOTHER'S TEARS FROM THAT NIGHT, AND NEVER HELD IT AGAINST HER.
AND SILENTLY, HE WORKED FOR HIS FATHER TO REPAY THE DEBT...
...ALL THE WHILE CLUTCHING THE SWEATER, FRAGRANT WITH HIS MOTHER'S LOVE...
OOOOAH!
bounce

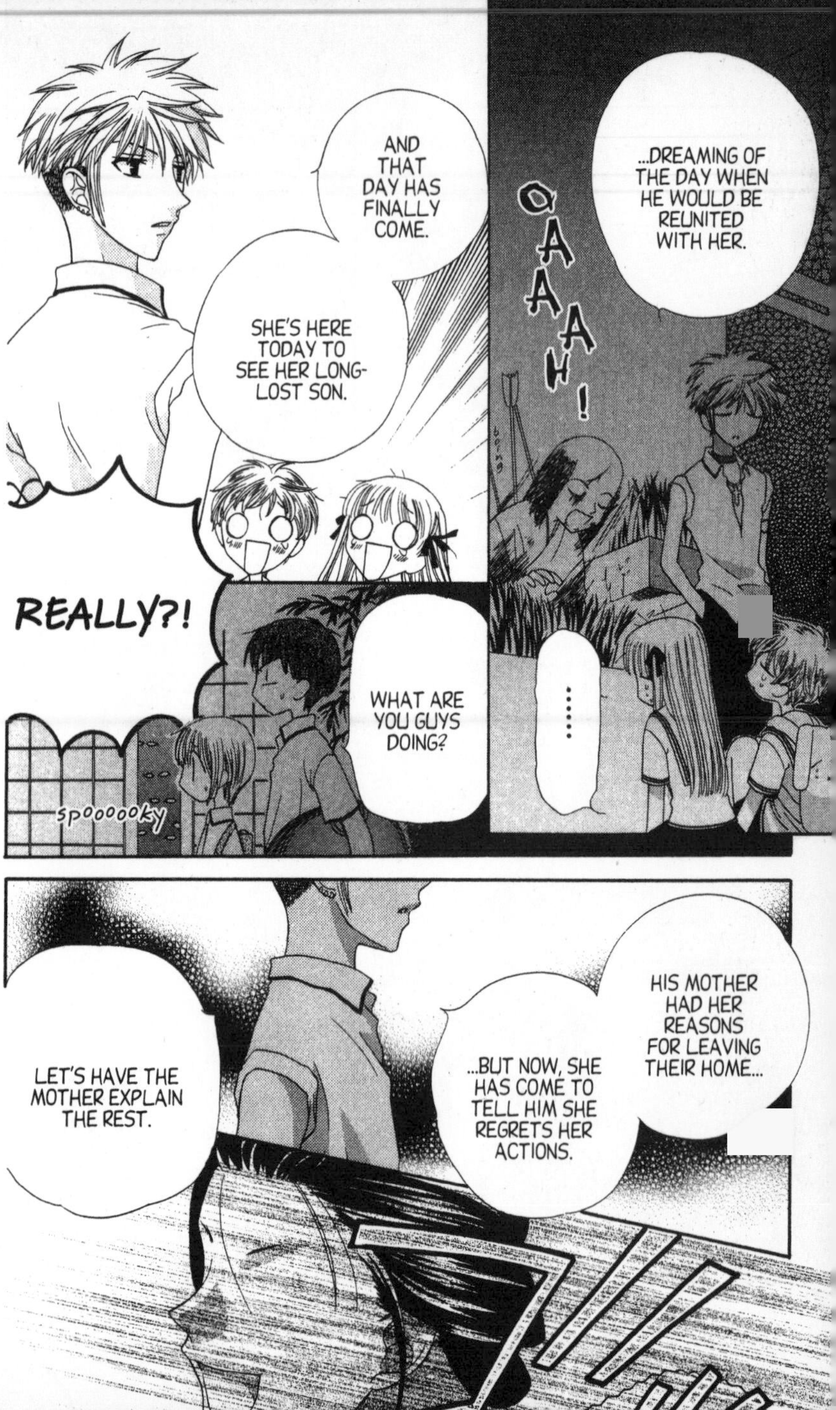
...DREAMING OF THE DAY WHEN HE WOULD BE REUNITED WITH HER.
OAAAH!
......
AND THAT DAY HAS FINALLY COME.
SHE'S HERE TODAY TO SEE HER LONG-LOST SON.
REALLY?!
WHAT ARE YOU GUYS DOING?
spooooky
HIS MOTHER HAD HER REASONS FOR LEAVING THEIR HOME...
...BUT NOW, SHE HAS COME TO TELL HIM SHE REGRETS HER ACTIONS.
LET'S HAVE THE MOTHER EXPLAIN THE REST.

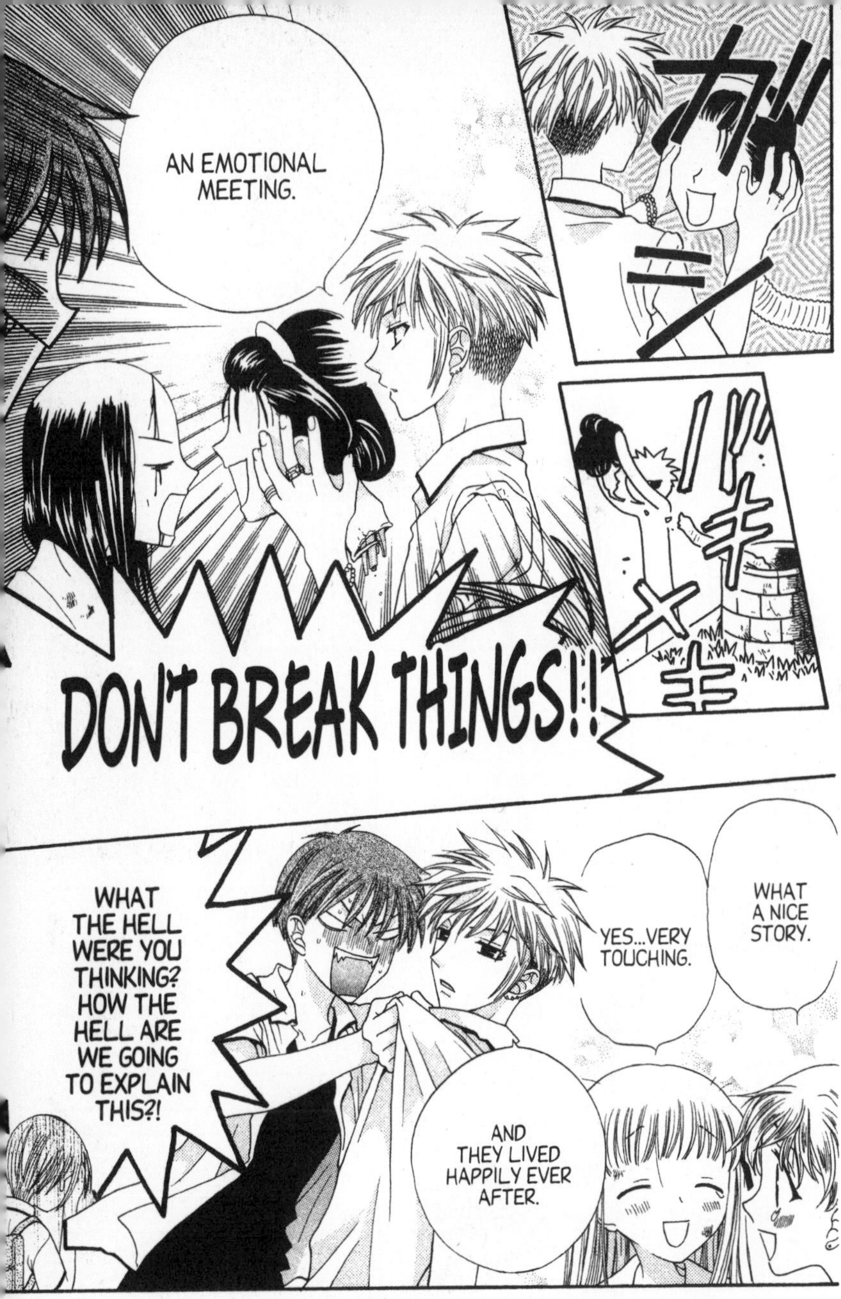
AN EMOTIONAL MEETING.
DON'T BREAK THINGS!!
WHAT A NICE STORY.
YES...VERY TOUCHING.
AND THEY LIVED HAPPILY EVER AFTER.
WHAT THE HELL WERE YOU THINKING? HOW THE HELL ARE WE GOING TO EXPLAIN THIS?!

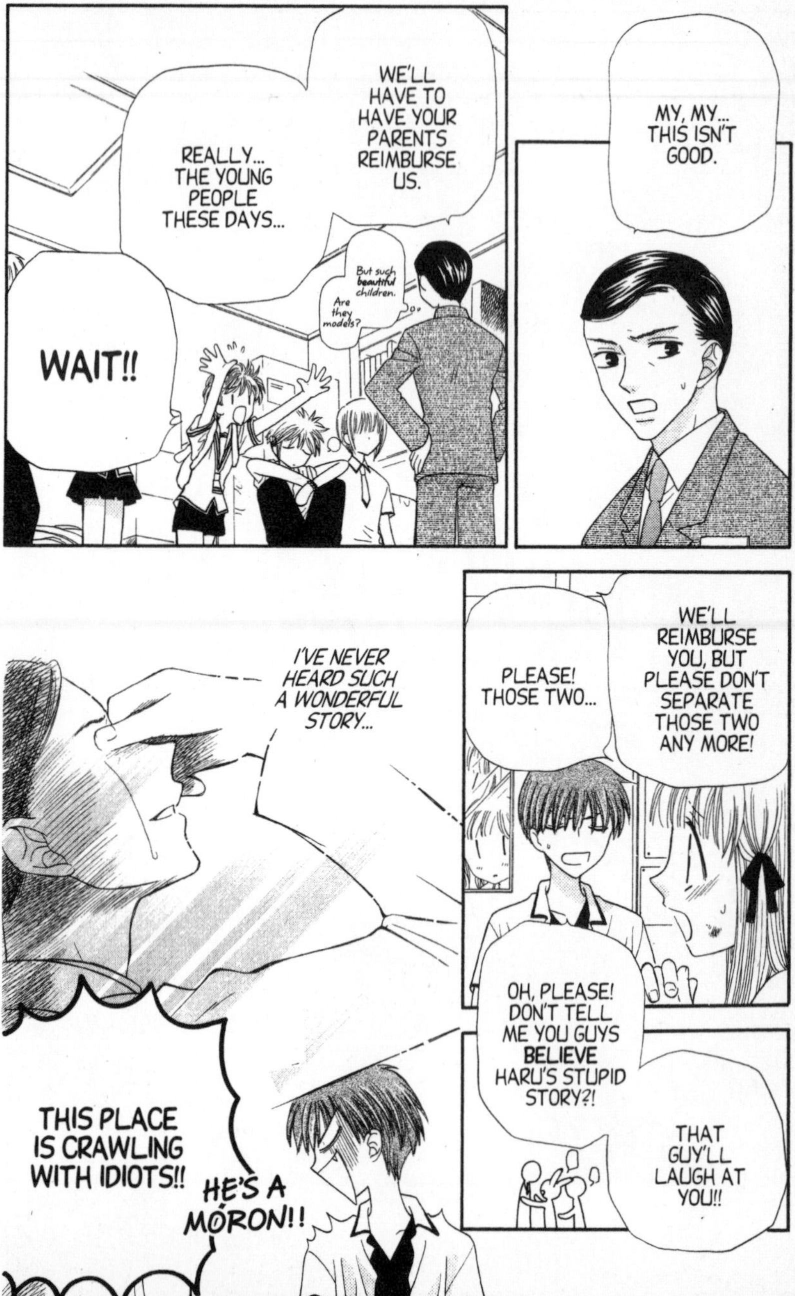
MY, MY... THIS ISN'T GOOD.
WE'LL HAVE TO HAVE YOUR PARENTS REIMBURSE US.
REALLY... THE YOUNG PEOPLE THESE DAYS...
But such beautiful children. Are they models?
WAIT!!
WE'LL REIMBURSE YOU, BUT PLEASE DON'T SEPARATE THOSE TWO ANY MORE!
PLEASE! THOSE TWO...
OH, PLEASE! DON'T TELL ME YOU GUYS BELIEVE HARU'S STUPID STORY?!
THAT GUY'LL LAUGH AT YOU!!
I'VE NEVER HEARD SUCH A WONDERFUL STORY...
THIS PLACE IS CRAWLING WITH IDIOTS!!
HE'S A MORON!!

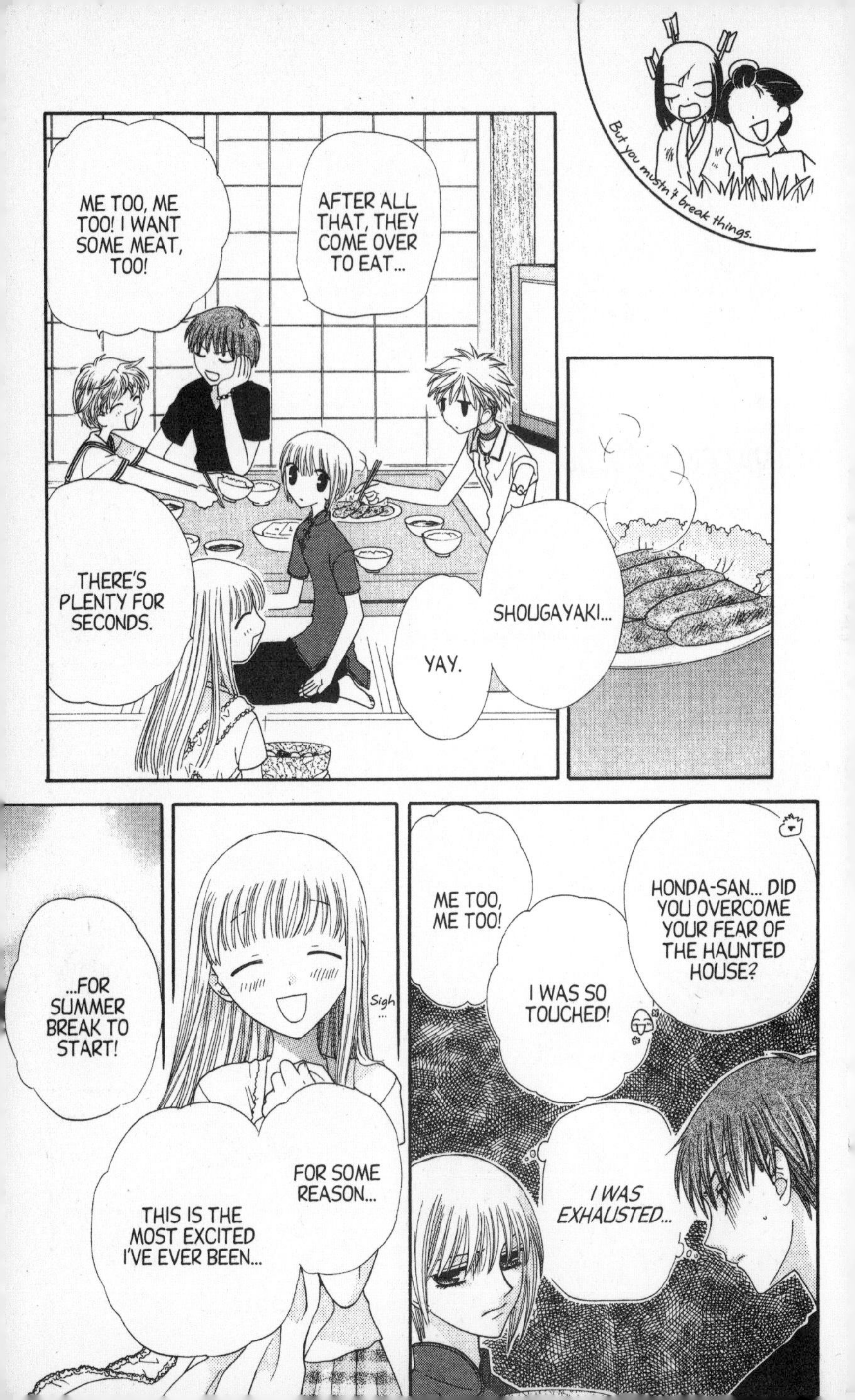
But you mustn't break things.
SHOUGAYAKI...
YAY.
AFTER ALL THAT, THEY COME OVER TO EAT...
ME TOO, ME TOO! I WANT SOME MEAT, TOO!
THERE'S PLENTY FOR SECONDS.
HONDA-SAN... DID YOU OVERCOME YOUR FEAR OF THE HAUNTED HOUSE?
ME TOO, ME TOO!
I WAS SO TOUCHED!
I WAS EXHAUSTED...
Sigh...
FOR SOME REASON...
THIS IS THE MOST EXCITED I'VE EVER BEEN...
...FOR SUMMER BREAK TO START!

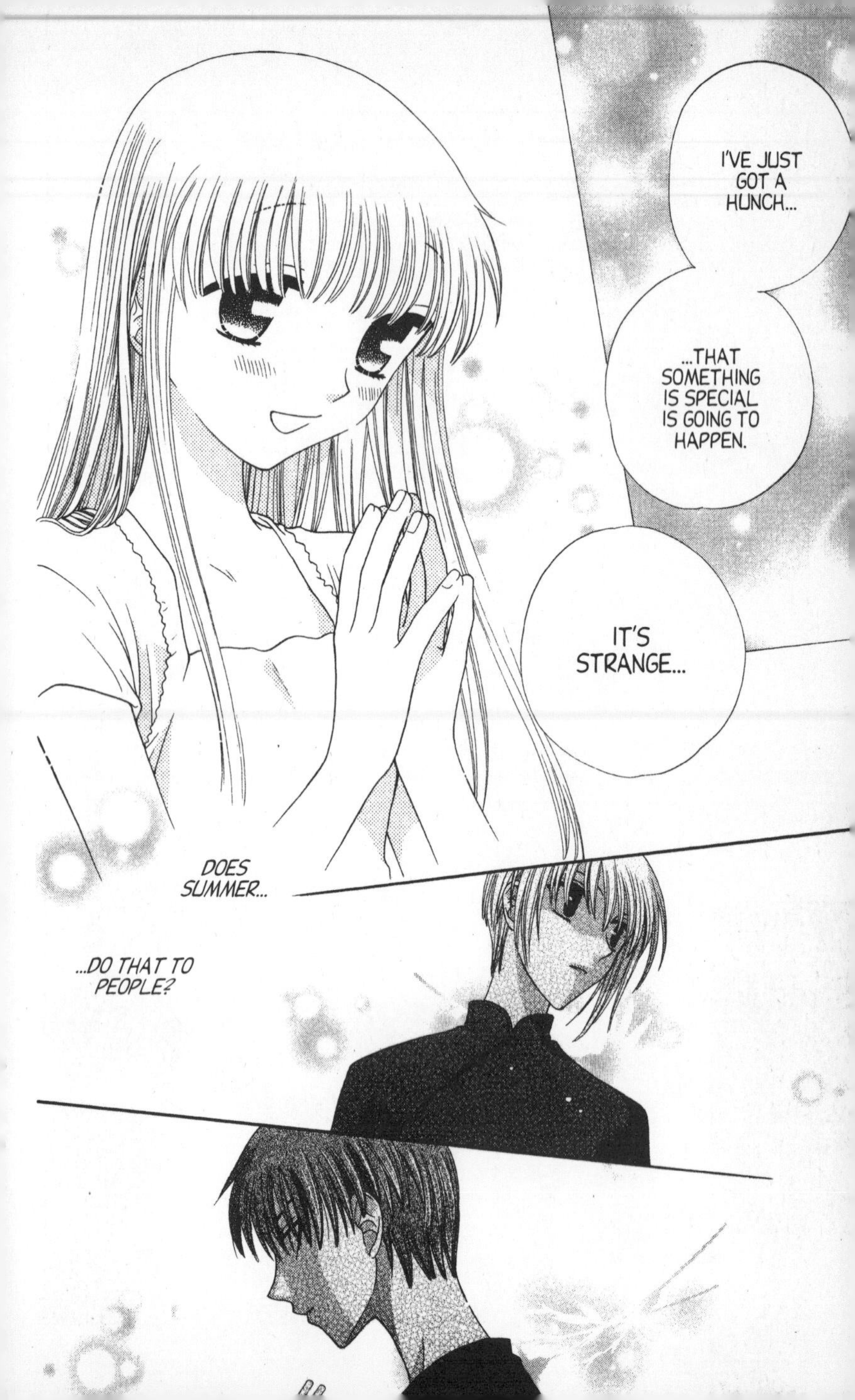
I'VE JUST GOT A HUNCH...
...THAT SOMETHING IS SPECIAL IS GOING TO HAPPEN.
IT'S STRANGE...
DOES SUMMER...
...DO THAT TO PEOPLE?

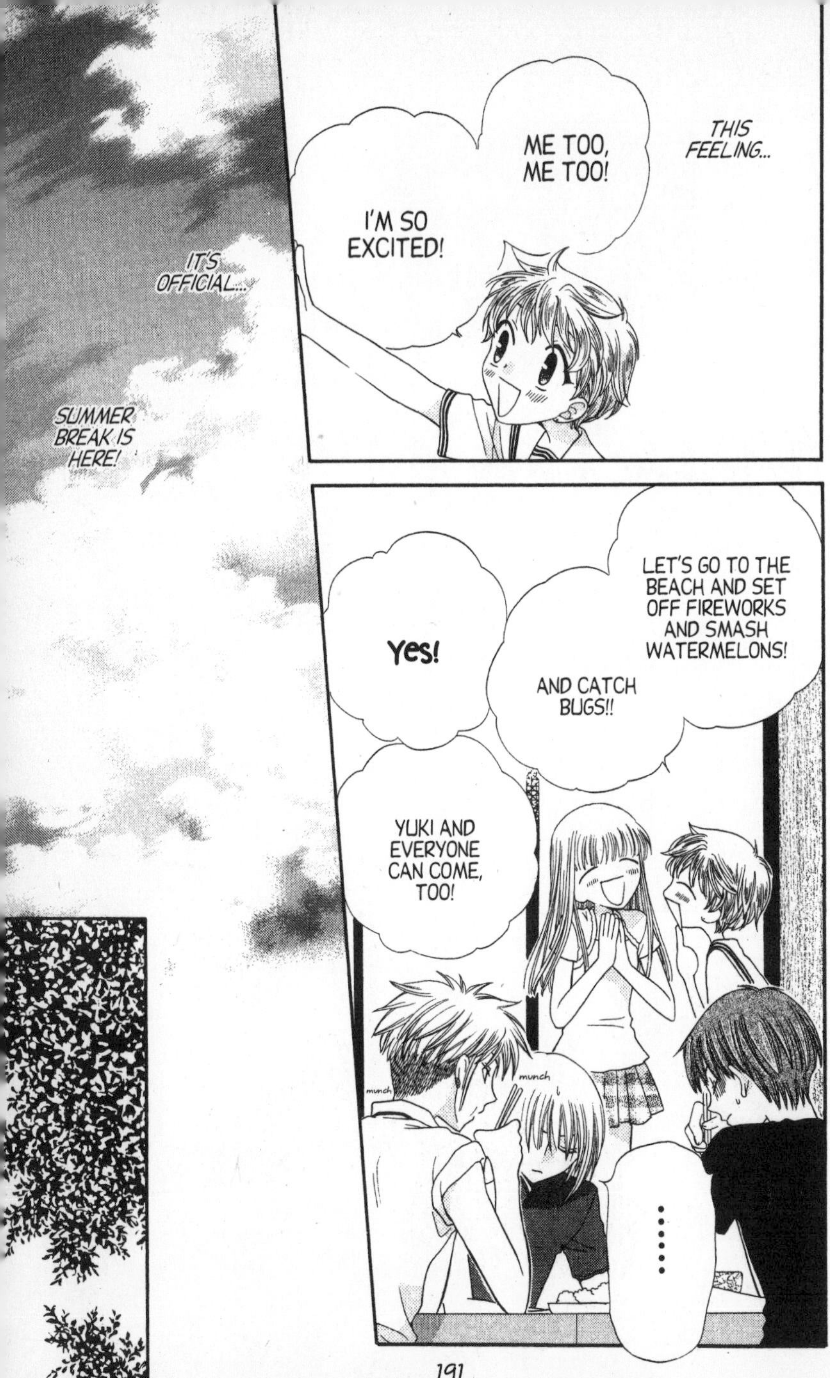
THIS FEELING...
ME TOO, ME TOO!
I'M SO EXCITED!
LET'S GO TO THE BEACH AND SET OFF FIREWORKS AND SMASH WATERMELONS!
AND CATCH BUGS!!
Yes!
YUKI AND EVERYONE CAN COME, TOO!
munch
munch
......
IT'S OFFICIAL...
SUMMER BREAK IS HERE!

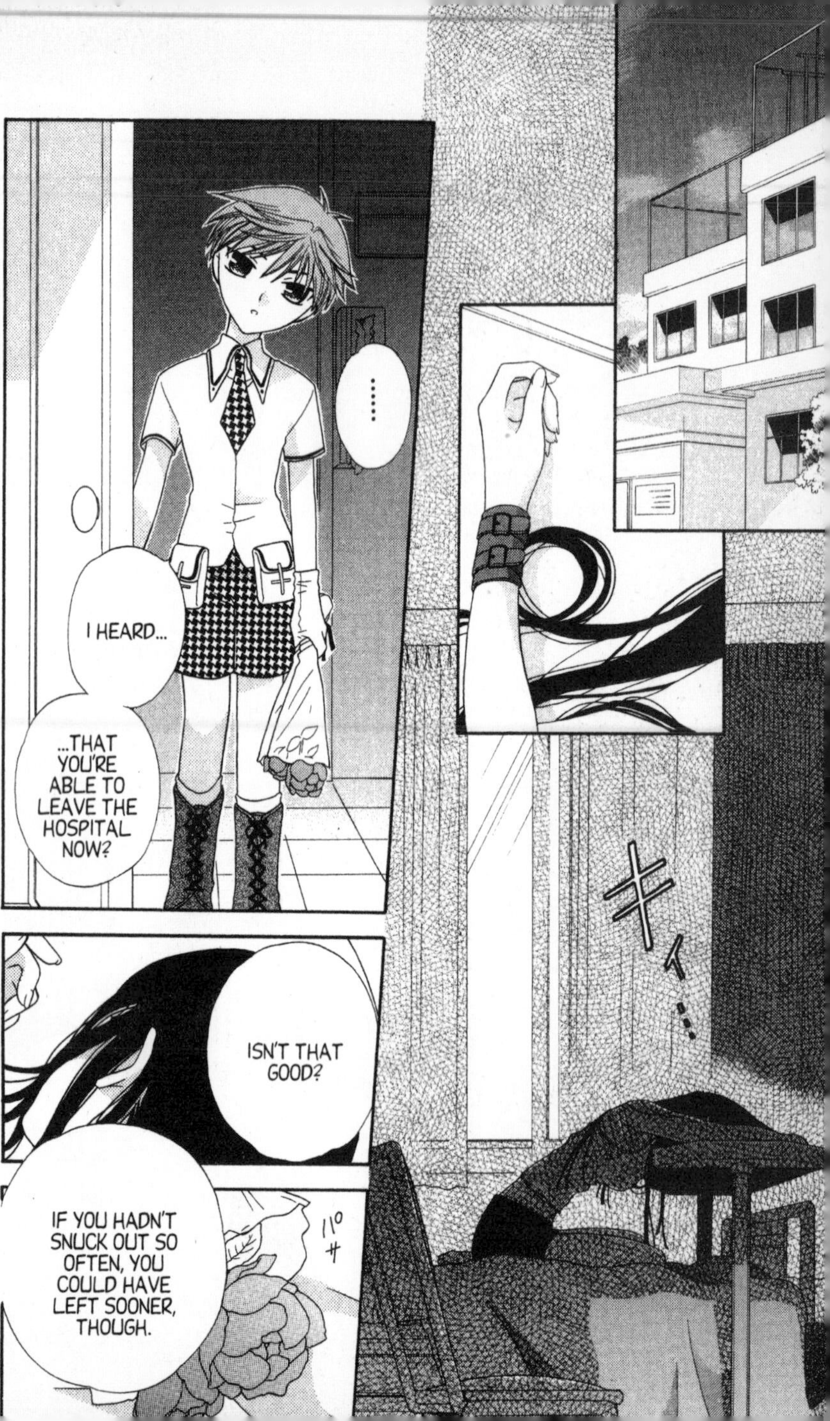

キィ…
……
I HEARD...
...THAT YOU'RE ABLE TO LEAVE THE HOSPITAL NOW?
ISN'T THAT GOOD?
IF YOU HADN'T SNUCK OUT SO OFTEN, YOU COULD HAVE LEFT SOONER, THOUGH.
パサ

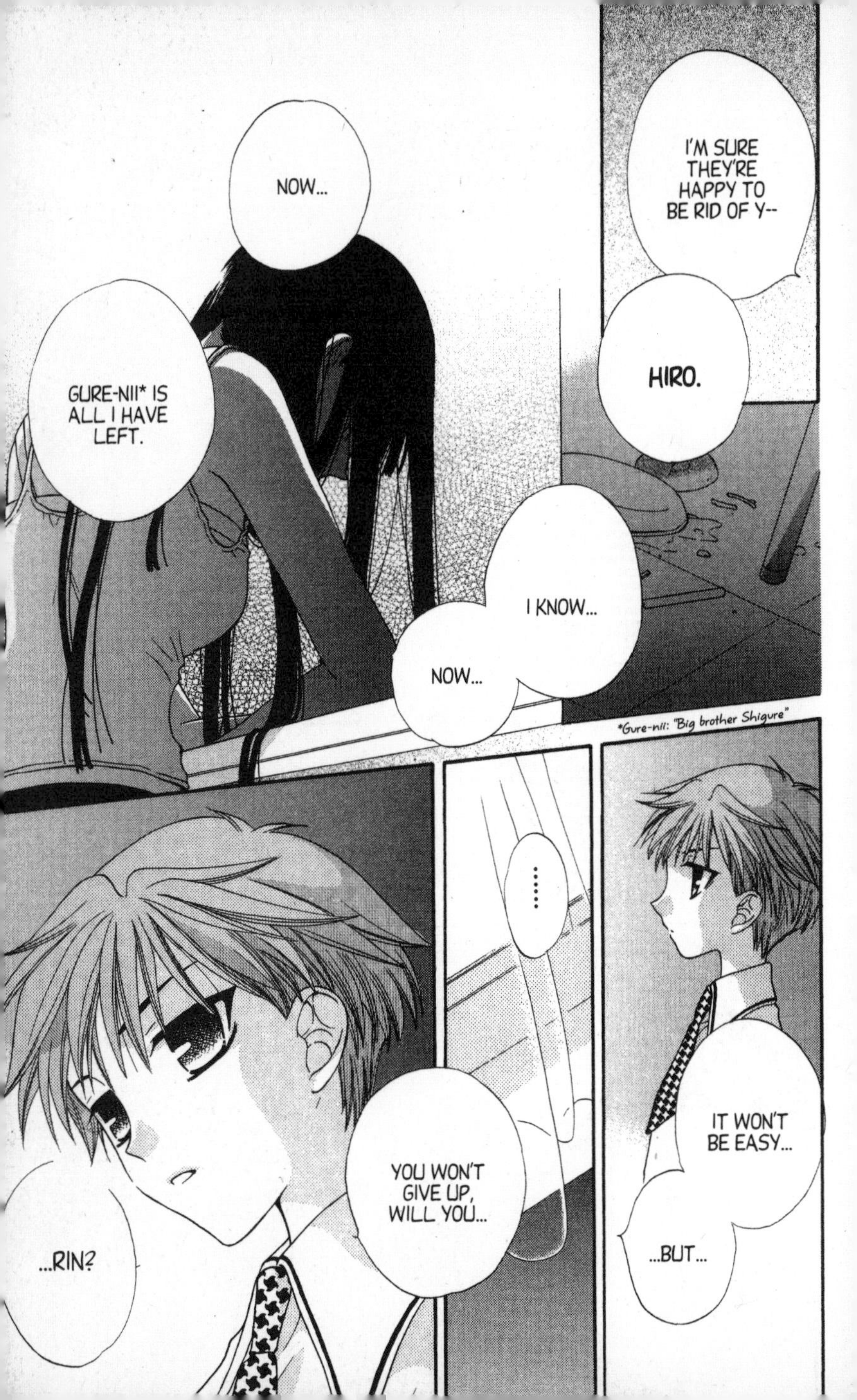
I'M SURE THEY'RE HAPPY TO BE RID OF Y--
HIRO.
NOW...
GURE-NII* IS ALL I HAVE LEFT.
I KNOW...
NOW...
IT WON'T BE EASY...
...BUT...
......
YOU WON'T GIVE UP, WILL YOU...
...RIN?

*Gure-nii: "Big brother Shigure"

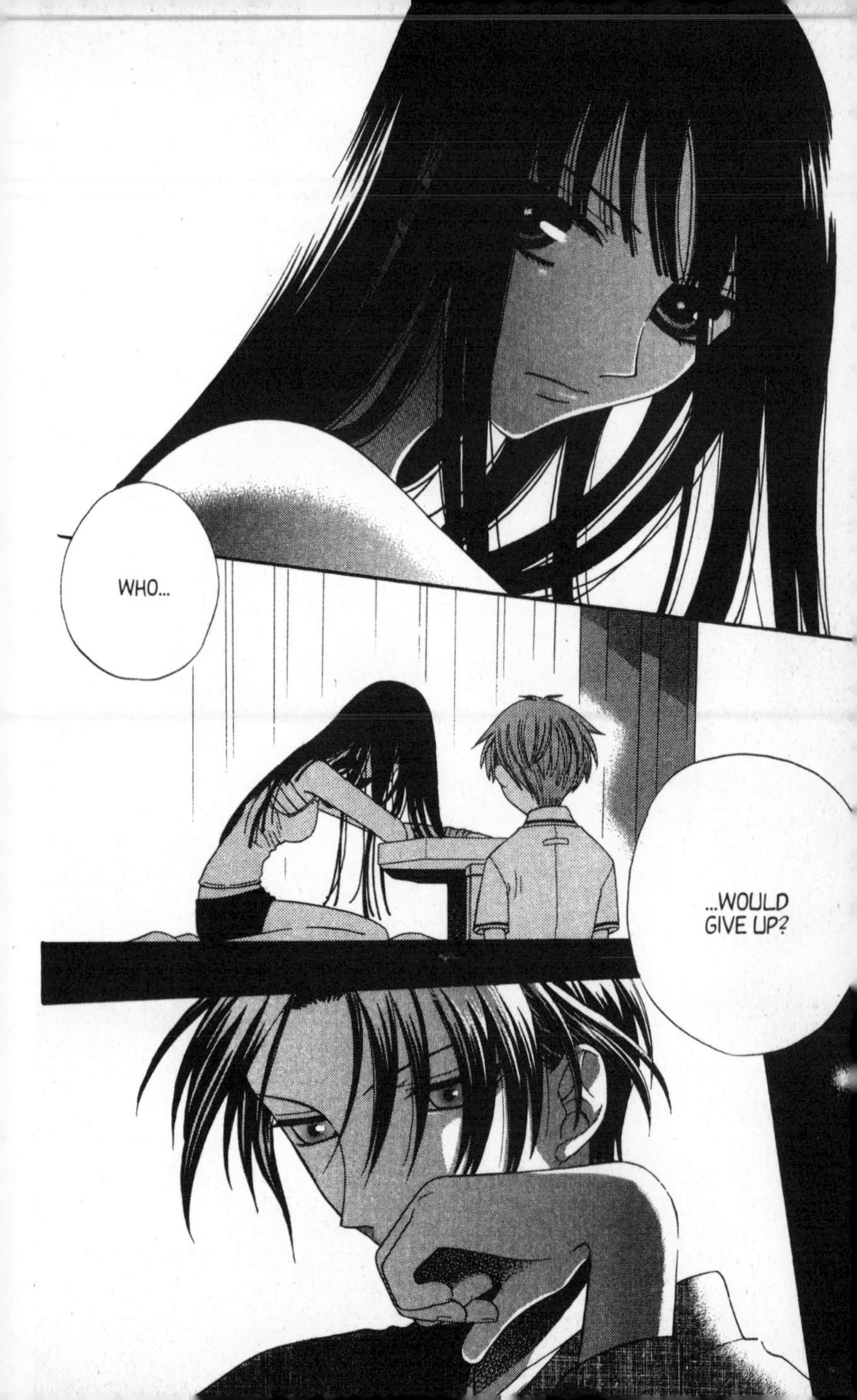
WHO...
...WOULD GIVE UP?

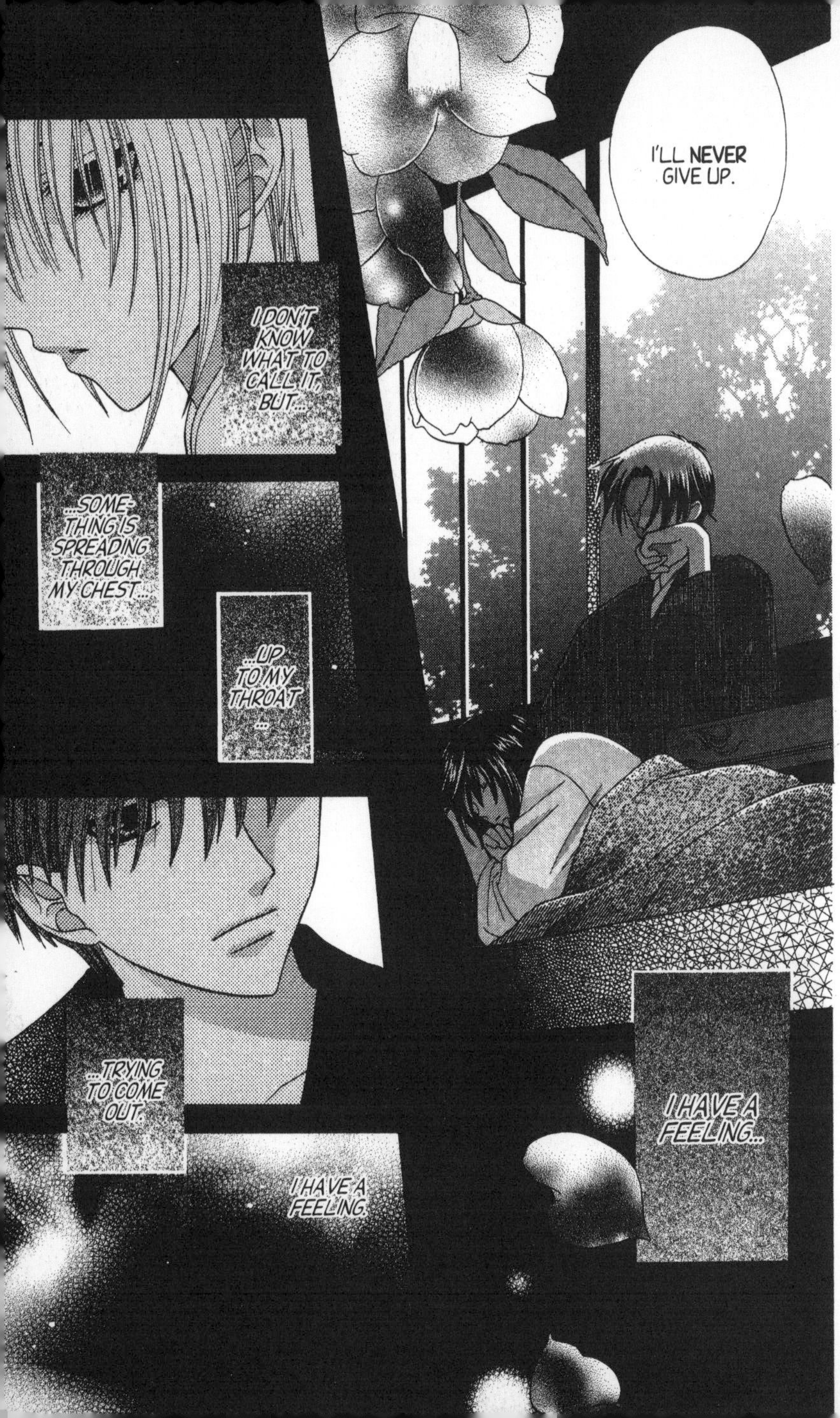
I'LL NEVER GIVE UP.
I DON'T KNOW WHAT TO CALL IT, BUT...
...SOME-THING IS SPREADING THROUGH MY CHEST...
...UP TO MY THROAT...
...TRYING TO COME OUT.
I HAVE A FEELING...
I HAVE A FEELING.

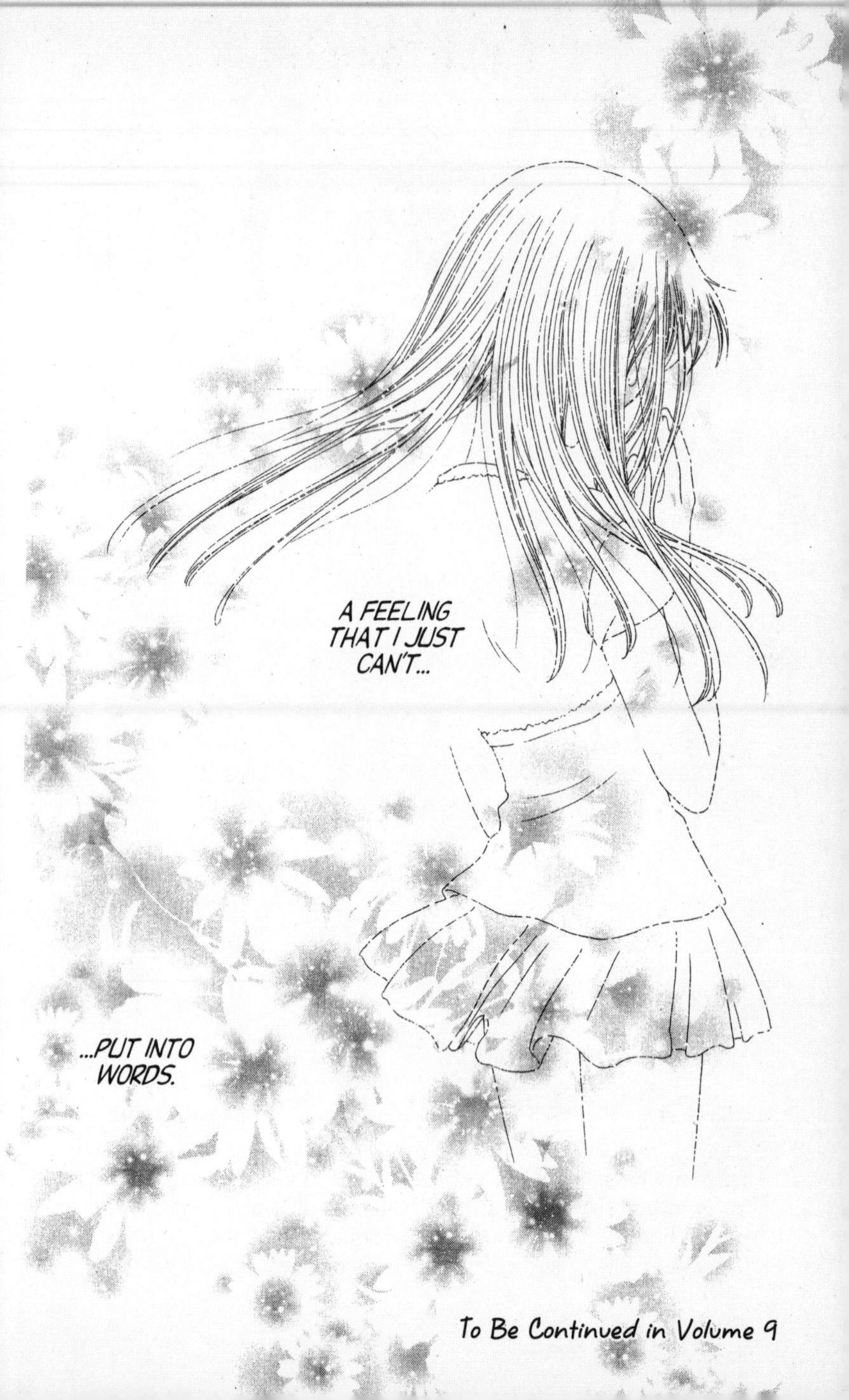
A FEELING THAT I JUST CAN'T...
...PUT INTO WORDS.
To Be Continued in Volume 9

Next time in...

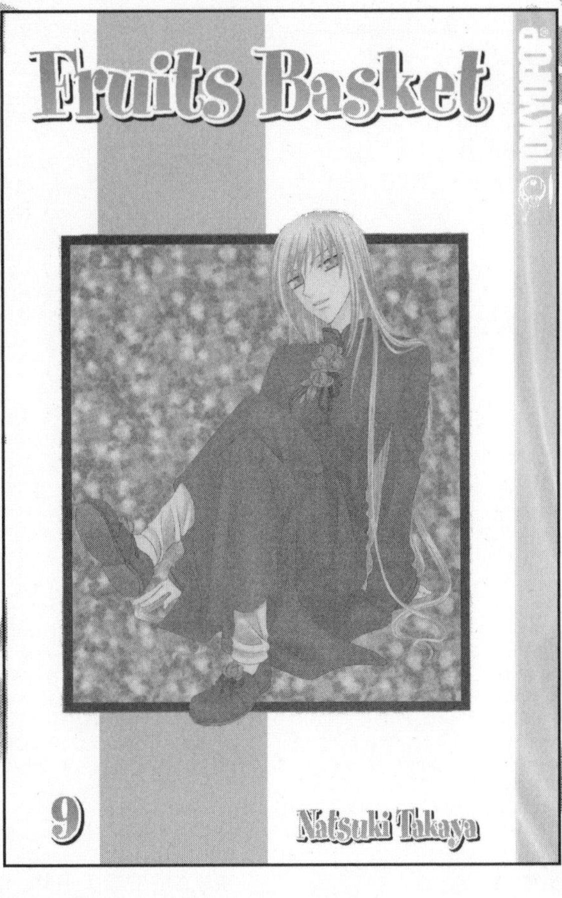
Fruits Basket
TOKYOPOP
9
Natsuki Takaya

Sizzlin' Summer Lovin'...

Finally--summer has arrived! While Tohru struggles through bipolar days of hope and anxiety, what will happen when Yuki comes face-to-face with the new member of the student council?! And…is Uo-chan crazy in love?! Who's that she's hanging out with?! Plus, Hana-chan's past is finally disclosed in a bonus feature! Come join the party in the 9th volume of the super-popular *Fruits Basket!*

Fruits Basket Volume 9
Available June 2005

Year of the Dragon: Hot Headed

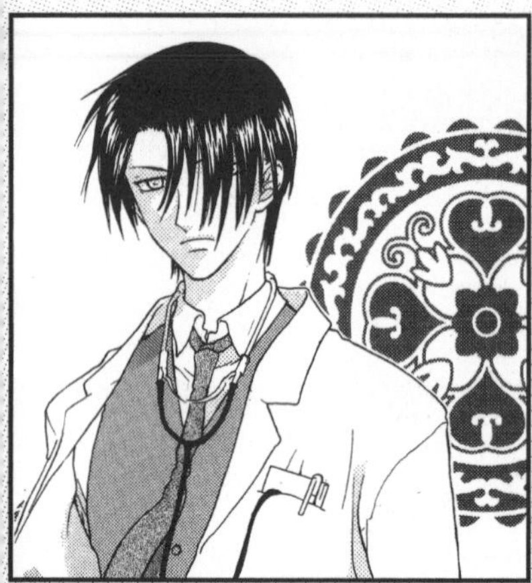

Dragon

Years*: 1940, 1952, 1964, 1976, 1988, 2000, 2012, 2024, 2036
Qualities: Intelligent, Enthusiastic, Softhearted, Lucky, Imaginative
Grievances: Bossy, Loud, Flamboyant
Suitable Jobs: Polictician, Priest, Artist, Film Director
Compatible With: Rat, Snake, Monkey, Rooster
Must Avoid: Dog, Sheep
Ruling Hours: 7 AM to 9 AM
Season: Spring
Ruling Month: April
Sign Direction: East-Southeast
Fixed Element: Wood
Corresponding Western Sign: Aries

At first glance, the dragon is by far the most mysterious of all the animals of the Chinese Zodiac, and the one most up to interpretation as to what the dragon is. A Komodo Dragon might come to mind for a Westerner, but *Fruits Basket* takes a very Eastern view by having Hatori Sohma transform into a Sea Horse, literally "tatsu no otoshigo" or "dragon's child," showing a glimmer of the awe the creatures emit.

For the Chinese, who proclaim themselves "Lung Tik Chuan Ren" or "Descendents of the Dragon," these Dragons bring about good fortune and the year itself is a grandiose one full of ambition. This brave and energetic nature races ten-fold through the very core of anyone born under the Dragon's banner.

Dragons themselves are naturally healthy and loving individuals that are quite eccentric, but are easily excited and prone to stubborn outbursts. Dragons are pioneering individuals with their futures well thought out in advance.

However, success is not necessarily a needed outcome as the very experience of trying is reward enough for a Dragon. Naturally softhearted, Dragons should be careful to not let themselves become too vulnerable by being too trusting of others.

Women born in this year are noble without exception and never submit to pressure when they have the chance to outshine another individual--especially men. Females tend to be quite practical in their clothing choices as they hate being restricted--meaning they shy away from tight and flashy and go for loose and comfortable. Love for a Dragon comes from the very bottom of their heart and is the kind that is sincere and the truest of trues.

Celebrity Dragons:
Sandra Bullock
Courteney Cox
Shannon Elizabeth
Colin Farrell
Melissa Joan Hart
Teri Hatcher
Haley Joel Osment
Reese Witherspoon
Malecifent (Sleeping Beauty)

* Note: It is important to know what day Chinese New Year's was held on as that changes what Zodiac animal you are. Example: 1988 actually began on February 17 and anyone born before that date is actually a Rabbit.

Year of the Ox: Beast of Burden

Ox

Years*: 1937, 1949, 1961, 1973, 1985, 1997, 2009, 2021, 2033
Qualities: Inspiring, Conservative, Steadfast, Dependable, Eloquent
Grievances: Methodical, Stubborn, Eccentric, Fierce Temper
Suitable Jobs: Surgeon, General, Hairdresser, Investment Banker
Compatible With: Snakes, Roosters and Rats
Must Avoid: Sheep
Ruling Hours: 1 AM to 3 AM
Season: Winter
Ruling Month: January
Sign Direction: North-Northwest
Fixed Element: Water
Corresponding Western Sign: Capricorn

Men born in this year are highly impressionable and any scrap of unhappiness tends to leave lasting marks on their personality--especially where girls are concerned. Put an Ox up against a lady and they turn to mush, literally, on the spot--a stark contrast to their brash stubbornness to be sure.

On the other hand, women tend to be serious, but also neat and punctual. Their cooking is to die for and they are very loving and motherly. Perfectionists at heart, woman born in this year try to turn a deaf ear on flattery, as the knowledge of a job well done is more than thanks enough in their eyes. A good deed though, never goes unpaid with an Ox.

Celebrity Oxen:
Neve Campbell
Adam Garcia
Whoopi Goldberg
Andy Lau
Heather Locklear
Frankie Muniz
Jack Osbourne
Sigourney Weaver

During the great race, the cunning Rat hitched a ride atop the Ox's head and jumped across the finish line at the last moment. To say the Ox was angry would have been the understatement of a lifetime. Oxen are unyieldingly stubborn and hate feeling opposed. In fact, the only thing they hate more is failing. For these reasons, people born in the year of the Ox are natural born leaders and powerfully successful ones at that.

While an Ox might seem like a scary person to go up against, they tend to be quiet, very patient of others and highly trusted. Much like Hatsuharu, Ox (or Cows, if you prefer) have a certain yin-yang type of duality to their personalities meaning they can be kind and calm at times and at others completely rude and arrogant. Nonetheless, they enjoy listening to others and usually take a friend or colleague's advice whenever given. Oxen are very orderly and strictly by-the-book when it comes to their jobs and chores.

*Note: It is important to know what day Chinese New Year's was held on as that changes what Zodiac animal you are. Example: 1985 actually began on February 20 and anyone born before that date is actually a Rat.

Fans Basket

Shyrah Esteban
Age 16
Kaneohe, HI

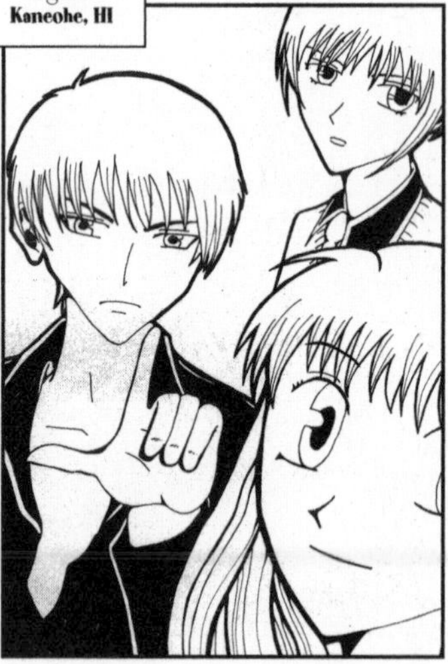

Aloha, Shyrah! I love your unique style. Very bold, very artsy. You have a knack for graphic design!

Katch
Age 16
Oceanside, CA

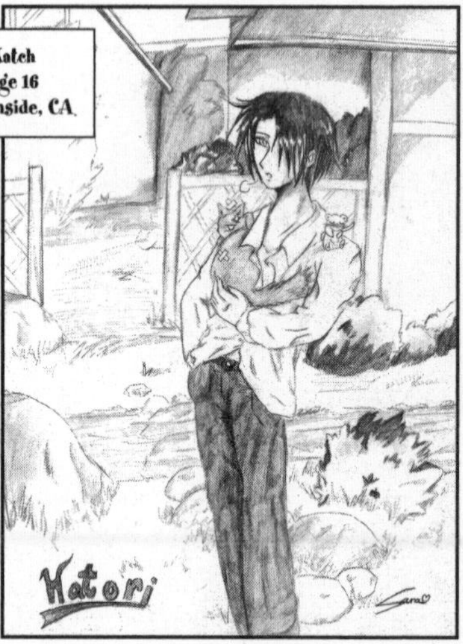
Hatori
Sara

Poor Hatori. He looks exhausted. I guess patching up Kyo and Yuki all the time keeps his mind off his broken heart, right, Katch?

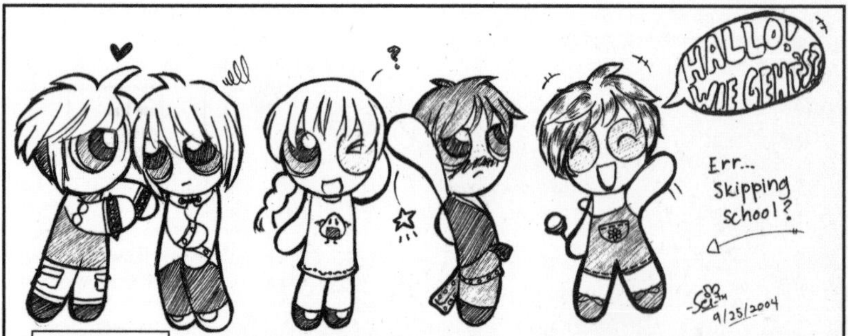
HALLO! WIE GEHT'S?
Err... Skipping school?
9/25/2004

Sei-chan
Age 17
Duluth, MN

This is seriously adorable! All our favorite *Fruits Basket* characters illustrated Craig McCracken-style! Craig McWho, you ask? He's the creator of the *Powerpuff Girls,* of course! Awesome work, Sei-chan!

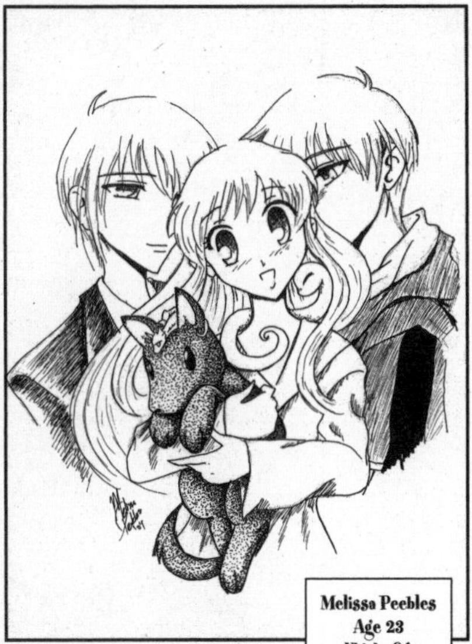

Melissa Peebles
Age 23
Ukiah, CA

I liked all of your art, Melissa, including your heavily illustrated envelope! I picked this piece, though, because I loved the "toning technique" you used for Shigure.

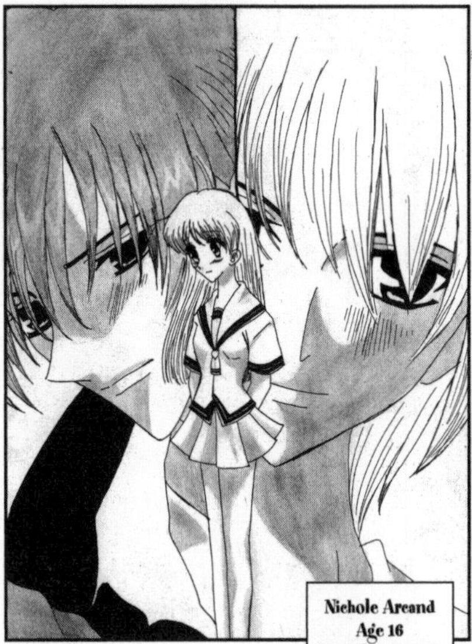

Nichole Areand
Age 16
King George, VA

I really like this drawing. It simply and effectively portrays Tohru's romantic dilemma.

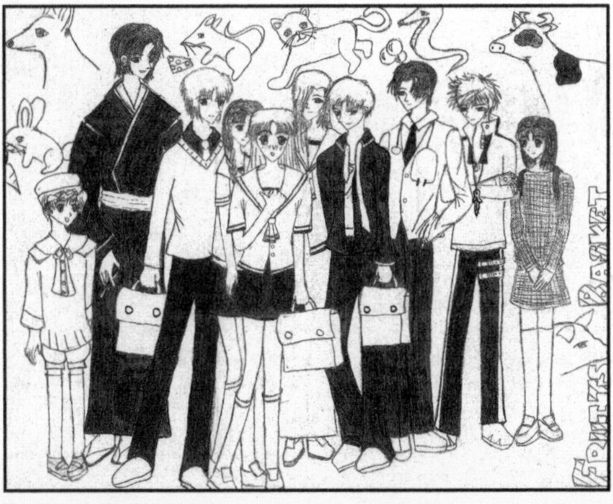

Jane Luo
Age 11
Springfield, VA

A lot of people draw the entire *Fruits Basket* cast when they submit fan art, and Jane is no exception. Surprisingly, Jane is only 11! Somebody has been encouraging her to draw, that's for sure! Her composition is great, and all of her animals are super cute!

Honda Tohru 本田透

Sara Wright-Avila
Age 16
Covina, CA

Sara is a **huge** *Fruits Basket* fan! She has submitted several pieces of art, and at long last, she's getting one published! Kyo looks furious, and poor Yuki looks terrified of falling out of Tohru's basket. Nicely done, Sara.

Sara Hendricks
Age 13
Lake Worth, FL

Keep penciling, Sara! You're only 13 and showing a lot of drawing talent. Tohru's dress looks fabulous!

Do you want to share your love for *Fruits Basket* with fans around the world? "Fans Basket" is taking submissions of fan art, poetry, cosplay photos, or any other Furuba fun you'd like to share!

How to submit:

1) Send your work via regular mail (NOT e-mail) to:

"Fans Basket"
c/o TOKYOPOP
5900 Wilshire Blvd.
Suite 2000
Los Angeles, CA 90036

2) All work should be in black-and-white and no larger than 8.5" x 11". (And try not to fold it too many times!)

3) Anything you send will not be returned. If you want to keep your original, it's fine to send us a copy.

4) Please include your full name, age, city and state for us to print with your work. If you'd rather us use a pen name, please include that, too.

5) IMPORTANT: If you're under the age of 18, you must have your parent's permission in order for us to print your work. Any submissions without a signed note of parental consent cannot be used.

6) For full details, please check out our website: http://www. tokyopop.com/aboutus/ fanart.php

Disclaimer: Anything you send to us becomes the exclusive property of TOKYOPOP Inc. and, as we said before, will not be returned to you. We will have the right to print, reproduce, distribute, or modify the artwork for use in future volumes of Fruits Basket or on the web royalty-free.

Arian Applewhite
Age 20
Mt. Sterling, KY

I knew Arian's art would be difficult to scan and reproduce in the book, but it was too funny and clever to pass up! We're definitely not in Kansas anymore--especially when our favorite *Fruits Basket* cast members are dressed like *Wizard of Oz* characters! Shigure as Toto is brilliant!

Kayla Throm
aka "Myoga Jiichan"
Age 16
Snohomish, WA

Momiji is one of my favorite characters, and I laughed when I saw the slippers he's wearing here! Myoga's pencils have a loose, breezy quality that make her art stand out.

TOKYOPOP SHOP

WWW.TOKYOPOP.COM/SHOP

HOT NEWS!
Check out
TOKYOPOP.COM/SHOP
The world's best
collection of manga in
English is now available
online in one place!

SOKORA REFUGEES

PLANET BLOOD

THE TAROT CAFÉ

WWW.TOKYOPOP.COM/SHOP

```
0 00000 00000 0
```

- **LOOK FOR SPECIAL OFFERS**
- **PRE-ORDER UPCOMING RELEASES!**
- **COMPLETE YOUR COLLECTIONS**

Sokora Refugees © Kurt Hassler and TOKYOPOP Inc. Planet Blood © 1996 Kim Tae-Hyung, Daiwon C.I. Inc.
The Tarot Café © 2005 Sang Sun Park/ SIGONGSA

SPOTLIGHT TOKYOPOP MANGA SUPPLEMENT

IN DREAM WORLD: FOLLOW YOUR DREAMS... BUT BEWARE OF THE NIGHTMARES!

Nightmares are bad enough when you are asleep, but in In Dream World, nightmares are real monsters! Drake, Hanee and Kyle battle these night terrors with special "In Dream Cards," magical cards that have unusual and devastating powers. Those who wield the cards gain the power of the elements, and our heroes must master the cards before they are put into a permanent state of sleep!

OT OLDER TEEN AGE 16+

For more information visit: **www.TOKYOPOP.com**

© YOON JAE-HO, DAIWON C.I. Inc.

VAN VON HUNTER™

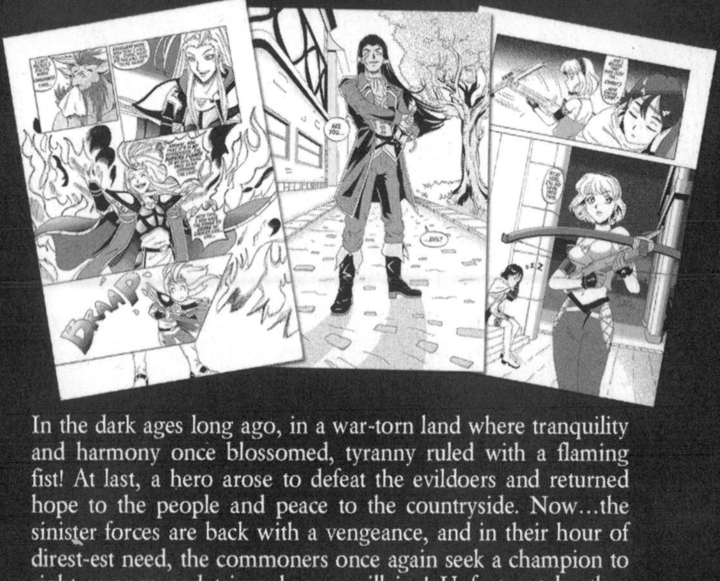

In the dark ages long ago, in a war-torn land where tranquility and harmony once blossomed, tyranny ruled with a flaming fist! At last, a hero arose to defeat the evildoers and returned hope to the people and peace to the countryside. Now...the sinister forces are back with a vengeance, and in their hour of direst-est need, the commoners once again seek a champion to right wrongs and triumph over villainy! Unfortunately, they could only get the mighty warrior Van Von Hunter, Hunter of Evil...Stuff!

Together with his loyal, memory-challenged sidekick, Van Von Hunter is on a never-ending quest to smite the bad guys—and believe us, they're real bad!

Preview the manga at:

www.TOKYOPOP.com/vanvonhunter
www.VanVonHunter.com

TEEN
AGE 13+

© Pseudome Studios LLC.

VAN VON HUNTER

EVIL NEVER DIES...
BUT EVIL STUFF DOES!

FROM THE
WINNERS OF
TOKYOPOP'S FIRST
RISING STARS OF
MANGA™
COMPETITION

STOP!

This is the back of the book.
You wouldn't want to spoil a great ending!

This book is printed "manga-style," in the authentic Japanese right-to-left format. Since none of the artwork has been flipped or altered, readers get to experience the story just as the creator intended. You've been asking for it, so TOKYOPOP® delivered: authentic, hot-off-the-press, and far more fun!

DIRECTIONS

If this is your first time reading manga-style, here's a quick guide to help you understand how it works.

It's easy... just start in the top right panel and follow the numbers. Have fun, and look for more 100% authentic manga from TOKYOPOP®!

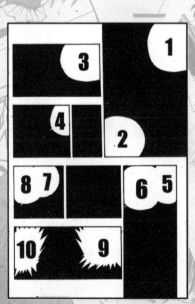